The DB2 Replication Certification Guide

IBM DB2 Certification Guide Series

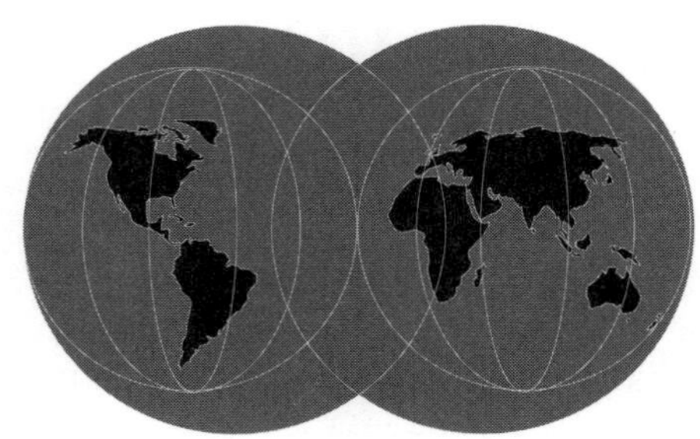

DB2 Universal Database Certification Guide, Second Edition
edited by Janacek and Snow

DB2 Cluster Certification Guide
by Cook, Janacek, and Snow

DB2 Universal DRDA Certification Guide
by Brandl, Bullock, Cook, Harbus, Janacek, and Le

DB2 Replication Certification Guide
by Cook and Harbus

DB2 Universal Database and SAP R/3 Version 4
by Bullock, Cook, Deedes-Vincke, Harbus, Nardone, and Neuhaus

Universal Guide to DB2 for Windows NT
by Cook, Harbus, and Snow

INS.

The DB2 Replication Certification Guide

JONATHAN COOK ■ ROBERT HARBUS

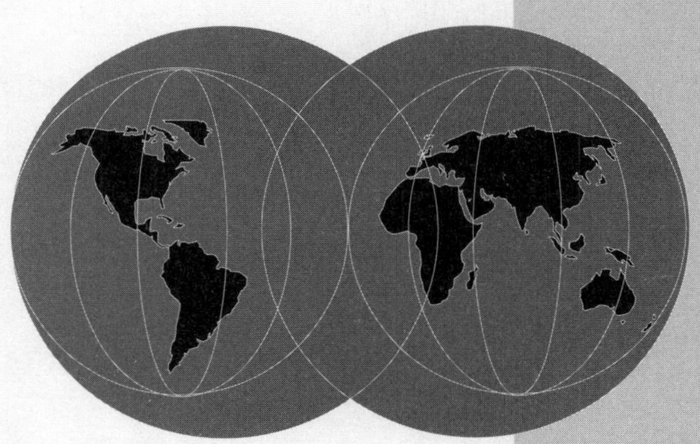

International Technical Support Organization
Austin, Texas 78758

PRENTICE HALL PTR, UPPER SADDLE RIVER, NEW JERSEY 07458
http://www.phptr.com

Editorial/production supervision: *Jane Bonnell*
Cover design director: *Jayne Conte*
Cover designer: *Bruce Kenselaar*
Manufacturing manager: *Pat Brown*
Marketing manager: *Bryan Gambrel*
Acquisitions editor: *Michael Meehan*
Editorial assistant: *Bart Blanken*

Published by Prentice Hall PTR
Prentice-Hall, Inc.
Upper Saddle River, NJ 07458

Prentice Hall books are widely used by corporations and government agencies for training, marketing, and resale. The publisher offers discounts on this book when ordered in bulk quantities.
For more information, contact
Corporate Sales Department
Phone 800-382-3419; FAX: 201-236-7141
E-mail (Internet): corpsales@prenhall.com
Or Write: Prentice Hall PTR
Corporate Sales Department
One Lake Street
Upper Saddle River, NJ 07458

DB2 information on the Internet—http://www.software.ibm.com/data/db2
DB2 certification information on the Internet—http://www.ibm.com/certify

Printed in the United States of America
10 9 8 7 6 5 4 3 2 1

ISBN 0-13-082424-0

Prentice-Hall International (UK) Limited, *London*
Prentice-Hall of Australia Pty. Limited, *Sydney*
Prentice-Hall Canada Inc., *Toronto*
Prentice-Hall Hispanoamericana, S.A., *Mexico*
Prentice-Hall of India Private Limited, *New Delhi*
Prentice-Hall of Japan, Inc., *Tokyo*
Prentice-Hall (Singapore) Pte. Ltd., *Singapore*
Editora Prentice-Hall do Brasil, Ltda., *Rio de Janeiro*

Contents

Figures

Tables

Preface

This guide helps you prepare for the IBM Data Replication certification exam, which is one of the tests towards the certification IBM Certified Advanced Technical Expert - DB2 Universal Database V5. The path to this level of certification involves the following:

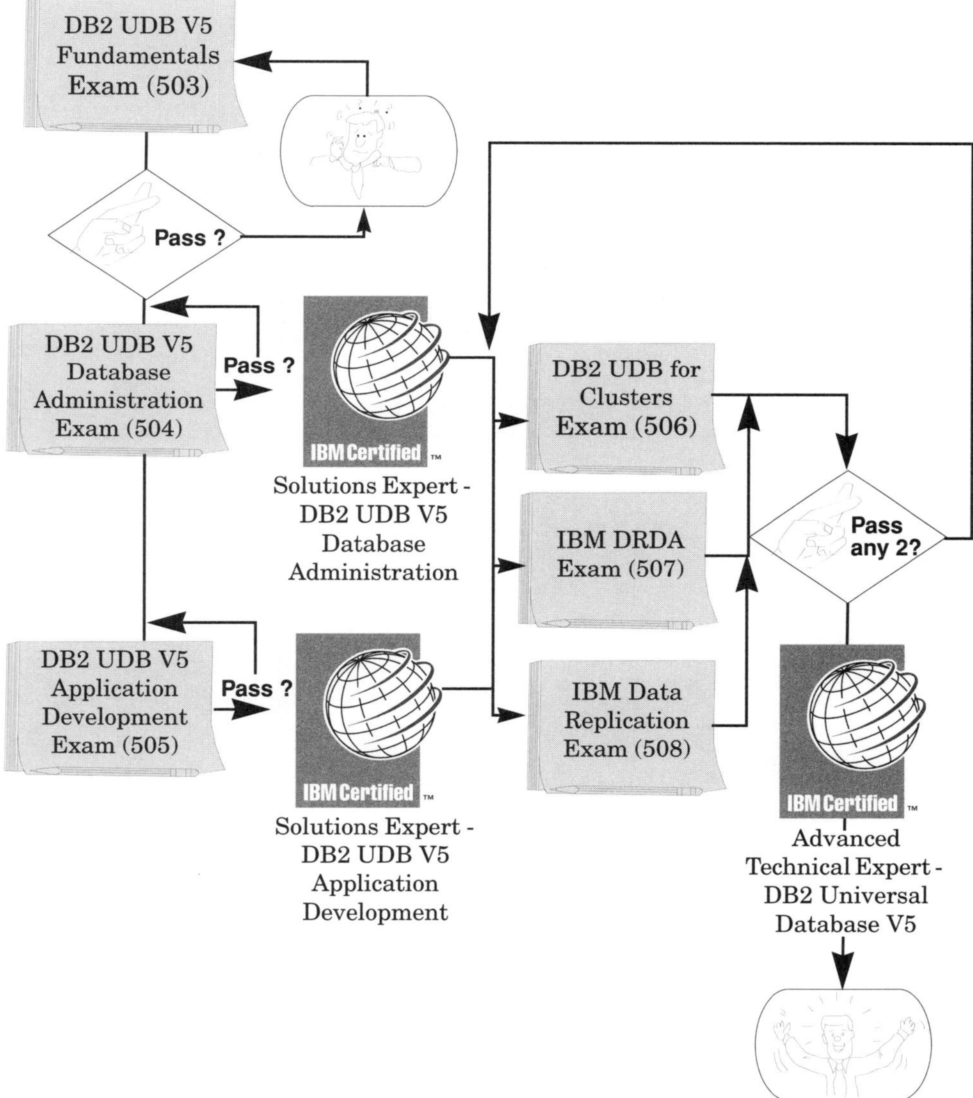

Figure 1. The Path to Certification

To become an IBM Certified Advanced Technical Expert - DB2 Universal Database V5, you must do the following:

1. Be either an IBM Certified Solutions Expert - DB2 UDB V5 Database Administration or an IBM Certified Solutions Expert - DB2 UDB V5 Application Development

   To possess either of the IBM Certified Solutions Expert levels, you must have successfully passed:

   1. DB2 UDB V5 Fundamentals - Exam (503)
   2. One or both of the following:
      - DB2 UDB V5 Database Administration - Exam (504)
      - DB2 UDB V5 Application Development - Exam (505)

2. Pass any two of the following three advanced exams:

   3. DB2 UDB for Clusters - Exam (506)
   4. IBM DRDA - Exam (507)
   5. IBM Data Replication - Exam (508)

Those interested in taking the IBM Data Replication Exam (508) should review the sample questions found in Appendix A, "Sample Certification Questions and Test Objectives" on page 375. This test is one of the three advanced tests; passing any two of these tests along with the pre-requisites will give you the Advanced Technical Expert - DB2 Universal Database V5 certification.

This book is divided into the following areas:

- Overview: This chapter is a short introduction to IBM Data Replication. It covers some features and functions and some of the terminology and conventions used throughout the book.
- Managing the replication components: Chapters two and three cover the principal components in a replication configuration: the administration component, the Capture component, and the Apply component.
- Practical Replication: Chapters four through seven cover some real-life replication scenarios. These include: replicating DB2 data from OS/390 to Windows NT, using staging tables, setting up update-anywhere configurations, and using mobile replication.
- Advanced Techniques: Chapter eight covers some more advanced replication topics, including using views to replicate data, and replicating between DB2 and non-DB2 data sources.

- Troubleshooting: Chapter nine provides an introduction to troubleshooting your replication environment, including all the log and trace files that can be generated by the various components.

How This Book was Created

This book was a joint effort between the Austin ITSO (International Technical Support Organization) and the IBM Toronto Lab. The ITSO is a group within IBM whose mission is to provide skills transfer on new products and emerging technology on a worldwide basis. We provide direct feedback to the IBM software labs as we gather input from various groups of DB2 users, including IBM support personnel, customers and business partners.

The ITSO provides a working envionment for interested individuals to work with new IBM software products. These individuals (who may include IBM employees and customers) work in a team and develop a workshop or a book.

> **Note**
>
> Check out the ITSO web site for more information including a listing of available ITSO redbooks at: **http://www.redbooks.ibm.com**.

The DB2 Replication Certification Guide was produced by many people from all over the world.

Jonathan Cook is the DB2 Project Leader at the International Technical Support Organization (ITSO), Austin Center. He has ten years of experience as a database specialist working in the areas of application development and database administration. He has been with IBM since 1992, working in both the United Kingdom and France before joining the Austin ITSO. He writes extensively and teaches IBM classes worldwide on DB2 for the UNIX and Intel platforms.

Robert Harbus is the DB2 Universal Database Certification and Education coordinator at the IBM Toronto Lab. A member of the DB2 UDB team since its inception in 1991, Robert provided Technical Marketing and electronic customer support and direct customer support most recently as a member of the DB2 Universal Database Enterprise - Extended Edition (EEE) support team. Robert is currently responsible for the DB2 UDB certification program and testing, and works with the ITSO and Education & Training to ensure that DB2 UDB education courses, training and material are available to meet the needs of DB2

UDB users. Robert teaches DB2 internals and certification courses worldwide and is involved in producing certification guides and redbooks.

Tadakatsu Azuma is a leading DPROPR specialist with IBM Japan, having implemented several major customer replication solutions. He has particular expertise in using DPROPR for replication to and from non-IBM databases. Azuma-san was a major contributor to the following ITSO publications: *Data Where you Need It, the DPropR Way!* (GG24-4492-00) and *DPROPR Planning and Design Guide* (SG24-4771-00).

David Hepple is a data management support specialist for IBM Ireland. For the previous three years, he was a member of the EMEA Data Management Centre of Competence based in Dublin. Prior to that, he worked on replication product development and support.

Jieun Lee is a Sales Specialist for IBM Korea. She has been supporting IBM's Business Intelligence solutions, including Datawarehousing and DataMining for the last 3 years. For the 2 years previous to this, Jieun was working extensively on IBM DB2 technical support.

Carlos Mendoza works for IBM Global Services in Ireland as an IT Specialist supporting IBM Server Group's plant operation in Dublin. He is a Certified DB2 Database Administrator. At the time the book was written he was working in the IBM Data Management Centre of Competence for EMEA, providing pre- and post-sales technical support for DB2 and the Data Replication family of products. He worked on the team that developed the education program for IBM Data Replication when version 5 of the product was launched in 1997.

Yu-Phing Ong has worked in the IBM Australia Support Centre for the last 4 years. He is the country specialist for DB2 on the PC and UNIX platforms, and is a member, and the team leader, of the ISC group, which supports the IBM Data Management and Business Intelligence products for the Asia Pacific (South) region.

Thanks to the following people who provided very valuable feedback on the technical content:

Rob Goldring
IBM Santa Teresa Laboratory

Ray Houle
The Fillmore Group, Inc

Christian Lenke
IBM Global Services, Germany

Dave Romack
IBM Eduaction and Training, Dallas

Nick Smith
IBM Global Services, UK

The following people were invaluable for their proof-reading expertise and moral support:

John Owczarzak
IBM ITSO Austin

Catherine Cook
IBM France

Chapter 1. An Overview of DB2 Data Replication

What is data replication? Why replicate data in the first place? What can it gain you? In this chapter we try to answer these questions for you. We tell you what data replication is, why you may wish to consider using it in your environment, and then follow this up with explanations of the major concepts and topics in DB2 data replication. We do not cover the basic DB2 database concepts, as it is assumed that the reader is already familiar with DB2.

The need to provide easy and rapid access to vital data to end users is a major issue with most companies today. In a typical situation, data is kept in a single location, and users access the data either remotely or locally. This requires that they have access to the database server where the data is located when they want to access the data. This database server access is not always possible. As an example, take the growing base of mobile users with laptop computers who require access to company data on the road; they do not have the ability to connect to the corporate database at all times.

In some situations, you may choose to have your own local copy of the data that you need. This is sufficient as long as the original data does not change. If the original data is not static, then you have to worry about keeping your own local copy up-to-date with the master copy of the data. This can be a tedious and time consuming exercise if you have to make a new copy of the required data on a regular basis.

You may find that you need to have a history of the changes that have been made to your data over time. In this situation, a point-in-time picture of the data will not meet your needs.

DB2 data replication (also known as DPropR) is the key technology which enables management of multiple copies of redundant data. The copies can be different from the source. The copies can be generated once or may be resynchronized on an on-going basis. Using DB2 data replication, you can make your data available to local, remote, and mobile users in a timely and up-to-date manner. It provides efficient means to:

- Automate the copying of data.
- Give you the option to fully refresh or only replicate changes.
- Enhance your data using all the functionality available in SQL.
- Administer your environment easily through a single graphical user interface.

All these functions can be accomplished by DB2 data replication without the need to schedule a batch processing window nor any specific knowledge of the business applications running in your environment.

Data replication function is built into version 5 of the DB2 UDB product. It is available as separate products or features for DB2 products on MVS, OS/390, OS/400, and VSE and VM.

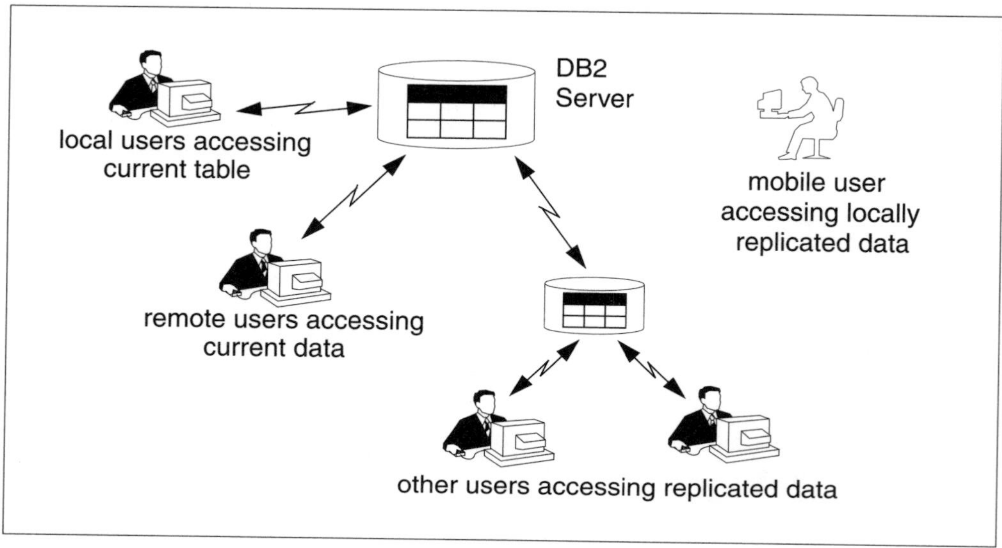

Figure 2. DB2 Data Replication

Figure 2 shows you how you can have numerous access paths to your corporate data; either through local or remote direct connections or through access to replicated data on other servers or personal machines.

Having your database data replicated to other locations and using the DB2 replication features to keep your data up-to-date can allow your users to have quicker access to your corporate data. It also allows them to have access to up-to-date data without the need for a connection to the primary corporate database server (or servers).

1.1 What is Data Replication?

Data replication is a copy management service that involves two processes: initial setup, and on-going or continuous data resynchronization.

During the initial setup:

1. A copy (target) is created, based on a given DB2 table or view (source).
2. An initial data transfer is performed from the source into the target.
3. The source and target data now have a point of synchronization.

During the on-going maintenance of data consistency:

1. Updates occur to the source which create a delta with the target.
2. Updates are captured.
3. Captured updates are asynchronously applied to the target.
4. The source and target data have a new point of consistency.

You can think of Data Replication as comprising three main components working independently of each other, but coordinating their activities through DB2 control structures:

1. Determining the data that has changed in the source tables or views you have chosen to be replicated, and making those changes available for copying (**Capture**).
2. Taking the changes made available above and copying them to target tables (**Apply**). These target tables can be in the same or different databases (or both) as the tables chosen to be replicated.
3. The replication administration features that are included in the DB2 UDB Control Center. The Control Center enables you to easily define and manage your source and target tables. In contrast, the **Capture** and **Apply** programs actually do the work of determining the changes that have occurred to the source tables and applying them to the target tables.

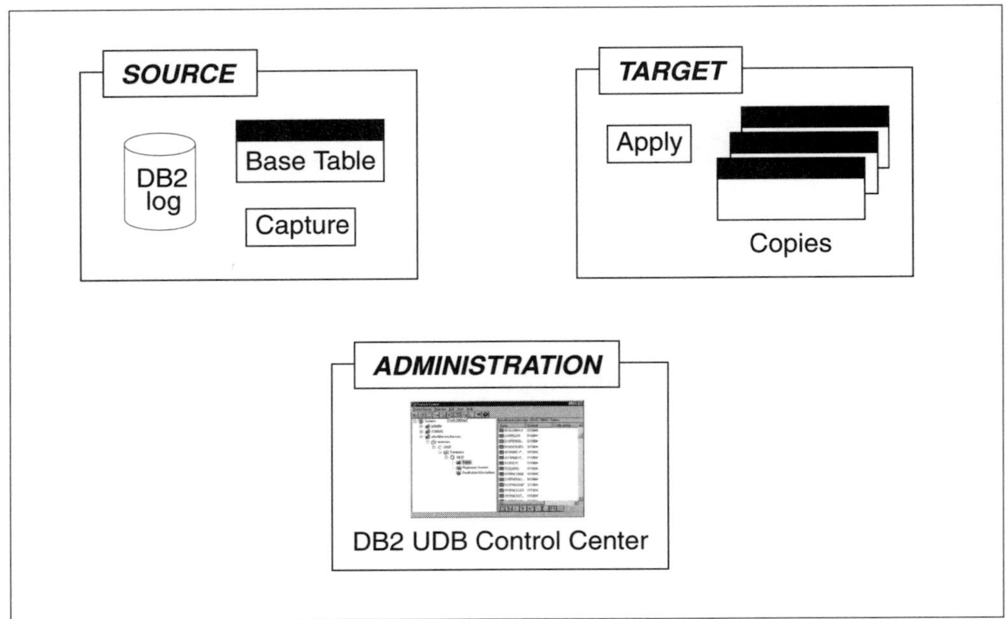

Figure 3. DB2 Data Replication Components

Figure 3 shows these major components. Now that we know what we are aiming for and what we have to work with, let's discuss the major concepts in DB2 data replication. We start with what we want to copy, where we want to copy it to, and how to set this up.

1.1.1 Data Replication Sources

A **replication source** can be a DB2 table or a view and can be located in any database accessible on the network. What constitutes a replication source will be dictated by your particular business and user needs. These tables and views are the foundation for your replication scenario.

Once you have determined the tables and/or views to use as sources, you need to consider such things as: which columns in the source table are to be available for replication and whether the before image of a column's data should be captured as well as the after image (for example, as a result of an update to the column's data). When you define a replication source, you can select these types of options, among others.

A table or view only needs to be defined as a replication source once. Many different targets may then share this same replication source.

1.1.2 Data Replication Targets

A **data replication target** is always in the form of a table. This table may be enhanced as compared to the format of it's associated replication source(s). There are several ways which replication can transform the data in order to enhance its value:

- Filter out, or subset rows, from the source data to a more meaningful amount. For example, a sales representative does not require the corporate database on his laptop, he simply requires his or her accounts.
- Filter out columns of sensitive data which are not appropriate for this given user. For example, a user may require access to the name and phone number from a personnel record, but not the salary.
- The source may be a single table, or a join of several tables in the form of denormalized data.
- Columns in the target table may be derived from, or calculated based on, columns in the source table. For example, using SQL aggregation functions such as AVG or SUM.
- The updates which occur at the source can be enriched with a timestamp, and multiple updates to a single source row may each be stored independently. For example, this can be used to determine how many items were sold between 9 AM and 11 AM, versus how many are now in stock.

Relative to the source tables, target tables can be in the same or different databases and can be on the same server or other servers on your network. It is important to note that the target tables do not have to have a 1-to-1 relationship to the source tables.

Together, the replication source and target tables define the players in your replication environment. Later in this chapter, we provide more details on the types of target tables you can define.

1.1.3 Registrations and Subscriptions

Once you have determined the data to be replicated, and the destination for this replicated data, you need to define the exact behavior of your replication scenario. **Registration** is the process of *publishing* a table or view as a replication source. When you register a replication source you define which columns will be available for replication and whether before as well as after images are to be kept. A given source table or view is registered just once, independent of how the data is actually distributed. A registration itself can only be associated with one database.

Subscription is the process of establishing the relationship between a registered replication source and the target table. When you define your subscription, you specify the target tables and their structure, the source tables for each of the target tables, and finally, the schedule for the replication. Each such definition is termed a **subscription member**.

1.1.4 Administration through the Control Center

You can administer your entire replication system from a single point of control, running on a workstation that's either local to or remote from the data involved. The replication system can be changed dynamically without a negative impact on the entire replication network.

The administration component of DPROPR is integrated into the DB2 Universal Database V5 Control Center. It uses SQL connectivity to enable remote operation with any DB2 database server. The administration component allows you to:

- Register a table or view as a source for change capture and replication.
- Create a replication target table.
- Using subscriptions, define the conditions under which the data from a source table is copied to a target table.

In Figure 4 on page 7, you can see the Replication Sources and Replication Subscriptions folders associated with a database in the DB2 UDB Control Center:

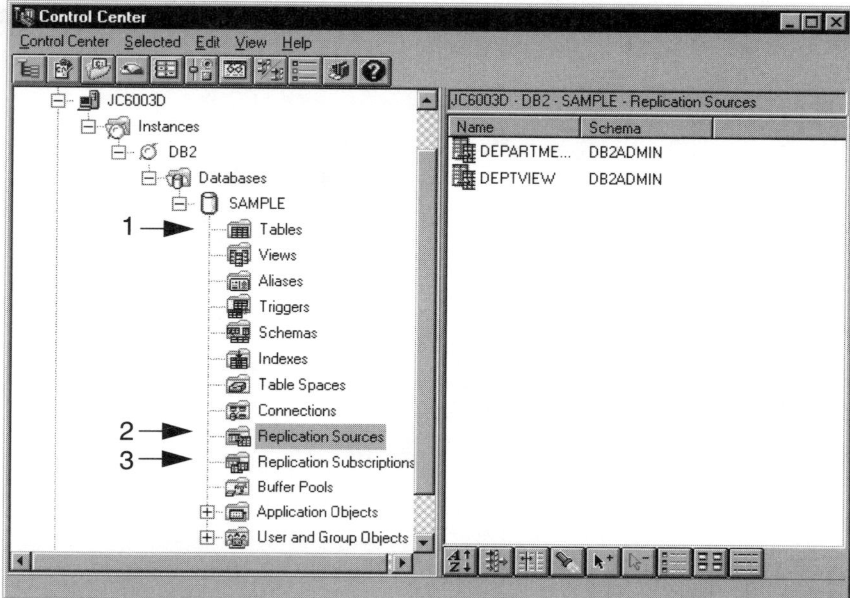

Figure 4. DB2 UDB Control Center - Replication Sources

In Figure 4, these are the important folders:

1. **Tables folder**, which contains your database tables. This includes the DB2 system catalog tables as well as any user-defined database tables. It is on these tables that you define your replication sources.
2. **Replication Sources folder**, which shows you which tables or views have already been defined as replication sources. These can include any tables in the tables folder, any views defined on registered sources, or replication target tables that are being also used as source tables.
3. **Replication Subscriptions folder**, which lists the subscriptions that you have defined. An example of this folder's contents is shown in Figure 5 on page 8.

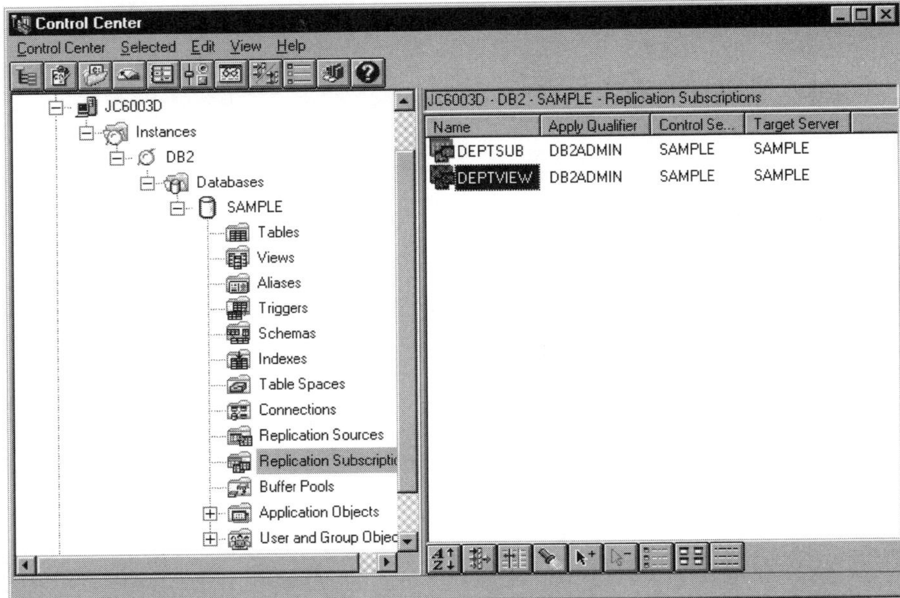

Figure 5. DB2 UDB Control Center - Replication Subscriptions

It is important to be aware that while you use the DB2 UDB Control Center to manipulate your replication sources and subscriptions, you do not operate the actual Capture and Apply programs from the Control Center, nor does the Control Center need to be active for replication to occur.

1.1.5 Subscription Sets

You can have more than one subscription member in a subscription. If you do have more than one member defined in a subscription, that subscription is termed a **subscription set**. The Apply program will process all the subscription members within a set in one commit scope. This allows related tables to be copied with application integrity by ensuring that the changes to multiple source tables are applied to the target tables in the same unit of work.

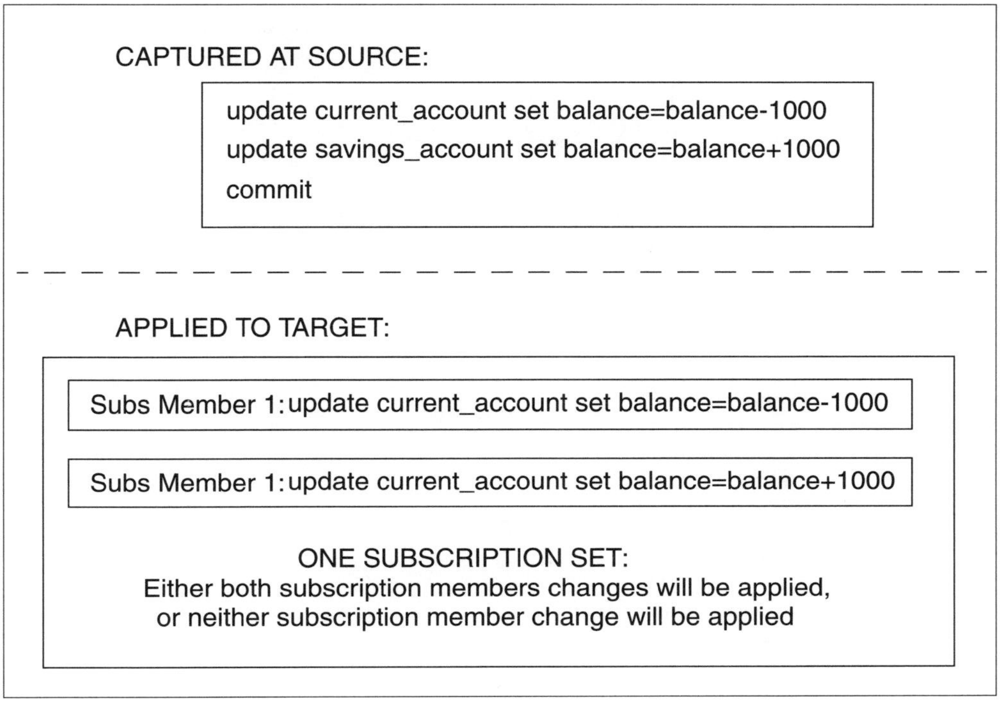

CAPTURED AT SOURCE:

```
update current_account set balance=balance-1000
update savings_account set balance=balance+1000
commit
```

APPLIED TO TARGET:

Subs Member 1: update current_account set balance=balance-1000

Subs Member 1: update current_account set balance=balance+1000

ONE SUBSCRIPTION SET:
Either both subscription members changes will be applied,
or neither subscription member change will be applied

Figure 6. Subscription Sets

Figure 6 shows a transaction involving a transfer of money from a current account to a savings account. This is a typical database unit of work, where either both updates must complete, or neither one complete, to ensure the integrity of the data. When replicating these changes to another system, two different subscription members are defined, one for the current_account table, and one for the savings_account table. The only way to ensure that data integrity is preserved at the target server is to define both of these subscriptions in the same subscription set.

When source tables are linked using referential integrity (RI) constraints, subscription sets should be used to ensure the integrity of the changes which are applied to the target tables.

You can view your subscription sets, and the members of these sets, in the DB2 Control Center.

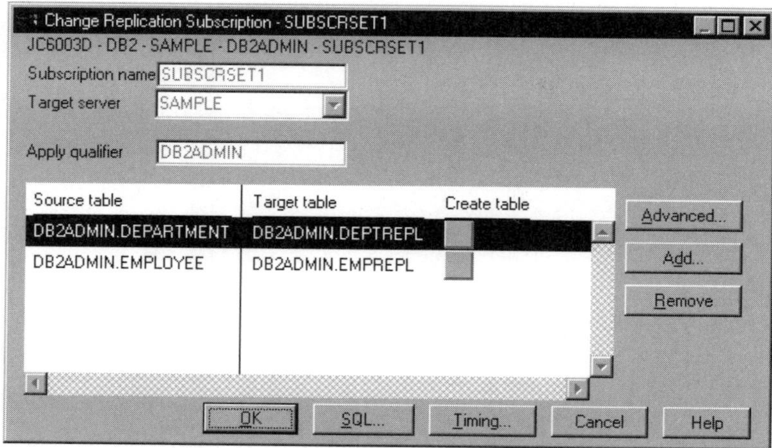

Figure 7. A Subscription Set in the Control Center

Figure 7 shows a subscription called SUBSCRSET1 with two subscription members defined in it.

For more details about subscription sets, see Chapter 2, "Managing Replication Sources and Subscriptions" on page 35.

1.1.6 The Capture Process

As we have indicated, data replication can be viewed as being comprised of three pieces: Capture, Apply, and administration.

The **Capture** process, running at the source server, determines what changes were made against your source and makes those changes available to be replicated to the target. It does this by reading the DB2 database log file (or journal) and retrieving any changes made to any DB2 tables that have been defined as replication sources. Note that the Capture process never accesses the actual source table. When using a table in a DB2 Universal Database V5 database as a source, the database must be made recoverable by enabling LOGRETAIN or USEREXIT (or both). The source table must also be altered with the DATA CAPTURE CHANGES option.

After reading data from the log files (or journal), the Capture process stores it in a **Change Data** (CD) table. For each registered source, there is one CD table, which is created during the registration process. In addition, the Capture process writes information on committed units-of-work to the **unit-of-work** (UOW) table. Both these control tables are later used by the Apply process. By using both tables, the Apply process can determine which transactions were actually committed and then only apply those. If uncommitted transactions were applied, this would cause your database to become inconsistent; by using the UOW table, the Capture process maintains transaction consistency.

As we have already discussed, you need to register the source tables to be used. The scope of the **Capture** process is one database. In other words, all the registrations defined in a single database are actioned by a single Capture process.

Figure 8 shows that Capture updates the CD and UOW tables on the source server based on information read from the DB2 logs:

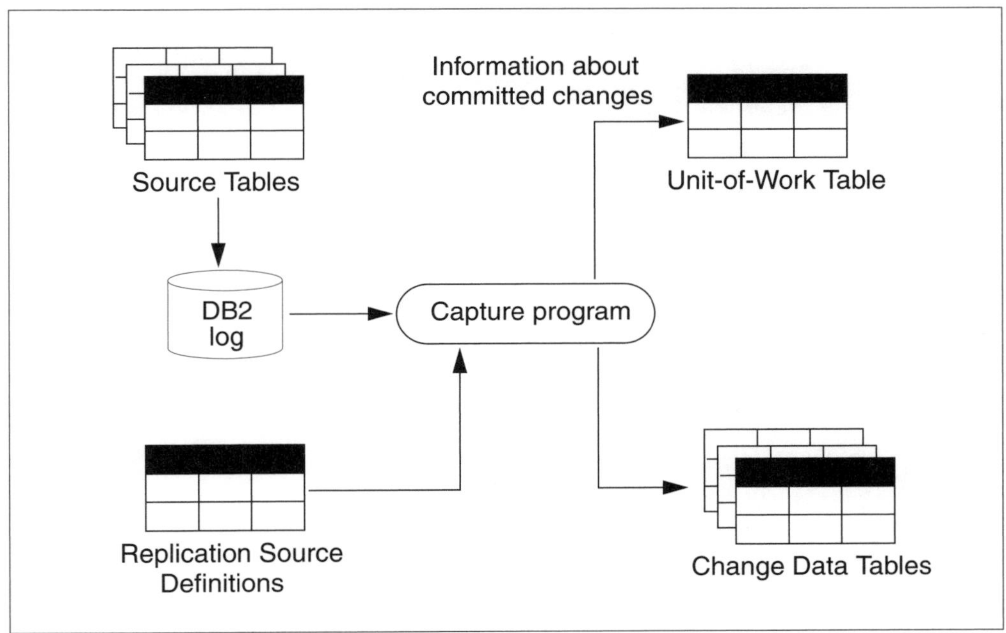

Figure 8. Capture Process - Overview

1.1.7 The Apply Process

Once the Capture process starts capturing changes to the source tables, you then need to start a process to copy the changes to the target tables.

The **Apply** process takes changes from the replication sources and applies them to your target tables. It takes the data that the Capture process has written to the Change Data control tables (in conjunction with the information in the Unit Of Work control table), and then based on the subscription definition, determines which data to apply to the target tables. In the event of a **full refresh copy** operation, the Apply process will read information directly from the source tables, since it is copying the entire source table in this operation. The Apply process runs totally independently of the Capture process and communicates with Capture only through DB2 tables.

Note

Capture and Apply do not need to be running simultaneously for replication to take place. After capture has captured changes, Apply can be run at some later time to apply these changes.

The target server is generally the location for the Apply process; however, it may be run on any machine in the network, including at the source server. The Apply process is associated with one or more subscriptions and is responsible for connecting to each database or server participating in the replication scenario.

Figure 9 shows how the Apply process applies the captured data to the target tables:

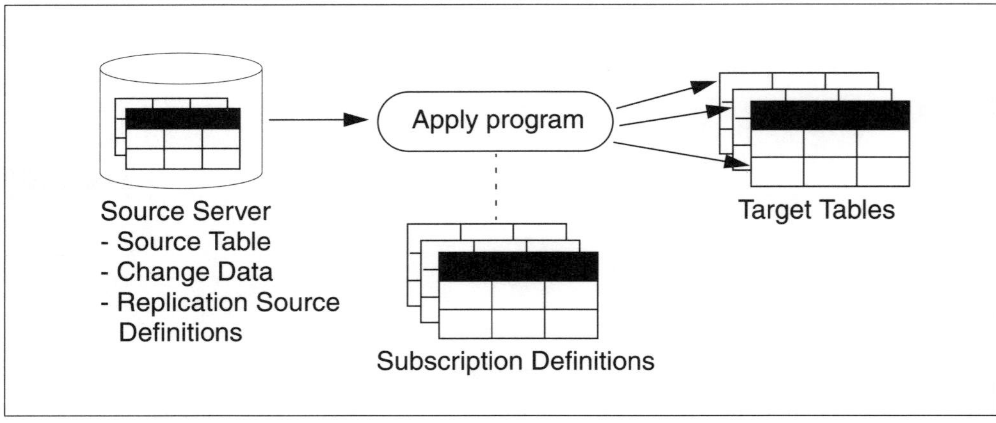

Figure 9. Apply Process - Overview

Push versus Pull Apply Configurations

Apply offers you the flexibility of running in either a push or a pull configuration.

- In a **push** configuration, the Apply program runs on the source server and therefore connects locally to the source database to retrieve the changes. Once these have been retrieved locally, the Apply program then connects to the remote target database and sends, or *pushes,* the changes to that server.
- In a **pull** configuration, the Apply program connects to the remote source database, and retrieves the data to be replicated. Once all the data has been *pulled* to the target server, the Apply program then connects to the target database and applies the changes to the target table.

Generally, a pull configuration performs better than a push configuration because it allows more efficient use of the network. It takes advantage of DB2 block fetching, which sends blocks of data, each containing many rows, across the network. In a push configuration, data is sent row by row. However, under the following circumstances a push configuration is a better choice:

- When there is no Apply program for the target server platform, for example, as with VSE or VM.
- The source table changes very infrequently, but when it changes, it should be replicated as soon as possible.

Figure 10 on page 14 shows both a push and a pull configuration:

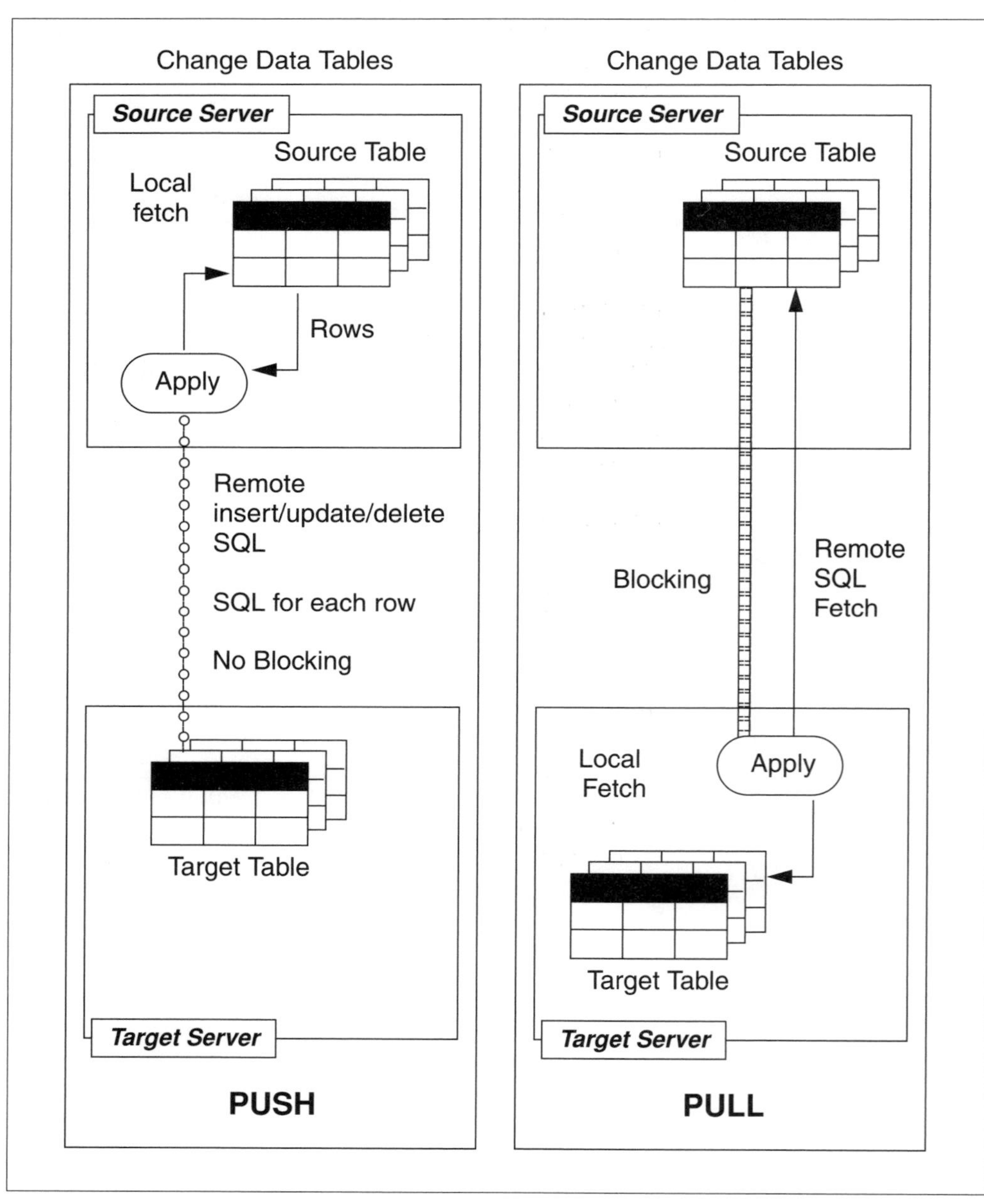

Figure 10. Apply Process - Push Versus Pull

Differential Refresh versus Full Refresh

As we now know, the Apply program copies source table data from the source server to the target server. You have two choices on how to configure this data transfer, thereby determining the amount of data to transfer and which components are involved in the work: a **full refresh** or a **differential refresh**.

In a **full refresh** operation, the Apply program directly accesses the entire source table and copies it to the target table. In this case, the Capture program is not involved at all; no changes are captured, and no control tables are written to. Full refresh is used for the initial load of the target table. If you have large tables, you might want to use a fast load program to simulate an initial full refresh copy.

A **differential refresh** involves copying all the desired source data once initially, and then only replicating the subsequent changes. The Capture process and the control tables are involved. The default method that is used is differential refresh. If you wish to have a full refresh performed every time Apply processes a subscription, you must specify this when you define the replication source.

The first time the Apply program copies data to the target table or after a cold start of the Capture program, the Apply program uses full refresh copying to populate the target table. This establishes a synchronization point between source and target. After the target table is populated, differential refresh is used.

In both the case of a full or a differential refresh, you have the option of using SQL to capture a subset of the source data and also modify the data before copying it to the target table, if you so choose.

Now that we have covered the basic concepts, Figure 11 shows you a high level view of the tasks involved in setting up and managing a DB2 replication system:

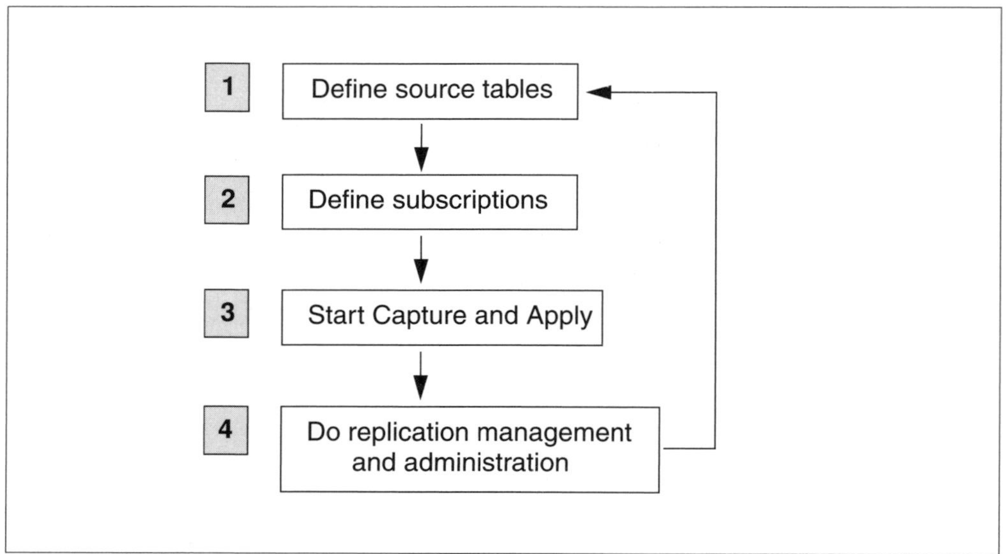

Figure 11. DB2 Replication System - Task Overview

We have now discussed the basic concepts and the major components included in DB2 data replication, and we are ready to discuss some of the more detailed replication concepts. These include the tables used by DB2 Replication and also some of the features of DB2 Replication.

1.1.8 Source, Target, and Control Servers

Up to this point we have discussed the tables that are involved in a replication scenario and also the steps to be taken to setup such a scenario. Let's step back a bit and look at the database servers that exist in a replication environment and look at how they relate to the above tables. There are three servers to consider: the **source server**, **target server**, and **control server.**

The source server is the database server (or database) where your replication source tables are defined. The Capture program always runs at the source server.

Conversely, your target server is the server (or database) where the database tables to receive the replicated changes are defined. Very often, this will also be located where the Apply program runs.

The control server is the database server (or database) that contains the replication subscription control tables (the control tables used by Apply). The Apply process must be able to connect to the control server using standard

SQL. The relationship between control server and Apply processes is one to many. Since each Apply process is associated with a subscription, each Apply process is associated with a control server; however, multiple Apply programs can share a control server.

For better performance, the control server should be located at the server where the Apply program runs because the Apply program frequently reads the tables in the control server. However, locating the control server at the source server, if it is a server in a secure environment, can provide improved security and ease of monitoring.

1.1.9 Control Tables

Control tables are the brains behind IBM data replication. They contain information about:

- How the replication is to be performed:

  The control tables contain the identification, description and location of the source, target, and staging tables. They also hold the parameters dictating how the scenario is to work, such as frequency, refresh type, included columns, WHERE predicates and so on.

- How it is performing:

  The control tables track where in time the various stages of the replication scenario are, and if there are any problems. They also contain the measure of data latency and the degree of data currency.

The DB2 UDB Control Center is used to create the replication control tables automatically for you when you use it to do your administration tasks. These tables will be created for you at all servers involved in the replication environment, so you must be able to connect to all of the required databases (source, target and control) from the Control Center on the system where you perform the replication administration. (The one exception to this is the mobile environment, which we discuss later in Chapter 7, “Mobile Replication” on page 249).

Some of the Control Tables are summarized below in Table 1:

Table 1. Control Tables

	Control Table Name	**Control Table Function**
Used by Capture (Only)	Warm Start	Allows capture to restart and continue processing from the last position in the DB2 log or journal that it processed.
	Trace	Used for concurrency between Capture and Apply.
	Tuning Parameters	Performance tuning information for Capture.
Used by Capture and Apply	Register	Contains name of the source tables and name of the change data table associated with the source.
	Unit-Of-Work	Contains committed unit-of-work information written by Capture and used by Apply.
	Change Data	Contains changed data read by Capture and is the source of data for update copies.
	Pruning Control	Used by Capture to prune the Change Data table.
	Critical Section	Trace information for Capture.
Used by Apply (Only)	Apply Trail	Records statistics about full and differential refresh copies performed during each subscription cycle.
	Subscription Set	Defines the characteristics of each subscription set.
	Subscription Statement	Contains the SQL statements or names of stored procedures to be run before/after the subscription set is processed.
	Subscription Events	Contains timing information for copying the subscription set based on events.
	Subscription Target Member	Information for an individual subscription set that maps a specific source table to a specific target table.
	Subscription Columns	Additional information about each copied column in the target table.

1.1.10 Data Transformation

There will be times when you want to massage or transform the data as it passes from the source to target tables. This could include taking a subset of the data, changing the contents of the data, or adding to the data. Having this ability gives you the flexibility to store, and therefore present, the data in a fashion that is more suited to your particular requirements (for example, in Data Warehousing, Decision Support, and other such environments).

Through the DB2 UDB Control Center, you have a very rich selection of types of transformations to use. You can specify the basic type of transformation you want to occur when you setup your replication subscription. Some of the supported transformations are listed below, and we discuss each one in turn:

- Choosing your target table type.
- Choosing a subset of the source data to be copied to your target.
- Choosing to do run-time processing on the data before or after the replication subscription is run.
- Renaming columns or computing columns.
- Replicating both the before and after images of changes.
- Defining a table join as a replication source.

1.1.10.1 Choosing your Target Table Type

When you setup your replication subscription, you decide how you want to have the data copied from your source to your target table. This is done through the DB2 Control Center, as shown in Figure 12:

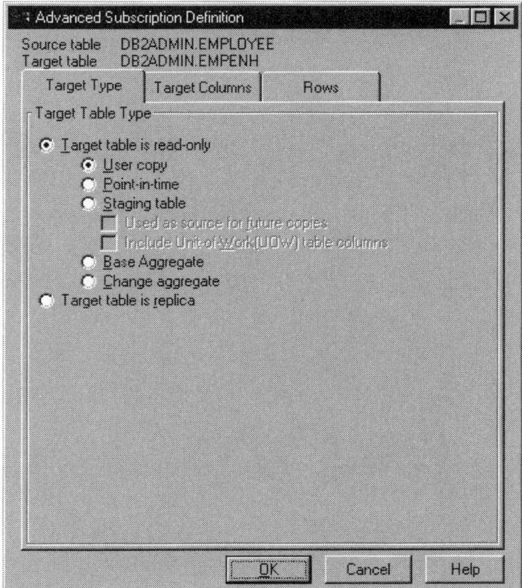

Figure 12. Data Transformation - Target Table Type

First, the target table type will depend on whether you want the target table to be a **read-only** or an **updateable** table. In this context, read-only means that only the Apply process should change the target table. Users or other applications should not change the target table, as it will then cease to be a consistent copy of the source table. In contrast, if users or applications change an updateable target table, then these changes are replicated back to the source table, and the two versions are kept in synchronization.

Read-Only Target Table Types

There are several different types of read-only target tables:

- **User Copy**. This table type is the most commonly used in data replication and is basically a simple copy of the replication source table. It can be subsetted by row or column.
- **Point-in-Time**. This table type is a simple copy of the replication source table with the addition of a timestamp column to indicate when the update occurred. It can also be subsetted by row or column.
- **Aggregate tables**. These tables have their contents based on calculations (such as SUM or AVG) to compute summaries of the contents of the source tables or of the changes made to the source tables. Rows are added over time. There are two types of aggregate tables:
  - **Base Aggregate**. This is a history table that summarizes the contents of the source table itself. Each new row in the table is a result of a changed row in the source table, which in turn, results in an SQL column function calculation against the source table. For example, a daily summary of inventory totals.
  - **Change Aggregate**. This table holds an aggregation of the changes that have occurred since the last aggregation request. Basically, we are *aggregating* changes. The aggregation is done against the change data in the control tables, and does not access the actual source table itself. As above, SQL column functions are involved in the aggregation. This type of aggregate table can be used to track changes made between each Apply subscription processing cycle.
- **Staging Tables (CCDs)**. These tables can be used as sources for future copies and to improve the efficiency of your replication system. They can be used as history or audit trail tables (if non-condensed), and can contain just the changes made to the original source table (if non-complete), or additionally, the entire original source table (if complete). If condensed, you can use a staging table to track the last state of a row in a table. The benefits of staging tables are covered in more detail in "Staging Tables" on page 23, and the different options (like condensed, complete and so on) are covered in Chapter 5, "Staging Tables" on page 169.

Updateable Target Table Types

There is only one type of updateable target table, the **Replica**. The default for this table type is to have the same after-image columns and primary key fields as the source table. Replica tables can be used for copying updates back to the source table in an update-anywhere scenario. In this sense, they can be considered as source tables also. A more complete discussion of update-anywhere is given in "Update Anywhere" on page 25 and step-by-step examples of using update-anywhere are given in Chapter 6, "Update-Anywhere Replication" on page 211.

1.1.10.2 Subsetting Source Data in Target Tables

You can subset your source data at both the row and column level, giving you the flexibility to determine exactly what data you want replicated. When you define your replication source table, you choose which source table columns to include for replication processing. In the DB2 UDB Control Center, you choose your target columns and your target rows when you define your subscription. This is shown Figure 13:

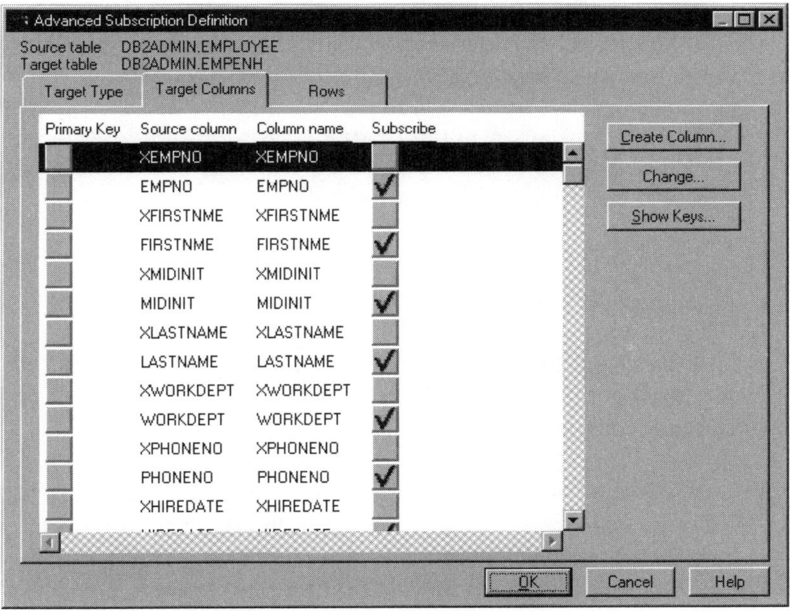

Figure 13. Data Transformation - Subsetting Source Data

In this panel, you have the ability to choose exactly which source columns you wish to replicate. In addition, the **Rows** tab in this panel allows you to subset which rows you want replicated by using a WHERE predicate.

1.1.10.3 Run-time Processing on the Data

In your environment, you may find it necessary to massage the source and/or target data before or after the subscription cycle. You can do this using SQL statements or stored procedures at the target server just before or after the Apply subscription processing is done. You also have the ability to specify that this run-time processing should be done at the source server before the Apply subscription is processed. This feature gives you a lot of flexibility and functionality in the way data is replicated, and allows you to do such things as:

- Pruning staging tables to delete data that is no longer required.
- Posting an event in the events table to control the start of the next subscription that should follow the current one. This allows you to specify the order your subscriptions should be run. For more details, see "Triggering Replication" on page 70.
- Providing enhancements to your data.

1.1.10.4 Renaming or Computing Columns

Your target table does not have to have the same column names as the source table. When defining your subscription, you have the option to rename the target table columns.

You can also add new columns to your target table and have their values determined by the results of an SQL expression. Any valid SQL arithmetic expression or aggregate function can be used.

1.1.10.5 Replicating Before and After Images

If your application or environment needs to know not only the current data but what it was before the change was made, you have the option of specifying that the source table should contain the before images of the data. As part of your replication subscription, you also have the additional option to indicate which of these before columns you wish to replicate.

1.1.10.6 Defining a Table Join as a Replication Source

When your target table needs to contain columns from multiple tables in the source database, DB2 replication provides the ability to define a replication source that is a view. Views can be based upon multiple replication source tables and can be used as sources for subscription definitions. This is all setup through the DB2 Control Center. You may find this feature of use if you need to restructure your data, and it can be used to enable easier querying of the replicated data.

1.1.11 Staging Tables

An important concept in the architecture of DB2 Replication is the *staging* of data. The changed data is copied from the source to an intermediate target staging table. At some future time, this data is then copied to its final target destination. You can consider a **staging table** as a special kind of data replication table that can be used to make your environment more flexible and efficient.

In a basic replication scenario, the Capture program determines the source table changes from the database log files (or journal) and inserts information about the changes into the Change Data tables and transaction commit information into the Unit-of-Work table. The Apply process then has to do a join of the Change Data and Unit-of-Work tables to get the final result set of changes that have been committed. In this manner, regardless of how many Apply processes are running, the Capture process only has to update the CD and UOW tables once. Unfortunately, in this scenario, Apply must do the join of these two tables each and every time a subscription is processed.

If you define a staging table (or **Consistent Change Table (CCD table)**) in your environment, this table will hold the committed changes against a source table. A CCD table is a join of the CD and UOW tables, and contains only committed changed data.

Once a staging table is defined, it can then be used as a source in a replication scenario with other target tables. The Apply process will no longer have to do a join of two tables to get the replication data; instead, it only has to access a single table.

In Figure 14 on page 23, you can see how a CCD table fits into the total replication picture. A CCD table can be located on the source or target servers, or on another server on the network.

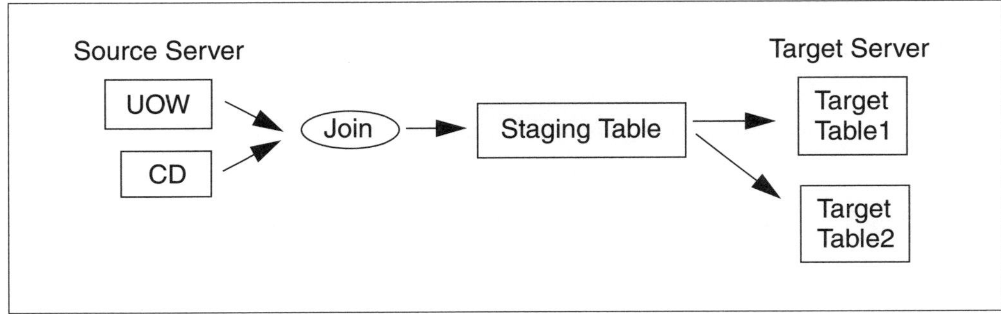

Figure 14. CCD or Staging Table

Some of the benefits of having a staging table include:

- Maintaining complete histories of data changes.
- Minimizing change data and unit-of-work table processing by removing the need for the Apply process to do a join.
- Lower network loads by reducing the amount of data sent between source and target servers.

There are many ways to define a staging table, and these are discussed in much more detail in Chapter 5, "Staging Tables" on page 169.

1.1.12 Scheduling Replication

Now that you understand what goes into a replication scenario and the pieces you need to have, the next step you need to do is to tell DB2 when to do the replication for you. This schedule is associated with the replication subscription, and you set it up using the DB2 Control Center when you create the subscription, as shown in Figure 15 on page 24.

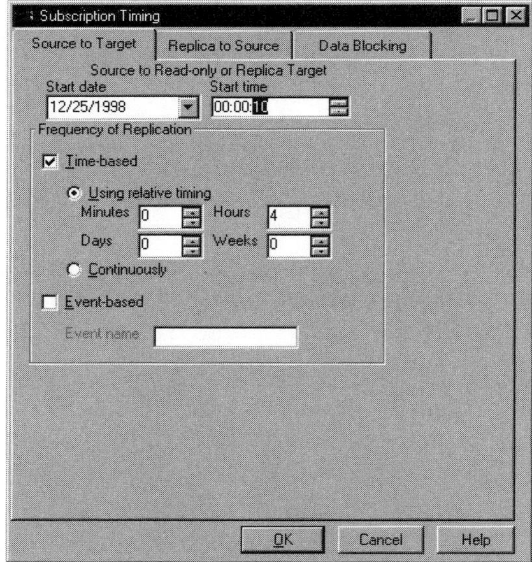

Figure 15. Scheduling Replication

As shown in this panel, you have two options you can use in scheduling. You can choose to replicate at a defined interval, for instance, once a day or once a month (this is called **interval** or **relative timing**). You can also choose to have the replication subscription run when an external event occurs (known as **event timing**). You can choose to use either or both of these options with your subscription. In the panel shown above, we chose to start replication on Christmas morning just after midnight and to have replication initiated every four hours.

In addition to specifying how often and when to do the replication, you can limit the length of time that Apply will copy data at a time. The time parameter does not directly limit the time apply runs, but the maximum time block of captured data which is to be processed in one cycle. This cuts the workload of Apply into smaller pieces in order to prevent resource utilization problems.

This is also done through the Control Center through the **Data Blocking** panel, as shown in Figure 16:

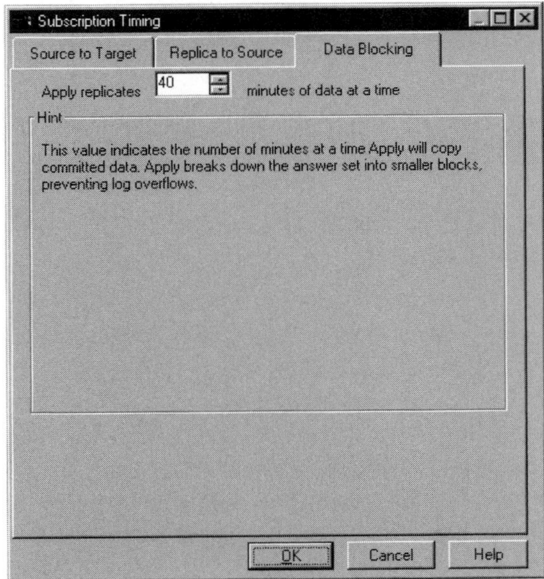

Figure 16. Setting Data Blocking

1.1.13 Update Anywhere

So far, we have discussed the ability to replicate from a source table to a target table in a one-way direction. In this configuration, the target table is considered read-only, in that any changes made to it will not be copied back to the source table. You may find it desirable in your environment to be able to update the target tables any time you want and then at some other time synchronize the targets with each other and with the source.

Figure 17 on page 26 shows the model of **updating** your target and source tables **anywhere** in which a replication source has its target table(s) defined as read/write copies. In this scenario, you define your target table type as a **replica** table.

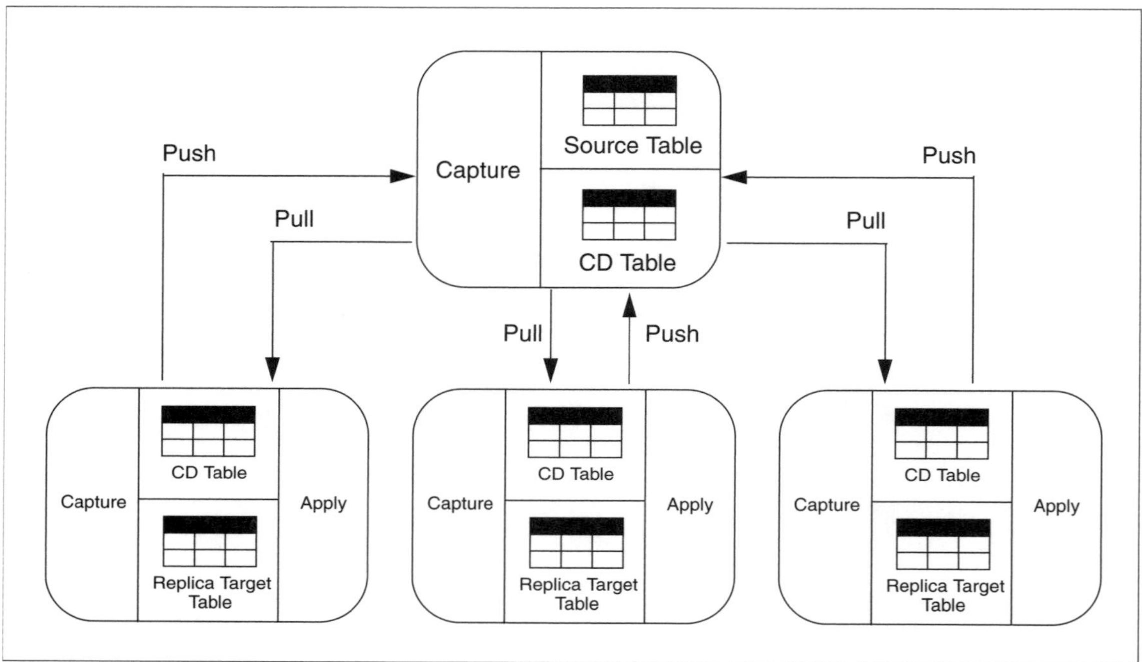

Figure 17. Update Anywhere Scenario

In this example, we have three target tables and one source table. In addition to the Capture process running at the source with a change data table, we now require a Capture process and change data table at each replica site. The Apply process will run at each replica, pull down changes remotely captured at the source and push up changes captured locally at each replica. Once replicated to the source server, the changes will be available to the other target servers for replication. The source server maintains the most up-to-date data.

In this type of situation, conflicting updates may occur. In the case of conflicts, the source becomes the point of reference and will be the winner in the case of any conflicts. The losing replica will receive compensatory SQL to undo its updates. For more details, see Chapter 6, “Update-Anywhere Replication” on page 211.

1.1.14 Pruning Data

Up to this point, we have discussed the methodology for copying your data to where you need it. As part of this process, certain control tables, such as the UOW and Change Data tables, will grow continuously. Obviously, from a space management point of view, this can be a problem.

To resolve this situation, you **prune** your tables either automatically or manually. The pruning process involves the following:

1. Apply updates the pruning control table with information about the updates it has applied to the target tables.
2. Capture goes though the CD and UOW tables removing unwanted records based upon the information supplied by Apply.

We discuss pruning in more detail in "Pruning" on page 80.

1.1.15 Mobile Replication

Mobile users are becoming more and more prevalent in today's industries. Take, for example, the insurance industry. It is not uncommon for a company's sales force to be equipped with laptop computers and be on the road most of the time. In situations such as this, it is very important that the sales force have access to the latest information regarding new offers, special packages, and so on. Since the sales force does not come into the office often, they rely on their laptop computers for the latest data.

Such a mobile environment not only requires the ability for an **update anywhere** type of configuration, but it goes a step beyond since the individual is only **occasionally connected** to the primary servers at the corporate office. They rely on dial-in downloads of the latest information and uploads of changes made to their local copies, and they only stay connected to the source server long enough to synchronize the local database tables. A direct connection is not feasible, nor required.

In such a situation, it is necessary for the mobile client to initiate and control the replication process. DB2 Replication supports this mobile environment by providing:

- On-demand connection and execution of both Capture and Apply processes on and from the mobile target server. Connection to the required source sites is dynamic.
- Both Apply push and pull configurations are supported, so that the target server may not only receive changes from the source but also send updates to the source server.

- A mobile replication enabler and associated graphical user interface program to invoke the replication process. This allows the end user to accomplish the required replications without needing detailed knowledge about DB2 Replication.

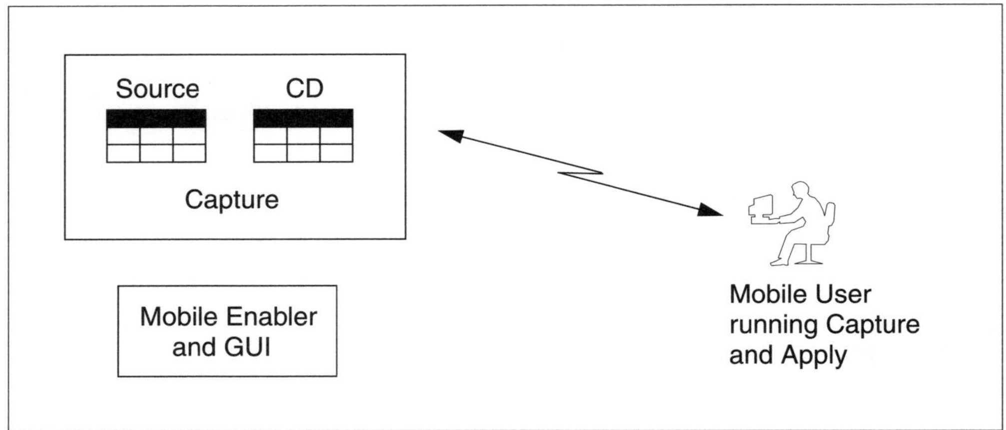

Figure 18. Occasionally Connected (Mobile) Users

In this situation, the mobile site initiates and controls the replication and the central source server does not know about the mobile site until it initiates a connection. Any changes from the mobile site (new or changed data) are pushed to the central server. Any changes from the central server are pulled to the mobile site.

For further details on mobile replication, please see Chapter 7, “Mobile Replication” on page 249.

1.2 IBM Data Replication Products

IBM provides a very complete set of data replication products and tools across its DB2 product platforms. All these products function together to provide a single data replication solution for your environment. The products that are currently available include:

- IBM Replication products:
  - Included in DB2 Universal Database V5.0 and V5.2 are the replication administration functions provided by the DB2 UDB Control Center and the Capture and Apply programs for the supported UDB platforms.
  - IBM Capture and Apply for MVS Version 5.1.
  - Capture for VSE and VM Version 5.1: these are integrated into the IBM DB2 Server for VSE and VM Version 5.1 product.
- DPROPR Version 1 allows you to support IBM DB2 DataJoiner Version 2.
- DataPropagator Relational Capture and Apply for OS/400.
- IBM DataPropagator NonRelational (DPROPNR): provides you with change capture capability for IMS.
- IBM DataRefresher: use this for IMS, VSAM and Flat Files and to provide a transformation mapping for DPROPNR.
- IBM DB2 DataJoiner and the DataJoiner Replication Administration Tool: DataJoiner adds a heterogeneous capability to DPROPR for non-IBM database servers such as Oracle, Sybase, Informix and Microsoft SQL Server.
- Lotus NotesPump: this allows you to update from your DB2 database server to Lotus Notes databases.

Table 2 on page 30 shows you the DB2 Replication relational product lineup and how the Capture, Apply and Administration components are packaged. The non-relational products are not listed. Please refer to the appropriate product documentation for information on these products.

Table 2. DB2 Replication Products and Features

Product Name	Platforms	Replication Features	Includes Host and OS/400 Connectivity
DB2 Enterprise Edition	OS/2, Windows NT, AIX, HP/UX, Solaris, SCO UnixWare 7	Capture program, Apply program, and DPROPR V1 Migration program on OS/2, Windows NT, Windows 95	Yes
DB2 Workgroup Edition	OS/2, Windows NT, AIX, HP/UX, Solaris, SCO UnixWare 7	Capture program, Apply program, and DPROPR V1 Migration program on OS/2, Windows NT, Windows 95	No
DB2 Personal Edition (see note 1 below)	OS/2, Windows NT, Windows 95/98	Capture program, Apply program, and DPROPR V1 Migration program on OS/2, Windows NT, Windows 95	No
DB2 Connect Personal Edition (see note 2 below)	OS/2, Windows NT, Windows 95/98, Windows 3.1	DPROPR V1 Migration program on OS/2, Windows NT, Windows 95	Yes, single-user
DB2 Connect Enterprise Edition (see note 1 below)	OS/2, Windows NT, AIX, HP/UX, Solaris, SCO UnixWare 7	DPROPR V1 Migration program on OS/2, Windows NT, Windows 95	Yes
DPROPR Capture for MVS, V5.1	MVS	Capture Program	Yes, packaged with DB2 Connect Personal Edition
DPROPR Apply for MVS, V5.1	MVS	Apply Program	Yes, packaged with DB2 Connect Personal Edition
DB2 Server for VSE or VM V5.1	VSE or VM	Capture Program	Yes, packaged with DB2 Connect Personal Edition
DPROPR Capture and Apply for OS/400	AS/400	Capture and Apply Programs	Yes, packaged with DB2 Connect Personal Edition

Note:
1. Both products are required at a minimum for the mobile environment.
2. Included in the Capture and Apply program packages for MVS, and Capture program packages for VSE and VM.

1.2.1 Software Requirements

The software requirements for each Data Replication product as of DB2 Universal Database Version 5.2 are provided for you in Table 3:

Table 3. DB2 Replication Products - Software Requirements

Product	Software Requirements
Capture and Apply programs on DB2 Universal Database V5.0 or V5.2	- Both the Capture and Apply programs are shipped with DB2 UDB and therefore the software requirements for DB2 UDB are in effect. Please refer to the *DB2 Universal Database Quick Beginnings* document for your operating system platform.
Capture for MVS, 5.1 Apply for MVS, 5.1	- IBM MVS/ESA Version 3 Release 1 Modification 3 (5695-047) or higher (data sharing requires MVS/ESA Version 5 Release 1 (5655-068) or higher). - DFSMS Version 1 Release 1 (5695-DF1) or MVS/DFP Version 3 Release 3 (5665-XA3) or higher. - IBM C/370 Library Version 2 or IBM SAA AD/Cycle Language Environment/370 Version 1 Release 3 or higher, including any PTFs. - IBM DATABASE 2 Server for OS/390, Version 5, Release 1 (5648-158), or IBM DATABASE 2 for MVS Version 3 Release 1 or higher, including any PTFs. - IBM System Modification Program/Extended Version 1 Release 8 (5668-949).
Capture for VSE, 5.1 Capture for VM, 5.1	- IBM DATABASE 2 Server for VSE & VM Version 5, Release 1 (5648-158). - IBM Language Environment for VSE Version 1 Release 4 (5685-094) or the equivalent C & CEL run-time support provided in the base of VSE/ESA Version 2 Release 2. (for Capture for VSE). - IBM Language Environment Version 1 Release 5 (5688-198) or higher, or the equivalent C & CEL run-time support provided in the base of VM/ESA Version 2 (for Capture for VM).
Data Propagator Relational Capture and Apply for OS/400	- AS/400 Version 4.1 or higher.

1.2.2 Hardware Requirements

You should also be aware of the hardware requirements for the particular platform configurations you may deal with. They are listed for you in Table 4:

Table 4. DB2 Replication Products - Hardware Requirements

Product	Hardware Requirements
Capture and Apply programs on DB2 Universal Database V5.0 or V5.2	- Both the Capture and Apply programs are shipped with DB2 UDB and therefore the hardware requirements for DB2 UDB are in effect. Please refer to the *DB2 Universal Database Quick Beginnings* document for your operating system platform.
Capture for MVS, 5.1 Apply for MVS, 5.1	- Any hardware configuration that supports MVS/ESA Version 5 Release 1 (5655-069) or higher (for data sharing) or MVS/ESA Version 3 Release 1 Modification 3 (5695-047) or higher (without data sharing). - System/390 Parallel Sysplex is required for data sharing.
Capture for VSE, 5.1 Capture for VM, 5.1	- Any hardware that supports VSE/ESA Version 2 Release 1 Modification 2 or higher (for Capture for VSE). - Any hardware that supports VM/ESA Version 2 Release 1 or higher (for Capture for VM 5.1).
Data Propagator Relational Capture and Apply OS/400	- Any hardware that supports AS/400.

1.3 Replication Connectivity Configurations

To be able to use the IBM Replication features you need to understand under which conditions and platforms the products are currently supported. At the time of writing, data can be replicated:

- Among DB2 for MVS, DB2 for VSE & VM, DB2 Universal Database V5, and DB2 for OS/400 database servers.
- Across platforms for MVS, VM, VSE, OS/400, AIX, HP-UX, SCO UnixWare 7, OS/2, Windows NT, Windows 95/98, and the Solaris operating environment.
- On non-DB2 sources and targets through DB2 DataJoiner.

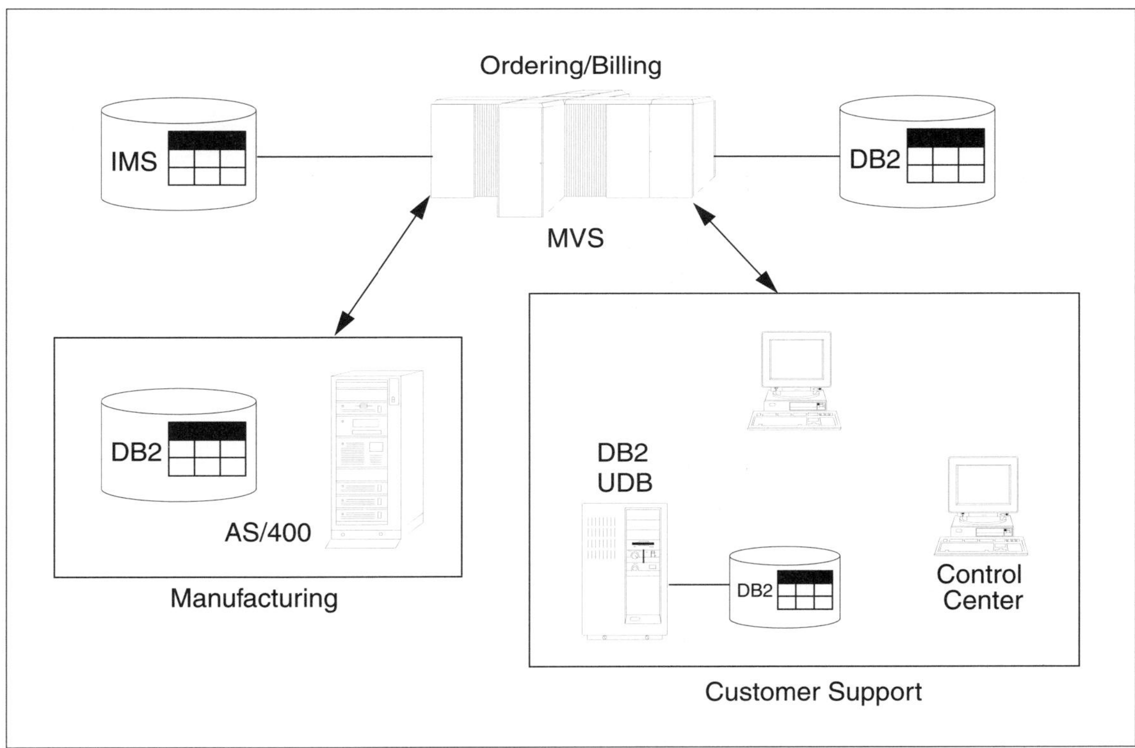

Figure 19. Data Replication Connectivity Options

As we have discussed earlier in this chapter, the Capture process is always local to the source data and must be able to connect to the local database.

From an administrative point of view, the DB2 Control Center must be able to connect to the source, control and target servers.

In most cases, the Apply process must also be able to connect to the target, control and the source servers.

In any situation where you have network connectivity (any non-local connection), you will either use a protocol supported by DB2 Universal Database V5 for client-server connectivity or DRDA. The actual protocols that you will use depend on the platforms being connected:

- If you are connecting between DB2 Universal Database V5 platforms you can use any of the supported network protocols for the operating system platforms you are using including TCP/IP, NetBIOS, SNA, and IPX/SPX.
- Connections to host database servers such as DB2 for MVS, DB2 for VSE/VM or DB2/400 require a protocol supported under DRDA.

  At the time of writing, DB2 for OS/390 V5.1 running on OS/390 V1R3, DB2/400 V4R2, and DB2 for VM V6.1 support native TCP/IP connections.

  All other DRDA based connections must use SNA.

Note

It is important to note that any connections between DB2 Universal Database V5 databases and DB2 for MVS, DB2 for VSE, or DB2 for VM require a DB2 Connect product.

1.4 Summary

In this chapter we discussed the major concepts of DB2 Data Replication, including the different kinds of tables involved and how to perform administrative functions.

In the following chapters of this book, we concentrate on giving you more details on how the replication process is actually accomplished and show you example scenarios with detailed step-by-step guides to help you setup your own replication environment.

Chapter 2. Managing Replication Sources and Subscriptions

This chapter explains how to define replication sources and subscriptions using the DB2 UDB Control Center, how to change the overall replication defaults, and how to change the default control table definitions.

2.1 Overview

First, let's review the principal components that we reference in this chapter:

- Replication Source.

  A table can be defined as a *Replication Source*. To use a table as the source in a subscription, the table must already be defined as a replication source.

- Replication Target.

  A *Replication Target* is the table into which the replicated changes are inserted, updated or deleted.

- Replication Subscription.

  A *Replication Subscription* defines the way data is replicated between a replication source table and a replication target table.

Before configuring replication sources and subscriptions, you can optionally review or change the default settings for replication. If you are setting up replication for the first time, you should probably accept these default settings. Changing the default settings requires you to have detailed knowledge of how replication works. For details on how to review and change these default settings, see "Managing Defaults for Replication Sources and Subscriptions" on page 56.

A table defined as a replication source table can be a normal user-defined table or one of a list of advanced types. See "Other Types of Replication Sources" on page 40 for more details. Here, we will start by discussing user-defined tables.

2.1.1 Defining a Replication Source

There are two ways to define a replication source, *Quick* and *Custom*. The Quick option is recommended if you are setting up replication for the first time and want to understand more about replication sources. To use the Quick option:

From the Control Center, click on **Tables** in the required database. Right-click against the required table, and then from the pop-up, select **Define as Replication Source->Quick**:

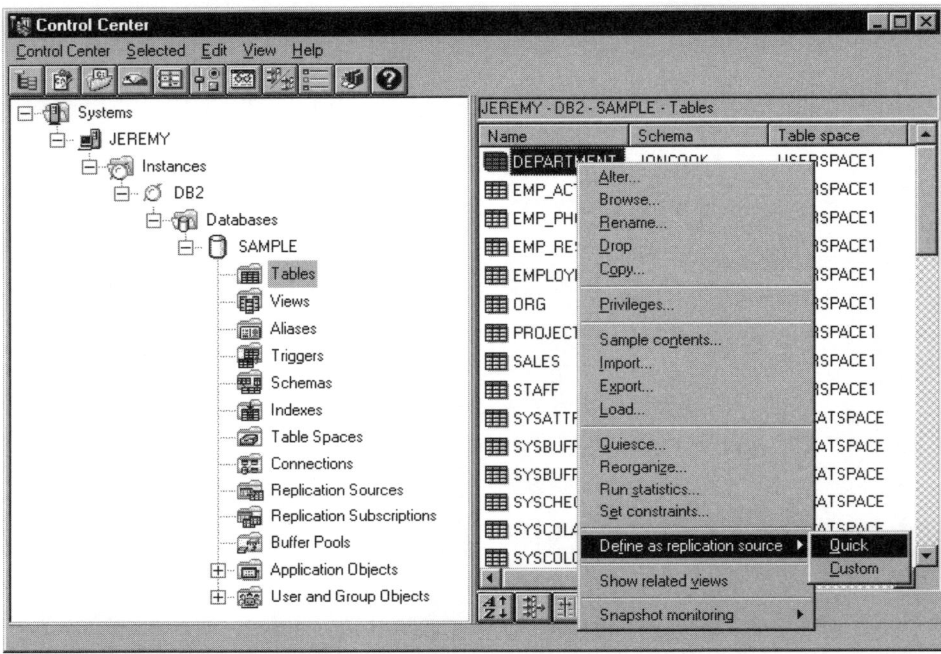

Figure 20. Define Replication Source - Quick

In this example, we have chosen the DEPARTMENT table. The following pop-up is displayed:

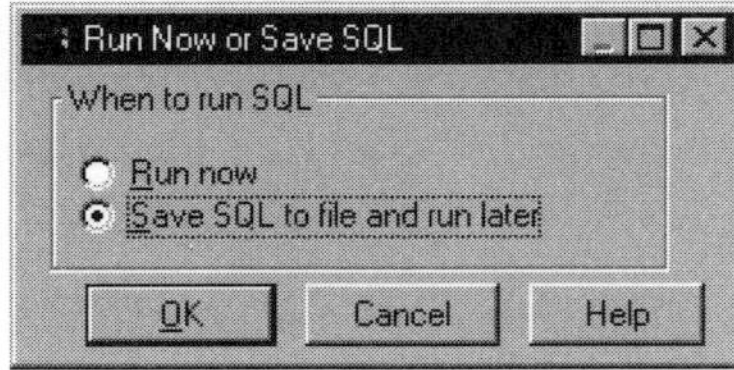

Figure 21. Run Now or Later Pop-up

You can choose to run the SQL immediately, or save it to a file and run it later. If you choose the second option, you must then enter a file name for the SQL file. You can then examine the file to see the generated SQL, and modify it if required. For example, you can choose the table space where the Change Data (CD) table is stored.

To run the SQL saved in a file, right-click on **Replication Sources** in the Control Center, and then select **Run SQL files**:

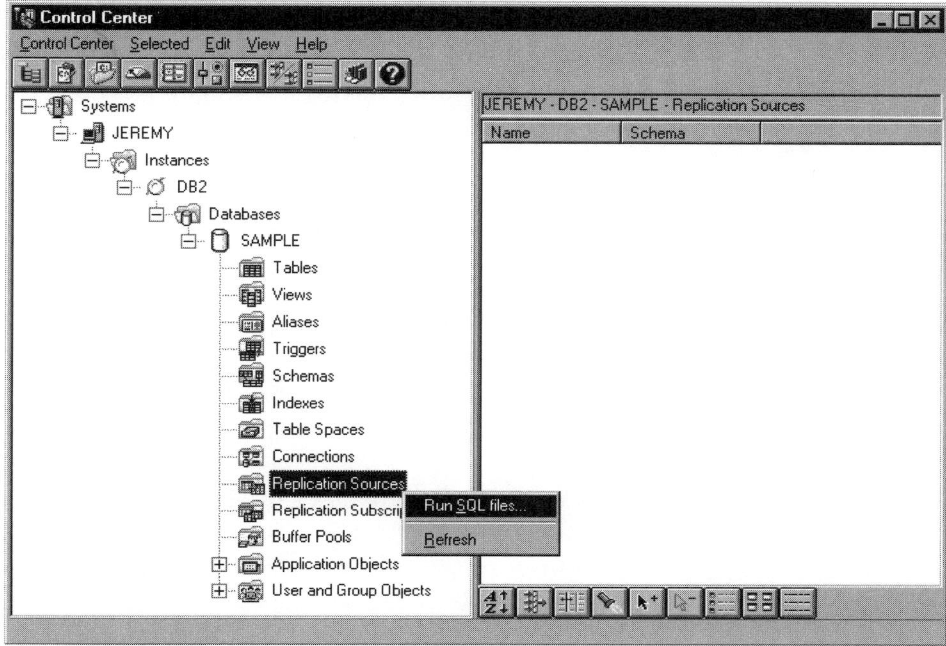

Figure 22. Run SQL Files

You then choose the name of the SQL file to run. By default, this is the file you just created.

When the SQL finishes successfully, the table has been defined as a replication source. If you click on **Replication Sources->Refresh**, you will see an entry in the contents pane at the right. In this case, the SQL performs the following:

1. The DEPARTMENT table is altered for DATA CAPTURE CHANGES. This tells DB2 to record additional information in the DB2 logs about the changes made to the table. Capture will use this information.
2. A change data (CD) table for DEPARTMENT is created. This table will hold all the changes to the DEPARTMENT table. For each column in the DEPARTMENT table, there are two columns in the CD table, one for the column value before the change, and one for the column value after.
3. An index is created on this CD table.

4. A row is inserted into the REGISTER table (ASN.IBMSNAP_REGISTER). There is one row per replication source in this table.

Note

If you need to define many replication sources at once, you can select multiple tables using the **Shift** or **Ctrl** keys. In this case, only the Quick option is possible.

2.1.2 Defining a Custom Replication Source

If you choose to define a Replication Source using the Custom option, you can:

- Setup full refresh copies.
- Exclude individual source columns from the replication process.
- Configure update-anywhere replication.

To use the Custom option, from the Control Center, click on **Tables** in the required database. Right-click on the required table, and select **Define as Replication Source->Custom** (see Figure 20 on page 36). The following panel is displayed:

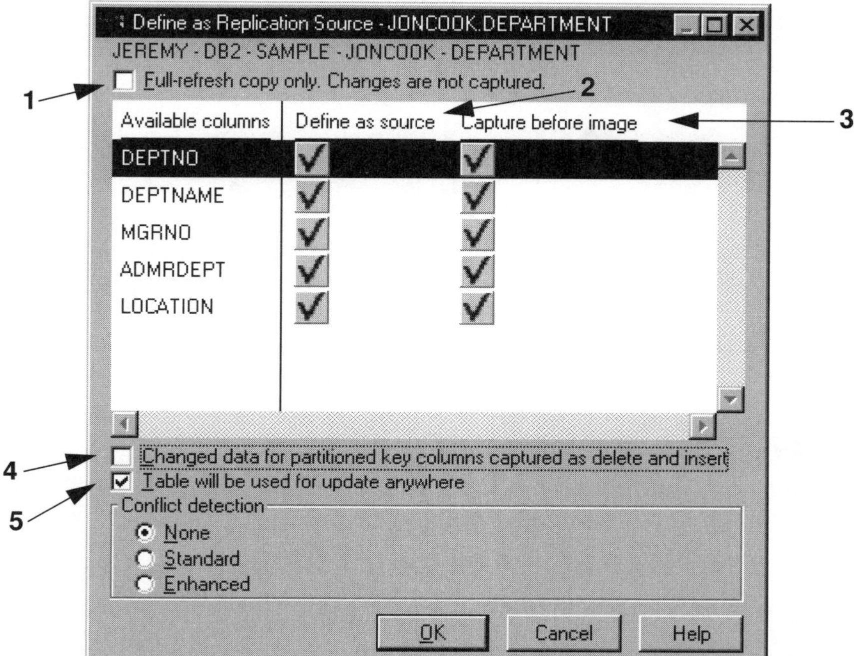

Figure 23. Define Replication Source - Custom

From the panel shown in Figure 23, these options are available:

1. **Full-refresh copy only**. If you choose this option, all the rows of the source table will be copied to the target table. Changes to the source table will not be captured. By default, this setting is not selected.
2. **Define as source**. You can choose to include or exclude each column in the replication process. A check in this column means that changes to this column will be captured. The default is to include every column. For update-anywhere replication, you must include every column.
3. **Capture before image**. You can choose to include or exclude each column's before image. In update changes, the before image contains the column's value before the update took place. The default is to include every column's before image.
4. **Partitioned key columns**. If you select this option, an update of a partition key is captured as a delete and an insert. The default is off. See "Replicating Updates" on page 60 for more details.
5. **Update Anywhere**. If you are configuring update-anywhere replication, then you can select the mode of conflict detection. These are the choices:

- **None**: This means that no conflict detection will take place. This is the default.
- **Standard**: This means that the Apply program will look in the CD tables of the source and replica for conflicts.
- **Enhanced**: This means that the Apply program will not only use CD tables for conflict detection, but also wait for transactions in progress to complete when looking for conflicts.

Chapter 6, "Update-Anywhere Replication" on page 211 contains a full discussion about update-anywhere, including a step-by-step example.

As for a Quick definition, you are given the option of running the SQL immediately, or saving it to a file for later execution.

2.1.3 Other Types of Replication Sources

In addition to a normal user-defined table, there are other types of objects that can be defined as replication sources:

- A join of user-defined tables. See the next section for more details.
- A replication target table.
- A CCD (staging) table. When a CCD table is defined as the target table during the definition of a subscription, it can be defined as a replication source at the same time. See Chapter 5, "Staging Tables" on page 169 for more details.
- A Replica table. This is used in update-anywhere configurations and is automatically defined as a replication source. See Chapter 6, "Update-Anywhere Replication" on page 211 for more details.
- An external CCD table. This is a CCD table that is maintained by a user-defined program. See "CCD Table Considerations" on page 314 for more details.

2.1.4 Defining Join Replication Sources

You define the join of two or more tables as a replication source. This can be used to perform data transformation between the source and target tables.

First, you must define the tables involved in the join as replication sources. In Figure 24 on page 41, the DEPARTMENT and EMPLOYEE tables are shown in the right pane:

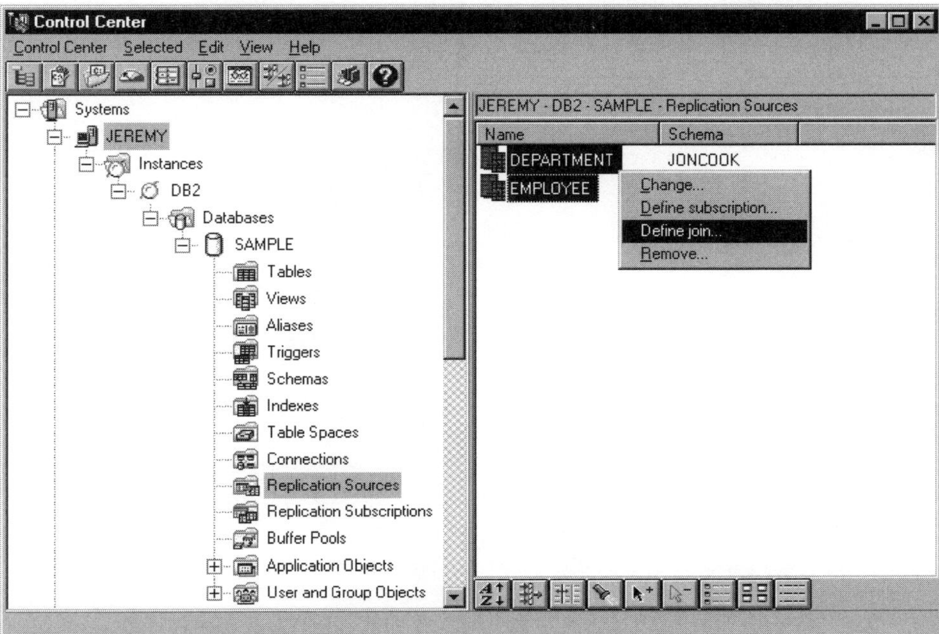

Figure 24. Define Join Replication Source

The next step is to hold the **Ctrl** key and click on each replication source to highlight each one, then right-click and select **Define join**. The Define Join panel is displayed:

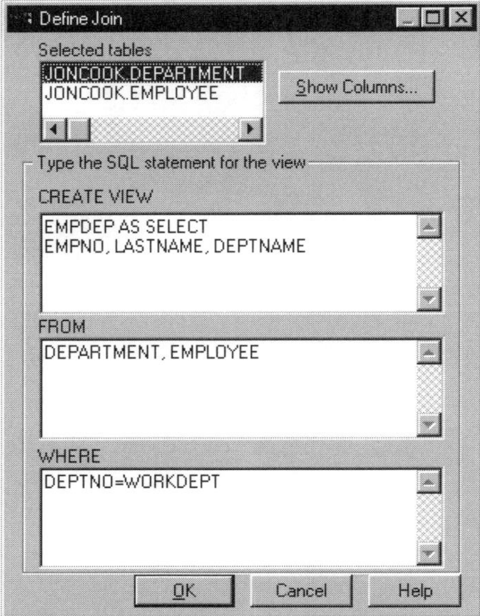

Figure 25. Define Join

In this panel, you can:

- Select a table, then click on **Show Columns** to display its columns.
- Enter the view definition, as shown in Figure 25 above.

When entering the view definition, do not enter the CREATE VIEW, FROM, or WHERE keywords - they are automatically supplied. When you have finished, click **OK**. You are given the option to run the SQL immediately, or save it to a file for later execution.

Note

The two (or more) tables that you join together to form a join replication source MUST be tables, not views.

2.1.5 Managing Replication Sources

Once you have defined replication sources, you can perform certain tasks on them. If you need to make any changes, you must first make sure that the Capture program is not running.

- **View/change**. To view or change a replication source, right-click on the replication source in the contents pane and select **Change**. You can only change the definition if the replication source was originally defined for update-anywhere usage and you chose a conflict level greater than 'None'. In this case, the level of conflict detection may be changed.

- **Remove**. When you remove a replication source, any subscriptions that use this replication source will also be deleted, as well as any join replication sources that use this replication source.

2.2 Replication Subscriptions

Before you define any subscriptions, you should first catalog the remote databases that will be used in the replication process (for example, the target database).

2.2.1 Defining a Subscription

Let's start by looking at how to define a basic subscription. Later on, we cover the advanced options.

Select **Replication Sources** to display the replication sources in the contents pane. Right-click on the desired replication source and select **Define subscription**:

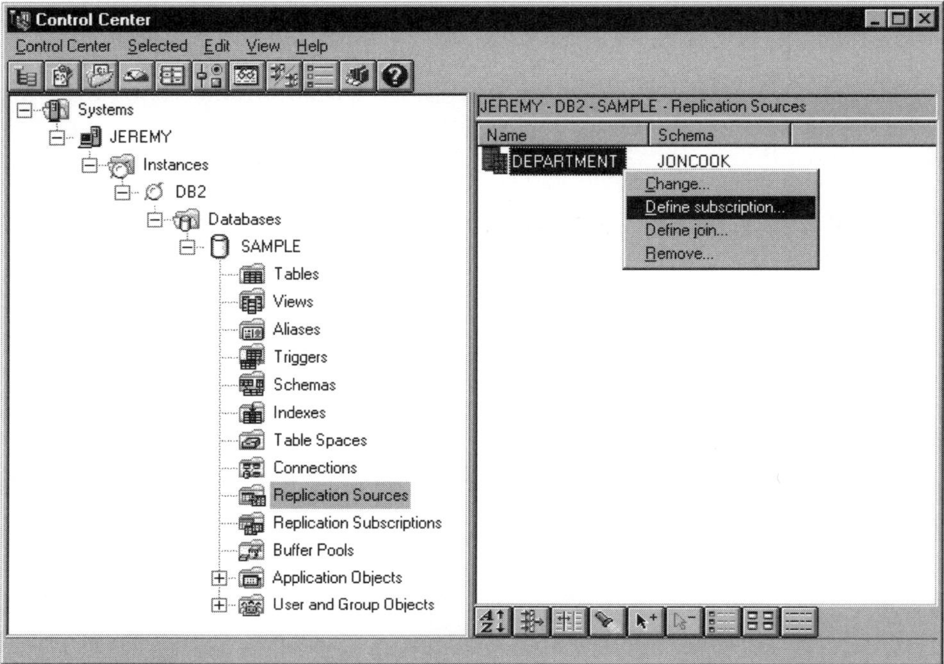

Figure 26. Define Subscription

> **Note**
>
> You can also select multiple registration sources by using the **Shift** or **Ctrl** keys. This can be useful if you need to use many replication sources in the same subscription set.

The following panel is displayed:

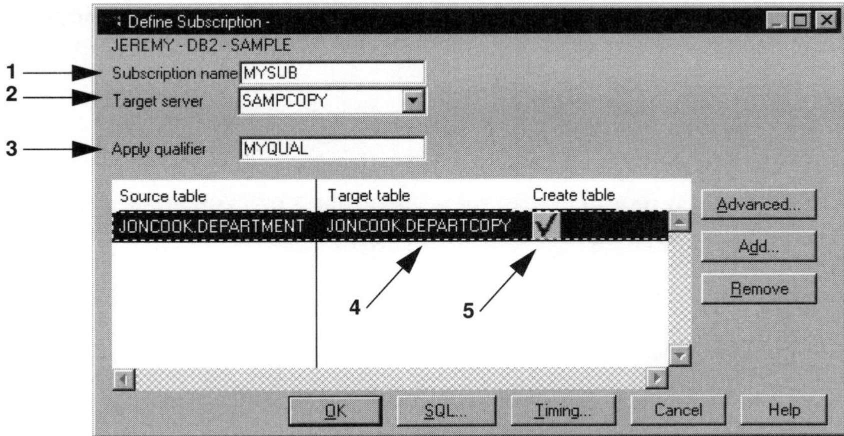

Figure 27. Define Subscription Panel

In the Define Subscription panel shown in Figure 27, you can:

1. Enter a **Subscription name**. You can use this name to group together many subscriptions into one subscription set. A subscription set is identified by the:
   - Subscription name. This is also known as the *set name*.
   - Apply qualifier (entered on this screen).
   - Name of the database holding the control tables (control server). This is specified in the next panel (see Figure 28 on page 46).

   You can use the **Add** button on this panel to add more subscriptions to the same subscription set, and the **Remove** button to remove them. If you have tables that are linked together by referential integrity contraints, then you should group all the subscriptions in the same subscription set to ensure data integrity at the target database.

2. In the **Target server** field, select a database using the pull-down list. The list will display all the databases, local and remote, that are cataloged on the local system. If you don't see all the cataloged databases, you may have to expand the required systems in the Control Center. You should select the database that will hold your target table(s).

3. Enter an **Apply qualifier**. When the Apply program is started later, this qualifier is used as a parameter.

4. By default, the **Target table** name is the same as the source table name. You can change this name by clicking on this field and editing the name.

5. To have the target table created in the target database, click on **Create Table**. If you don't select this option, then you must create the target table yourself. Alternately, you can configure the replication default settings so that the target table is automatically created. In this case, the option will be automatically checked. See "Replication Defaults Using Tools Settings" on page 56 for more details.

You can continue and create the subscription by clicking **OK**. If you want to use a target table that is not a simple copy of the source table, specify the replication timing or perform any data transformation between the source and target, then see "Defining Subscriptions - Advanced Options" on page 47.

After clicking **OK**, the following panel is displayed:

Figure 28. Define Subscription - Run Now or Save SQL

Enter the name of the database where you want to store the control tables. In this example, we have chosen the target database, SAMPCOPY. As we saw when defining replication sources, you can choose to run the SQL immediately, or save it to a file and run it later.

In this case, the SQL performs the following:

- In the database that holds the subscription control tables, rows are inserted into these tables:
  - ASN.IBMSNAP_SUBS_SET - one row per subscription set.
  - ASN.IBMSNAP_SUBS_MEMBER - one row per member of a subscription set.
  - ASN.IBMSNAP_SUBS_COLS - one row per column per subscription set member.
- In the source database:
  - A row is inserted into the Pruning Control table (ASN.IBMSNAP_PRUNCNTL). This is used during the pruning operation to delete old entries from the CD and UOW tables. See "Pruning" on page 80 for more details.

To verify that the Subscription has been created, right-click on **Subscriptions** (in the source database) and select **Refresh**. You should see your newly-created subscription in the contents pane at the right.

2.2.2 Defining Subscriptions - Advanced Options

You should use the advanced options when defining subscriptions if you need to:

- Configure n-tier replication (staging tables) or configure update-anywhere replication (replica tables) or use history or aggregate tables.
- Perform data transformations between the source and target tables.
- Perform SQL statements during the processing of subscriptions.
- Change the default timing for replication, or make replication dependant on a certain event taking place.

2.2.3 Defining Target Table Types

If you want to use a target table apart from user copy (the default), click on **Advanced** from the Define Subscription panel (Figure 27 on page 45) to display the Advanced Subscription Definition panel:

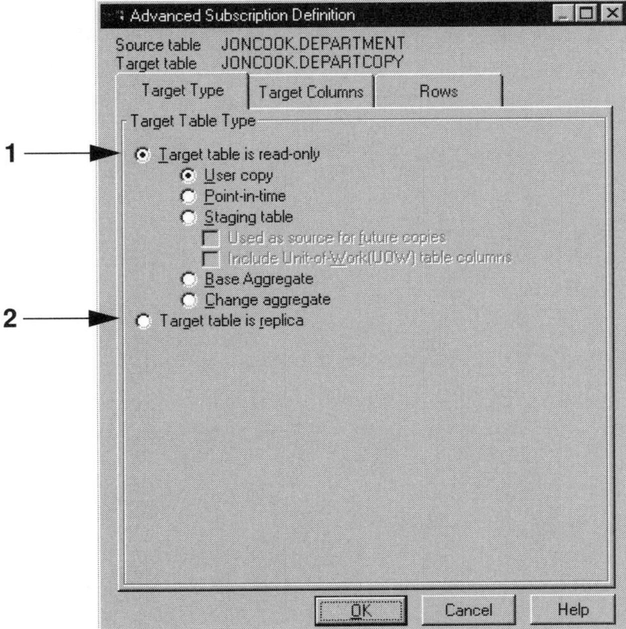

Figure 29. Advanced Subscription Definition

By default, the target table is a *read-only* copy. You can perform inserts, updates, or deletes on a read-only target table, but it is *read only* in terms of replication, as any changes will not be replicated back to the source table.

1. You can select one of these read-only target table types:

   - **User copy**: Matches the data in the source table exactly at the time of the copy. This choice is the default and must have a primary key.
   - **Point-in-time**: Similar to a user copy table with a timestamp column added.
   - **Staging table**: Can be used as a replication source for further copies in multi-tier replication. If you select this target type, you can optionally append unit-of-work table columns to the target table by selecting the Unit-of-Work (UOW) table columns check box. For more details, see Chapter 5, "Staging Tables" on page 169.
   - **Base aggregate**: Contains aggregated data for a user table appended at specified intervals. A new row is appended for each changed row in the source table. This results in an SQL column function calculation against the existing user table.
   - **Change aggregate**: Contains aggregated data based on changes to the change data table. The source table is not accessed.

2. Alternatively, you can choose to make the target table a **replica** table. You should do this if you are setting up update-anywhere replication. Changes to a replica table can be replicated back to the source table. See Chapter 6, "Update-Anywhere Replication" on page 211 for more details.

In the case of staging tables and replicas, the target tables themselves are used as replication sources. The definition of these types of target tables as replication sources is performed during the definition of the subscription. For a staging table, the **Used as source for future copies** option must be selected for auto-registration to take place.

2.2.4 Defining Target Columns

You can define extra columns in your target table whose values are computed, or rename columns (both with respect to the source table).

To do this, click on the **Target Columns** tab in the Advanced Subscription Definition panel (Figure 30 on page 49):

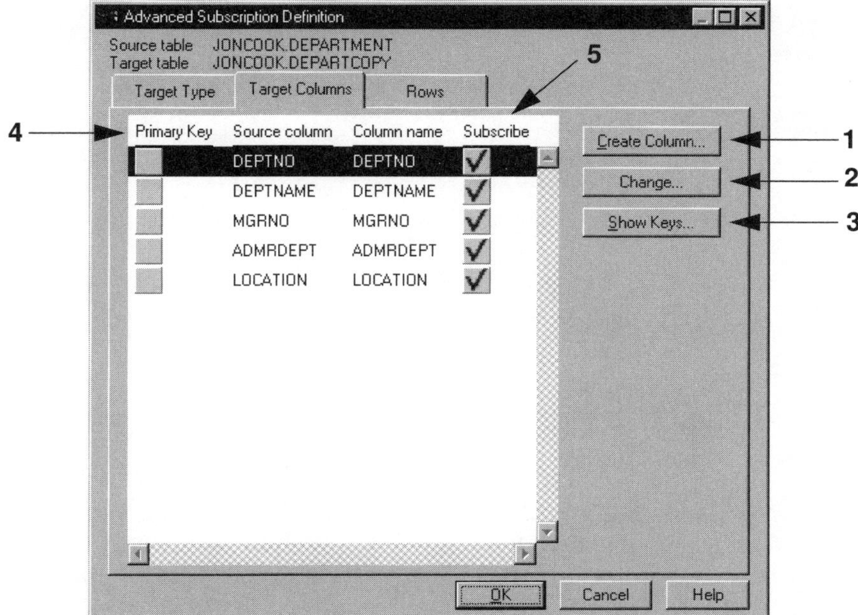

Figure 30. Advanced Subscription Definition -Columns

In this screen, you can define how the target table columns differ from source table columns. You can:

1. **Add new columns**: To add a new column based on an expression, click on **Create Column**. In the next panel (Figure 31 on page 50), specify an SQL expression for the column value.

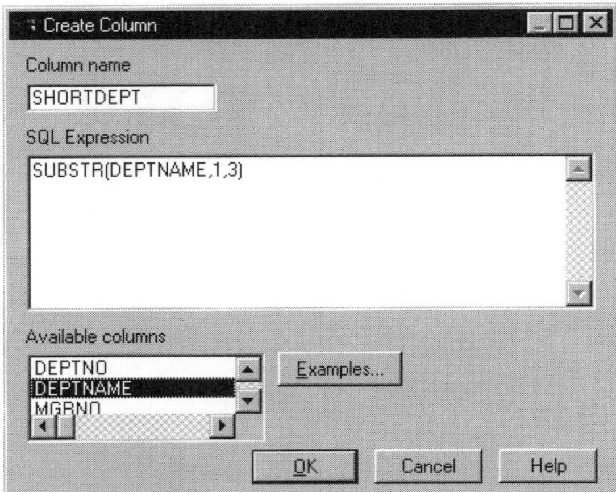

Figure 31. Create Column

2. **Change or Rename Columns**: From the Target Columns tab (Figure 30 on page 49), highlight the column you wish to work with, click on **Change**. In the next panel (which is identical to Figure 31 apart from the title bar), enter an SQL expression for the column value. You can also rename the column.

   If you do enter an SQL expression when adding or changing a column, you can get some guidance by clicking **Examples**. In particular, if your SQL expression uses an aggregate function (SUM, AVG, and so on), then you will need to enter a GROUP BY clause in the ROWS panel. This is known as a *computed column*. The columns you can use are listed in the 'Available Columns' box.

> **Note**
>
> A quick way to rename a target column is to click on the required column and edit the name.

3. **Display the Source Table Primary Key or Unique Indexes**: Click on **Show Keys** to display the list of columns that make up the primary key of the source table (if defined) or any unique indexes on the source table.

4. **Define Primary Key of Target Table**: Click on the check-box for the required columns to define the primary key of the target table. If you don't select any columns, the columns that make up the primary key of the source table are used.

5. **Exclude Columns**: To exclude a source table column from the target table, deselect the **Subscribe** check against the column.

2.2.5 Defining Target Rows

You can restrict the source rows to replicate by using a WHERE clause, or define a GROUP BY clause for aggregation functions.

To do this, click on the **Rows** tab in the Advanced Subscription Definition panel, as shown in Figure 30:

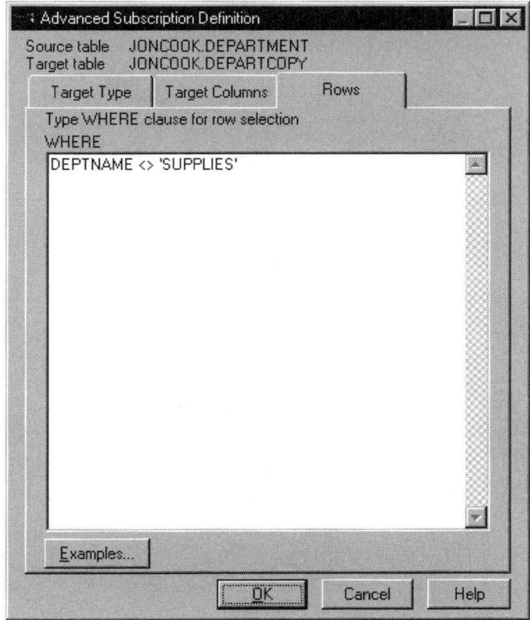

Figure 32. Advanced Subscription

In this screen, you can enter a WHERE clause for row selection from the source table. This can be used to:

- Restrict the rows that are copied from the source table to the target table.
- Provide a GROUP BY clause if you are using a computed column (SUM, COUNT, AVG and so on) in the target table. In this case, if you do not have any WHERE condition, you must provide a dummy WHERE clause (such as WHERE 1=1).

As for the target columns, click on **Examples** for guidance in specifying the WHERE clause.

Note

Don't type the word WHERE - it is automatically supplied.

2.2.6 Specifying SQL Statements

You can specify SQL statements to be performed during replication processing by clicking on **SQL** in the Define Subscription panel (Figure 27 on page 45).

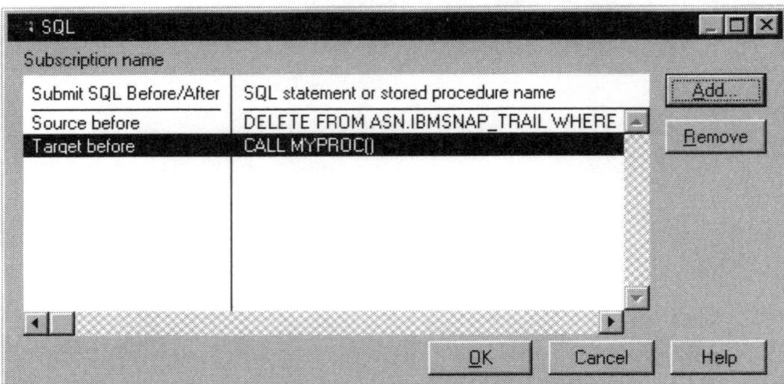

Figure 33. SQL Statements List

In addition to SQL statements, you can also specify the name of a stored procedure. You can add or remove statements or procedures by using the **Add** and **Remove** buttons. Click on **Add** to add a new statement or procedure:

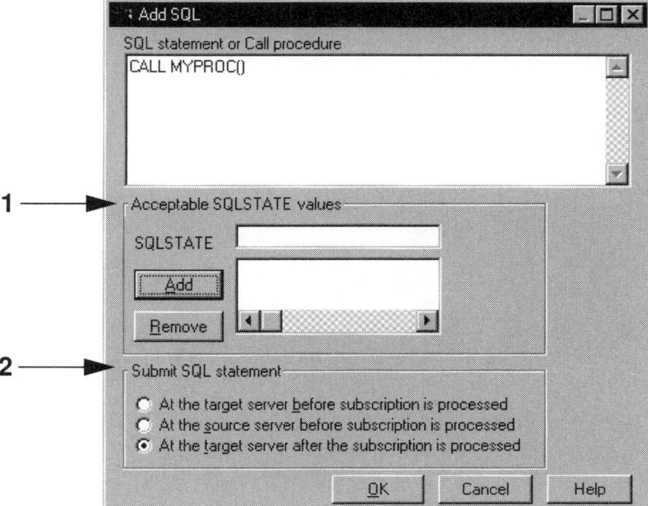

Figure 34. Add SQL Statement

You can also:

1. Supply a list of SQLSTATEs to ignore, so that replication processing can continue in the event of one of these SQLSTATEs being returned.
2. Choose when the SQL or stored procedure is executed. This can be at the source server before subscription processing or at the target server before or after subscription processing. Note that this cannot be at the source server before subscription processing.

Any statements or procedures that you define are stored in the Statements control table (ASN.IBMSNAP_SUBS_STMTS).

2.2.7 Defining Timing and Event-based Settings

You can choose to have replication triggered on a time interval basis, or as the result of an event taking place.

To specify timing and event-based settings, click on **Timing** in the Define Subscription panel (Figure 27 on page 45).

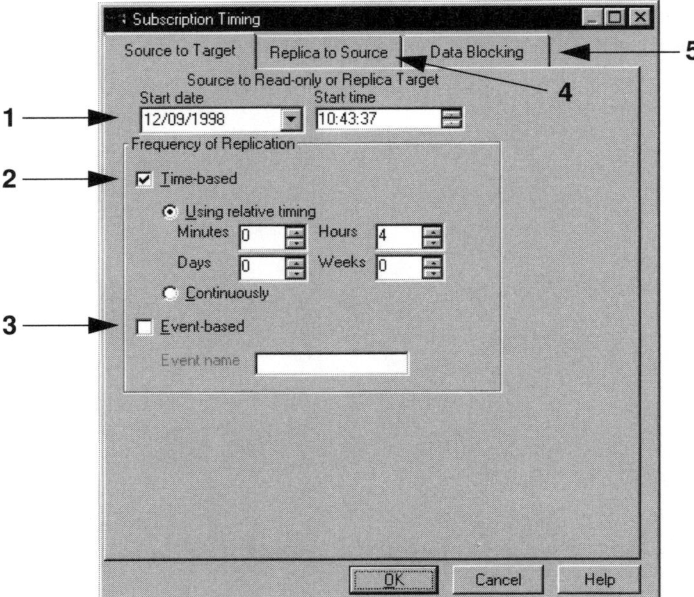

Figure 35. Advanced Replication - Timing and Events

1. In the **Source to Target** tab, you can define the start date and time for replication. By default, the current date and time is used.
2. Replication can either be triggered by a time interval, or an event, or a combination of the two. For time-based, choose an interval, or select continuously. By default, the interval is set to 4 hours.
3. In event-based timing, you specify an event name. Replication is triggered when a row is inserted into the Events control table (ASN.IBMSNAP_SUBS_EVENT) with this EVENT_NAME.
4. You can select the **Target to Source** tab if you have selected a target table type of replica (update anywhere replication). In the panel that is displayed, you can specify the timing and event settings for replication from the target to the source table.
5. If you select the **Data Blocking** tab, this panel is displayed:

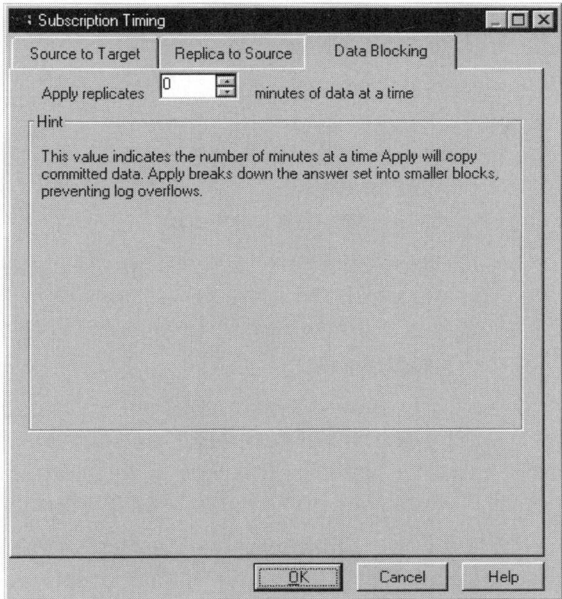

Figure 36. Data Blocking

In this panel, you can enter a number of minutes (default 0) for the Apply program to copy data in blocks. You can use this setting to prevent overflow of the database log files and Apply spill files. This value is stored in the MAX_SYNCH_MINUTES column of the Subscription Sets control table (ASN.IBMSNAP_SUBS_SET).

2.2.8 Managing Subscriptions

Once you have defined subscriptions, you can perform the following tasks on them:

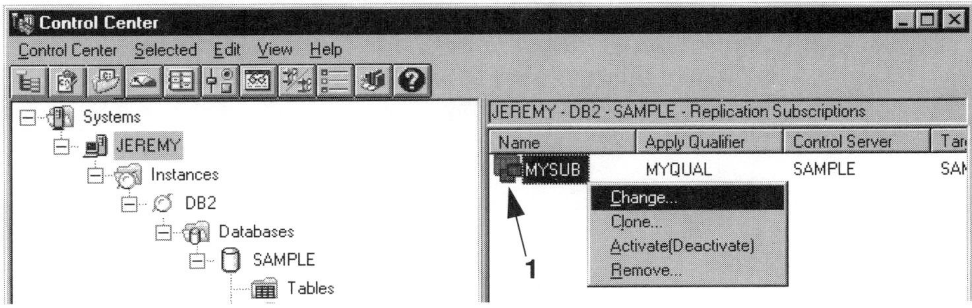

Figure 37. Managing Subscription Definitions

- **View/Change**. To view or change a subscription, right-click against the subscription in the contents pane and select **Change**. The changes you can make are limited to the following:
  - The row predicate (WHERE clause) in the Rows panel can be changed.
  - SQL statements and stored procedures can be added or removed.
  - Timing settings can be changed.
  - The data blocking value can be changed.
- **Clone**. You can easily copy (or clone) a subscription to another system by selecting **Clone**. You are prompted to enter a new Apply Qualifier and the new Target server (this is the new target database). This database must be cataloged at the local system.
- **Deactivate/Activate**. If you want to temporarily stop using a subscription, you can deactivate it by selecting **Activate(Deactivate)**. When the subscription is deactivated, its icon (marked 1 in Figure 37) is greyed out. When you want to start using it again, select **Activate(Deactivate)** again.
- **Remove**. By default, when you remove a subscription, the target table will remain after the deletion. You can have the target table deleted automatically when removing a subscription by changing the replication defaults in Tools Settings. This also applies if the subscription is removed as the result of removing a replication source. See the next section for more details.

2.3 Managing Defaults for Replication Sources and Subscriptions

There are certain characteristics of replication behavior that can be modified to apply to all replication-related objects. You should review these settings before configuring a production replication environment.

2.3.1 Replication Defaults Using Tools Settings

To view or alter the replication defaults, select **Tools Settings** from the Control Center Tool bar or choose **Start->Programs->DB2 for Windows NT->Administration Tools->Tool Settings** (on Windows NT). The following panel is displayed:

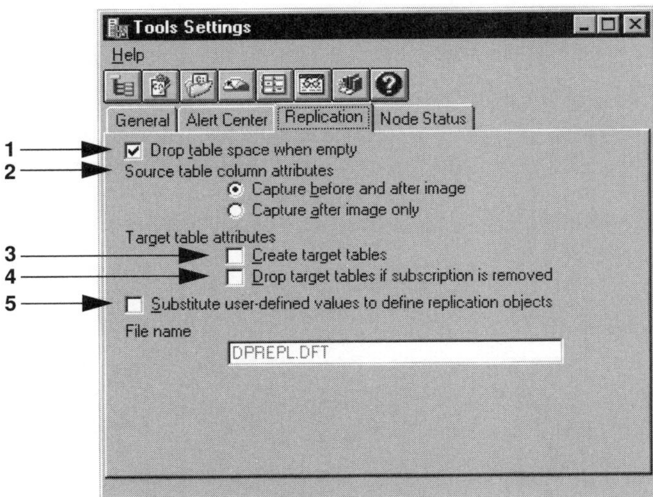

Figure 38. Tools Settings - Replication

The panel shown in Figure 38 allows you to choose the following options:

1. **Drop Table spaces when empty**: If you select this option, then any table spaces used to hold Change Data (CD) tables or target tables will be dropped automatically if they become empty. By default, this setting is on.
2. **Capture Before and After Images**: You can choose to make the before images of source tables unavailable for Capture when defining a Quick Replication Source. By default, both before and after images are captured when defining a Quick Replication Source. When defining a Custom Replication Source, you can choose to include the before images independent of this setting.
3. **Create Target Tables**: Check this tick-box to change the defaults for creating target tables when defining subscriptions. If this option is chosen, then the Create Table option in the Define Subscription panel (see Figure 27 on page 45) is selected by default.
4. **Drop Target Tables if Subscription Removed**. If this option is selected, then when a subscription is removed, the target table is dropped.
5. **Replication Objects Defaults**: This option allows you to specify a file (by default DPREP.DFT) that overrides the default settings for replication source and subscription definitions. There is an example file in SQLLIB\SAMPLES\REPL. This file can be useful if, for example, you want to define many change data (CD) tables in a specific table space, or many target tables in a specific table space.

A similar function can be achieved by modifying the SQL generated when defining replication sources or subscriptions. The benefit of using this file is that the user-specified settings only need to be entered once.

This file is included in Appendix C, “Replication Defaults File - DPREP.DFT” on page 391 for your reference. Full details about how to use this file are given in the comments section at the start of the file.

When you have finished, close the **Tools Settings** panel to save your changes.

2.3.2 Replication Control Tables Defaults

The default CREATE TABLE and CREATE INDEX statements that are used to create the replication control tables can be changed by using the DPCNTL file for the required platform. There are four versions, all in the SQLLIB\REPL\SAMPLES directory:

- DPCNTL.UDB - For all DB2 UDB platforms.
- DPCNTL.MVS - For MVS and OS/390.
- DPCNTL.400 - For AS/400.
- DPCNTL.VM - For VSE and VM.

You can use this file, for example, to define additional indexes for performance reasons or to place control tables/indexes in specific table spaces.

To use the DPCNTL file, you should first make any required changes to the file. If the database is remote, catalog the database on the local system. Next, connect to the database chosen to hold the control tables and run this command, where xxx is the platform:

```
db2 -tvf DPCNTL.xxx
```

There is also an equivalent file for each platform, called DPNCNTL.xxx, that can be used to drop the control tables. The DPCNTL file for the UDB platform is included in Appendix D, “Script to Create Control Tables - DPCNTL.UDB” on page 393 for your reference.

2.4 Summary

This chapter has provided you with an overview of how to define replication sources and subscriptions, and how to modify them after creation.

We will provide more details on replication sources and subscriptions in the step-by-step examples provided in the subsequent chapters.

Chapter 3. Capture and Apply

The Capture and Apply programs were introduced in Chapter 1, "An Overview of DB2 Data Replication" on page 1. In this chapter, we explain how to run and control Capture and Apply, and explain in more detail how the Capture and Apply programs work and interact with each other.

At the end of this chapter, the steps required to set up a very simple replication configuration are explained.

3.1 The Capture Program

The Capture program is the IBM Replication component that captures the changed data and makes it available for replication by inserting it into the change data (CD) tables. It must always run at the source server database.

Capture reads data from the DB2 log or journal (in DB2 for AS/400) to detect changes made to the tables that have been registered for replication. It places the captured changes into change data tables for the Apply program to process. There is only one Capture program per:

- DB2 Universal Database database.
- DB2 for OS/390 subsystem in a non-data-sharing environment.
- DB2 for OS/390 data-sharing group (located with the member where the logs are merged).
- DB2 for VM or DB2 for VSE database.

In the case of Capture for AS/400, one Capture job can process up to 50 different journals at the same time. It is possible to have more than one Capture job running at the same time. All members of a subscription set must be using the same journal.

The Capture program usually runs continuously, but it can be stopped while running utilities or modifying replication sources. It runs independently of the Control Center, but uses control information created by the Control Center.

3.1.1 How the Capture Program Works

DB2 records every transaction in a log file for recovery purposes. However, this information is not enough for the Capture program to capture changes made to the source table. For this to occur, the source table must have the **data capture changes** attribute set. The data capture changes attribute indicates that extra information regarding SQL changes to this table will be written to the log.

Note

If the source table doesn't have the data capture changes attribute set, the Control Center will generate the necessary SQL statements to alter the table when the table is defined as a Replication Source.

Furthermore, in order for the Capture program to capture changes, log retention must be enabled. For more details, check the documentation for your platform.

Once a table has been defined as a replication source via the Control Center, the Capture program reads change records from the DB2 log or journal (in the case of DB2 for AS/400) and stores the changes in the change data (CD) tables. The Capture program also maintains information about committed units of work in the unit-of-work (UOW) table. These tables are joined to identify and replicate committed updates. The Apply program can then copy the committed updates to the target site and apply them to the target table.

3.1.2 Replicating Updates

By default, the Capture program captures an update to the source table as an UPDATE statement. However, in some cases, it may be necessary to replicate updates as DELETE and INSERT statements. This function is referred to as *logical partitioning key support*. For example:

- When one or more columns of a table primary key are updated.
- When one or more columns of a table partitioning key (either the target table is in a partitioned database managed by DB2 Enterprise-Extended Edition (EEE), or in a DB2 for MVS partitioned table space).
- When the source application updates one or more columns referenced in a subscription predicate.

Without replication logical partitioning key support, when the primary keys of the source or target tables are being updated, the Capture program would capture the changed rows for the update as an update. The Apply program would then attempt to make an update to a row on the target table with the new key value. This new key value would not be found in the target table, so the Apply program would convert the update into an insert. The new row would be correct, but the old row with the old key value would remain in the table incorrectly. This is illustrated in Figure 39:

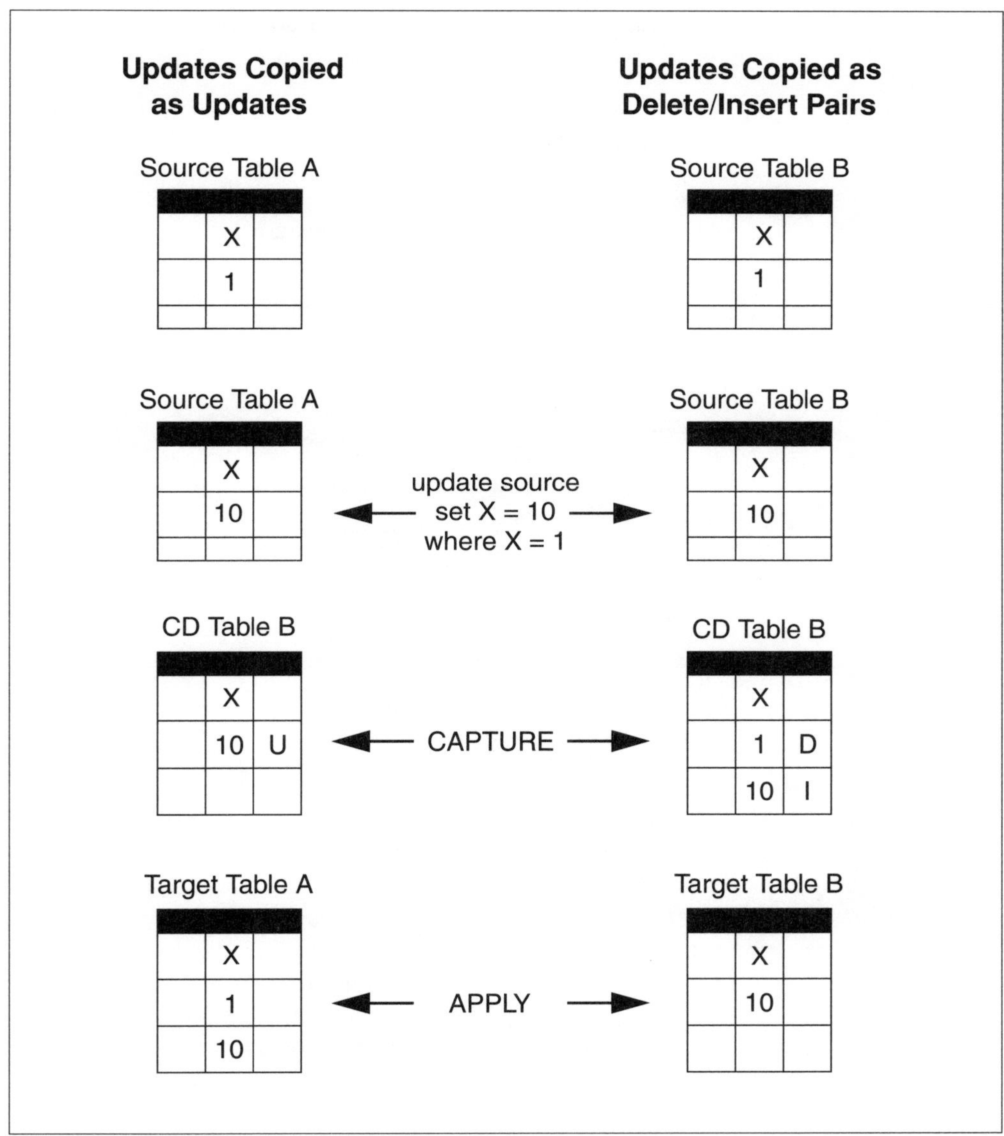

Figure 39. Logical Partitioning Key Support

3.1.3 Authorization Requirements

The security for IBM Replication is handled by DB2 directly. The entire system is table driven. DB2 provides security mechanisms for all objects involved.

The user ID that runs the Capture program must be able to access the system catalog tables, be able to access and update the control tables, and have execute privilege on the Capture program plan.

These are the basic authorities needed to run the Capture program on various platforms:

- **OS/390**:
  - DBADM or SELECT, UPDATE, INSERT, and DELETE privilege for all Capture related tables.
  - SELECT privilege for SYSIBM.SYSTABLES and SYSIBM.SYSCOLUMNS.
  - TRACE privilege.
  - MONITOR1 and MONITOR2 privilege.
  - EXECUTE privilege for the capture plan.
- **VM/VSE**:
  - DBA authority.
- **Universal Database**:
  - Have DBADM or SYSADM authority
  - Write authority on the directories from where the program is invoked.

3.1.4 Running the Capture Program on Windows NT

In this section, we focus on the commands used to control Capture on the Windows NT platform. While the syntax and usage considerations of these commands on the other supported workstation platforms are very similar, you should refer to the *Replication Guide and Reference* for exact details. The commands used to control Capture for the OS/390 platform are covered in Chapter 4, “Replicating DB2 Data from OS/390 to Windows NT” on page 89. For the other supported platforms, such as OS/400, VM, and VSE, please also refer to the relevant chapter in the *Replication Guide and Reference*.

Before running Capture, you should perform the following steps:

1. Logon as a user ID with DBADM or SYSADM privileges for the source database. For example, the user ID who created the source server database.
2. Make sure that the source database is enabled for roll-forward recovery. You can do this in one of two ways:

- From the Control Center, right-click on the source database. Select **Configure** from the pop-up menu and choose the **Logs** tab. One or both of 'Retain log file for forward recovery' or 'Invoke user exit for log file archiving' must be set to ON. If either one is already set, you do not have to make any changes.
- From a Command Window, enter the following command. Substitute `SAMPLE` with the name of your source database:

  ```
  db2 get db cfg for SAMPLE
  ```

  If neither LOGRETAIN nor USEREXIT is ON, then use either or both of these commands:

  ```
  db2 update db cfg for SAMPLE using LOGRETAIN ON
  db2 update db cfg for SAMPLE using USEREXIT ON
  ```

Changes to the database configuration will take effect once all users disconnect from your database and the first connection or activation after that occurs.

3. Changing the roll-forward recovery settings puts the database into a backup pending state. To make the database accessible, you must first perform a off-line backup. You can either:
   - From the Control Center, right-click on the required database. Select **Backup->database** from the pop-up menu. Follow the prompts to specify where the backup is stored.
   - From a Command Window, use the DB2 BACKUP DB command. For example:

     ```
     db2 backup db SAMPLE to C:\BACKUP
     ```

     In this case, `SAMPLE` is the database name, and `C:\BACKUP` is the directory where the backup image is to be stored.
4. Bind the Capture packages:

   The Capture packages contain embedded SQL statements that are used by the Capture program. They must be bound to any database that the Capture program needs to connect to.

   Change to the C:\SQLLIB\BND directory (assuming DB2 UDB is installed on C:). Connect to the source database (in this case, SAMPLE) and bind the capture packages:

   ```
   db2 connect to sample
   db2 bind @capture.lst isolation ur blocking all
   ```

   Where:

   - `isolation ur` - specifies an isolation level of uncommitted read.

• `blocking all` - for remote connections, return data in large blocks where possible.

3.1.5 Starting Capture on Windows NT

Follow these steps to start the Capture program on Windows NT:

1. From the Control Center, check that replication sources have been defined.
2. Now you are ready to start the Capture program. You can either do this from a command line or as an NT service (see “Setting up Capture and Apply as Windows NT Services” on page 75).

   If the database for which you want to capture changes is not defined in the default DB2 instance, set the DB2INSTANCE environment variable to the instance you require. For example:

   ```
   SET DB2INSTANCE=myinst
   ```

   Change directory to C:\SQLLIB\BIN and run the ASNCCP command:

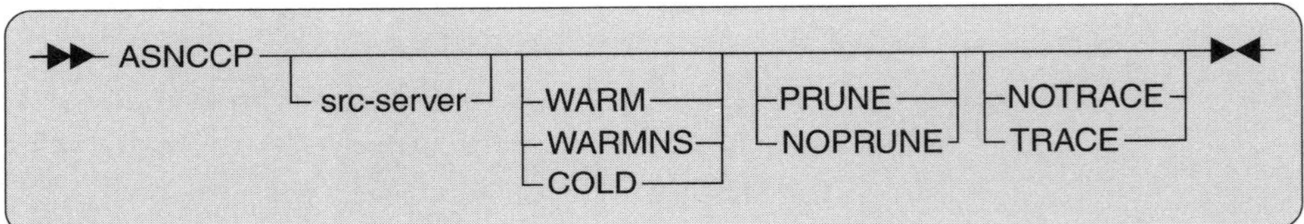

The parameters are as follows:

Table 5. Capture Parameters

Parameter	Description
src-server	The name of the database against which Capture will run. If not specified, the value of DB2DBDFT is used.
WARM (Default) WARMNS COLD	- If warm start information is available, then capture resumes processing where it ended its previous run. If warm start information is not available, then a cold start is performed. - Like WARM, except that if warm start information is not available, a message is displayed and Capture terminates. - Capture deletes all information generated from previous runs if it exists (CD, OUW tables).
PRUNE (Default) NOPRUNE	- The CD and UOW tables are pruned automatically by Capture. - Automatic pruning is disabled.
NOTRACE (Default) **TRACE**:	- No trace is taken. - Trace information is written to standard output.

For more details about warm and cold starting Capture, see “Starting Capture” on page 119. Pruning is explained in more detail in “Pruning” on page 80.

When capture is running, messages are written to a log file called <instance><database>.CCP, which is created in the directory from which capture was started. These messages are also recorded in the ASN.IBMSNAP_TRACE control table.

For example, to run capture against the `SAMPLE` database in the DB2 instance, with a warm start, automatic pruning enabled and write trace information to `c:\tmp\trace.out`:

```
c:\sqllib\bin\asnccp sample trace > c:\tmp\trace.out
```

When running this command from a command line, if the prompt is not returned, it means that capture is running normally. If the prompt is returned, then capture has terminated. In this case, you should check the messages file <instance><database>.CCP and the trace file.

Refer to Chapter 9, “Troubleshooting” on page 355 for more information.

3.1.6 Controlling Capture

In addition to starting capture, you can control capture on Windows NT using the ASNCMD command. To use this command, start a new command window and change directory to C:\SQLLIB\BIN. Make sure that DB2INSTANCE is set to the required instance, and that DB2DBDFT is set to the source server database.

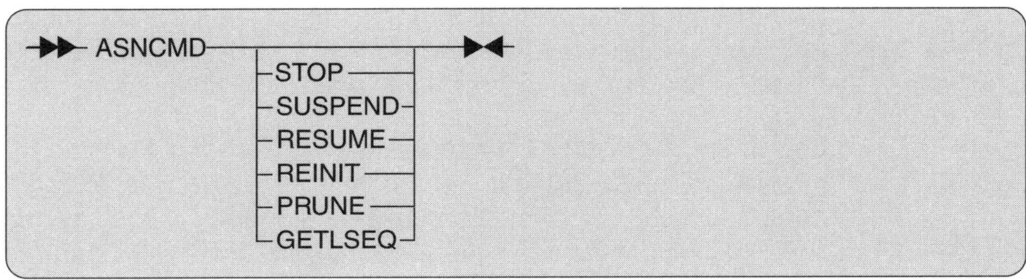

The parameters for all DB2 UDB platforms are as follows:

Table 6. ASNCMD Parameters

Parameter	Description
STOP	Stop the Capture program in an orderly way. If Capture was started as a Windows NT service, you can stop it using the Windows NT Services panel. You should always stop the Capture program before deleting or modifying a replication source.
SUSPEND	Suspend the Capture program. This can be used to release resources to other processes on the system. Capture processing can be resumed using the RESUME option.
RESUME	Resume the Capture program. Use this option after a SUSPEND.
REINIT	Force the Capture program to re-read the tables that hold the replication sources (ASN.IBMSNAP_REGISTER) and the tuning parameters (ASN.IBMSNAP_CCPPARMS). Use this option to add a new replication source or alter capture tuning parameters without stopping capture.
PRUNE	Prune the CD and UOW tables. Use this option if capture was started with the NOPRUNE option.
GETLSEQ	Display the timestamp and current log sequence number. Use this option to determine which point capture has reached in the DB2 log.

3.1.7 Specifying Tuning Parameters for Capture

To control the performance of the Capture program, you can specify the following tuning parameters in the ASN.IBMSNAP_CCPPARMS tuning parameters table:

Retention limit: The number of minutes to keep the change data table rows and the unit-of-work (UOW) table rows. The default value is 10,800, which is 7 days. The rows are deleted up to where the changes have been applied.

Lag limit: The number of minutes the Capture program can be backlogged from the current local time before shutting itself down. The default value is 10,800 (which is 7 days). This value is higher for a busy system; therefore, a lower lag limit shuts down the Capture program. If the Capture program shuts itself down, you may have to perform a cold start if the database does not have or support an archive log.

Commit interval: The number of seconds to wait before issuing a COMMIT statement. The default value is 30 seconds. Set the interval smaller than the DB2 time-out interval if the Capture and Apply programs are running at the same time. This precaution helps to avoid locking overhead. If the Apply program is not running at the same time as the Capture program, you can set the commit interval no higher than the DB2 time-out interval.

Prune interval: The number of seconds to wait before pruning the staging tables. The default value is ten times the commit value or 300 seconds, whichever is larger. This parameter is ignored if you start the Capture program with the NOPRUNE option.

To specify the tuning parameters, do one of the following tasks:

- Modify the DPCNTL file in the C:\SQLLIB\SAMPLES\REPL directory before you define the first replication source for a database. See Appendix D, "Script to Create Control Tables - DPCNTL.UDB" on page 393 for more details.
- Update the table with the following SQL statement after you create the tuning parameters table:

```
UPDATE TABLE ASN.IBMSNAP_CCPPARMS
SET RETENTION_LIMIT=number_of_minutes,
LAG_LIMIT=number_of_minutes,
COMMIT_INTERVAL=number_of_seconds,
PRUNE_INTERVAL=number_of_seconds
```

If you need to change the values and refresh the tuning parameters while the Capture program is running, use the ASNCMD REINIT command after changing the table values.

3.2 The Apply Program

The Apply program is the IBM Replication component that propagates the data from the source to the target tables by reading the changes captured and stored in CD tables and applying these changes to the target tables. The Apply program can also read data directly from the source table when copying the entire source table (full refresh) or from staging tables (see Chapter 5, “Staging Tables” on page 169).

The Apply program generally runs at the target server, but it can run at any server in your network that can connect to the source, control, and target servers.

When the Apply program resides with the target server and is copying the data from the source server, the configuration is usually known as a *pull configuration*. If, on the other hand, the Apply program resides with the source server and is copying the data to the target server, the configuration is known as a *push configuration.*

3.2.1 How the Apply Program Works

Usually the Apply program connects to the control server to read the control tables, to the source server to pick up changed data, and then to the target server to apply that data. Table 7 describes the Apply program cycle.

Table 7. The Apply Program Cycle

Step	Server
Look for work, check the subscription control tables	Control server
Pick up recent change data to be applied to the target table	Source server
Write the answer set into a local spill file (possibly an in-memory file)	Target server
Apply the change data in the spill file to the target table	Target server
Update subscription status	Control server
Report subscription progress in the pruning control table	Source server

3.2.1.1 Selecting What to Do

The Apply program must first select which subscription to process. This selection can be determined by the relative time or an event, and a single subscription might be eligible under either criteria. Among these two, possibly overlapping lists, the eligible subscriptions are ordered based on the last time they were processed, using the LASTRUN column from the IBMSNAP_SUBS_SET table. This way, the Apply program prevents one subscription from getting all the machine resources. There are then, logically, two round-robin lists of subscriptions; one for relative time driven subscriptions, and one for event driven subscriptions. A subscription is eligible based on the timestamp of the last time it ran successfully, represented by the LASTSUCCESS column of the IBMSNAP_SUBS_SET table. This means that a failing subscription remains eligible, but goes to the end of the round-robin list after every attempted cycle.

The Apply program looks for work every 5 minutes, or more frequently if there are subscriptions with intervals of less than 5 minutes.

Once the Apply program has selected which target tables it will refresh or update, it chooses from a list of potential source tables in the following order:

1. The CCD table associated with the defined replication source table.
2. The CD table associated with the replication source table.
3. The replication source table associated with the replication subscription.

In some cases, the source table considered first might not be the one that the Apply program reads from. For example, if the target table is a point-in-time table, but has not yet been initialized, the Apply program must use a source table that is complete. If the CCD table is not complete (that is, CCD_COMPLETE=N in the Register control table), the replication source table is selected as the refresh source.

3.2.2 The Apply Qualifier

When the Apply program is started, it is supplied with a job qualifier, called an Apply qualifier, independent from a logon user ID. The Apply qualifier is associated with individual replication subscriptions and is responsible for replicating only those replication subscriptions. You specify a value for the Apply qualifier when you define a subscription.

The Apply qualifier can be up to 18 characters long and is case sensitive. It is usually a good idea to provide a name that is meaningful to the operation of a particular Apply program. You cannot easily change the Apply qualifier, so it is important to plan carefully.

By using different Apply qualifiers, it is possible to use one ID to run more than one instance of the Apply program.

3.2.3 Authorization Requirements

The security for IBM Replication is handled by DB2 directly. The entire system is table driven. DB2 provides security mechanisms for all objects involved. Additionally, the Apply program uses a qualifier that must be coordinated, but the same user ID can be used to run multiple Apply program instances.

The user ID used to run the Apply program, must be a valid logon ID on the source, control, and target servers, and the workstation where the Control Center is installed. At the same time, the user ID must at least be able to select from all source tables, select from and update the control tables, and update the target tables. In addition, this user ID must be able to execute the access plan or package for the Apply program on both source and target servers. The user ID must also have enough authority to execute the Apply program.

Apply Password File

When running on DB2 Universal Database on Windows or Unix, the Apply program may require a password file to connect to the source server if DB2 authentication is set to SERVER or DCS. The password file must meet the following criteria:

- Be named as shown:

  ```
  <APPLYQUAL><instname><CNTLSRV>.PWD
  ```

  Where `<APPLYQUAL>` is the Apply qualifier. It is case sensitive and must match the value of APPLY_QUAL in the subscription set table. `<instname>` is the value of DB2INSTANCE, and `<CNTLSRVR>` is the name of the control server in upper case.

- Reside in the directory from which Apply is to be run.
- Contain one or more records using the following format:

  ```
  SERVER=<server_name> PWD=<password> USER=<userid>
  ```

  Where `<server_name>` is the source, target, or control database. The file cannot include blank lines or comment lines.

By using the password file, it is possible to use different passwords or even different user IDs to connect to the servers. It is recommended that the access to this file is limited to the user ID that will run the Apply program.

3.2.4 Triggering Replication

Determining how often the data must be replicated depends on the particular requirements of each implementation, and it must reflect the need for data currency. IBM Replication can use two different mechanisms to trigger the replication of data: relative timing and event timing.

Both timing methods can be specified during the subscription definition process and can be used together for the same subscription.

When using relative timing, the Apply program will copy the data at specified intervals; it is the simplest method of controlling subscription timing. The interval can be continuous or set from one minute to one year. The interval applies for the entire subscription set; meaning that all the tables within one set are replicated at the same time. The intervals are approximate. The Apply program will begin processing the subscription as soon as it can, depending on its work load and the resources available. The interval can be changed using the Control Center (see Figure 48 on page 85 for an example) or by issuing standard SQL against the control tables.

External events can be used to trigger Apply by associating a subscription with an event name. Then, when the external event occurs, it updates the event table (ASN.IBMSNAP_EVENT) with the event name. Apply sees the new record in the event table and knows it can begin processing the subscription

The ASN.IBMSNAP_EVENT table has three columns:

EVENT_NAME The event specified while defining the replication subscription.

EVENT_TIME The timestamp for the time when the Apply program begins processing the replication subscription.

END_OF_PERIOD An optional value that indicates that the transactions after this time should be deferred until a future date.

END_OF_PERIOD is checked against the clock at the source server, while EVENT_TIME is checked against the clock of the control server.

It is important to notice that it is not the Control Center who posts the events; it is up to the user or to a user application to post the events. The replication activity can be tied to the user applications through named events. As soon as there is a row inserted with a particular event name and the current timestamp, all subscriptions tied to this event will be eligible to run. The events can be posted in advance, for the next few hours, days, or even years.

See “Event Timing” on page 148 for a detailed example of event driven replication.

3.2.5 Running the Apply Program on Windows NT

In this section, we focus on the commands used to control Apply on the Windows NT platform. While the syntax and usage considerations of these commands on the other supported workstation platforms are very similar, you should refer to the *Replication Guide and Reference* for exact details. The commands used to control Apply for the OS/390 platform are covered in "DB2 ODBC Catalog" on page 333. For the other supported platforms, such as OS/400, VM, and VSE, please also refer also to the relevant chapter in the *Replication Guide and Reference*.

Before running Apply, you should perform the following steps:

1. Logon as a user ID with the necessary privileges, as explained in "Authorization Requirements" on page 70.
2. The database(s) that the Apply program needs to connect to should be cataloged at the local system. This includes any source, target, or control databases. You can do this using one of the following tools:
   - The Client Configuration Assistant (CCA) using the Add Database function.
   - The Control Center using the Add System, Add Instance, and Add Database functions.
   - A Command Window using the DB2 CATALOG NODE and DB2 CATALOG DB commands.
3. Bind the Apply packages.

   These packages contain embedded SQL statements that are used by the Apply program, and must be bound to any database that the Apply program needs to connect to.

   Change to the C:\SQLLIB\BND directory (assuming DB2 UDB is installed on C:). Connect to the source database and bind the apply packages:

   ```
   db2 connect to <source-database>
   db2 bind @applycs.lst isolation cs blocking all grant public
   db2 bind @applyur.lst isolation ur blocking all grant public
   ```

   Where:

   - `isolation cs` - specifies an isolation level of cursor stability.
   - `isolation ur` - specifies an isolation level of uncommitted read.
   - `blocking all` - for remote connections, return data in large blocks where possible.
   - `grant public` - gives execute permission to all users.

The same two BIND commands should be run against the target database and the control database (if it is not the same as the source or target databases).

4. Create the password file as explained in “Authorization Requirements” on page 70.

3.2.6 Starting Apply

Follow these steps to start the Apply program on Windows NT:

1. From the Control Center, check that replication sources and subscriptions have been defined. For subscriptions, verify they are activated - they will be as long as you did not de-activate them.
2. Now you are ready to start the Apply command itself. You can either do this from a command line or as a Windows NT service (see “Setting up Capture and Apply as Windows NT Services” on page 75).

   Ensure that your DB2INSTANCE variable is set correctly for Apply.

   For example:

   ```
   SET DB2INSTANCE=myinst
   ```

   Change directory to C:\SQLLIB\BIN and run the ASNAPPLY command:

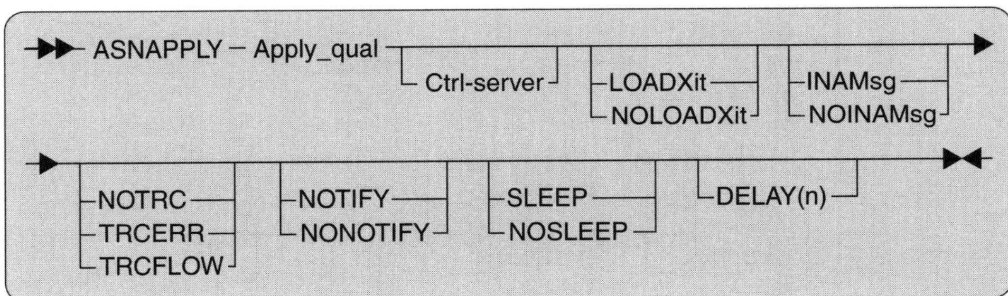

The parameters are as follows:

Table 8. Apply Parameters

Parameter	Description
Apply_qual	The name of the apply qualifier. This is used to identify the subscriptions to apply. It must match the case of the qualifier in the subscription set control table.
Ctrl_server	The name of the server where the replication control tables reside. If you do not specify this optional positional parameter, the default is the value of DB2DBDFT.

Parameter	Description
LOADXit **NOLOADXit** (Default)	- Apply will invoke the ASNLOAD user exit to initialize a target table. - Apply will not invoke ASNLOAD.
INAMsg (Default) NOINAMsg	- Apply will issue a message when it becomes inactive. - No inactive message is displayed
NOTRC (Default) TRCERR TRCFLOW	- Apply will not generate a trace - Apply will generate a trace with only error information. - Apply will generate a trace with error and execution flow information
NOTIFY **NONOTIFY** (default)	- Apply will invoke the ASNDONE user exit when apply processing ends. - Apply will not invoke ASNDONE.
SLEEP (default) NOSLEEP	- Apply will sleep if no new subscriptions are available - Apply will not sleep if no new subscriptions are available. It will terminate
DELAY(n) (default is 6 seconds)	- Specifies the delay at the end of each apply cycle when continuous replication is used. Valid values are 0, 1, 2, 3, 4, 5 or 6.

For more details about the LOADXit option, see "LOADX Option to Refresh the Target Table" on page 143, and for more details about the NOTIFY option, see "ASNDONE User Exit" on page 141.

On Windows NT Apply writes a log of its actions to a file called <APPLYQUAL><INSTANCE><CTRL-SRV>.LOG and also to the apply trail table (ASN.IBMSNAP_APPLYTRAIL) at the control server database.

3.2.7 Stopping Apply

You can stop the Apply program on Windows NT using the ASNASTOP command. To use this command, start a new command window and change directory to C:\SQLLIB\BIN. Make sure that DB2INSTANCE is set to the Apply instance.

The Apply qualifier must be in upper case.

You can also press **Ctrl+C** or **Ctrl+Break** from the command window that Apply was started from.

3.3 Setting up Capture and Apply as Windows NT Services

The Capture and Apply programs under Windows NT can be configured as Windows NT Services as an alternative to running them from a Command Prompt. This allows you to have these programs start automatically at boot time. To do this:

1. Install the Replication Windows NT Service. Enter this command from a command prompt (assuming that DB2 UDB has been installed in C:\):

   ```
   asninst c:\sqllib\bin\asnserv.exe
   ```

   After running this command, check that the Replication service is displayed in the NT Services Panel. Select **Start->Settings->Control Panel->Services**.

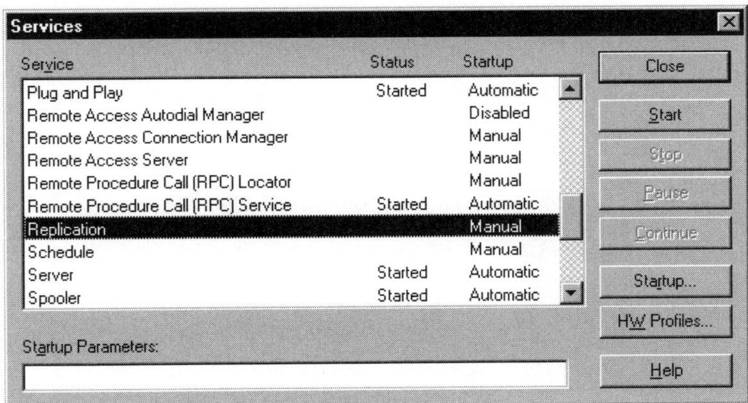

Figure 40. Windows NT Services Panel

2. From this panel, to change the startup options, click on **Startup**:

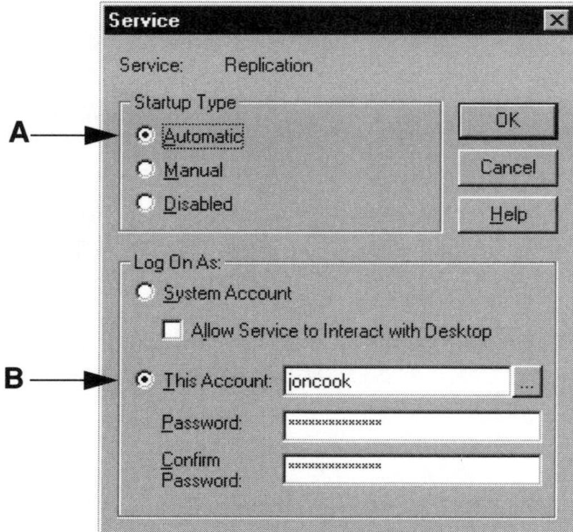

Figure 41. NT Service Startup Options

A. In Startup Options, click on **Automatic** to have this service started at boot time.

B. In Log On As, enter a user and password. This user should have all the privileges necessary to run the Capture and Apply programs as previously explained.

Click on **OK** to save the changes.

3. Add a new System Environment variable called ASNPATH. Select **Start->Settings->Control Panel->System**, then select the Environment tab:

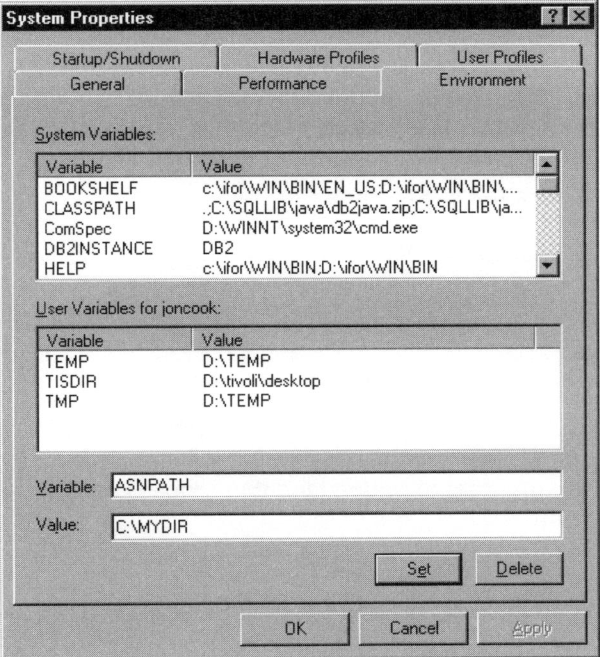

Figure 42. Windows NT System Environment Variables

First click on existing System Environment variable. You will see the variable name and value appear in the Variable and Value fields at the bottom of the panel. Type over these fields, and enter ASNPATH for Variable, and a directory for Value (here, C:\MYDIR).

Click on **Set** to save your changes. You should see the ASNPATH variable in the list of System Environment variables. Click on **OK**.

4. Create a text file that contains the Capture and Apply commands with the parameters you wish to use. The commands should be in this format:

```
<capture_db> <path>\asnccp <parameters>
<apply_db> <path>\asnapply <parameters>
```

Where:

- `<capture_db>` is the database against which the capture program is to run.
- `<apply_db>` is the database which holds the control tables for the apply program.
- `<path>` is the full path of the relevant program.
- `<parameters>` are the parameters for each program.

For example:

```
sample c:\sqllib\bin\asnccp
sampcopy c:\sqllib\bin\asnapply myqual sampcopy
```

The name of this text file must be NTSERV.ASN, and it must be placed in the directory pointed to by ASNPATH (here, C:\MYDIR). Be careful if you use Notepad or Wordpad to create this file, as you will find that these tools may add a **txt** suffix to the filename.

To remove the Replication Windows NT service, use the ASNREMV command.

3.4 Communications between Capture and Apply

This section explains how the Capture and Apply programs work together to exchange information. Although most of the following information is internal to the product, it is important to understand it in order to be able to manage a replication solution.

Capture and Apply exchange information in order to be able to maintain data consistency when copying and for pruning purposes. Using information from the control tables, Capture and Apply can address the following issues:

- How and when to start capturing updates for a table.
- How to maintain data consistency.
- How to maintain transaction consistency across all the members of a subscription set.
- How to detect which changes from the CD table are ready for pruning, given the fact that more than one Apply program can be using the same CD table.
- How to detect a gap in the chain of updates.
- How to communicate to the Apply program the need of a full refresh due to a Capture cold start.

IBM Replication always guarantees table consistency and transaction consistency across sets of tables. In other words, it guarantees that all data in the target table has been committed at the source, and that all the members of a subscription set are bound and copied together to the same point in time based on the transaction number, maintaining this way, referential constraints that exist among the members of a subscription set.

In order to achieve synchronization between the sources and the targets, IBM Replication uses two values: SYNCHPOINT and SYNCHTIME.

SYNCHPOINT Is a sequence value usually related to the log sequence number. It represents a point in the logs that has been processed.

SYNCHTIME Is the timestamp equivalent to the SYNCHPOINT. It is an approximate value that represents the time the transaction was committed.

In order to select which data must be copied, the Apply program connects to the control server to find out the subscription set lower bound, that is, the last point of consistency. It gets the value of the SYNCHPOINT column from the IBMSNAP_SUBS_SET table.

Then, the Apply program connects to the source server to find the upper bound, that is the highest point of consistency for the subscription set. The highest bound can be calculated in three different ways:

1. It will use the lowest value from the CD_NEW_SYNCHPOINT column of the IBMSNAP_REGISTER table for the members of the set. Figure 43 on page 80 represents the calculated SYNCHPOINT that the Apply program would use to replicate the data from a subscription set. Even though there is more data captured from tables 1 and 2, Apply will only copy what is common across the whole set.
2. When using events, if the value of the END_OF_PERIOD column for the event is set, the Apply program will calculate the SYNCHPOINT using any value from the IBMSNAP_COMMITSEQ column of the CD tables, trying to find the closest match between the value in END_OF_PERIOD on the event and IBMSNAP_LOGMARKER on the CD table.
3. When using MAX_SYNCH_MINUTES in the subscription, the technique is similar to that used for END_OF_PERIOD. The Apply program will calculate a higher bound using the time of the last successful copy plus the value of MAX_SYNCH_MINUTES. The limit is automatically recalculated if the Apply program encounters a resource constraint making the set limit unfeasible.

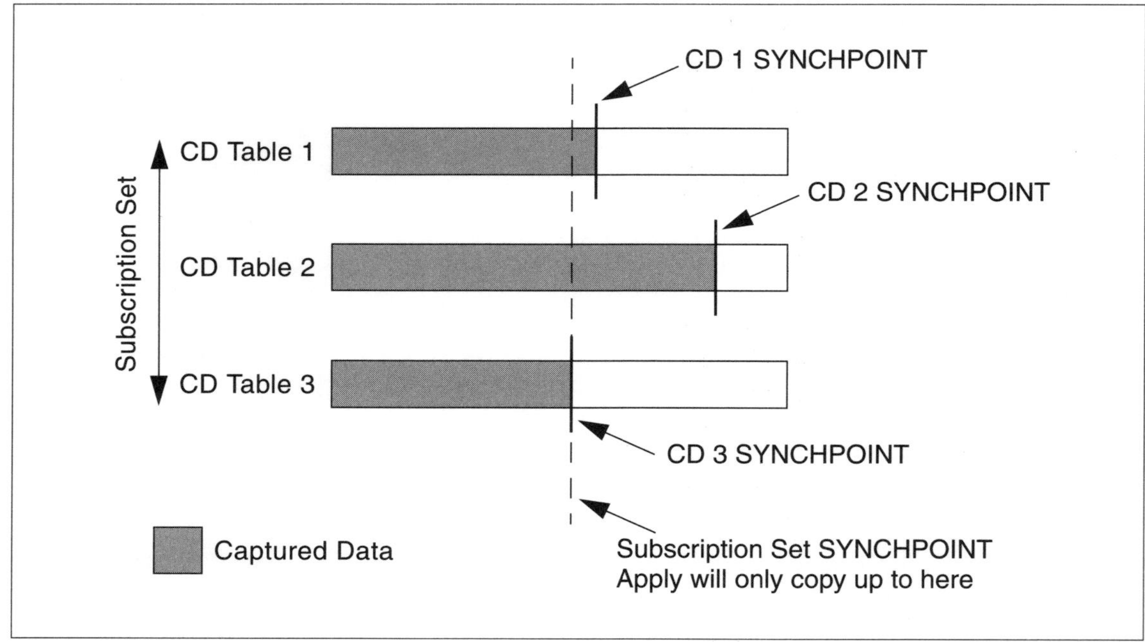

Figure 43. SYNCHPOINT

For a detailed example of how Capture and Apply use SYNCHPOINT to communicate, see "Communication between Capture and Apply in Full Refresh" on page 135.

3.4.1 Pruning

Pruning is the process of deleting unneeded records from the CD and UOW tables, that is, all records that have been replicated by all subscriptions associated with a given source table. The Capture program can either prune automatically, if pruning was enabled when it was started, or by request using Capture commands.

If PRUNE is enabled, the Capture program will use the value in the PRUNE_INTERVAL column from the IBMSNAP_CCPPARMS table to determine how often to prune.

The pruning control table coordinates the pruning of the CD and UOW tables, which have the potential for unlimited growth. There is one pruning control table at each source server.

The Capture program prunes the CD and UOW tables based on information inserted into the pruning control table by the Apply program. The Apply program maintains the log sequence number of the last transaction replicated for a particular subscription set in the SYNCHPOINT column of the pruning control table. Initially, the Apply program sets this sequence number to zero when it performs a full refresh. A zero value signals the Capture program to start capturing. When the Apply program copies changes from the CD table to the target table, it updates the SYNCHPOINT column. The Capture program can then prune changes in the CD and UOW tables that have less or equal log sequence number s than that from the pruning control table.

A detailed example of using manual pruning is given in "Manual Pruning" on page 140.

3.5 Setting up a Simple Replication Configuration

The following example will help you get familiarized with the IBM Replication architecture, providing a high level overview of the process. Although it was tested running under Windows NT, it should run on any DB2 UDB workstation platform (AIX, OS/2, Windows 95, and so on).

We are assuming that DB2 Universal Database was installed successfully and that the Control Center is running, either locally or remotely, to access the source and target databases. For more information, please refer to the DB2 Universal Database Quick Beginnings book for your platform.

For the example, we will use the ORG table from the SAMPLE DB2 database as a source to copy to a target DB2 database for Windows NT. This type of copy is known as a user copy, which is a complete, condensed copy of the replication source table without the timestamp columns.

These are the objects used during the example:

Source server database	**SAMPLE**
Target server database	**TARGETDB**
Source table	**ORG**
Target table	**ORGCOPY**
Set Name	**ORGREP**
Apply qualifier	**ORGQUAL**

In order for the Capture program to capture changes, the database must be enabled for roll-forward recovery, either by enabling Log Retain for Recovery or the User Exit For Logging. Please refer to the DB2 Universal Database on-line information to learn more about logging.

The following sections explain the steps required for this operation.

3.5.1 Defining a Replication Source

1. Start the Control Center and expand the Systems tree to display the tables for the SAMPLE database:
2. Right click on ORG and select **Define as Replication source->Custom** from the pop-up menu:

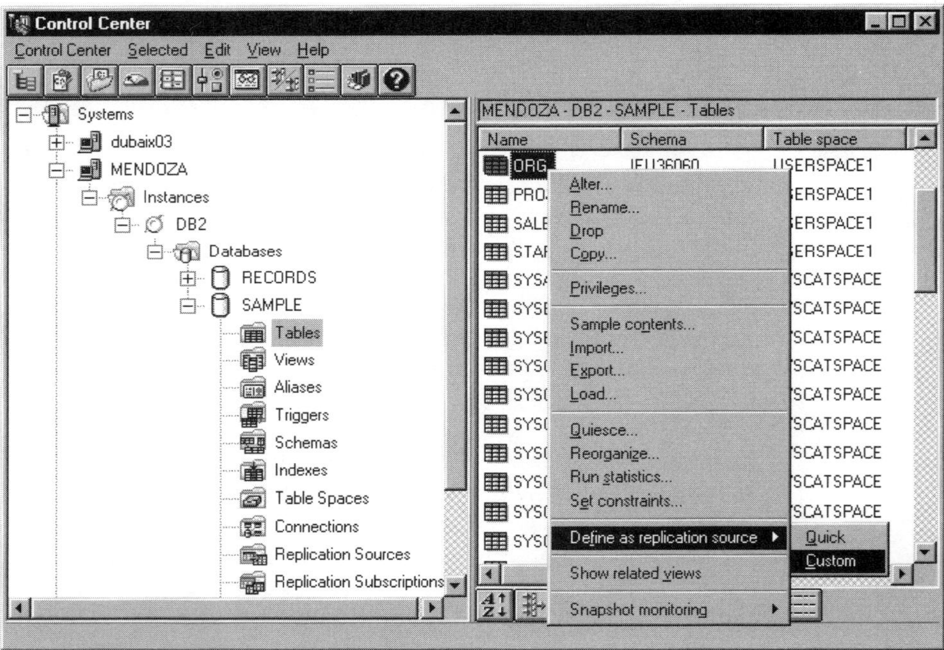

Figure 44. Defining a Custom Replication Source

3. The Define as Replication Source panel is displayed:

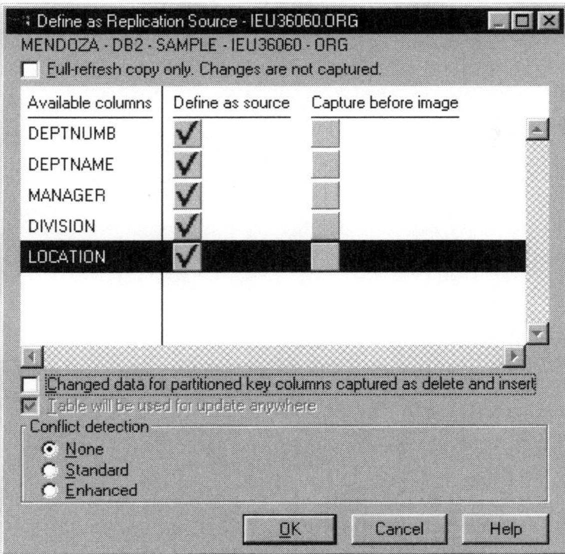

Figure 45. Defining a Table as a Replication Source

4. Make sure that all source columns are selected, and that no before images are captured for any of the columns. Also, make sure that the Full-refresh copy option is not selected. Click on **OK**.
5. Select the option to **Run Now** and click on **OK**.

Note

If the table doesn't have the attribute set for data capture changes, the Control Center will generate the necessary alter table statement to modify this attribute. Also, if there are no control tables defined at the source server, the Control Center will generate the necessary SQL statements to create these tables.

3.5.2 Defining a Replication Subscription

1. Start the Control Center and expand the Systems tree to display the replication sources for the SAMPLE database. A list of all the tables defined as replication sources will appear in the right pane.
2. Right click on the table ORG and select **Define subscription**:

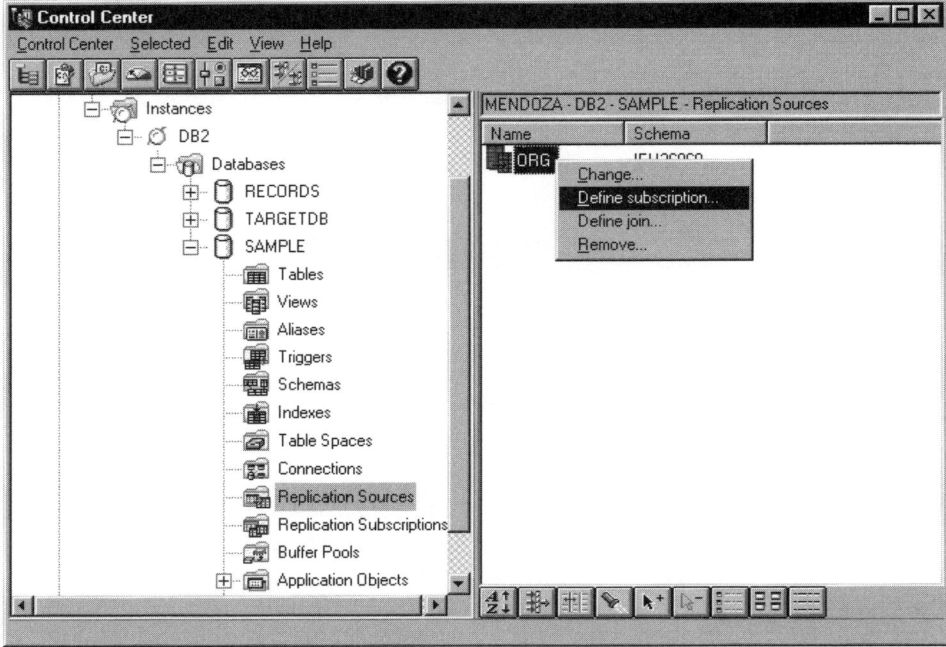

Figure 46. Defining a Replication Subscription

The Define Subscription panel is displayed:

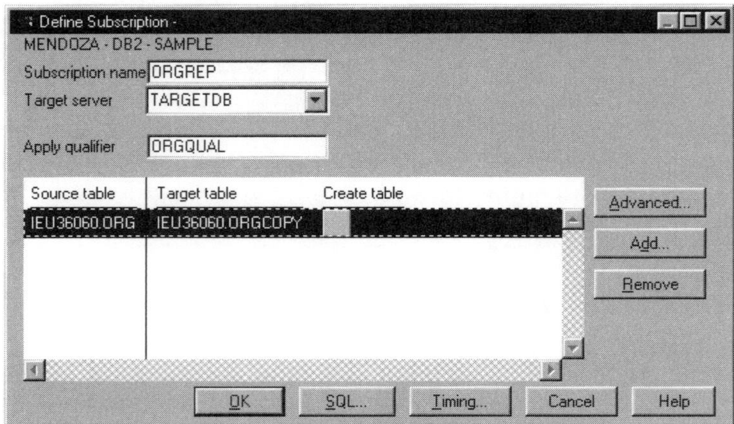

Figure 47. Defining the ORGREP Subscription

3. Enter ORGREP as the Subscription name. For the Target Server, select TARGETDB from the drop down list. Set the Apply qualifier to ORGQUAL.

Change the name of the target table to ORGCOPY and make sure that the **Create Table** check box is selected.

4. Click on the **Advanced** button and go to the **Target Columns** tab. Make sure that all the columns are selected and that DEPTNUMB is selected as the Primary Key.

> **Note**
>
> In this panel, you can add predicates to filter rows for the target table, or change the type of the target table.

For this example, the defaults will suffice. Click on **OK**.

5. Click on the **Timing** button and set the interval to relative timing every two minutes. Click on **OK**.

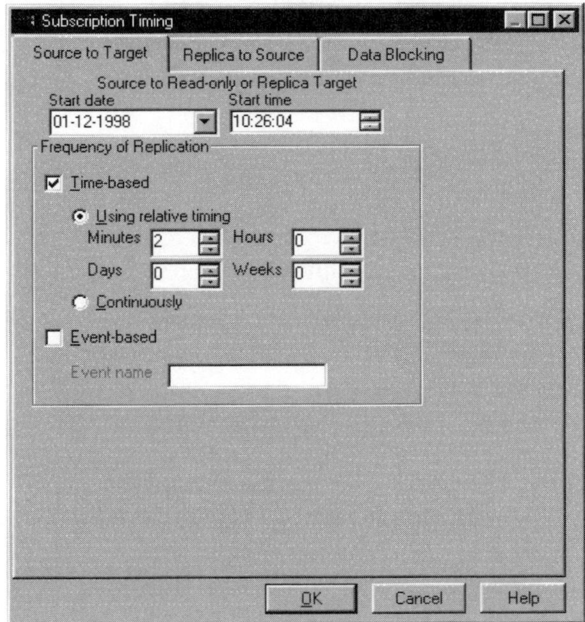

Figure 48. Subscription Timing

The following panel is displayed:

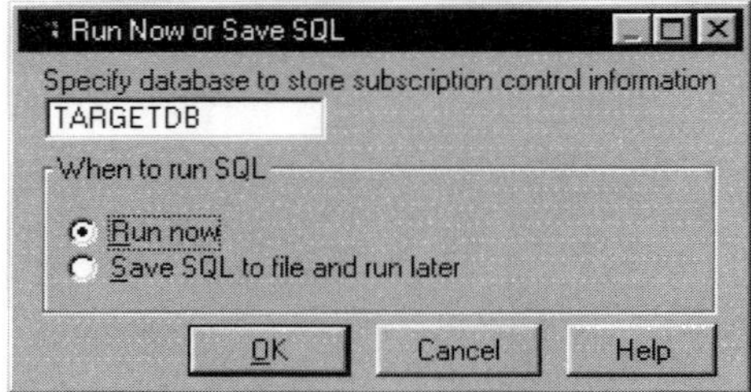

Figure 49. Choosing the Appropriate Control Server

6. Specify TARGETDB as the Control Server, select **Run now**, and click on **OK**.

> **Note**
>
> If the control tables are not defined at the target or control servers, the Control Center will generate the necessary SQL statements to create the tables.

3.5.3 Binding the Capture Program

1. From a DB2 Command Window, connect to the SAMPLE database:

```
DB2 CONNECT TO SAMPLE
```

2. Bind the CAPTURE.LST file from the \SQLLIB\BND directory:

```
DB2 BIND @CAPTURE.LST ISOLATION UR BLOCKING ALL
```

3.5.4 Binding the Apply Program

1. From a DB2 Command Window, connect to the SAMPLE database:

```
DB2 CONNECT TO SAMPLE
```

2. Bind the APPLYUR.LST and APPLYCS.LST files from the \SQLLIB\BND directory:

```
DB2 BIND @APPLYUR.LST ISOLATION UR BLOCKING ALL
DB2 BIND @APPLYCS.LST ISOLATION UR BLOCKING ALL
```

3. Connect to the TARGETDB database:

```
DB2 CONNECT TO TARGETDB
```

4. Bind the APPLYUR.LST and APPLYCS.LST files from the \SQLLIB\BND directory:

```
DB2 BIND @APPLYUR.LST ISOLATION UR BLOCKING ALL GRANT PUBLIC
DB2 BIND @APPLYCS.LST ISOLATION UR BLOCKING ALL GRANT PUBLIC
```

3.5.5 Creating the Password File

1. Change to the directory from which the Apply program will be started (for example, C:\REPL)
2. Create a text file named ORGQUALDB2TARGETDB.PWD.
3. Add these two lines. Do not include any blank or comment lines in the file:

   ```
   SERVER=SAMPLE USER=USERID PWD=PASSWORD
   SERVER=TARGETDB USER=USERID PWD=PASSWORD
   ```

   Make sure that you are using a valid userid/password combination, with enough privileges to run Capture and Apply.

3.5.6 Starting the Capture Program

From a Command Window enter:

```
ASNCCP SAMPLE
```

The Capture program has successfully started if it is running and no command prompt appears.

To stop the Capture program, you should use the ASNCMD STOP command.

3.5.7 Starting the Apply Program

From a Command Window enter:

```
ASNAPPLY ORGQUAL TARGETDB
```

The Apply program has successfully started if it is running and no command prompt appears.

To stop the Apply program, just use Ctrl+C or Ctrl+Break, or use the ASNASTOP <apply qualifier> command.

3.6 Summary

This chapter has given more details about how Capture and Apply function and interact with each other. You should now have a basic understanding of these two primary components of DB2 Replication.

Chapter 4. Replicating DB2 Data from OS/390 to Windows NT

This chapter explains how to implement replication using DB2 for OS/390 as the source and DB2 UDB for Windows NT as the target. It goes into detail on the many general DB2 replication concepts and shows you step by step how to setup and configure this replication environment.

4.1 Replication Overview

In this section, we review some of the major replication concepts before going into more detail later.

Recall that the data replication Capture component runs local to the data replication source. Capture *reads* the source database log activity using the log read API for the database, recognizes database updates of interest (as specified by the user), and stores information related to updates in local DB2 tables. For each change (insert, update, or delete) to a source table, a row is inserted in a *change data* (CD) table. There is one change data table for each source table. DB2 commit points for units of work that include such captured updates are stored in a global table known as the *unit-of-work* (UOW) table. The Apply program determines the committed changes by joining the CD and UOW tables and then propagates them to the target table.

The scope of the Capture program is always restricted to the local database, subsystem, or data sharing group depending on the operating system platform. Capture must be able to connect to the source server database. The Apply program must be able to communicate with both the source and target databases. This connectivity is always performed using DRDA or a DB2 Universal Database LAN-based protocol. DB2 Connect is required for connections between DB2 Universal Database and DB2 for OS/390 (also known as DB2/MVS) where a connection must be made to the DB2 for OS/390 system. Either TCP/IP or SNA can be used with DB2 for OS/390 5.1 when DB2 UDB is the application requester.

Communication can be an important factor in a replication design that involves staging data at a server that is different from the source database. For example, in a typical replication scenario between DB2 for OS/390 5.1 and DB2 for Windows NT, the best connectivity scenario might be to use TCP/IP rather than SNA when considering the network configuration workload.

The Apply program generally runs at the target server. This is known as a *pull* configuration. In pull mode, the Apply program connects to the remote source server to retrieve the data. In this configuration, it may be possible to use block fetch to efficiently pass the data across the network. After retrieving all the data for a particular table, the Apply program can establish a local connection to the target server and apply the changes to the target table. When the Apply program resides on the source server and copies the data to the target server, this is known as a *push* configuration.

Before we get into the details of setting up this configuration, let's first look at some considerations when implementing replication from DB2/MVS to DB2 UDB for Windows NT.

4.2 Capture for OS/390 V5 Considerations

DPropR Capture/MVS V1 did not support archive log retrieval and data compression. These functions are implemented in Capture for OS/390 V5 (also known as Capture/MVS). In addition, DB2 for MVS V4.1 introduced the Instrumentation Facility Interface (or IFI). As shown in Figure 50 on page 91, Capture/MVS V5 uses the new IFI READ macro calls (IFCID 306) to utilize these functions if the level of DB2 for MVS is V4.1 or higher.

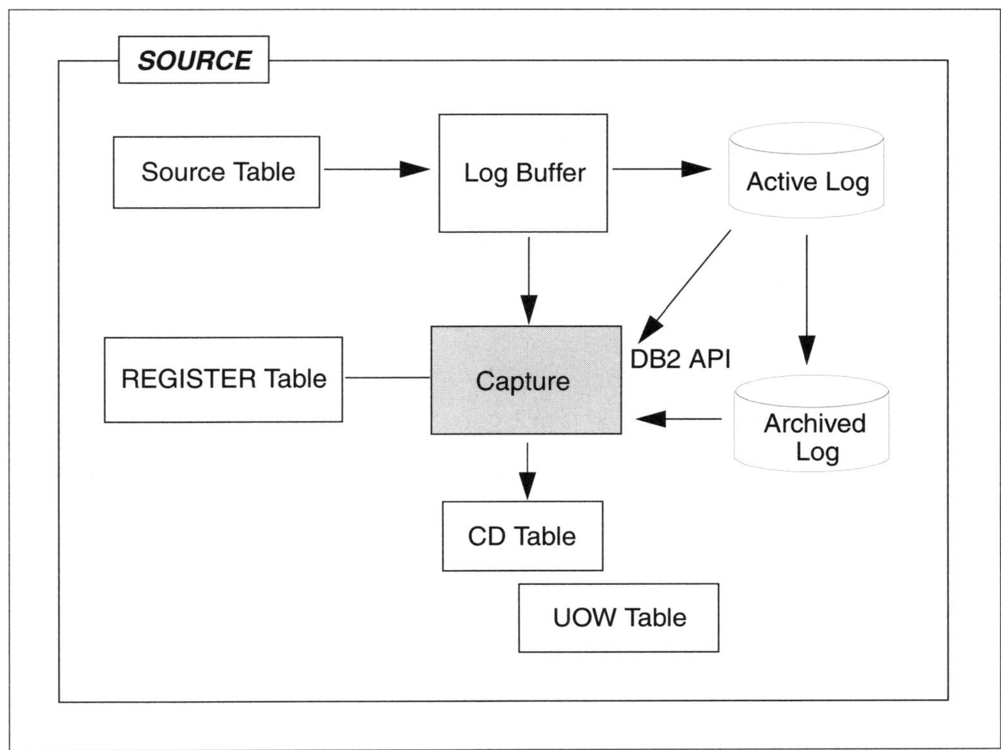

Figure 50. Capture/MVS Process Overview

4.2.1 Archived Log Read Support

Capture/MVS V5 retrieves log records that have been archived in the archive log. This is necessary if Capture/MVS is lagging far behind transactions for some reason (perhaps a heavy load on the CPU or contention over DB2 resources). In this case, uncaptured data overflows to the archive log. Archive log record reading by Capture/MVS requires DB2 for MVS V4.1 or higher. If you are running DB2 for MVS V3.1, the size of the active log should be large enough to handle at least 24 hours of transaction data.

4.2.2 Compression Data Support

Capture/MVS captures changes made to compressed tables using OS/390 compression hardware or software emulation. Hardware or software compression has been available for DB2 since version 3.1. The compression dictionary is used to compress the row. Before issuing a REORG for compressed replication source tables, you should perform one of the following tasks:

- Ensure that the Capture program has completed capturing all of the existing changes.
- Use the KEEPDICTIONARY option on the REORG command to preserve the existing compression dictionary.

Data compression is also possible through the use of EDITPROC and FIELDPROC, but the Capture program does not yet support data that is compressed using EDITPROC or FIELDPROC.

4.2.3 Data Sharing Support

In DB2 for MVS V4.1 or higher, DB2 also supports the data sharing option. Up to 32 DB2 subsystems can share the same data when running in data share mode on a Sysplex hardware configuration. This means that the same DB2 table can be updated by more than one DB2 subsystem. Since each DB2 subsystem maintains its own log, there is a need for a global sequencing system that extends over all the logs with a granularity small enough to guarantee that no two updates have the same sequence number. DB2 uses a sequencing system called LSN (log sequence number) that is a value associated with each log record. Capture/MVS V5 uses LRSN instead of RBA since the LRSNs generated by a given DB2 data sharing group will form a strictly increasing sequence for each DB2 log and a strictly increasing sequence for each page across a DB2 group. See “Communication between Capture and Apply in Full Refresh” on page 135 for more details. One instance of Capture/MVS can be run per source data sharing group. To maximize the Capture throughput, Capture should be run on its own member or on the most lightly loaded member. Using Capture in a data sharing environment can dramatically improve throughput performance.

4.2.4 Authorization for Running Capture for MVS

To run Capture for MVS, you must have:

- SELECT, UPDATE, INSERT, and DELETE privilege for all Capture-related tables
- SELECT privilege for the DB2 catalog tables
- TRACE privilege
- MONITOR1 and MONITOR2 privilege
- EXECUTE privilege for the Capture plan

4.3 Apply for Windows NT V5 Considerations

IBM Replication products are packaged as part of other products or are available separately. DB2 Universal Database for Windows NT contains both the Capture and the Apply components for the Windows NT platform. In this example configuration, Apply for Windows NT fetches the data it requires (which has been inserted by Capture for MVS into the DB2/MVS change data tables) by using the DRDA protocol. It stores the fetched rows into one or more *spill files* and applies each change, one row at a time, to the target tables. This process is shown in Figure 51:

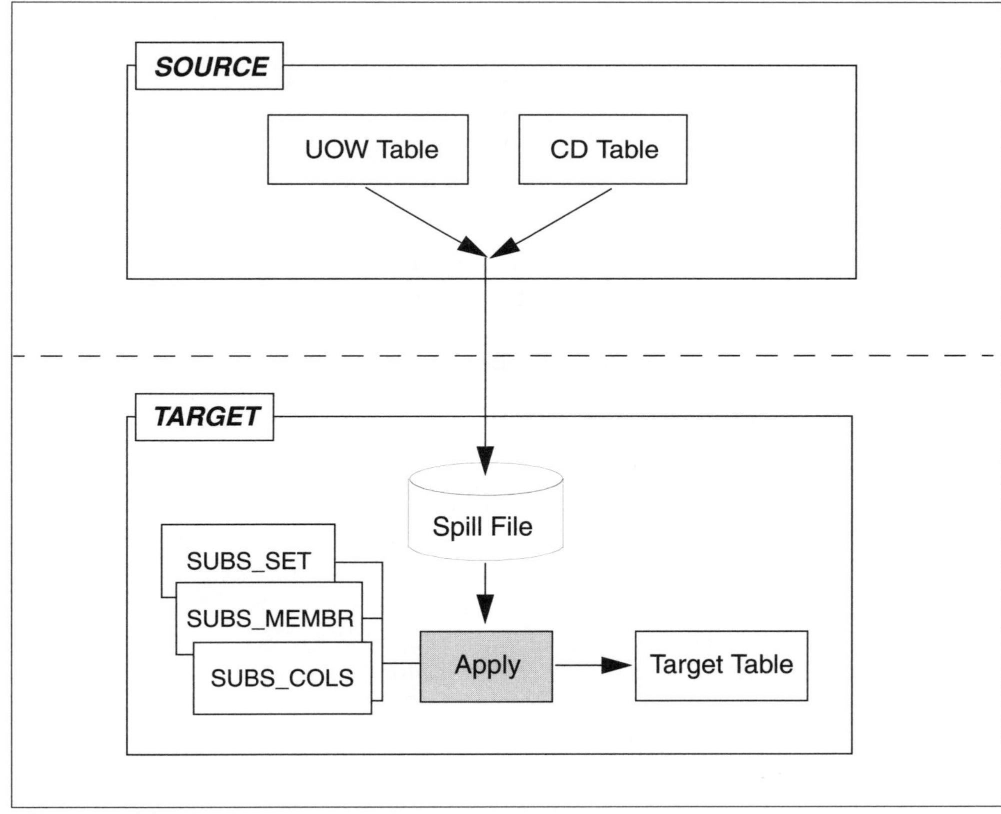

Figure 51. Apply for Windows NT Process Overview

4.3.1 Uncommitted Read (UR) Isolation Level Support

In DPropR V1, Capture for MVS takes an exclusive lock on the critical section table before it starts capturing changes. During this time, Apply for Windows NT cannot access this table. Conversely, Apply for Windows NT needs to take a share lock on the critical section table at the source server before it starts processing. Capture for MVS becomes inactive during this time allowing one or more Apply for Windows NT processes to take the share lock.

In DPropR V5, the change data tables can now be used simultaneously by Capture and one or more Apply tasks with these exceptions:

- While Capture is pruning the change data tables.
- When databases involved do not support the UR isolation mode, such as DB2 for MVS V3.1.

During insert operations by Capture, an exclusive lock still must be taken on the change data tables that are to be updated. However, at each commit point, Capture now tracks the highest commit log sequence number captured as part of that commit interval (default of 30 seconds). Apply reads the change data tables with a *dirty read* (using the Uncommitted Read or UR isolation level) to fetch new data but limits the search to data that has been previously committed by using the sequence number provided by Capture at its most recent commit point.

This new mode of operation provides for much higher throughput rates by Capture and Apply since they are not constantly in lock contention. Running with the UR isolation level also means that there is no penalty for increasing the number of Apply components in a replication environment, which results in improved scalability.

4.3.2 Subscription Sets

Another new feature of IBM Data Replication V5 is the support for *subscription sets*. Users can group multiple target table subscriptions (known as members) to run within a subscription set. Apply will handle all target table subscription members within a set in one commit scope. This is a great functional improvement since related tables can be copied with application integrity. It is also a potential performance improvement since the overhead required to process a group of target tables together is reduced. The resource savings are dependent on the number of subscription members grouped within a set. Bear in mind that multiple Apply components can be run in parallel to increase the total throughput of Apply, whereas, a subscription set will be processed serially by a single instance of Apply. Note that multiple spill files are used for the replication subscriptions with multiple target tables if the user groups together multiple target tables. The total spill file size should be enough to store the data selected for all subscription members at each interval, including the full refresh case (unless you are using the ASNLOAD exit program). This is shown in Figure 52 on page 95:

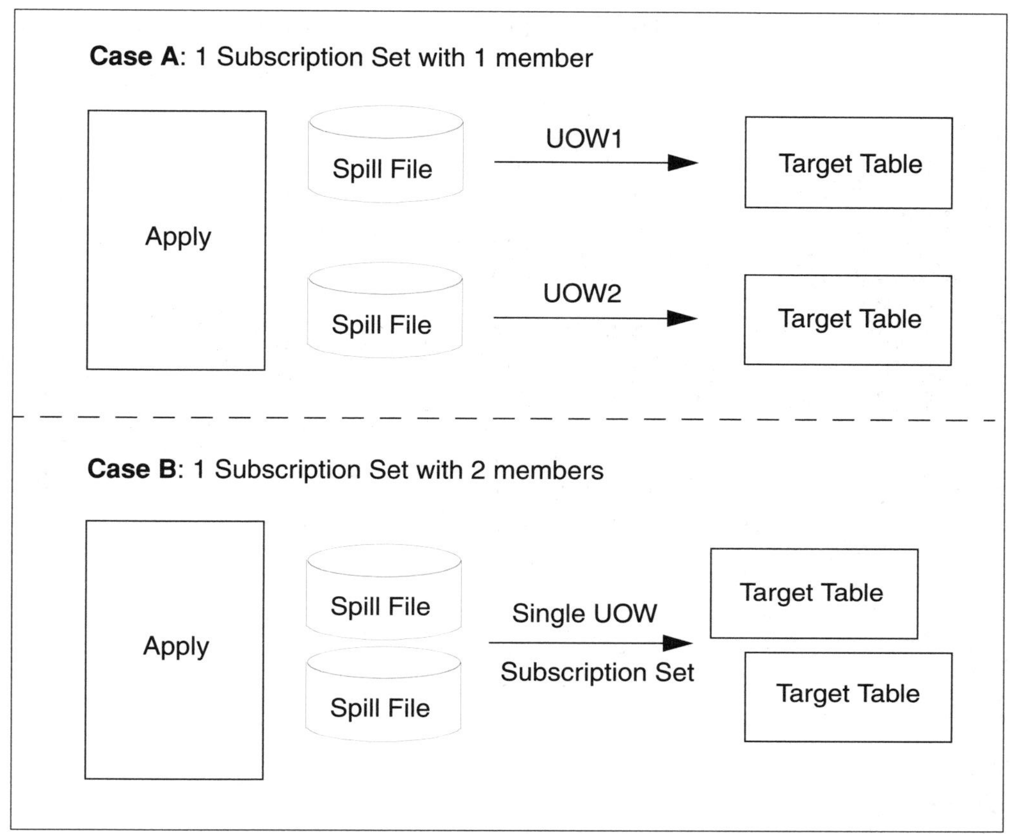

Figure 52. Subscription Sets

4.4 Test Environment for OS/390 and Windows NT Replication

In this example, DB2 for OS/390 V5.1 is used as the source server, and DB2 UDB for Windows NT V5.2 is used as the target and control server. The location name of DB2 for OS/390 is DB2C, and the COPYDB1 database on the Windows NT machine is the target database. We will replicate the EMPLOYEE table in the DB2C subsystem to the EMPLCOPY table in the COPYDB1 database on the Windows NT machine.

Table 9 summarizes the test environment:

Table 9. Test Environment Configuration for OS/390 to Windows NT Replication

Machine Name	OS/ DB Software	Database or (Instance)	Description
wtsc42oe	DB2 for OS/390 V5.1	DB2C (DB2C)	- Used as replication source - Capture runs here
jc6003c	Windows NT4.0 / DB2 UDB V5.2	COPYDB1 (DB2)	- Used as replication target - Remote USER COPY table in COPYDB1 - Apply runs here

An overview of the replication to be performed is shown in Figure 53:

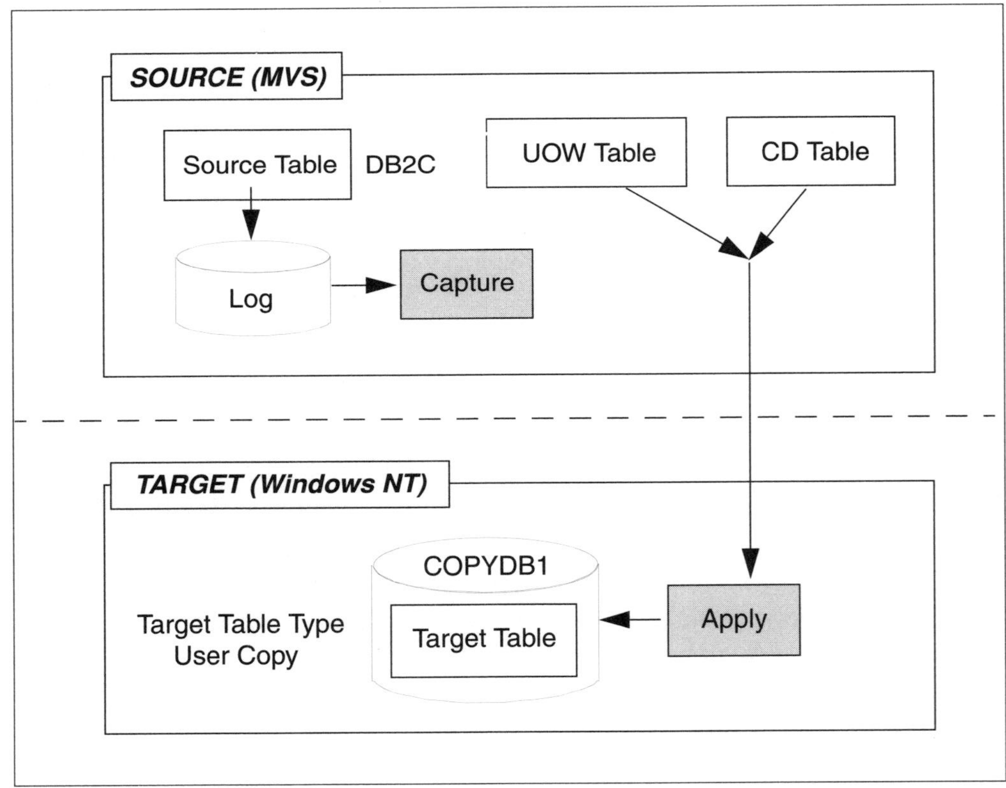

Figure 53. Replication Overview - DB2 OS/390 to DB2 for Windows NT

4.4.1 Configuring TCP/IP DRDA for DB2 for OS/390

This section explains how to configure TCP/IP communications between the DB2 Connect workstation (here Windows NT) and the DRDA server running DB2 for OS/390 Version 5.1. It assumes that:

- You are connecting to a single host database using TCP/IP. Multiple host connections are handled in exactly the same way, although the port numbers and service numbers required in each case may be different.
- The target database resides on DB2 for OS/390 Version 5.1.
- All the necessary software prerequisites are installed.
- DB2 clients have been set up as required.

DB2 for OS/390 has the Application Server function built into the *Distributed Data Facility* (DDF). DDF gets its connection data for inbound connections only from the *Bootstrap Data Set* (BSDS). The DDF definition looks like this:

```
//SYSADMB JOB ,'DB2 5.1 JOB',CLASS=A
//*
//*        CHANGE LOG INVENTORY:
//*        UPDATE BSDS WITH
//*             - DB2 LOCATION NAME FOR NEW_YORK3
//*             - VTAM LUNAME (NYM2DB2)
//*             - DB2/VTAM PASSWORD
//*
//*             - GENERIC LU NAME
//*             - TCP/IP PORT FOR DATABASE CONNECTIONS
//*             - TCP/IP PORT FOR RESYNCH OPERATIONS
//*
//DSNBSDS EXEC PGM=DSNJU003
//STEPLIB  DD  DISP=SHR,DSN=DSN510.DSNLOAD
//SYSUT1   DD  DISP=OLD,DSN=DSNC510.BSDS01
//SYSUT2   DD  DISP=OLD,DSN=DSNC510.BSDS02
//SYSPRINT DD  SYSOUT=*
//SYSUDUMP DD  SYSOUT=*
//SYSIN    DD  *
  DDF     LOCATION=DB2C,LUNAME=SCPDB2C,PASSWORD=PSWDBD1,
          GENERICLU=name,PORT=33302,RESPORT=33303
/*
//*
```

Two suitable TCP/IP port numbers must be assigned by your network administrator. By default, DB2 for OS/390 uses port number 446 for database connections and port number 5001 for resynchronization requests (used during two-phase commit). In this case, the database connection port number is 33302. You can review the current setting by looking up the DDF start-up message:

```
DSNL519I =DB2C DSNLILNR TCP/IP SERVICES AVAILABLE 276
           FOR DOMAIN wtsc42oe.itso.ibm.com AND PORT 33302
DSNL519I =DB2C DSNLIRSY TCP/IP SERVICES AVAILABLE 277
           FOR DOMAIN wtsc42oe.itso.ibm.com AND PORT 33303
DSNL004I =DB2C DDF START COMPLETE 278
           LOCATION  DB2C
           LU        USIBMSC.SCPDB2C
           GENERICLU -NONE
           DOMAIN    wtsc42oe.itso.ibm.com
           TCPPORT   33302
           RESPORT   33303
```

Configuration of the Application Requester (AR) component in DB2 Connect consists of these steps:

4. Setup and verify the TCP/IP stack.

   The easiest way to verify that we have a working TCP/IP configuration is to ping the Application Server from the DB2 Connect system.

5. Update the node directory.

   The node directory holds all protocol specific information concerning the the remote DBMS.

6. Update the database directory.

   The database directory maps a database alias on the DB2 Connect system to an entry in the node directory.

7. Update the DCS directory.

   The DCS directory holds the DRDA specific parameters.

Here are the definitions we used in this example configuration. The DB2 for OS/390 Location Name is DB2C:

```
catalog tcpip node db2c remote wtsc42oe.itso.ibm.com server
        33302 ostype MVS ;
catalog db db2c at node db2c authentication dcs;
catalog dcs db db2c;
```

You can also use the Client Configuration Assistant (CCA) to configure these directories. Since DB2 UDB Discovery is not supported for DRDA Application Servers, you cannot use the Search the network option. You must select **Manually configure a connection to a DB2 database** and click on **Next** to get to the other pages.

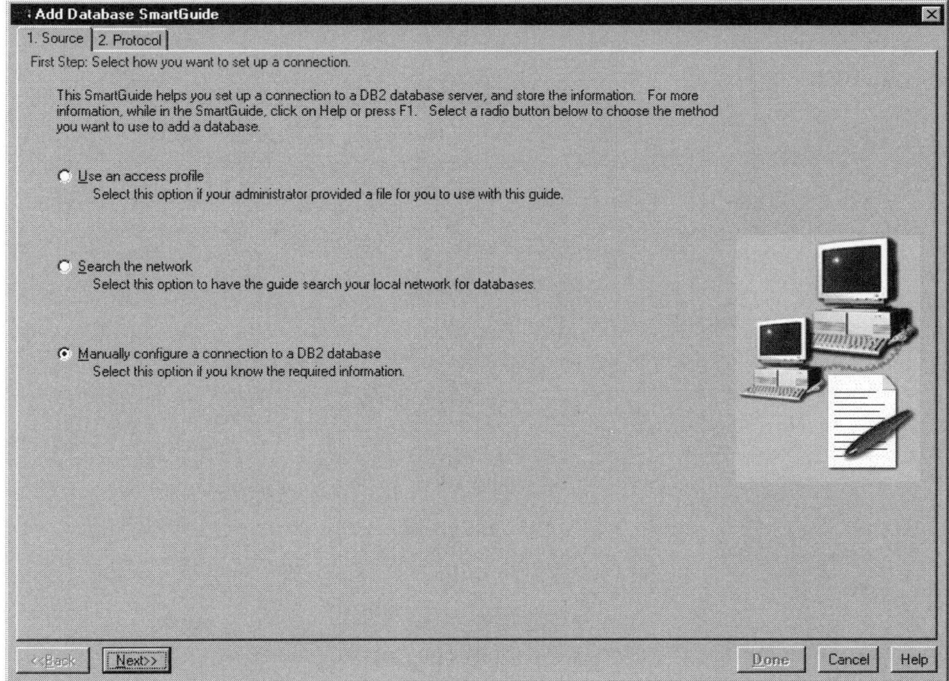

Figure 54. CCA - Add Database SmartGuide

We can examine the contents of the directories using the LIST NODE DIRECTORY SHOW DETAIL, LIST DATABASE DIRECTORY and LIST DCS DIRECTORY commands. Here is the output obtained by running these commands in this example:

```
list node directory show detail
Node Directory
Node 1 entry:
Node name                      = DB2C
Comment                        =
Protocol                       = TCPIP
Hostname                       = wtsc42oe.itso.ibm.com
Service name                   = 33302
Remote instance name           =
System                         =
Operating system type          = MVS

list db directory
System Database Directory
Database 1 entry:
Database alias                  = DB2C
Database name                   = DB2C
Node name                       = DB2C
Database release level          = 8.00
Comment                         =
Directory entry type            = Remote
Authentication                  = DCS
Catalog node number             = -1

list dcs directory
Database Connection Services (DCS) Directory
Number of entries in the directory = 1
DCS 1 entry:
Local database name                = DB2C
Target database name               =
Application requestor name         =
DCS parameters                     =
Comment                            =
DCS directory release level        = 0x0100
```

4.5 Initial Configuration for the Replication Scenario

Having presented the connectivity issues and also the considerations per platform, we now move ahead to setting up a simple replication from source to target table. Initially, the whole source table will be copied to the target table, then any source table changes will be replicated individually to the target table. In this kind of replication environment, the target table is known as a *user copy*. Here are the basic procedures to setup this replication environment:

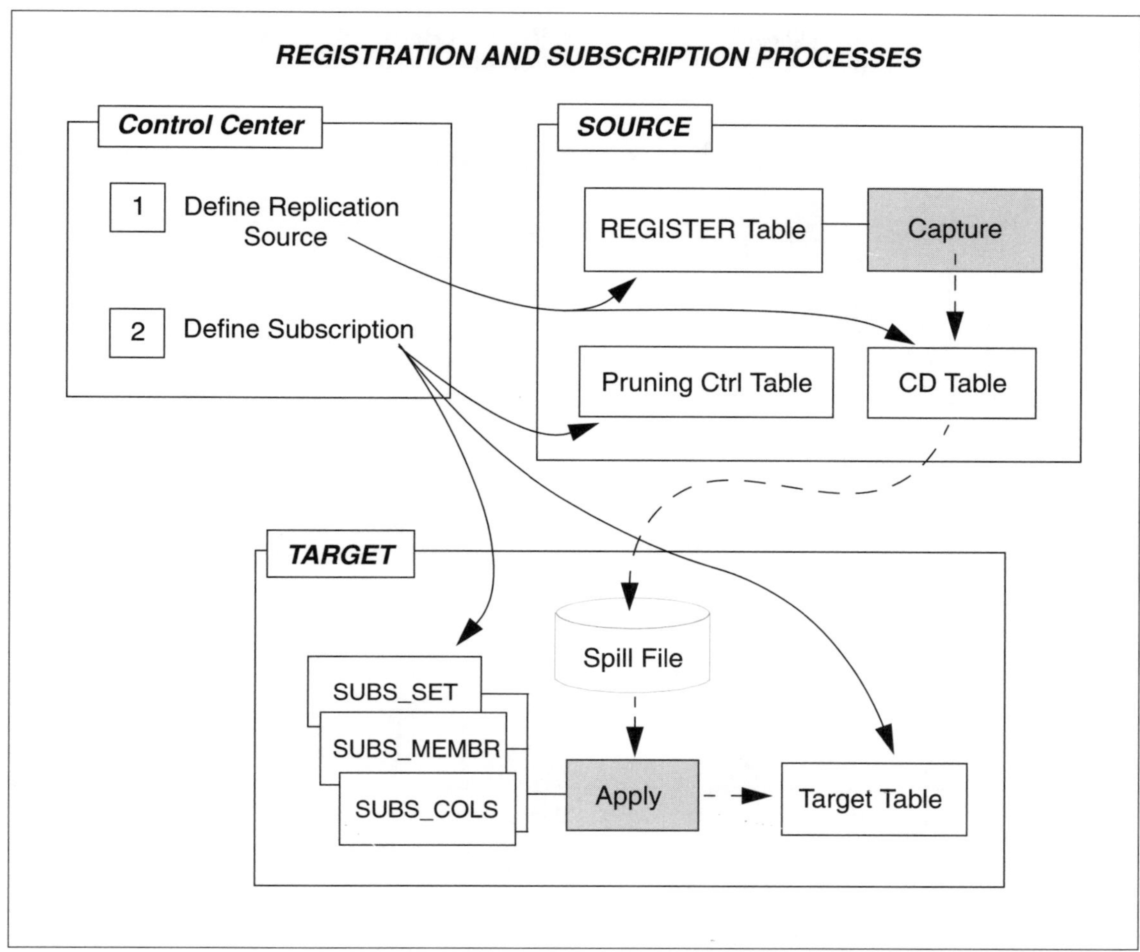

Figure 55. Registration and Subscription Processes

Figure 55 shows an overview of the steps we will follow. We will explain these steps in detail in this section.

Note that when the Capture and the Apply programs are running, the Control Center does not have to be active, and that the Control Center can not be used to operate the Capture and Apply programs.

4.5.1 Defining a Replication Source

To define a replication source, you should use the DB2 UDB Control Center.

1. Start the Control Center on the Windows NT machine and expand the object trees **System->wtsc42oe.itso.ibm.com->DB2C**. Click on the **Tables** folder to display the list of tables in the DB2C database in the right hand pane:

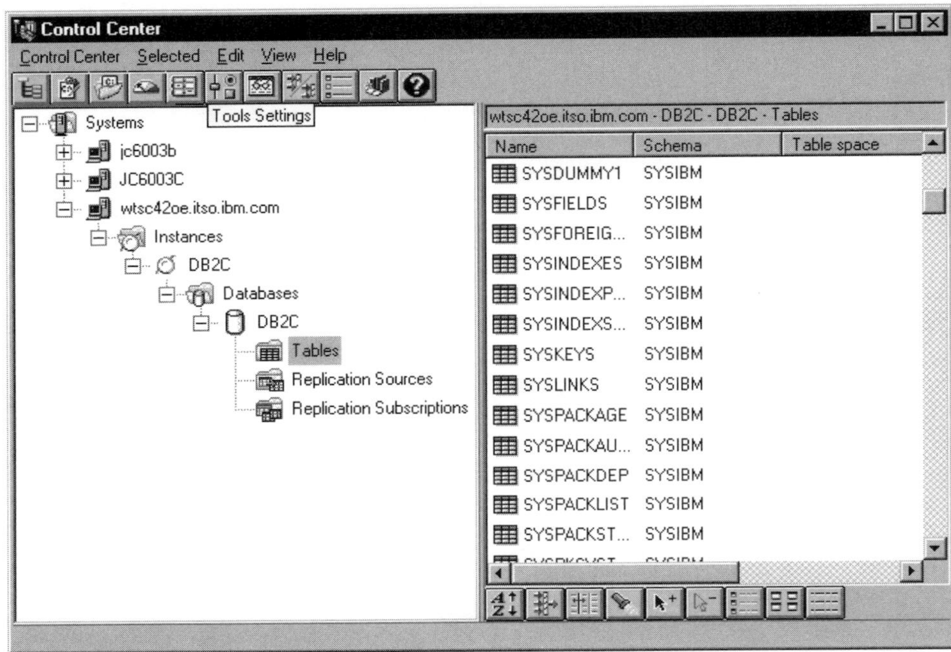

Figure 56. DB2 UDB Control Center - Define a Replication Source

2. Before we define our replication source, let's review the tools settings for replication and understand what you can and cannot set. Click on the **Tools Settings** icon in the tool bar to set the replication default values. The Tools Settings Notebook is displayed as shown in Figure 57 on page 103.

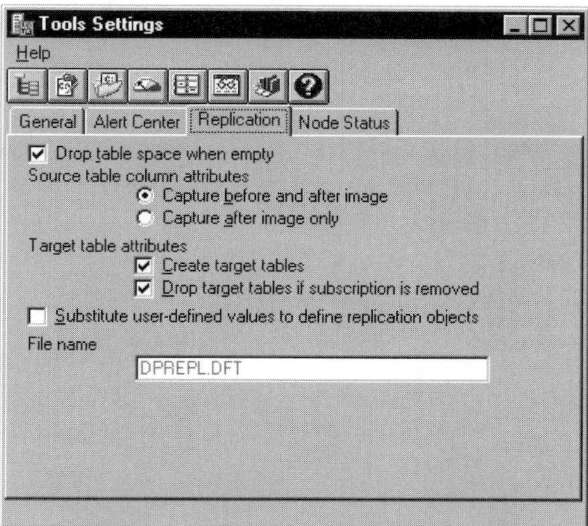

Figure 57. DB2 UDB Control Center - Tools Settings Notebook

3. Clicking on the **Replication** tab will show you the options you can set for DB2 Replication:

   Note the **Drop table space when empty** option. You may choose to have this option enabled depending on your particular site requirements. The default is to drop the table spaces.

   This setting means that both the table spaces for the CD tables at the source server and those for the target table at the target server will be dropped when empty. This applies to the MVS, VM/VSE, and UDB platforms.

   Make sure the **Capture before and after image** option is selected.

   This is the default and means that both the before and after images of the source table columns are captured and can be replicated to the target table. The before image columns will contain the following data depending on the type of change made to the source column:

Table 10. Before/After Image Column Values

SQL operation	Before-Image Column	After-Image Column
INSERT	NULL	After-Image value
DELETE	Before-Image value	Before-Image value
UPDATE	Before-Image value	After-Image value

Make sure that the **Create target tables** option is selected, which is the default.

This means that target tables will automatically be created while defining a replication subscription.

In our example, we chose to have the **Drop target tables if subscription is removed** option selected, which is also the default. You may or may not wish to do this for your site implementation.

This option means that the relevant target tables (and their related control tables) will be dropped when the subscription set is removed.

Close the **Tools Settings** notebook to save your changes.

4. Back in the Control Center, choose a table to be a replication source (here, EMPLOYEE) and click the right mouse button. Select **Define as replication source->Custom**:

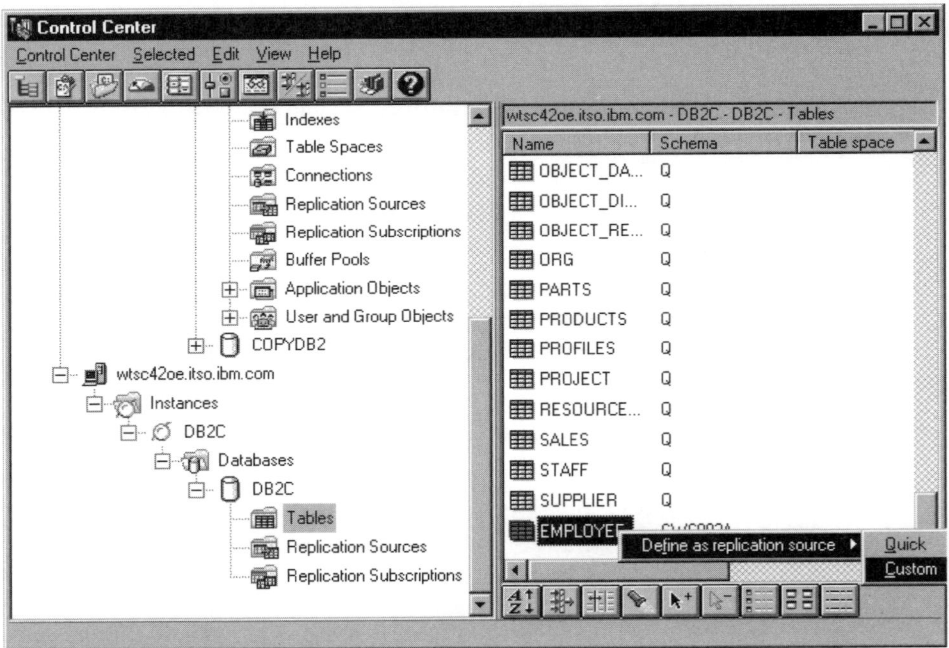

Figure 58. Define a Replication Source - Custom

The Define as Replication Source panel is displayed:

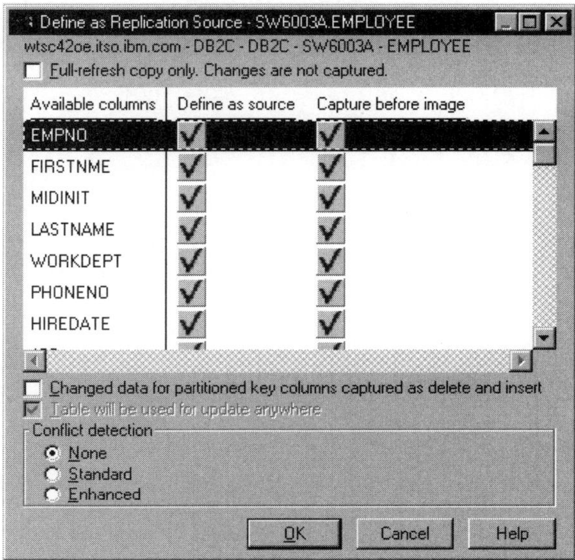

Figure 59. Define as Replication Source Panel

5. Make sure the **Define as source** and **Capture before image** check boxes are selected for all columns.

   If you select **Full-refresh copy only**, the Capture program will not capture changes to the source and the Apply program will copy all the data from the source table at every Apply cycle. Although you will be defining a replication source, a CD table will not be created.

6. Make sure that Conflict Detection is set to **None** as we are not using update-anywhere in this scenario. You can also choose to not select the **Table will be used for update anywhere** option.

7. Select **OK** to save the options and close the window. The Run Now or Save SQL window is displayed:

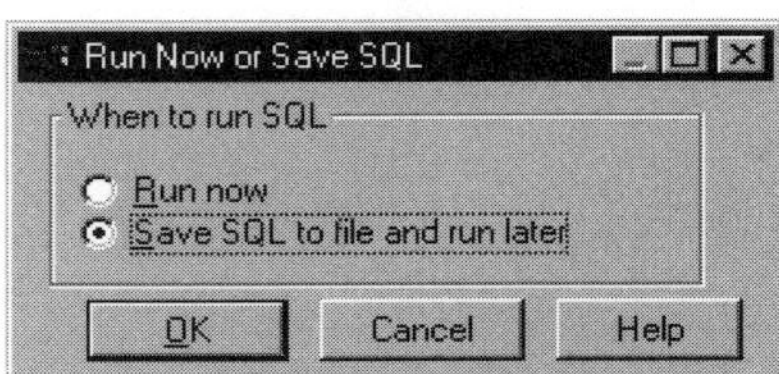

Figure 60. Define Replication Source - Run Now or Save SQL

You have the option to run the SQL to create this replication source immediately or save the SQL generated for later execution. If you do the latter, then the SQL files can be customized, for example, to allow you to:

- Create multiple copies of the same replication action, customized for multiple servers.
- Customize CD table names or other settings, such as:
  - The database name for DB2 for MVS.
  - The nodegroup name for DB2 UDB EEE.
  - The table space name and size for DB2 UDB EE or DB2 for VM/VSE.

8. Select the **Save SQL to file and run later** option and click **OK**. The Save SQL file window is displayed:

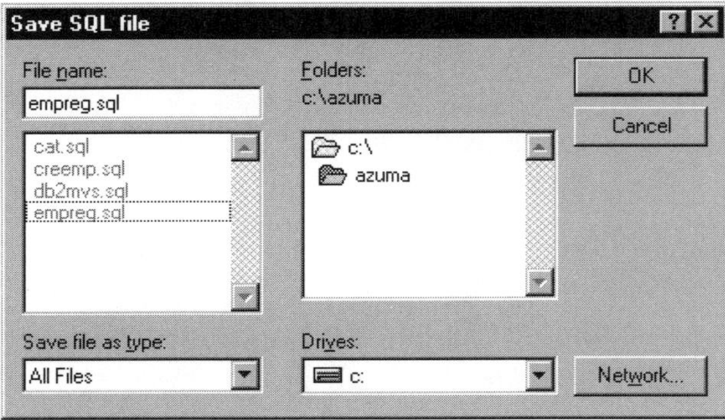

Figure 61. Choose SQL File

9. Enter the file name (here, empreg.sql). Click **OK** to save the SQL file. You will see a confirmation message saying that the SQL file has been saved for later execution.

10. Examine the SQL file with a text editor. It should contain these SQL statements:

- Part one:

```
CONNECT TO DB2C;

ALTER TABLE SW6003A.EMPLOYEE
DATA CAPTURE CHANGES;
```

After connecting to the source server database (DB2C) where the EMPLOYEE table resides, an ALTER TABLE statement with the DATA CAPTURE CHANGES option will be run against the source table. The

DATA CAPTURE CHANGES option will cause DB2 to log full before images and partial after images for any update made to a source table that has been selected for replication. Note that we must add the USER and USING clause on the CONNECT SQL statement when the source server requires that a user and password be provided for a connection. Otherwise, we will get the connection error message SQL30081N when the connect statement is invoked. So, in this case, we modify the CONNECT statement to:

```
CONNECT TO DB2C USER SW6003A USING xxxxx;
```

• Part two:

```
CREATE TABLE SW6003A.CD19981125119436 (
IBMSNAP_UOWID CHAR ( 10 ) FOR BIT DATA NOT NULL,
IBMSNAP_INTENTSEQ CHAR ( 10 ) FOR BIT DATA NOT NULL,
IBMSNAP_OPERATION CHAR ( 1 ) NOT NULL,
XEMPNO CHAR ( 6 ),
EMPNO CHAR ( 6 ) NOT NULL,
XFIRSTNME VARCHAR ( 12 ),
FIRSTNME VARCHAR ( 12 ) NOT NULL.......
```

Here is the create table statement for the CD table of the replication source table, EMPLOYEE. The CD table holds the changes (inserts, updates, or deletes) to the source table. For each source column, there is a column with the same column name but prefixed with X (by default), for example, XEMPNO. This column is used to store the before image.

A CD table receives all the changed data rows from the Capture program. The changes are not condensed, so ten updates to the same row will result in ten rows inserted in the CD table. The CD table has no knowledge of transaction boundaries or whether the transaction issuing the updates is committed. The Apply program joins the CD tables with the unit of work (UOW) table to determine the committed changes to copy. Uncommitted and incomplete changes can appear in rows in a CD table but will not be copied until committed.

It is important to point out that the name of the CD table can be changed by changing the SQL statement above. If you choose to change the name of the CD table, ensure that you also change the references to the CD table name in the remaining SQL statements in this file.

• Part three:

```
CREATE TYPE 2 UNIQUE INDEX SW6003A.IX19981125875570
ON SW6003A.CD19981125119436
( IBMSNAP_UOWID ASC, IBMSNAP_INTENTSEQ ASC );
```

This is a unique ascending index created on the CD table for the EMPLOYEE table. We must use a TYPE 2 index for DB2/MVS V4.1 or higher.

Do not specify a TYPE 1 index if the table space containing the identified table has a LOCKSIZE of ROW. If you specify a TYPE 1 index in a data sharing environment, a warning message is issued if you specify a value greater than one for SUBPAGES. Also, you can't use an isolation level of UR with an access path that uses a TYPE 1 index.

Apply usually reads the change data tables with a *dirty read* (UR isolation level) to fetch new data. Type 2 indexes are a new type in DB2/MVS version 4, and the locking used on their index pages allows for more concurrency, which, in turn, reduces deadlock and time-out problems.

• Part four:

```
INSERT INTO ASN.IBMSNAP_REGISTER ( GLOBAL_RECORD, SOURCE_OWNER,
SOURCE_TABLE, SOURCE_VIEW_QUAL, SOURCE_STRUCTURE, SOURCE_CONDENSED,
SOURCE_COMPLETE, CD_OWNER, CD_TABLE, PHYS_CHANGE_OWNER,
PHYS_CHANGE_TABLE,
CD_OLD_SYNCHPOINT, CD_NEW_SYNCHPOINT, DISABLE_REFRESH, CCD_OWNER,
CCD_TABLE, CCD_OLD_SYNCHPOINT, SYNCHPOINT, SYNCHTIME, CCD_CONDENSED,
CCD_COMPLETE, ARCH_LEVEL, DESCRIPTION, BEFORE_IMG_PREFIX,
CONFLICT_LEVEL,
PARTITION_KEYS_CHG ) VALUES (
'N', 'SW6003A', 'EMPLOYEE', 0, 1,'Y', 'Y', 'SW6003A',
'CD19981125119436',
'SW6003A', 'CD19981125119436', NULL, NULL, 0, NULL, NULL, NULL, NULL,
NULL, NULL, NULL, '0201', NULL, 'X', '0', 'N');
```

This is the insert statement to the Register table that contains information about the replication source table. Unless you use the view registration technique, the values of CD_TABLE and PHYS_CHANGE_TABLE should match. The initial values of SYNCHPOINT and SYNCHTIME are NULL.

Note that the CONFLICT_LEVEL is set to zero, which indicates that there is no need for conflict detection for the User Copy. Conflict detection is only required if the target table type is Replica.

> **Note**
>
> New registrations may be added at any time, but a *REINIT* command is required when you add new registrations after the Capture program has started. The *REINIT* command forces the Capture program to read the REGISTER and CCPPARMS tables.

4.5.2 Defining a Replication Subscription

You also use the DB2 UDB Control Center to define the replication subscription:

1. From the Control Center, expand the object trees until you see the replication sources folder (**System->wtsc42oe->DB2C**). Click on **Replication sources** to display the list of defined replication sources in the right hand pane.

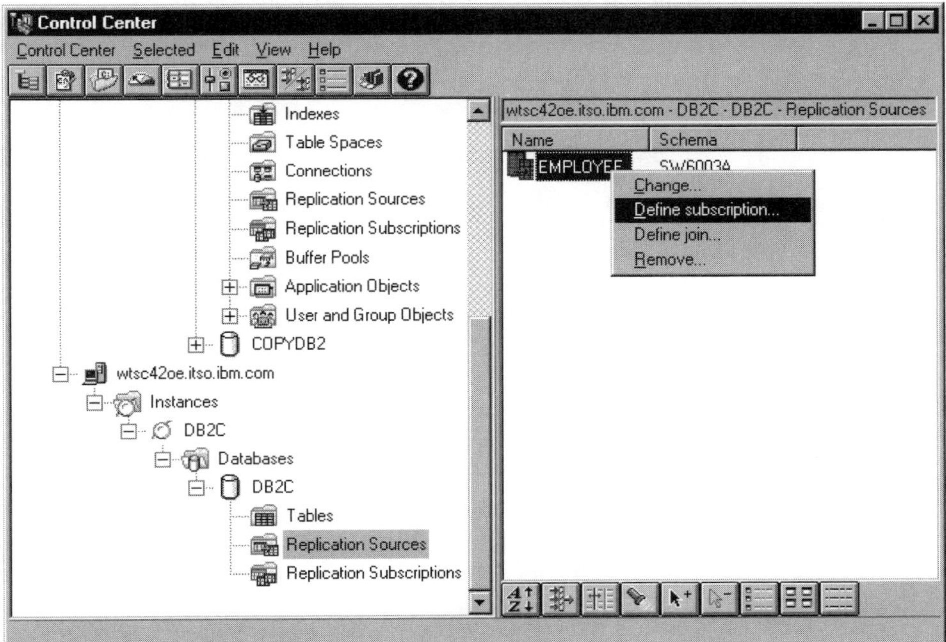

Figure 62. Define Subscription in the DB2 UDB Control Center

2. Choose a replication source (here, EMPLOYEE) and click the right mouse button. From the pop-up menu, select **Define subscription**. The Define Subscription panel is displayed:

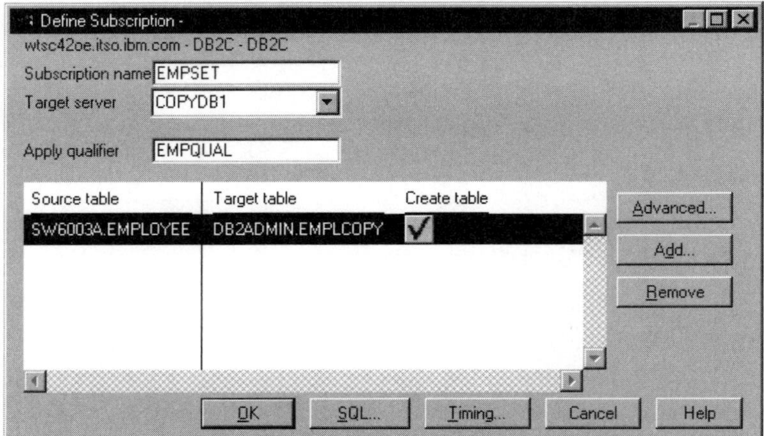

Figure 63. Define Subscription Panel

3. Fill in the Define Subscription window as shown in Figure 63.

   Enter the **Subscription name** (here, EMPSET). This is user defined and up to 18 characters in length.

   Select the **Target server** (here, COPYDB1). This is the database on the Windows NT machine.

   Enter the **Apply Qualifier** (here, EMPQUAL). This name will be used later when we invoke the Apply program.

   Change the name of the **Target table** (here, EMPLCOPY). This is to make the target table easily identifiable.

4. Select **Advanced** to display the Advanced Subscription Definition panel:

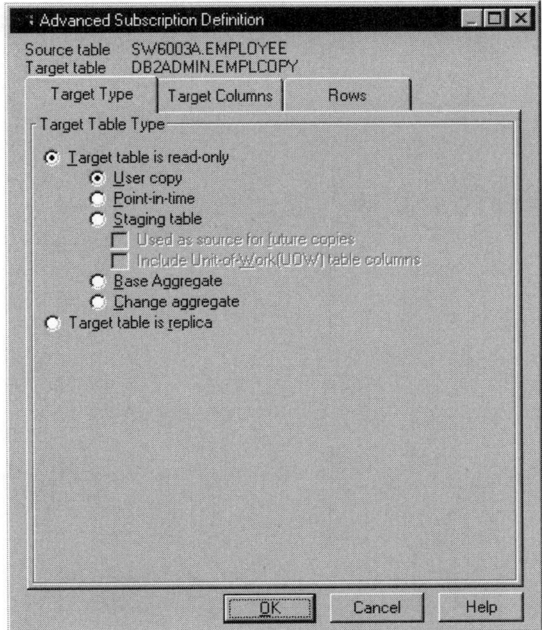

Figure 64. Advanced Subscription Definition

5. Make sure the **User Copy** option is selected. This target table type is the default. Click on the **Target Columns** tab:

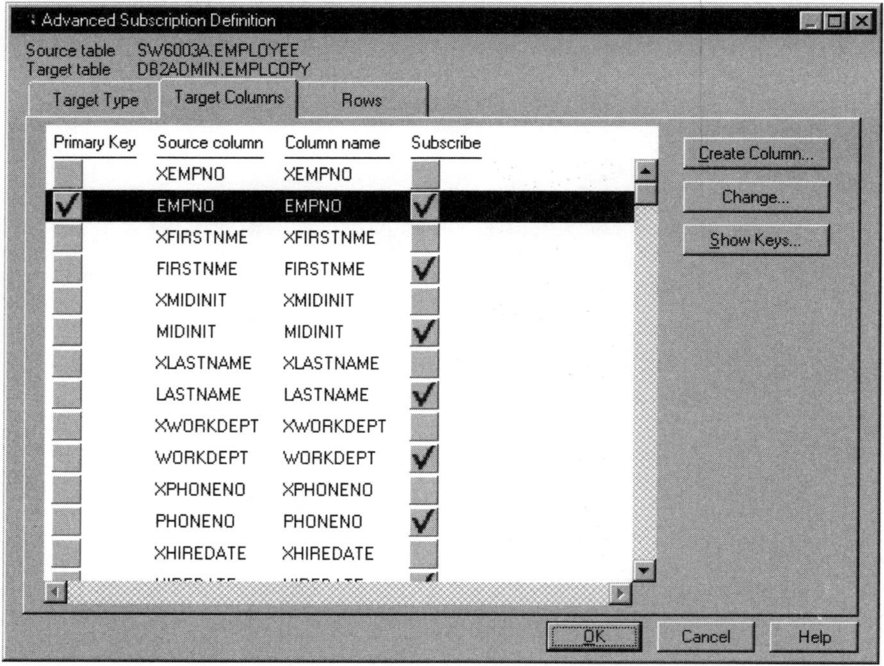

Figure 65. Define Subscription - Primary Key

6. Check the Primary Key check box against the EMPNO column. A user copy target table always requires a primary key. If this is not the case, Apply will fail when it tries to replicate the changed data.

   Click on **OK** to return to the Define Subscription panel (Figure 63 on page 110). Click on the **Timing** button:

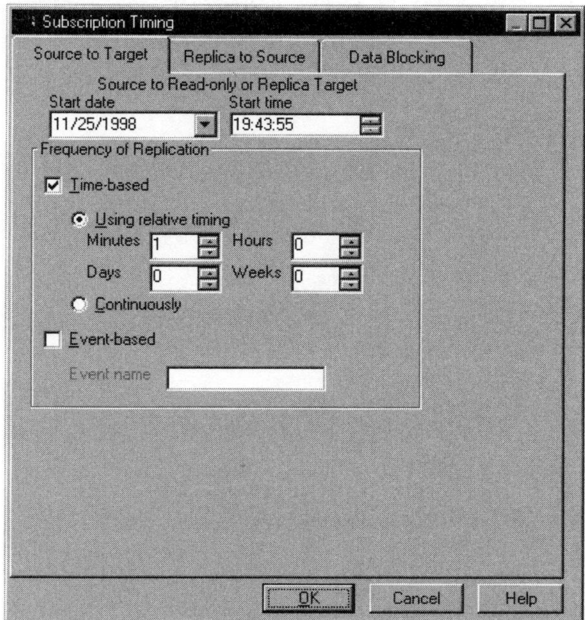

Figure 66. Define Subscription - Timing

7. As this is a test environment, change minutes to one and hours to zero. You can use the spin buttons to change these values or just overtype the fields. The start date and time defaults to the current date and time. Click **OK** to take you back to the Define Subscription screen. Click **OK** again to display this panel:

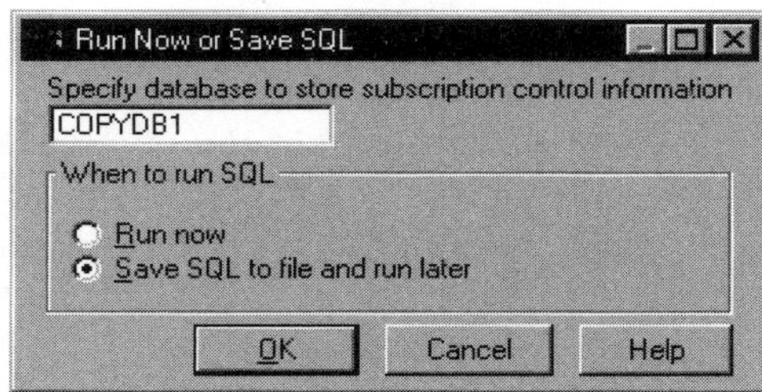

Figure 67. Define Subscription - Run Now or Save SQL

8. Enter the name of the database where the subscription control information will be stored. In this example, we chose the target database, COPYDB1. Choose **Save SQL to file and run later** and click **OK**.

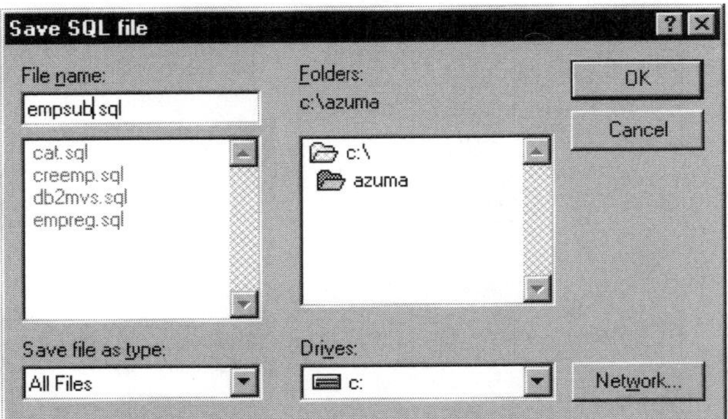

Figure 68. Define Subscription - Save SQL File

9. Enter a file name (here, empsub.sql). Click **OK** to save this file.

After you save this subscription definition SQL file, open the SQL file with a text editor to examine some of the contents:

- Part one:

```
CONNECT TO COPYDB1;

INSERT INTO ASN.IBMSNAP_SUBS_SET ( ACTIVATE, APPLY_QUAL, SET_NAME,
WHOS_ON_FIRST, SOURCE_SERVER, TARGET_SERVER, STATUS, LASTRUN,
REFRESH_TIMING, SLEEP_MINUTES, EVENT_NAME, LASTSUCCESS, SYNCHPOINT,
SYNCHTIME, MAX_SYNCH_MINUTES, AUX_STMTS, ARCH_LEVEL, SOURCE_ALIAS,
TARGET_ALIAS ) VALUES ( 1, 'EMPQUAL', 'EMPSET', 'S', 'DB2C',
'COPYDB1', 0, '1998-11-25-19.43.55.000000', 'R', 1, NULL,
'1998-11-25-19.43.55.000000', NULL, NULL, NULL, 0, '0201', 'DB2C',
'COPYDB1' );
```

First, a connection is made to the control database, COPYDB1.

Next, subscription information is inserted into the control tables. Look at the insert statement for the IBMSNAP_SUBS_SET table. This table contains information regarding the source and target servers with detailed subscription information, such as the copy interval (SLEEP_MINUTES=1).

```
INSERT INTO ASN.IBMSNAP_SUBS_MEMBR ( APPLY_QUAL, SET_NAME,
WHOS_ON_FIRST, SOURCE_OWNER, SOURCE_TABLE, SOURCE_VIEW_QUAL,
TARGET_OWNER, TARGET_TABLE, TARGET_CONDENSED, TARGET_COMPLETE,
TARGET_STRUCTURE, PREDICATES )
VALUES ( 'EMPQUAL', 'EMPSET', 'S', 'SW6003A', 'EMPLOYEE', 0,
'DB2ADMIN', 'EMPLCOPY', 'Y', 'Y', 8, NULL;
```

The insert statement for IBMSNAP_SUBS_MEMBR has the table name mapping information between the source and target table. In our case, the source table is SW6003A.EMPLOYEE, and the target is DB2ADMIN.EMPLCOPY.

```
INSERT INTO ASN.IBMSNAP_SUBS_COLS ( APPLY_QUAL, SET_NAME,
WHOS_ON_FIRST,
TARGET_OWNER, TARGET_TABLE, COL_TYPE, TARGET_NAME, IS_KEY, COLNO,
EXPRESSION )
VALUES ( 'EMPQUAL', 'EMPSET', 'S', 'DB2ADMIN',
'EMPLCOPY', 'A', 'EMPNO', 'Y', 0, 'EMPNO');
```

Here we see an insert into the subscription columns table. This table has information on each column that is being copied in a replication subscription. You can see 'Y' as the value of IS_KEY in IBMSNAP_SUBS_COLS table for the EMPNO column telling us that the EMPNO column is part of the primary key.

- Part two:

```
CREATE TABLE DB2ADMIN.EMPLCOPY (
EMPNO CHAR ( 6 ) NOT NULL,
FIRSTNME VARCHAR ( 12 ) NOT NULL,
MIDINIT CHAR ( 1 ) NOT NULL,
LASTNAME VARCHAR ( 15 ) NOT NULL,
WORKDEPT CHAR ( 3 ),
PHONENO CHAR ( 4 ),
HIREDATE DATE,
JOB CHAR ( 8 ),
EDLEVEL SMALLINT NOT NULL,
SEX CHAR ( 1 ),
BIRTHDATE DATE,
SALARY DECIMAL ( 9, 2 ),
BONUS DECIMAL ( 9, 2 ),
COMM DECIMAL ( 9, 2 ) ,
PRIMARY KEY ( EMPNO ) );
```

This is the target table creation statement. The structure is the same as the source table (SW6003A.EMPLOYEE). Since the target table type is User Copy, each row must be uniquely identifiable in the target table. A primary key is defined as we selected it in the subscription definition.

• Part three:

```
CONNECT TO DB2C;

INSERT INTO ASN.IBMSNAP_PRUNCNTL ( TARGET_SERVER, TARGET_OWNER,
TARGET_TABLE, SYNCHTIME, SYNCHPOINT, SOURCE_OWNER, OURCE_TABLE,
SOURCE_VIEW_QUAL, APPLY_QUAL,
SET_NAME, CNTL_SERVER, TARGET_STRUCTURE, CNTL_ALIAS ) VALUES (
'COPYDB1',
'DB2ADMIN', 'EMPLCOPY', NULL, NULL, 'SW6003A', 'EMPLOYEE', 0,
'EMPQUAL',
'EMPSET', 'COPYDB1', 8, 'COPYDB1');
```

After connecting to the source server database (DB2C), one row is inserted in the IBMSNAP_PRUNCNTL table. Note that we must add a USER and USING clause on the CONNECT statement when the source server requires a password. Therefore, this statement was modified to:

```
CONNECT TO DB2C USER SW6003A USING xxxxx;
```

The initial values of SYNCHPOINT and SYNCHTIME in the Pruning Control table are NULL. After the full refresh, these two values will be maintained by the Apply component at each execution cycle. The value of the TARGET_STRUCTURE column is 8, which means User Copy table.

10. To run this SQL file, go back to the Control Center as shown below:

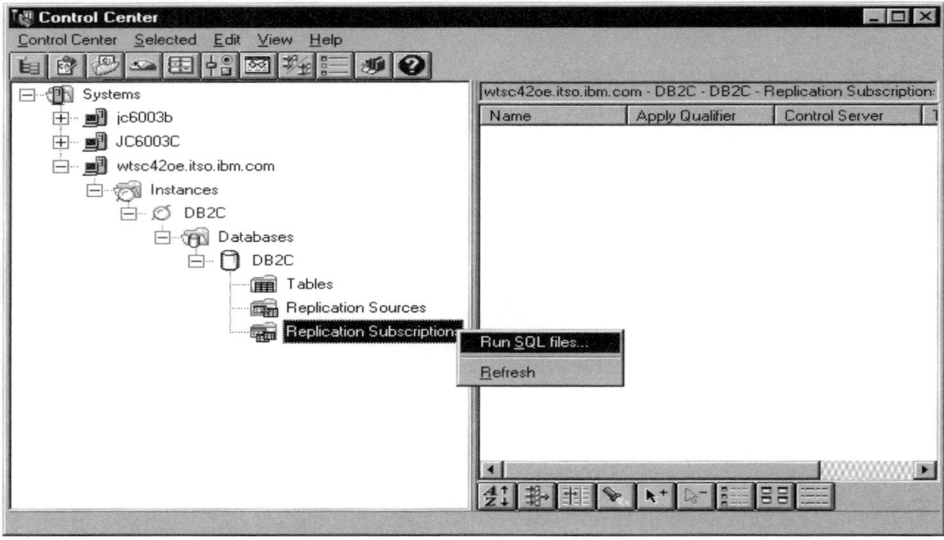

Figure 69. Define Subscription - Run SQL

11. Select **Replication Subscriptions->Run SQL files**. Select the file name (here, empsub.sql). Click **OK** to run this SQL file. If you get any error messages, check and correct the contents of this SQL file.

4.6 Setting up Capture for MVS

We have now defined the replication source and replication subscription for our replication scenario. We now need to ensure that the Capture and Apply processes will function correctly on their respective platforms. In this section, we discuss Capture for MVS. In the following section, we discuss Apply for Windows NT.

Capture for MVS uses the DB2 for MVS Instrumentation Facility Interface (IFI) to retrieve log records. Make sure to apply the correct DB2 maintenance before installing Capture for MVS. At the time of writing, there is one information APAR (II09636) regarding required DB2/MVS PTF information.

Capture for MVS is packaged in SMP/E format. The installation sequence is as follows:

1. Use SMP/E to install (RECEIVE/APPLY/ACCEPT)
2. Provide APF authorization
3. Link-Edit Capture/MVS
4. Create and load VSAM message files
5. You must create the control tables as a pre-installation task.These control tables must be created in the DB2C database:
   - ASN.IBMSNAP_REGISTER
   - ASN.IBMSNAP_PRUNCNTL
   - ASN.IBMSNAP_CCPPARMS
   - ASN.IBMSNAP_TRACE
   - ASN.IBMSNAP_WARM_START
   - ASN.IBMSNAP_UOW
   - ASN.IBMSNAP_CRITSEC
   - ASN.IBMSNAP_SUBS_SET
   - ASN.IBMSNAP_SUBS_MEMBR
   - ASN.IBMSNAP_SUBS_STMTS
   - ASN.IBMSNAP_SUBS_COLS
   - ASN.IBMSNAP_SUBS_EVENT
   - ASN.IBMSNAP_APPLYTRAIL

   You can create these control tables manually by running the SQL in the DPCNTL.MVS file under the SQLLIB\SAMPLES\REPL directory supplied with DB2 UDB for Windows NT. Please note that you may wish to consider modifying the DDL in this file to suit your particular installation.

6. Bind to the DB2 subsystem. Here is our example:

```
//ASNL2BD5 JOB (999,POK),'INSTALL ',CLASS=A,MSGCLASS=T,                  00040025
// NOTIFY=&SYSUID,TIME=1440,REGION=4M                                    00050025
/*JOBPARM L=999,SYSAFF=SC42                                              00060025
//*****************************************************************/
//* JOB NAME = ASNL2BD5                                            */
//*                                                                */
//* DESCRIPTIVE NAME = BIND JCL FOR THE IBM                        */
//*                    DATAPROPAGATOR RELATIONAL CAPTURE FOR       */
//*                    MVS FOR DB2 VERSION 5.1                     */
//*                                                                */
//* STATUS = VERSION 05  RELEASE 01  MODIFICATION LEVEL 00         */
//*                                                                */
//* FUNCTION = BIND THE DATAPROPAGATOR RELATIONAL                  */
//*            CAPTURE FOR MVS PLAN                                */
//* NOTES =                                                        */
//* 1) REVIEW ALL STATEMENTS.                                      */
//* 2) CHANGE THE HLQUAL FIELD(S) TO A VALID HIGH LEVEL            */
//*    QUALIFIER TO COMPLY WITH YOUR SITE'S NAMING STANDARDS.      */
//*    ASNL.V5R1M0 IS RECOMMENDED AS THE HIGH LEVEL QUALIFIER.     */
//* 3) BE SURE TO REMOVE THE TEXT THAT BEGINS WITH <== AT THE      */
//*    END OF SOME LINES                                           */
//*                                                                */
//*****************************************************************/
//*****************************************************************/
//*        FOR EXECUTION OF CAPTURE FOR MVS BIND PROCEDURE         */
//*****************************************************************/
//ASNL2BD5 EXEC PGM=IKJEFT01
//SYSPRINT DD  SYSOUT=*
//SYSTSPRT DD  SYSOUT=*
//SYSUDUMP DD  SYSOUT=*
//STEPLIB  DD  DISP=SHR,DSN=DB2V510.SDSNLOAD
//DBRMLIB  DD  DISP=SHR,DSN=ASNL.V5R1M0.SASNLDBM
//SYSTSIN  DD  *
 DSN S(DB2C)
 BIND PLAN(ASNLP510) MEMBER(ASNLDM51) ACTION(REP) ACQUIRE(USE) -
 RELEASE(COMMIT) ISOLATION(UR)
/*
//
```

7. Customize the invocation JCL and then invoke the JCL.

The Capture and the Apply programs both use the control tables. As a reference, Table 11 on page 119 shows a complete list:

Table 11. Control Table Reference List

	SERVER	Referenced by admin ?	Does Capture monitor this table using data capture changes?	Otherwise, referenced by Capture?	Referenced by Apply?
IBMSNAP_REGISTER	Source	Yes	No	Yes	Yes
IBMSNAP_PRUNCNTL	Source	No	Yes	Yes	Yes
IBMSNAP_CCPPARMS	Source	No	No	Yes	No
IBMSNAP_TRACE	Source	No	No	Yes	No
IBMSNAP_WARM_START	Source	No	No	Yes	No
IBMSNAP_UOW	Source	No	No	Yes	Yes
IBMSNAP_CRITSEC	Source	No	Yes	No	Yes
IBMSNAP_SUBS_SET	Control	Yes	No	No	Yes
IBMSNAP_SUBS_MEMBR	Control	Yes	No	No	Yes
IBMSNAP_SUBS_STMTS	Control	Yes	No	No	Yes
IBMSNAP_SUBS_COLS	Control	Yes	No	No	Yes
IBMSNAP_SUBS_EVENT	Control	No	No	No	Yes
IBMSNAP_APPLYTRAIL	Control	No	No	No	Yes

4.6.1 Starting Capture

One of the options when starting Capture defines the level of recovery that Capture will attempt. The Capture program can be started using a *warm* or *cold* start. Let's look at these options in detail.

4.6.1.1 Warm Start

When you start the Capture program with the WARM or WARMNS parameter, it searches for the warm start table, ASN.IBMSNAP_WARM_START, which is created during the first definition of a replication source or when the DPCNTL.* file is executed. This table contains information that enables the Capture program to quickly resynchronize to the time when it stopped. Essentially, the warm start table contains information about the units of work in progress and also starting sequence information that is necessary for

Capture to restart without needing to perform a full refresh to get back into synchronization. If the warm start table is empty, the Capture program can resynchronize using either the CD tables, the UOW table, or the register table ASN.IBMSNAP_REGISTER.

The process of a warm start can be listed as follows:

1. When Capture is started with the WARM or WARMNS parameters, the first thing it does is search for the presence of the warm start table.
2. If the table is found, and a restart point is located in the table:
    - Capture will do a WARM restart using the found information
3. If the table is not found, or the restart point information is not found:
    1. Capture will scan the CD, UOW and then Register tables to find the most recent log sequence number captured.
    2. If the log sequence number information is found and is available:
        - Capture will use this information to do a WARM start.
    3. If it is not available or not found, then Capture will initiate a COLD start.

In most cases, warm start information is saved . In extreme cases, warm start information might not be saved. For example, an operator might cancel the Capture program or stop DB2. In this case, the Capture program uses the CD, UOW, or Register tables to resynchronize to the time it was stopped. The Pruning Control table is not referenced at that time.

After a successful warm start, the old rows in the warm start table are deleted.

The Capture program switches to a cold start if you do not specify WARMNS and the warm start log sequence number is not available in the DB2 3.1 active log or if it is not available in the DB2 for OS/390 active or archived logs. The Apply program will perform a full refresh after a cold start.

If you prefer, or have reason to, you can manually do a full refresh into your target table rather than allowing an Apply initiated full refresh to occur. This is described in “Manual Loading” on page 145. Yet another alternative is to have Apply initiate the full refresh by means of the user exit approach indicated by using the LOADX option when starting Apply. This is described in “LOADX Option to Refresh the Target Table” on page 143.

4.6.1.2 Automatic Cold Start

Sometimes the Capture program automatically switches to a cold start even when you specify a warm start. The switch is made when:

- The warm start log sequence lags behind the current log sequence by more than the LAG_LIMIT value, as specified in the tuning parameters table ASN.IBMSNAP_CCPPARMS. You can use the GETLSEQ monitoring command to get the timestamp and current log sequence number to determine how far the Capture program lags behind the DB2 current log.
- The warm start log sequence is not available in the DB2 active log. This situation applies only for DB2 for MVS 3.1.
- You invoke the Capture program for the first time.

The first time that you invoke the Capture program, you will see a ASN0102W message indicating that the warm start failed. In this case, the Capture program has switched to a cold start. You can ignore this message when first invoking the Capture program. The message is:

```
ASN0102W: "The Capture program will switch to cold start because
the warm start information is insufficient."
```

4.6.1.3 Forcing a Warm Start Using WARMNS

In some situations, you might want to prevent the Capture program from cold starting . For instance, the Capture program cold starts if DB2 goes down or if someone brings down the DB2 table space containing the CD table. Forcing a warm start with the WARMNS parameter ensures that the control tables remain intact. You must correct the problem that caused the Capture program to terminate. If you do not correct the problem, the Capture program will continue to terminate or perform a cold start every time you start it.

The following message will be displayed when the warm start information is not available when the Capture program is started with the WARMNS option. The control table information is not changed in this case.

```
ASN0122E: An error occurred while reading the warm start
information or DB2 log. The Capture program will terminate."
```

4.7 Setting up Apply for Windows NT

We now take you through some of the steps required to ensure that Apply will function on your Windows NT environment. Seperate installation of Apply for Windows NT is not required because Apply for Windows NT is included in DB2 Universal Database. Roll-forward recovery does not have to be enabled for the target DB2 database if the Capture component does not run on the target database system.

4.7.1 Authorization

Ensure that the user that runs Apply for Windows NT has these privileges:

- Execute privilege for the Apply packages
- DBADM or SYSADM privilege for the database

4.7.2 Binding the Apply Packages

To bind the Apply packages, change directory to where the Apply bind files are located, which is the C:\SQLLIB\BND directory if DB2 UDB is installed on the C: drive. Then, perform the following BIND commands against the source server (DB2/MVS, DB2C):

```
connect to db2c user sw6003a using xxxxx

Database Connection Information
Database server        = DB2 OS/390 5.1.1
SQL authorization ID   = SW6003A
Local database alias   = DB2C

bind @applyur.lst blocking all isolation ur

LINE    MESSAGES FOR applyur.lst
------  -----------------------------------------------------
        SQL0061W  The binder is in progress.
        SQL0091N  Binding was ended with "0" errors and "0" warnings.

bind @applycs.lst blocking all isolation cs

LINE    MESSAGES FOR applycs.lst
------  -----------------------------------------------------
        SQL0061W  The binder is in progress.
        SQL0091N  Binding was ended with "0" errors and "0" warnings.
```

Perform these BIND commands against the target server (UDB for Windows NT, COPYDB1):

```
connect to copydb1

Database Connection Information
Database server        = DB2/NT 5.2.0
SQL authorization ID   = DB2ADMIN
Local database alias   = COPYDB1

bind @applyur.lst blocking all isolation ur

LINE    MESSAGES FOR applyur.lst
------  --------------------------------------------------
        SQL0061W  The binder is in progress.
        SQL0091N  Binding was ended with "0" errors and "0" warnings.

bind @applycs.lst blocking all isolation cs

LINE    MESSAGES FOR applycs.lst
------  --------------------------------------------------
        SQL0061W  The binder is in progress.
        SQL0091N  Binding was ended with "0" errors and "0" warnings
```

These commands create a list of packages. The package names that are created in DB2/MVS can be displayed using DB2 SPUFI:

```
 Menu  Utilities  Compilers  Help
 ssssssssssssssssssssssssssssssssssssssssssssssssssssssssssssssssssssssssssssss
 BROWSE    SW6003A.OUT                                 Line 00000000 Col 001 080
 Command ===>                                                   Scroll ===> PAGE
******************************** Top of Data *********************************
---------+---------+---------+---------+---------+---------+---------+---------+
SELECT COLLID,NAME,QUALIFIER,VALIDATE,ISOLATION,BINDTIME                00010006
FROM SYSIBM.SYSPACKAGE ORDER BY BINDTIME DESC ;                         00011005
---------+---------+---------+---------+---------+---------+---------+---------+
COLLID              NAME      QUALIFIER  VALIDATE  ISOLATION  BINDTIME
---------+---------+---------+---------+---------+---------+---------+---------+
NULLID              ASNNF013  SW6003A    R         S          1998-11-26-22.17.3
NULLID              ASNNP013  SW6003A    R         U          1998-11-26-22.17.3
NULLID              ASNNC013  SW6003A    R         U          1998-11-26-22.17.3
NULLID              ASNNA013  SW6003A    R         U          1998-11-26-22.17.3
NULLID              ASNNI013  SW6003A    R         U          1998-11-26-22.17.3
NULLID              ASNNB013  SW6003A    R         U          1998-11-26-22.17.3
NULLID              ASNNM013  SW6003A    R         U          1998-11-26-22.17.3
```

4.7.3 Apply Password File

Since DB2/MVS can not accept the DRDA TCP/IP flow from the UDB for Windows NT client without password information, we must create an Apply password file. The Apply program uses the information in this file to connect to the DB2C subsystem on DB2/MVS.

This password file must meet the following naming requirements:

```
<APPLYQUAL><instance><CNTL_SERVER>.PWD
```

where:

- `<APPLYQUAL>` is the Apply qualifier in upper case. The Apply qualifier is case sensitive and must match the value of `APPLY_QUAL` in the subscription set table (IBMSNAP_SUBS_SET) (the same as the qualifier specified when creating the subscription).
- `<instance>` is the instance name that the Apply program runs under (the value of DB2INSTANCE).
- `<CNTL_SERVER>` is the name of the control server in upper case.

In this example, the name of this file is `EMPQUALDB2COPYDB1.PWD`

Note that this naming convention is the same as the Apply log file and the spill file name but with a file extension of PWD.

This file must be placed in the directory from which the Apply for Windows NT program is started.

It must contain all the necessary server/password combinations. This enables you to have a different (or the same) password at each server. The entries use the following format:

```
SERVER=DB2C USER=SW6003A PWD=xxxxx
```

We don't need an entry for the COPYDB1 server because this database is the local, and Apply can connect to it without a password.

Table 12 describes how the Apply program retrieves the password information on each of the supported platforms:

Table 12. Apply Password File Requirements

Apply Platform	Password information
Apply for OS/2	OS/2 User Profile Management (UPM)
Apply for Windows	Password File
Apply for Windows NT	Password File
Apply for AIX	Password File
Apply for MVS	Communication Database (SYSIBM.SYSUSERNAMES or SYSIBM.USERNAMES)
Apply for AS/400	ADDSVRAUHE CL command (DRDA TCP/IP only)

4.8 Starting Capture for MVS

Before starting Capture for MVS, make sure the following post-installation tasks are completed:

- The Capture bind files have been bound to source server.
- The ASN.IBMSNAP_REGISTER table has at least one entry in it. This will be the case if you have defined a replication source, and the source table has been altered with the DATA CAPTURE CHANGES option.

You start Capture/MVS by specifying the appropriate invocation parameters in the PARM field of the ASNLRN*nn* DD statement. Tailor the JCL to meet your site's requirements. Here is the invocation JCL for this example:

```
//CAPTURE JOB (999,POK),'INSTALL ',CLASS=A,MSGCLASS=T,                  00040025
// NOTIFY=&SYSUID,TIME=1440,REGION=4M                                   00050025
/*JOBPARM L=999,SYSAFF=SC42                                             00060025
//*************************************************************/
//* JOB NAME = ASNL2RN5                                         */
//*                                                             */
//* DESCRIPTIVE NAME = INVOCATION JCL FOR THE IBM               */
//*                    DATAPROPAGATOR RELATIONAL CAPTURE FOR    */
//*                    MVS FOR DB2 VERSION 5.1                  */
//*                                                             */
//* STATUS = VERSION 05  RELEASE 01  MODIFICATION LEVEL 00      */
//*                                                             */
//* FUNCTION = INVOKE THE DATAPROPAGATOR RELATIONAL             */
//*            CAPTURE FOR MVS PROGRAM                          */
//*                                                             */
//* NOTES =                                                     */
//* 1) REVIEW ALL STATEMENTS.                                   */
//* 2) CHANGE THE HLQUAL FIELD(S) TO A VALID HIGH LEVEL         */
//*    QUALIFIER TO COMPLY WITH YOUR SITE'S NAMING STANDARDS.   */
//*    ASNL.V5R1M0 IS RECOMMENDED AS THE HIGH LEVEL QUALIFIER.  */
//* 3) IF YOU ARE RUNNING UNDER LE/370 ENVIRONMENT, ADD          */
//*    REGION=3M IN THE EXEC STATEMENT.                         */
//* 4) REPLACE D51A WITH YOUR SUBSYSTEM NAME                    */
//* 5) BE SURE TO REMOVE THE TEXT THAT BEGINS WITH <== AT THE   */
//*    END OF SOME LINES                                        */
//*                                                             */
//*************************************************************/
//*
//*************************************************************/
//*        FOR EXECUTION OF THE CAPTURE FOR MVS PROGRAM         */
//*************************************************************/
//ASNL2RN5 EXEC PGM=ASNLRP25,PARM='DB2C COLD NOPRUNE'
//*ASNL2RN5 EXEC PGM=ASNLRP25,PARM='DB2C WARMNS NOPRUNE'
//STEPLIB  DD  DISP=SHR,DSN=ASNL.V5R1M0.SASNLLNK
//         DD  DISP=SHR,DSN=DB2V510.SDSNLOAD
//         DD  DISP=SHR,DSN=EDC.V2R2M0.SEDCLINK
//         DD  DISP=SHR,DSN=PLI.V2R3M0.SIBMLINK
//MSGS     DD  DISP=SHR,DSN=ASNL.V5R1M0.MSGS
//CEEDUMP  DD  SYSOUT=*
//SYSTERM  DD  SYSOUT=*
//SYSUDUMP DD  SYSOUT=*
//SYSPRINT DD  SYSOUT=*
//x
```

In this example, the line that contains `EXEC PGM=ASNLRP25` includes the invocation parameters. The last two digits of `ASNLRP25` indicate the level of the Capture program:

- nn=23 - Capture for MVS that runs on DB2 for MVS V3.1
- nn=24 - Capture for MVS that runs on DB2 for MVS V4.1
- nn=25 - Capture for MVS that runs on DB2 for MVS V5.1

Submit the JCL and monitor the MVS console. Capture for MVS can run either as a batch job or as a started task.

Table 13 displays the parameters for starting Capture for MVS:

Table 13. Capture for MVS Startup Parameters

Parameter	Definition
DB2 subsystem name	The default is DSN. This must be the first parameter
TERM (Default) NOTERM	- Terminate the Capture program if DB2 is terminated. - Keep the Capture program running if DB2 is terminated with MODE(QUIESCE). When DB2 comes up again, the Capture program starts in WARM mode.
WARM (Default) WARMNS COLD	- The Capture program resumes processing where it ended in its previous run if warm start information is available. If the Capture program cannot warm start, it switches to a cold start. - The Capture program resumes processing where it ended in its previous run if warm start information is available. Otherwise, it issues a message and terminates. With WARMNS, the Capture program does not automatically switch to a cold start. The Capture program leaves the trace, UOW, CD and warm start tables intact. - The Capture program starts up by deleting all rows in its CD, UOW, and trace tables during initialization.
PRUNE (Default) NOPRUNE	- The Capture program automatically prunes rows from the CD and the UOW tables that the Apply program has copied since the last pruning. - Automatic pruning is disabled. The Capture program prunes the CD and UOW tables when you enter the PRUNE command.
NOTRACE (Default) TRACE	- No trace information is written. - Writes debug trace information to standard output, SYSPRINT

We specified COLD, NOPRUNE as the parameters. However, in many cases, you will want to prevent the Capture program from performing a cold start. If a CD table is dropped while Capture is running, Capture will terminate. All the changed data and UOW information will be deleted by the Capture program when you restart the Capture program with the COLD parameter again after correcting the problem caused the Capture program to terminate. It will also cause a full refresh when the Apply performs its next cycle. Many installations use the WARMNS parameter to ensure that the control tables remain intact.

The following message is displayed in the MVS console if Capture starts successfully:

```
ASN0100I The Capture program initialization is successful.
```

You can also confirm the invocation parameters that were used by selecting from the Trace table (IBMSNAP_TRACE) after Capture for MVS has been started:

```
select operation,description from asn.ibmsnap_trace;

OPERATION  DESCRIPTION
---------  ---------------------------------
PARM       ASN0103I The Capture program started
           with SERVER_NAME DB2C;
           the START_TYPE is COLD;
           the TERM_TYPE is TERM;
           the PRUNE_TYPE is NOPRUNE.
INIT       ASN0100I The Capture program
           initialization is successful.
```

4.9 Starting Apply for Windows NT

If all previous setup steps were completed successfully, then you should be ready to start your Apply for Windows NT process.

Change to the directory that holds the password file you created. Then, start the Apply program as follows: First ensure that the DB2INSTANCE environment variable is set correctly, and, if you wish, you can set the DB2DBDFT variable to point to the database where the Apply control tables are found. Issue the following command:

```
asnapply EMPQUAL COPYDB1 trcflow nosleep > fullcopy.trc
```

The full list of the parameters for Apply for Windows NT is given in Table 8 on page 73.

Make sure that the Apply qualifier is in upper case and matches the value you specified when defining the subscription.

The trace output for this example as follows:

```
Apply program compiled at 14:48:48 on Aug 12 1998 (Level 0053)
Apply qualifier is EMPQUAL.
Control srvr name is COPYDB1.
Issue Sleep msg.
Will not invoke ASNLOAD.
Will not invoke ASNDONE.
  IMSG: Instance name is DB2      .
  IMSG: The log file name is EMPQUALDB2COPYDB1.LOG.
   CEXPC: connect to COPYDB1
   CEXPC: CONNECT without USERID/PASSWORD
   CEXPC: serverIsolationUR is 1.
  CIMPC: serverIsolationUR is 1.
  CIMPC: The local_srvr is COPYDB1.
  CIMPC: Userid is AZUMA
    MSGF: MsgNumber is 45.
   The NLS msg is ASN1045I: The Apply program was started using database
COPYDB1.
The NLS msg is ASN1045I: The Apply program was started using database COPYDB1.
--- Process next subscription (1) ---
 CEXPC: connect to COPYDB1 <--------------------- 1
```

1. Apply looks for work and checks the subscription tables (Control Server). Note the the numbered arrow at the right above.

```
 GCST: Control server timestamp is 1998-11-28-16.49.01.015001
  R1NES: No eligible named event subscription at this moment
 Compiled(P) at 14:49:46 on Aug 12 1998 (Level 0053)
   CPGCI: numKeys is 1
  GMI: set type is READ_ONLY
  -------------------
      set_info
  -------------------
  ACTIVATE       = 1
  APPLY_QUAL     = EMPQUAL
  SET_NAME       = EMPSET
  WHOS_ON_FIRST  = S
  SOURCE_SERVER  = DB2C
  SOURCE_ALIAS   = DB2C
  TARGET_SERVER  = COPYDB1
  TARGET_ALIAS   = COPYDB1
................................................
................................................
PSET: Fetch answer set for member 0 <---------------------- 2
  Compiled(F) at 14:49:09 on Aug 12 1998 (Level 0053)
   USRSET: spill_file(0) = EMPQUALDB2COPYDB1.000
  FETSET: The number of rows fetched is 32. <------------- 3
 PSET: Commit3 ok
  CEXPC: connect to COPYDB1
  CEXPC: CONNECT without USERID/PASSWORD
  CEXPC: serverIsolationUR is 1. <------------------------- 4
 -------------------------
```

2. Pick up any recent changed data to be applied to the target (Source Server).
3. Write the answer set into a local spill file (Target Server).
4. Apply the changed data in the spill file to the target table (Target Server).

```
PSET: Commit4 ok
  Compiled(A) at 14:49:19 on Aug 12 1998 (Level 0053)
 PSET: Commit6 ok
  CEXPC: connect to COPYDB1
  CLOS: setRepeatCopy is 0 <---------------------------------- 5
  CLOS: activate = 1
  CLOS: status   = 0
  CLOS: lastrun = 1998-11-28-16.49.01.015001
  CLOS: lastsuccess = 1998-11-28-16.48.44.000000
  CLOS: synchpoint is null
  CLOS: synchtime = 1998-11-28-17.51.17.205147
  CLOS: apply_qual = EMPQUAL
  CLOS: set_name = EMPSET
  CLOS: sWhosOnFirst = S
  CEXPC: connect to DB2C
  CEXPC: CONNECT with USERID/PASSWORD
  CEXPC: serverIsolationUR is 1. <---------------------------- 6
```

5. Update the subscription status (Control Server).

6. Report the subscription progress in the pruning control table (Source Server). You can also see from the information below that a full refresh was done in this Apply cycle since MASS_DELETE = Y. In this case, we refreshed SET_INSERTED number of rows, or 32.

```
 CEXPC: connect to COPYDB1
  CEXPC: CONNECT without USERID/PASSWORD
  CEXPC: serverIsolationUR is 1.
  SAT: ASNLOAD = N, EFFECT_MEMBERS = 1
  SAT: MASS_DELETE = Y
  SAT: SET_INSERTED = 32
  SAT: SET_DELETED = 0
  SAT: SET_UPDATED = 0
  SAT: SET_REWORKED = 0
  SAT: SET_REJECTED_TRXS = 0
  SAT: STATUS = 0
  SAT: LASTRUN = 1998-11-28-16.49.01.015001
  SAT: LASTSUCCESS = 1998-11-28-16.48.44.000000
  SAT: SYNCHPOINT is null
  SAT: SYNCHTIME is 1998-11-28-17.51.17.205147
  SAT: SOURCE_ALIAS is DB2C
  SAT: SOURCE_SERVER is DB2C
  SAT: SOURCE_OWNER is
  SAT: SOURCE_TABLE is
  SAT: TARGET_ALIAS is COPYDB1
  SAT: TARGET_SERVER is COPYDB1
  SAT: TARGET_OWNER is
  SAT: TARGET_TABLE is
  SAT: SQLSTATE is null
  SAT: SQLERRM is null
  SAT: SQLCODE is null
  SAT: SQLERRP is null
  SAT: APPERRM is null
 PSET: mi(0): spill is 0, spillKey is 0
--- Process next subscription (2) ---
 CEXPC: connect to COPYDB1
 GCST: Control server timestamp is 1998-11-28-16.49.04.156001
  R1NES: No eligible named event subscription at this moment
  R1RTS: No eligible relative timer driven subscription at this moment
```

4.10 Managing the Replication Environment

Now that the initial configuration is completed, we will look at some typical tasks you can use to manage the replication environment.

4.10.1 Operating Capture for MVS

We can perform the following tasks on Capture for MVS:

- Stopping:

  Enter this command from the TSO or MVS console before removing or modifying an existing replication source:

```
F CAPTURE,STOP
ASN0008I The Capture program was stopped.
ASN0123I The highest log sequence number of a successfully
captured log record is 000000005EA8DB860000.
```

- Suspending:

  Do not use the SUSPEND command when removing a replication source. Instead, stop the Capture program by entering the STOP command:

```
F CAPTURE,SUSPEND
ASN0028I The Capture program is suspended by operator command.
```

- Resuming:

```
F CAPTURE,RESUME
ASN0029I The Capture program is resumed by operator command.
```

- Reinitializing:

  This command ensures that the Capture program recognizes a new replication source. It also rereads the ASN.IBMSNAP_CCPPARMS table for any changes made to the tuning parameters:

```
F CAPTURE,REINIT

ASN0024I The Capture program did not need to reinitialize the
register table. Table, reinit_register, did not change.
```

- Pruning:

The Capture program deletes data in the CD and UOW tables that has already been applied to the target tables:

```
F CAPTURE,PRUNE
ASN0124I The prune command was accepted; the pruning action is
        queued.
```

• Monitoring:

The Capture program issues the message ASN0125I indicating the position Capture has reached in the log:

```
F CAPTURE,GETLSEQ
ASN0125I The current log sequence number successfully
        processed is 000005EA9284C0000. The log timestamp is
        1998-12-07-18.00.16.199979.
```

You can use these commands from a TSO or MVS console.

Table 14 summarizes the commands that control Capture for MVS:

Table 14. Capture for MVS Commands

Action	Command	Definition
Stopping	F jobname,STOP	Stop Capture gracefully and commit the log records that it processed up to that point.
Suspending	F jobname,SUSPEND	Relinquish MVS resources to operational transactions during peak periods without destroying the Capture program environment.
Resuming	F jobname,RESUME	Restart the suspended Capture program
Reinitializing	F jobname,REINIT	Have the Capture program reread the REGISTER and CCPPARMS tables while it is running.
Pruning	F jobname,PRUNE	Start pruning the change data (CD) table and unit-of-work (UOW) tables if you used the NOPRUNE invocation parameter to disable pruning when you started the Capture program.
Monitoring	F jobname,GETLSEQ	Provide the timestamp and current log sequence number. You can use this number to determine how far the Capture program has read the DB2 log.

4.10.2 Removing a Replication Source

When you no longer need a replication source, you can remove the object from the Control Center and its control information from the control tables.

> **Note**
>
> Do *not* delete a replication source while the Capture program is running.

It is recommended that you check whether a dependent subscription table is being used as a source for another subscription. If this is the case, de-activate or remove the subscription before you delete the replication source.

By default, the Control Center drops the replication source table if it is empty. You can change the defaults in the Tools Settings notebook:

1. Stop the Capture program.

   Do not use the SUSPEND command. Use the *F jobname, STOP* command.

   ```
   F CAPTURE,STOP
   ASN0008I The Capture program was stopped.
   ASN0123I The highest log sequence number
            of a successfully captured log record
            is 000000005B7FFF5F0000.
   ```

   The Capture program stores the highest log sequence number in the WARM_START table. This information will be used if Capture is re-started with the WARM option.

2. From the Control Center, select the **Replication sources** folder. The replication sources are displayed in the contents pane.

3. Select the replication source that is to be deleted (here, EMPLOYEE) and select **Remove** from the pop-up menu:

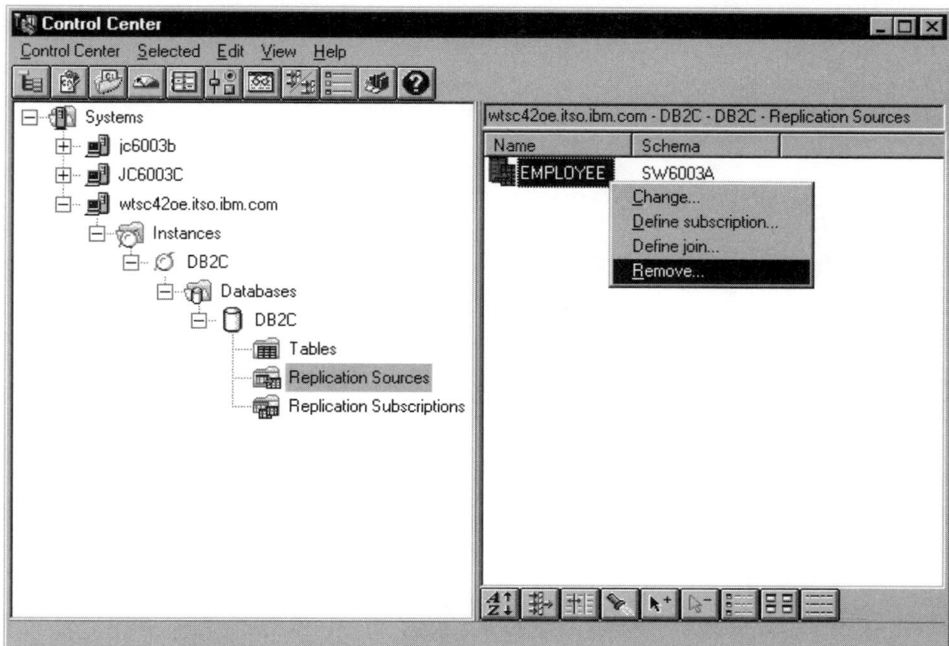

Figure 70. Removing a Replication Source

You are prompted to confirm that you want to remove the replication source:

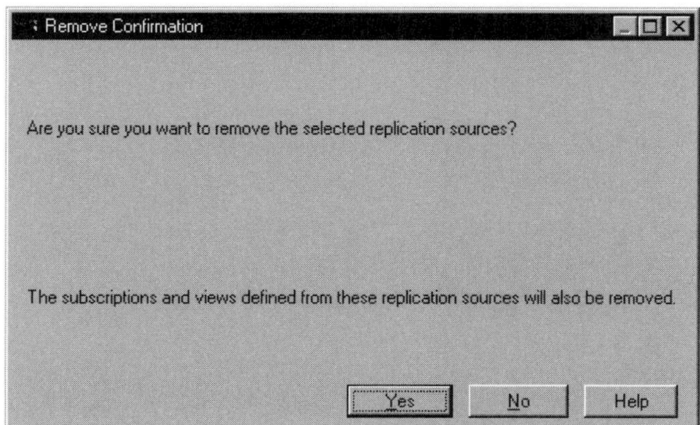

Figure 71. Removing a Replication Source - Confirmation

4. Click on **Yes** in the confirmation window to delete the replication source.
5. Choose the option to save the SQL file for future execution.

6. Use a text editor to modify the SQL file to add the USER and USING clause in order to connect to the source server.

```
CONNECT TO DB2C USER SW6003A USING xxxxx;

DROP TABLE SW6003A.CD19981125119436;

--DROP TABLESPACE DSNDB04.EMPLOYEE;

DELETE FROM ASN.IBMSNAP_REGISTER
WHERE SOURCE_OWNER = 'SW6003A'
AND SOURCE_TABLE = 'EMPLOYEE';
```

7. Run the saved SQL file.

If you wish to remove a replication source manually, the following sequence of tasks must be performed:

1. Stop the Capture program.
2. Delete the relevant row from the Register table.
3. Drop the relevant CD table.
4. Restart the Capture program.

It is important to remember that removing a replication source through the Control Center will also remove and cleanup associated replication subscriptions for you. If you manually remove a replication source, you will have to manually cleanup any other control tables and user tables in which this source is referenced or is associated.

4.10.3 Stopping Apply for Windows NT

Use the following command to stop Apply for Windows NT:

```
asnastop Apply_Qualifier
```

The Apply program will terminate at the end of the current subscription set if this command is issued while Apply is active on a DB2 UDB system. You can alternatively use one of the following key combinations from the window where the Apply program is running:

- Ctrl + C
- Ctrl + Break

To use this command, make sure that the following environment variables have been set:

- DB2INSTANCE: the value that was used when the Apply program started.

- DB2DBDFT: the control server specified when the Apply program was started.

4.10.4 Communication between Capture and Apply in Full Refresh

When a full refresh occurs, the Apply program reads the source table directly, fetches all the rows at the source server, and then writes them into a spill file at the target. Before reading the source table, the Apply program must internally update the Pruning Control table for each row that corresponds to a member of the replication subscription. This is done using the following SQL statement:

```
UPDATE ASN.IBMSNAP_PRUNCNTL
SET SYNCHPOINT=x'00000000000000000000'
, SYNCHTIME=CURRENT TIMESTAMP
WHERE SET_NAME='EMPSET' AND APPLY_QUAL='EMPQUAL';
```

This update will cause the Capture program to start capturing changes for the source table if it has not yet started to do so. The Capture program can recognize this update because the Pruning Control table has the DATA CAPTURE CHANGES attribute. The Capture program converts this hex zero value to the current log sequence number (known as RBA translation). Note that you might not see the hex zero value when the full refresh is done while Capture is running. In this way, the Pruning Control table is used for communication between the Apply and Capture programs. Capture records this behavior by writing a GOCAPT message in the ASN.IBMSNAP_TRACE table at the source server, for example:

```
GOCAPT    Change Capture started for owner SW6003A;
          the table name is EMPLOYEE at log sequence
          number (LSN) 00000000530A6C1B0000.
```

This converted log sequence value needs to match the CD_OLD_SYNCHPOINT and CD_NEW_SYNCHPOINT values in the Register table initially.

Capture for MVS, VM/VSE, and all UDB platforms (except UDB Enterprise-Extended Edition) can monitor the update of the Pruning Control (PC) table because of the DATA CAPTURE CHANGES attribute. Capture/400 works differently and uses a trigger program on the Pruning Control table to detect an update that sets SYNCHPOINT to hex zero.

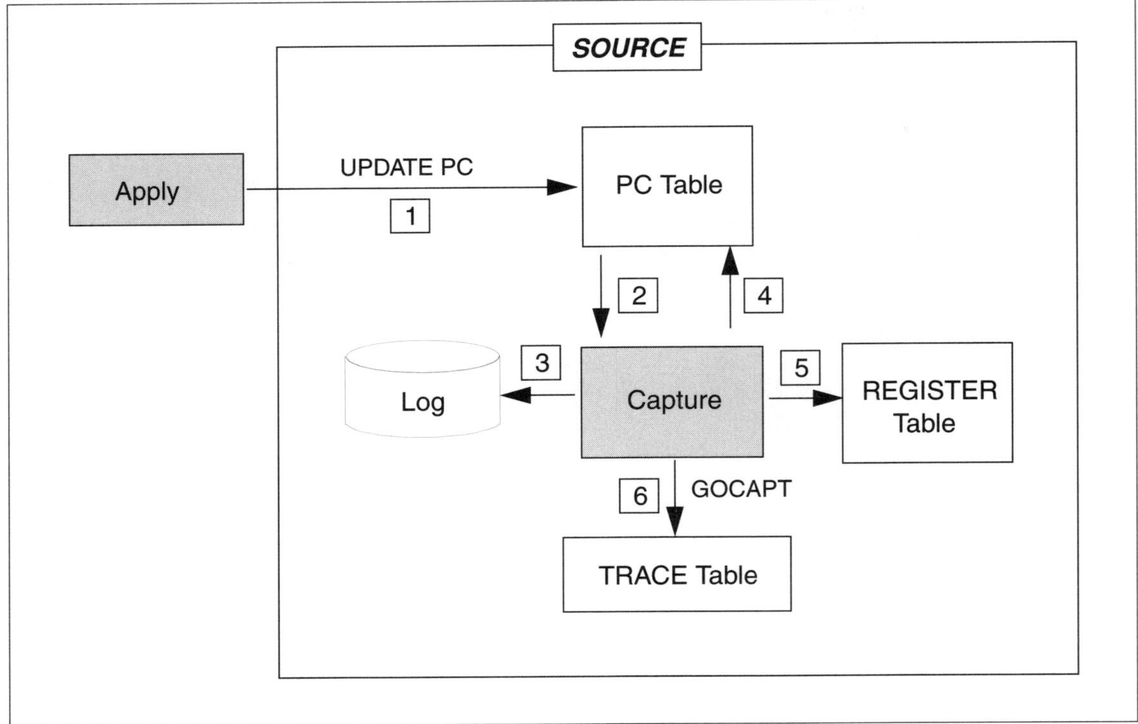

Figure 72. Communication between Capture and Apply

4.10.5 Differential Copy

In "Starting Apply for Windows NT" on page 127, we saw that when Apply was first started, it performed a full refresh as was noted in the trace with the MASS_DELETE=Y flag set. After this full refresh, normal processing should only have updates to the source table copied to the target table. When we have a full refresh, and then only replicate changes, we term this a differential refresh.

Now that we have confirmed that Capture has started capturing changes by seeing a GOCAPT message in the TRACE table (in "Communication between Capture and Apply in Full Refresh" on page 135), we can test the replication process by updating the source table:

```
 Menu  Utilities  Compilers  Help
 ssssssssssssssssssssssssssssssssssssssssssssssssssssssssssssssssssssssssssssss
 BROWSE    SW6003A.OUT                                  Line 00000000 Col 001 080
 Command ===>                                                     Scroll ===> PAGE
******************************** Top of Data **********************************
---------+---------+---------+---------+---------+---------+---------+---------+
DELETE FROM EMPLOYEE WHERE EMPNO='000010';                              00010000
---------+---------+---------+---------+---------+---------+---------+---------+
DSNE615I NUMBER OF ROWS AFFECTED IS 1
DSNE616I STATEMENT EXECUTION WAS SUCCESSFUL, SQLCODE IS 0
---------+---------+---------+---------+---------+---------+---------+---------+
---------+---------+---------+---------+---------+---------+---------+---------+
DSNE617I COMMIT PERFORMED, SQLCODE IS 0
DSNE616I STATEMENT EXECUTION WAS SUCCESSFUL, SQLCODE IS 0
---------+---------+---------+---------+---------+---------+---------+---------+
DSNE601I SQL STATEMENTS ASSUMED TO BE BETWEEN COLUMNS 1 AND 72
DSNE620I NUMBER OF SQL STATEMENTS PROCESSED IS 1
DSNE621I NUMBER OF INPUT RECORDS READ IS 1
DSNE622I NUMBER OF OUTPUT RECORDS WRITTEN IS 14
******************************* Bottom of Data ********************************



  F1=Help    F3=Exit    F5=Rfind  F12=Cancel
```

After this change was made, you will notice that only the CD_NEW_SYNCHPOINT value in the REGISTER table is advanced. Both the CD_OLD_SYNCHPOINT and CD_NEW_SYNCHPOINT values before this update were the same RBA number, as the GOCAPT message indicates.

```
 Menu  Utilities  Compilers  Help
 ssssssssssssssssssssssssssssssssssssssssssssssssssssssssssssssssssssssssssssss
 BROWSE    SW6003A.OUT                                  Line 00000000 Col 001 080
 Command ===>                                                     Scroll ===> PAGE
******************************** Top of Data **********************************
---------+---------+---------+---------+---------+---------+---------+---------+
SELECT HEX(CD_OLD_SYNCHPOINT),HEX(CD_NEW_SYNCHPOINT)                    00010000
FROM ASN.IBMSNAP_REGISTER WHERE SOURCE_TABLE='EMPLOYEE'                 00020002
WITH UR;                                                                00030002
---------+---------+---------+---------+---------+---------+---------+---------+

---------+---------+---------+---------+---------+---------+---------+---------+
00000000530A6C1B0000  000000005347957A0000
DSNE610I NUMBER OF ROWS DISPLAYED IS 1
DSNE616I STATEMENT EXECUTION WAS SUCCESSFUL, SQLCODE IS 100
---------+---------+---------+---------+---------+---------+---------+---------+
---------+---------+---------+---------+---------+---------+---------+---------+
DSNE617I COMMIT PERFORMED, SQLCODE IS 0
DSNE616I STATEMENT EXECUTION WAS SUCCESSFUL, SQLCODE IS 0
---------+---------+---------+---------+---------+---------+---------+---------+
DSNE601I SQL STATEMENTS ASSUMED TO BE BETWEEN COLUMNS 1 AND 72
DSNE620I NUMBER OF SQL STATEMENTS PROCESSED IS 1
DSNE621I NUMBER OF INPUT RECORDS READ IS 3
  F1=Help    F3=Exit    F5=Rfind  F12=Cancel
```

CD_NEW_SYNCHPOINT gives a hint to the Apply component. Capture provides additional information to Apply as to whether or not there is new data captured for any particular source table. Apply looks for these hints and avoids the expense of join queries in cases where there is no new data to be applied. If we check the CD table:

```
 Menu  Utilities  Compilers  Help
 ssssssssssssssssssssssssssssssssssssssssssssssssssssssssssssssssssssssssssssssss
 BROWSE    SW6003A.OUT                                 Line 00000000 Col 001 080
 Command ===>                                                  Scroll ===> PAGE
******************************** Top of Data **********************************
---------+---------+---------+---------+---------+---------+---------+---------+
SELECT                                                                  00010002
HEX(IBMSNAP_UOWID), HEX(IBMSNAP_INTENTSEQ)                              00011001
,IBMSNAP_OPERATION, XEMPNO, EMPNO                                       00012001
FROM CD19981125119436 WITH UR                                           00020001
---------+---------+---------+---------+---------+---------+---------+---------+
                                            IBMSNAP_OPERATION  XEMPNO  EMPNO
---------+---------+---------+---------+---------+---------+---------+---------+
0000000053478DDE0000  00000000534794540000  D                  000010  000010
DSNE610I NUMBER OF ROWS DISPLAYED IS 1
DSNE616I STATEMENT EXECUTION WAS SUCCESSFUL, SQLCODE IS 100
---------+---------+---------+---------+---------+---------+---------+---------+
DSNE617I COMMIT PERFORMED, SQLCODE IS 0
DSNE616I STATEMENT EXECUTION WAS SUCCESSFUL, SQLCODE IS 0
---------+---------+---------+---------+---------+---------+---------+---------+
DSNE601I SQL STATEMENTS ASSUMED TO BE BETWEEN COLUMNS 1 AND 72
DSNE620I NUMBER OF SQL STATEMENTS PROCESSED IS 1
DSNE621I NUMBER OF INPUT RECORDS READ IS 4
  F1=Help    F3=Exit    F5=Rfind  F12=Cancel
```

Then the UOW table:

```
 Menu  Utilities  Compilers  Help
 ssssssssssssssssssssssssssssssssssssssssssssssssssssssssssssssssssssssssssssssss
 BROWSE    SW6003A.OUT                                 Line 00000000 Col 001 080
 Command ===>                                                  Scroll ===> PAGE
******************************** Top of Data **********************************
---------+---------+---------+---------+---------+---------+---------+---------+
SELECT                                                                  00010001
HEX(IBMSNAP_UOWID),HEX(IBMSNAP_COMMITSEQ)                               00020002
,IBMSNAP_LOGMARKER,IBMSNAP_AUTHTKN                                      00021002
FROM ASN.IBMSNAP_UOW WITH UR                                            00030001
---------+---------+---------+---------+---------+---------+---------+---------+
                                            IBMSNAP_LOGMARKER           IBMSNAP_
---------+---------+---------+---------+---------+---------+---------+---------+
0000000053478DDE0000  000000005347957A0000  1998-11-29-14.07.13.441312  SW6003A
DSNE610I NUMBER OF ROWS DISPLAYED IS 1
DSNE616I STATEMENT EXECUTION WAS SUCCESSFUL, SQLCODE IS 100
---------+---------+---------+---------+---------+---------+---------+---------+
DSNE617I COMMIT PERFORMED, SQLCODE IS 0
DSNE616I STATEMENT EXECUTION WAS SUCCESSFUL, SQLCODE IS 0
---------+---------+---------+---------+---------+---------+---------+---------+
DSNE601I SQL STATEMENTS ASSUMED TO BE BETWEEN COLUMNS 1 AND 72
DSNE620I NUMBER OF SQL STATEMENTS PROCESSED IS 1
DSNE621I NUMBER OF INPUT RECORDS READ IS 4
  F1=Help    F3=Exit    F5=Rfind  F12=Cancel
```

Note that the value of UOWID in the CD and UOW tables match. During the Apply fetch phase, a join is performed between each CD table and the UOW table using the IBMSNAP_UOWID column.

Start the Apply program again:

```
asnapply EMPQUAL COPYDB1 trcflow nosleep > diffcopy.trc
```

Look at the end of the trace file:

```
PSET: Fetch answer set for member 0
  Compiled(F) at 14:49:09 on Aug 12 1998 (Level 0053)
   CDSET: spill_file(0) = EMPQUALDB2COPYDB1.000
  FETSET: The number of rows fetched is 1.
  UP1SYT: Synchtime is 1998-11-29-15.54.23.714752
 PSET: Commit3 ok
  CEXPC: connect to COPYDB1
  CEXPC: CONNECT without USERID/PASSWORD
  CEXPC: serverIsolationUR is 1.
 -------------------------
 PSET: Commit4 ok
  Compiled(A) at 14:49:19 on Aug 12 1998 (Level 0053)
 PSET: Commit6 ok
  CEXPC: connect to COPYDB1
  CLOS: setRepeatCopy is 0
  CLOS: activate = 1
  CLOS: status   = 0
  CLOS: lastrun = 1998-11-29-14.53.19.828001
  CLOS: lastsuccess = 1998-11-29-14.52.44.000000
  CLOS: Synchpoint is  000000005347957a0000
  CLOS: synchtime = 1998-11-29-15.54.23.714752
  CLOS: apply_qual = EMPQUAL
  CLOS: set_name = EMPSET
  CLOS: sWhosOnFirst = S
  CEXPC: connect to DB2C
  CEXPC: CONNECT with USERID/PASSWORD
  CEXPC: serverIsolationUR is 1.
  CEXPC: connect to COPYDB1
  CEXPC: CONNECT without USERID/PASSWORD
  CEXPC: serverIsolationUR is 1.
  SAT: ASNLOAD = N, EFFECT_MEMBERS = 1
  SAT: MASS_DELETE = N
  SAT: SET_INSERTED = 0
  SAT: SET_DELETED = 1
  SAT: SET_UPDATED = 0
  SAT: SET_REWORKED = 0
  SAT: SET_REJECTED_TRXS = 0
  SAT: STATUS = 0
```

In this case, we see that MASS_DELETE=N, indicating no full refresh (as expected); however, we do see that a row was deleted (as pointed to by SET_DELETED=1). This confirms for us that a copy was performed successfully by the Apply program.

4.10.6 Manual Pruning

Since we specified the NOPRUNE option when Capture for MVS was started, manual pruning is necessary to delete the rows from the CD and UOW tables when they are no longer required. Use the PRUNE command to start pruning. For example:

```
F Jobname,PRUNE
```

You can see the following message on the MVS console:

```
F CAPTURE,PRUNE
ASN0124I The prune command was accepted; the pruning action is
        queued.
```

To verify that the pruning task took place, look in the TRACE table:

```
MESSAGE ASN0124I The prune command was accepted;
        the pruning action is queued.
PRUNE   Data that has been copied was pruned from the change data table
        SW6003A.CD19981125119436   and the unit-of-work table.
PRUNE   ASN0105I Data that has been copied was pruned from the change
       data table LAST CD_TABLE and the unit-of-work table.
```

You can also check the CD and UOW tables:

```
 Menu  Utilities  Compilers  Help
 ssssssssssssssssssssssssssssssssssssssssssssssssssssssssssssssssssssssssssssssss
 BROWSE    SW6003A.OUT                                 Line 00000000 Col 001 080
 Command ===>                                                   Scroll ===> PAGE
******************************** Top of Data **********************************
---------+---------+---------+---------+---------+---------+---------+---------+
SELECT COUNT(*) FROM SW6003A.CD19981125119436 WITH UR;                 00010000
---------+---------+---------+---------+---------+---------+---------+---------+

---------+---------+---------+---------+---------+---------+---------+---------+
          0
DSNE610I NUMBER OF ROWS DISPLAYED IS 1
DSNE616I STATEMENT EXECUTION WAS SUCCESSFUL, SQLCODE IS 100
---------+---------+---------+---------+---------+---------+---------+---------+
SELECT COUNT(*) FROM ASN.IBMSNAP_UOW WITH UR;                          00020000
---------+---------+---------+---------+---------+---------+---------+---------+

---------+---------+---------+---------+---------+---------+---------+---------+
          0
DSNE610I NUMBER OF ROWS DISPLAYED IS 1
DSNE616I STATEMENT EXECUTION WAS SUCCESSFUL, SQLCODE IS 100
---------+---------+---------+---------+---------+---------+---------+---------+
---------+---------+---------+---------+---------+---------+---------+---------+
  F1=Help    F3=Exit    F5=Rfind  F12=Cancel
```

In your replication environment, you can choose between automatic and manual pruning. Manual pruning requires that the user trigger the pruning by running an operator command. Using the automatic pruning option, the user sets the frequency of pruning by updating the value of PRUNE_INTERVAL in the ASN.IBMSNAP_CCPPARMS table. The default value of PRUNE_INTERVAL is 300 seconds. Pruning needs to be performed on a regular basis; however, while Capture is pruning the CD and UOW tables, Apply is locked out, and Capture does not capture any new updates. Therefore, it is recommended that this activity be scheduled to run during off peak hours once or twice per day unless the volume of data demands that this activity be performed more often.

4.10.7 ASNDONE User Exit

If you specify the NOTIFY parameter when the Apply program starts, the ASNDONE user exit program is called after the processing for each subscription set is completed. It is always called regardless of the success or failure of the Apply program's actions. You can tailor the user exit to your specific needs. For example, the ASNDONE user exit can be used to examine the UOW table to discover rejected transactions and initiate further actions, such as issuing a message.

Running Apply with the NOTIFY parameter invokes the ASNDONE user exit program as you can see in the trace file:

```
asnapply QUAL1 SAMPLE TRCFLOW NOTIFY
```

Trace file contents:

```
Apply program compiled at 10:33:27 on Aug 12 1998 (Level 0053)
Apply qualifier is QUAL1.
Issue Sleep msg.
Will not invoke ASNLOAD.
Invoke ASNDONE.
  IMSG: Instance name is db2inst1.
  IMSG: The log file name is QUAL1db2inst1SAMPLE.LOG.
  CIMPC: serverIsolationUR is 1.
  CIMPC: The local_srvr is SAMPLE.
  CIMPC: Userid is DB2INST1
   INVV: app_qual is QUAL1, PID is 22988.
   INVV: pidfile is ASNAPPLYQUAL1.PID
   INVV: grpfile is ASNAPPLYQUAL1.GRP
   INVV: tmp_str is ps -p "37516" | grep -c "asnapply" > "ASNAPPLYQUAL1.GRP"
   INVV: rcde is 256. errno is 2.
   INVV: clean up grp file.
    CPMSGF: msg catalog is /home/db2inst1/sqllib/msg/en_US/asnapply.cat
    MSGF: MsgNumber is 45.
   The NLS msg is ASN1045I: "The Apply program was started using database SAMPLE
................................
SAT: ASNLOAD = N, EFFECT_MEMBERS = 1
  SAT: MASS_DELETE = N
  SAT: SET_INSERTED = 0
  SAT: SET_DELETED = 0
  SAT: SET_UPDATED = 6
  SAT: SET_REWORKED = 0
  SAT: SET_REJECTED_TRXS = 0
  SAT: STATUS = 2
  SAT: LASTRUN = 1998-12-08-10.33.40.642808
  SAT: LASTSUCCESS = 1998-12-08-10.33.23.680185
  SAT: SYNCHPOINT is 0000000000000177802f
  SAT: SYNCHTIME is 1998-12-08-10.29.20.000000
  SAT: SOURCE_ALIAS is SAMPLE
  SAT: SOURCE_SERVER is SAMPLE
  SAT: SOURCE_OWNER is
  SAT: SOURCE_TABLE is
  SAT: TARGET_ALIAS is SAMPLE
  SAT: TARGET_SERVER is SAMPLE
  SAT: TARGET_OWNER is
  SAT: TARGET_TABLE is
  SAT: SQLSTATE is null
  SAT: SQLERRM is null
  SAT: SQLCODE is null
SAT: SQLERRP is null
  SAT: APPERRM is null
  CEXPC: connect to SAMPLE
  DONE: child process created

ASNDONE
 argc = 7, pgmname = ASNDONE
 setName = SET1, appQual = QUAL1, whosOnFirst = S
 cntl_srvr = SAMPLE, trace_parm = yes, status = 2
  DONE: ASNDONE normal termination.
```

The ASNDONE user exit program receives the information below from the Apply program when Apply completes each subscription set. Note that ASNDONE will be called at the end of a mini-cycle UOW when you specify a value for MAX_SYNCH_MINUTES. We discuss MAX_SYNCH_MINUTES in

"Data Blocking Using MAX_SYNCH_MINUTES" on page 162. The information provided to ASNDONE is:

- Subscription Set name
- Apply qualifier
- Whos_on_first value
- Control server
- Trace option
- Status value

4.10.8 LOADX Option to Refresh the Target Table

Earlier in this chapter, we discussed how the Apply program can do a full refresh of the target table. Alternately, the Apply program can use a user exit load program to initialize the target table if you use the LOADX option.

The default Apply full refresh uses mass SQL DELETE and INSERT statements within a single unit of work. By default, the default user exit ASNLOAD.SMP uses an EXPORT/LOAD method. Since this is a sample program, you can modify it to best fit your needs. The source program is located under the SQLLIB\SAMPLES\REPL directory. When the LOADX option is used, Apply generates the following files instead of the spill file. We have listed the file types based on operating system platform for convenience in Table 15:

Table 15. ASNLOAD File Types

O/S Platform	File name and Extension	Description
MVS	No known facility	-
OS/2	<Apply Qualifier>.IXF	Exported source data
	<Apply Qualifier>.EXP	Export messages
	<Apply Qualifier>.LOA	Load messages
Windows NT and UNIX	ASNA<userid><database_instance_name><cntl_server>.IXF	Exported source data
	ASNAEXPT<userid><database_instance_name><cntl_server>.MSG	Export messages
	ASNALOAD<userid><database_instance_name><cntl_server>.MSG	Load messages

For example, if you start the Apply program with the LOADX option:

```
asnapply EMPQUAL COPYDB1 LOADX trcflow nosleep > fulloff.trc
```

Look at the end of the trace file:

```
API used: on_V1 = 0, on_V2 = 1
  datafile is ASNAAZUMADB2COPYDB1.IXF
  msgfile is  ASNAEXPTAZUMADB2COPYDB1.MSG
CONNECT to source server DB2C successful.

EXPORT:
Return from EXPORT: rc is 0
  Export number of rows is 31.
Connect to target server COPYDB1 successful.
LOG RETAIN : 0
USER EXIT  : 0

LOAD:
  datafile is ASNAAZUMADB2COPYDB1.IXF.
  string is REPLACE INTO DB2ADMIN.EMPLCOPY ASNALOADAZUMADB2COPYDB1.MSG.
  filetype is IXF.
  local msgfile ASNALOADAZUMADB2COPYDB1.MSG.
  remote msgfile (null).
Return from LOAD: Rc is 0:
  rows loaded 31
  rows committed 31
  USRX: return value from _spawnlp = 0
PSET: Commit6 ok
 CEXPC: connect to COPYDB1
 CLOS: setRepeatCopy is 0
 CLOS: activate = 1
 CLOS: status   = 0
 CLOS: lastrun = 1998-11-30-12.19.49.234001
 CLOS: lastsuccess = 1998-11-30-12.19.27.968000
 CLOS: synchpoint is null
 CLOS: synchtime = 1998-11-30-13.22.10.290718
 CLOS: apply_qual = EMPQUAL
 CLOS: set_name = EMPSET
 CLOS: sWhosOnFirst = S
 CEXPC: connect to DB2C
 CEXPC: CONNECT with USERID/PASSWORD
 CEXPC: serverIsolationUR is 1.
 CEXPC: connect to COPYDB1
 CEXPC: CONNECT without USERID/PASSWORD
 CEXPC: serverIsolationUR is 1.
 SAT: ASNLOAD = Y, EFFECT_MEMBERS = 1
 SAT: MASS_DELETE = Y
 SAT: SET_INSERTED = 0
 SAT: SET_DELETED = 0
 SAT: SET_UPDATED = 0
 SAT: SET_REWORKED = 0
```

Note that the SET_INSERTED counter value will always be zero when a full refresh is done using ASNLOAD. This is because Apply can't recognize the details of the LOAD activity and will receive only the return code from the LOAD exit program.

If an error occurs while the Apply program calls ASNLOAD, or if ASNLOAD returns a non-zero return code, the Apply program issues a message, stops processing that subscription, and moves on to the next subscription.

You may find the ASNLOAD user exit of use with referential constraints.You have to use ASNLOAD to fully refresh a table with referential integrity constraints in order to bypass referential integrity checking.

4.10.9 Manual Loading

So far in this chapter, we have discussed using Apply to do a full refresh, and also using a user exit to do this full target table refresh. There is a third option that involves doing your own full refresh.

The following example shows how to do a manual full refresh instead of the normal Apply full refresh. The Apply full refresh uses mass SQL DELETE and INSERT commands within a single unit of work. You might want to use a manual technique in the following situations:

- When loading to a DB2 for OS/390 source table.

  Capture for MVS does not capture any changes made by a DB2 utility even if you specify LOAD LOG(YES). Use a manual load to maintain consistency.
- To automate the loading of large copies of tables.
- To bypass referential integrity checking.
- As a way to resolve gap issues between source and target tables.

There are some variations on how to manage this process depending on the types of tables involved. In this example, we show you the case for a user copy target table.

> **Note**
>
> Capture must be running before you begin the following steps.

1. Optional: It is recommended that you disable the full refresh capability for the source table as shown in the following SQL statement. The Apply program will issue an error message rather than performing a full refresh if the following procedure is not performed correctly:

   ```
   UPDATE ASN.IBMSNAP_REGISTER SET DISABLE_REFRESH =1
   WHERE SOURCE_OWNER='SW6003A' AND SOURCE_TABLE='EMPLOYEE';
   ```

2. Ensure that the Apply program is inactive, or deactivate the applicable replication subscription, as shown in the following SQL statement:

   ```
   UPDATE ASN.IBMSNAP_SUBS_SET SET ACTIVATE=0
   WHERE SET_NAME='EMPSET' AND APPLY_QUAL='EMPQUAL';
   ```

3. Update the SYNCHPOINT and SYNCHTIME values in the ASN.IBMSNAP_PRUNCNTL table for each row that corresponds to a member of the replication subscription as shown in the following SQL statement:

```
--Connect to the data server
CONNECT TO DB2C USER SW6003A USING xxxx;

UPDATE  ASN.IBMSNAP_PRUNCNTL  SET
          SYNCHTIME =  current timestamp,
          SYNCHPOINT = X'00000000000000000000'
        WHERE
          TARGET_SERVER = 'COPYDB1'  AND
         TARGET_OWNER  = 'DB2ADMIN'  AND
          TARGET_TABLE  = 'EMPLCOPY'  AND
          TARGET_STRUCTURE  = 8  ;
```

4. Verify that the Capture program has performed RBA translation.

   You can verify the translation by selecting from the Pruning Control table and verifying that the SYNCHPOINT column has now been replaced from its original value of x'00000000000000000000'. This will happen if capture is already running or when you start capture.

5. Run your own unload/load procedure outside of DPropR.

6. Update the ASN.IBMSNAP_SUBS_SET table as shown in the following SQL statement. The NULL value in the ASN.IBMSNAP_SUBS_SET SYNCHPOINT column means that the subscription set is being processed for the first time, and a full refresh is required. However, by setting the SYNCHTIME to the current timestamp, Apply assumes a full refresh has just been completed and will do differential refreshes in the future:

```
--Connect to the control server
CONNECT TO COPYDB1;

UPDATE ASN.IBMSNAP_SUBS_SET   SET
         SYNCHTIME   = current timestamp,
         SYNCHPOINT = NULL,
         LASTSUCCESS= current timestamp,
         LASTRUN     = current timestamp,
ACTIVATE=1
       WHERE
APPLY_QUAL ='EMPQUAL'  AND
         SET_NAME ='EMPSET' ;
```

Table 16 shows a list of the above procedure:

Table 16. Manual Load Steps

Server	Action to be taken
Source Server	Update REGISTER to disable the full refresh (Optional)
Control Server	Update SUBS_SET to deactivate the subscription (Optional)

Server	Action to be taken
Source Server	Update PC to start capturing from the source table
Source Server	Confirm GOCAPT message by looking at Trace.
Source & Target Server	Run your own unload/load procedure
Control Server	Update SUBS_SET to avoid the full refresh by Apply and activate the subscription

7. Start the Apply program again:

```
asnapply EMPQUAL COPYDB1 trcflow nosleep > fulloff.trc
```

8. Look at the end of the trace file:

```
PSET: Fetch answer set for member 0
  Compiled(F) at 14:49:09 on Aug 12 1998 (Level 0053)
   CDSET: spill_file(0) = EMPQUALDB2COPYDB1.000
  FETSET: The number of rows fetched is 0.
  UP1SYT: Synchtime is 1998-11-30-12.50.47.196638
 PSET: Commit3 ok
  CEXPC: connect to COPYDB1
  CEXPC: CONNECT without USERID/PASSWORD
  CEXPC: serverIsolationUR is 1.
 -------------------------
 PSET: Commit4 ok
  Compiled(A) at 14:49:19 on Aug 12 1998 (Level 0053)
 PSET: Commit6 ok
  CEXPC: connect to COPYDB1
  CLOS: setRepeatCopy is 0
  CLOS: activate = 1
  CLOS: status   = 0
  CLOS: lastrun = 1998-11-30-11.50.57.734001
  CLOS: lastsuccess = 1998-11-30-11.50.27.968000
  CLOS: Synchpoint is  000000005391d1300000
  CLOS: synchtime = 1998-11-30-12.50.47.196638
  CLOS: apply_qual = EMPQUAL
  CLOS: set_name = EMPSET
  CLOS: sWhosOnFirst = S
  CEXPC: connect to DB2C
  CEXPC: CONNECT with USERID/PASSWORD
  CEXPC: serverIsolationUR is 1.
  CEXPC: connect to COPYDB1
  CEXPC: CONNECT without USERID/PASSWORD
  CEXPC: serverIsolationUR is 1.
  SAT: ASNLOAD = N, EFFECT_MEMBERS = 0
  SAT: MASS_DELETE = N
  SAT: SET_INSERTED = 0
  SAT: SET_DELETED = 0
  SAT: SET_UPDATED = 0
  SAT: SET_REWORKED = 0
  SAT: SET_REJECTED_TRXS = 0
```

No full refresh was done by the Apply program as MASS_DELETE=N and SET_INSERTED=0.

4.10.10 Event Timing

Earlier, when setting up our subscription, we chose to have the subscription processing based on interval timing. You may also choose to have subscription processing based on events where your applications may post (or activate) replication events.

The ASN.IBMSNAP_SUBS_EVENT table is used to manage timing dependencies between a batch application and the replication of the updates posted by the batch application. There are separate EVENT_TIME and END_OF_PERIOD timestamps in the event table, END_OF_PERIOD being optional. EVENT_TIME is the time to move the data with respect to the time at the control server. If a value exists for END_OF_PERIOD, then only transactions committed at or before this time will be propagated with respect to the time at the source server. Keep in mind that the control and source servers may exist in different time zones.

Some possible uses for event timing include:

- Have your batch applications post just the EVENT_TIME following the completion of an important batch job step to signal the start of propagation.
- Have your batch applications post the EVENT_TIME as some off-peak time a few hours later with END_OF_PERIOD defining which transactions should be propagated at EVENT_TIME. This implies that some transactions should be held for propagation until the end of the next business period (for example, the end of day or the end of week).

  For example, your application could post an event at 5:30 PM stating that the END_OF_PERIOD occurred at 5:15 PM, but that transactions should not propagate until 2:00 AM the following morning (EVENT_TIME).

Note that your application must post events; the Control Center cannot be used to do this. You tie your applications to subscription activity through named events. If you post an entry using CURRENT_TIMESTAMP for EVENT_TIME, then you trigger the event named by the EVENT_NAME. Any replication subscription tied to this event will then be eligible to run.

4.10.10.1 Change Subscription Timing

Let's look at a practical example of using event timing. We will use a subscription that we defined earlier and modify it from interval timing to event based timing.

First, to change the subscription settings:

1. Select the **Replication Subscriptions** folder from the object tree. The replication subscriptions appear in the contents pane:

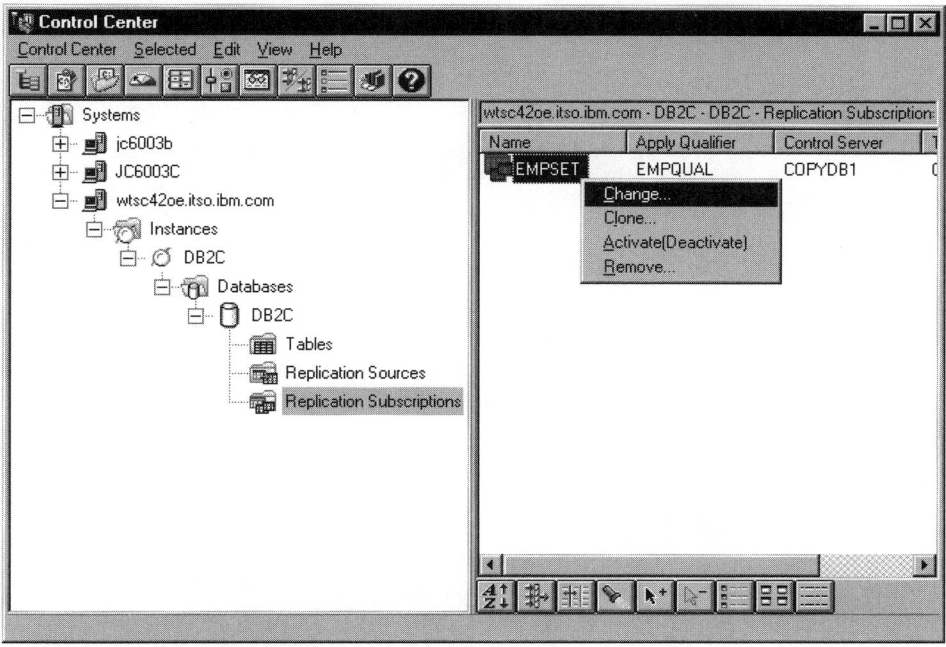

Figure 73. Change Subscription - Timing

2. Right-click on the subscription that you want to modify and select **Change** from the pop-up menu. The Change Replication Subscription panel is displayed:

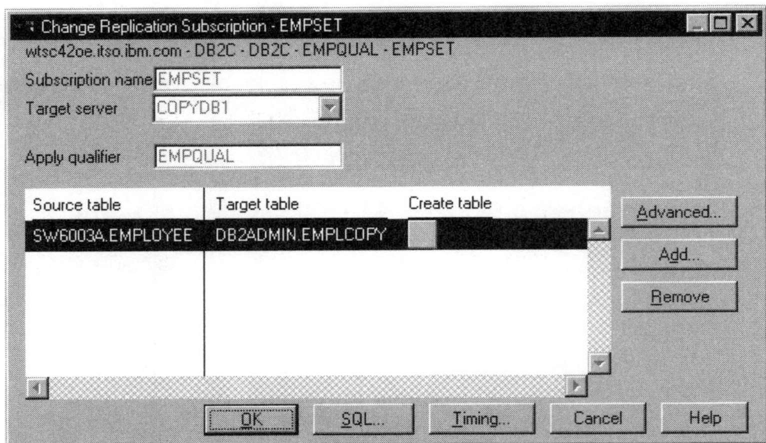

Figure 74. Change Subscription - Timing

3. Click on **Timing** to display the following panel:

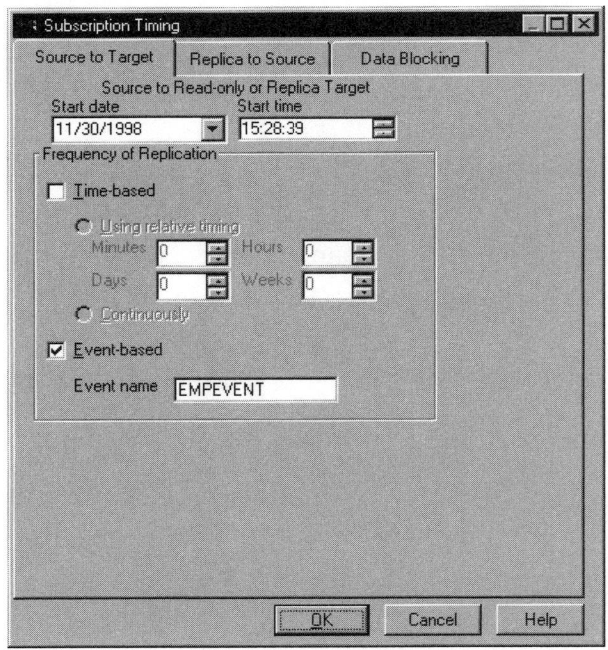

Figure 75. Change Subscription - Timing

4. You can change the timing values in the Subscription Timing panel. Enter EMPEVENT as the EVENT NAME after checking the Event based button.

Since we do not want interval timing, deselect the time based button. Click **OK**. This takes you back to the Change Replication Subscription screen. Click **OK** again.

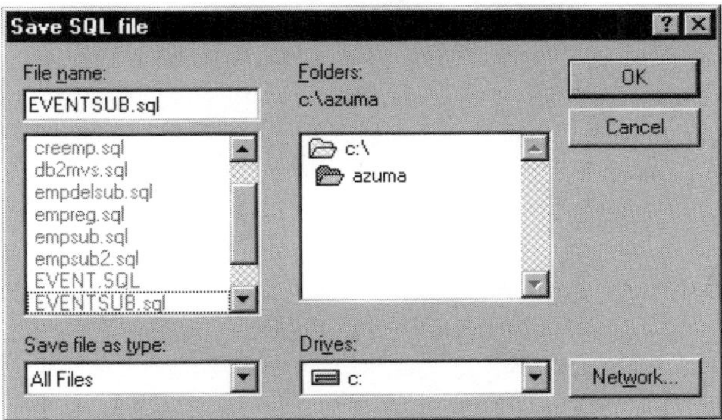

Figure 76. Save SQL

5. The Save SQL file window opens. Save the SQL as EVENTSUB.sql. Click **OK** to save this file.

Open the SQL file with a text editor to examine it:

```
CONNECT TO COPYDB1;

DELETE FROM ASN.IBMSNAP_SUBS_SET
WHERE APPLY_QUAL = 'EMPQUAL'
  AND SET_NAME = 'EMPSET';

UPDATE ASN.IBMSNAP_SUBS_MEMBR SET
PREDICATES = NULL
WHERE APPLY_QUAL = 'EMPQUAL'
  AND SET_NAME = 'EMPSET'
  AND SOURCE_OWNER = 'SW6003A'
  AND SOURCE_TABLE = 'EMPLOYEE'
  AND TARGET_OWNER = 'DB2ADMIN'
  AND TARGET_TABLE = 'EMPLCOPY'
  AND WHOS_ON_FIRST = 'S';

INSERT INTO ASN.IBMSNAP_SUBS_SET (
ACTIVATE, APPLY_QUAL, SET_NAME, WHOS_ON_FIRST,
SOURCE_SERVER, TARGET_SERVER, STATUS, LASTRUN,
REFRESH_TIMING, SLEEP_MINUTES, EVENT_NAME, LASTSUCCESS,
SYNCHPOINT, SYNCHTIME, MAX_SYNCH_MINUTES, AUX_STMTS,
ARCH_LEVEL, SOURCE_ALIAS, TARGET_ALIAS )
VALUES
( 1, 'EMPQUAL', 'EMPSET', 'S', 'DB2C', 'COPYDB1', 0,
'1998-11-30-12.19.49.000000', 'E', NULL, 'EMPEVENT',
'1998-11-30-12.19.49.000000', NULL, '1998-11-30-13.22.10.000290',
NULL, 0, '0201', 'DB2C', 'COPYDB1' );
```

Note that SLEEP_MINUTES is set to NULL, EVENT_NAME is set to EMPEVENT and REFRESH_TIMING is set to E.

6. Run the saved SQL file.

7. Start Apply as shown below:

```
asnapply EMPQUAL COPYDB1 trcflow
```

The trace looks like this:

```
Apply program compiled at 14:48:48 on Aug 12 1998 (Level 0053)
Apply qualifier is EMPQUAL.
Control srvr name is COPYDB1.
Issue Sleep msg.
Will not invoke ASNLOAD.
Will not invoke ASNDONE.
  IMSG: Instance name is DB2      .
  IMSG: The log file name is EMPQUALDB2COPYDB1.LOG.
   CEXPC: connect to COPYDB1
   CEXPC: CONNECT without USERID/PASSWORD
   CEXPC: serverIsolationUR is 1.
  CIMPC: serverIsolationUR is 1.
  CIMPC: The local_srvr is COPYDB1.
  CIMPC: Userid is AZUMA
    MSGF: MsgNumber is 45.
   The NLS msg is ASN1045I: The Apply program was started using database
COPYDB1.
The NLS msg is ASN1045I: The Apply program was started using database COPYDB1.
--- Process next subscription (1) ---
 CEXPC: connect to COPYDB1
 GCST: Control server timestamp is 1998-11-30-17.28.40.109001
  R1NES: No eligible named event subscription at this moment
  R1RTS: No eligible relative timer driven subscription at this moment
 TTOS: slpDay is 0; slpHour is 0, slpMin is 0, slpSec is 0, slpMSec is 0
 TTOS3: sleep_time = 300
 TTOS: delay_seconds = 300
 Delay_seconds = 300 seconds
  REST: Sleep time = 300 seconds.
    MSGF: MsgNumber is 44.
   The NLS msg is ASN1044I: The Apply program will become inactive for 5
minutes and 0 seconds.
The NLS msg is ASN1044I: The Apply program will become inactive for 5 minutes
and 0 seconds.
```

Since no event has been posted (or inserted) into the EVENT table, there is no eligible subscription at this moment. Apply will check the control tables every five minutes by default. Note that you can't control this timing check, as five minutes as the Apply checking interval is hardcoded in the Apply program.

8. Post an event to the EVENT table:

```
INSERT INTO ASN.IBMSNAP_SUBS_EVENT
VALUES ('EMPEVENT',CURRENT TIMESTAMP,NULL)
```

You should see the Apply program perform the replication within the following five minutes.

In some situations, you might need to trigger replication from the MVS site after the daily batch jobs have ended. To do this, you can update the EVENT table (on the Windows NT machine) from MVS by using the database on Windows NT as a DRDA Application Server.

4.10.10.2 Dealing with Capture Lag

If your END_OF_PERIOD is very close to the time of event posting, you may need to account for Capture lag. This is the possible delay in Capture processing the records in the log file. You would not want a transaction that occurred within the current period to be held back until the next business period because it has not yet been captured. To avoid this problem, you can have your applications post to a table similar to the event table (this could be an ASN.IBMSNAP_SUBS_EVENT table on another system or a similar table with a different name on the same system) and then define a subscription from this posting table into the event table. Assuming you've registered your posting table as a replication source, the postings made by your application will only be captured from the log after all preceding application updates have been captured. This means that by the time the posting makes its way into the real ASN.IBMSNAP_SUBS_EVENT table, all application updates within the current business period will have been captured.

The lag time to maintain the ASN.IBMSNAP_SUBS_EVENT entry with a subscription from the posting table adjusts for the lag time between the application updates and their capture into the UOW and change data tables. This scenario can be seen in Figure 77 on page 154 where, by following the sequence of steps, you can see how using this type of setup will allow you to compensate for the lag in Capture reading the log files for all relevant transactions.

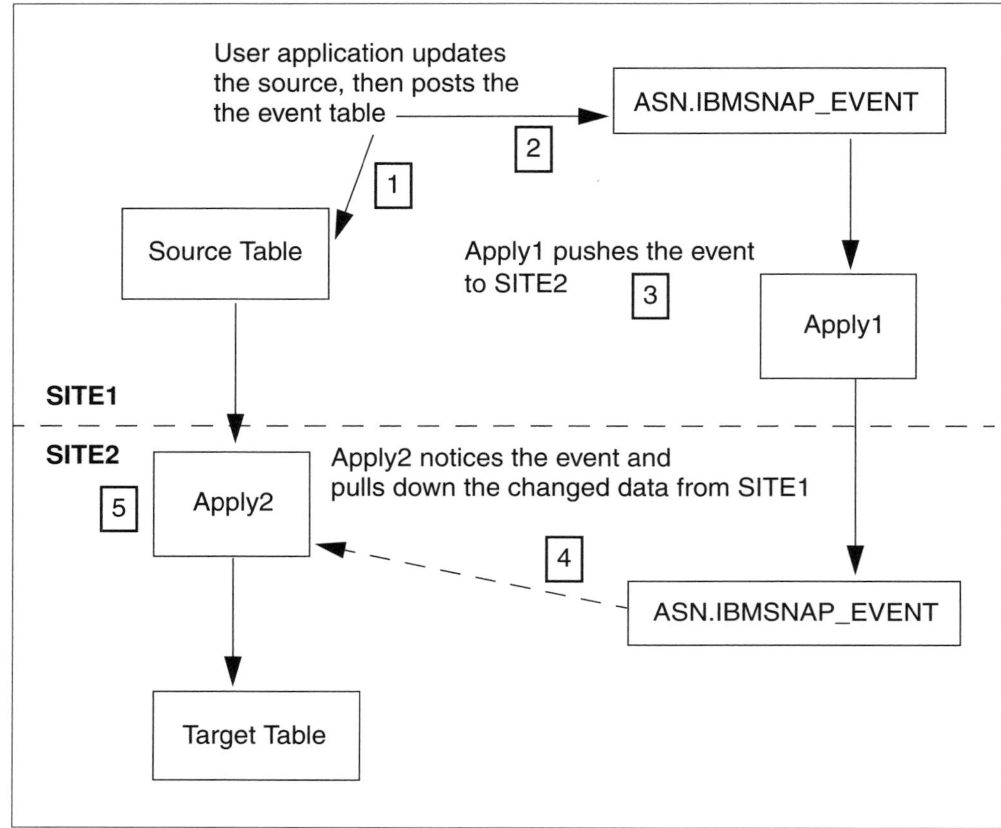
User application updates
the source, then posts the
the event table
ASN.IBMSNAP_EVENT
2
1
Source Table
Apply1 pushes the event
to SITE2
3
Apply1
SITE1
SITE2
Apply2
Apply2 notices the event and
pulls down the changed data from SITE1
5
4
ASN.IBMSNAP_EVENT
Target Table

Figure 77. Event Table Pushing and Pulling

4.10.10.3 Other Ways to Use Event Timing

There are other uses for replication events, such as customized scheduling. You can post events in advance, so it is possible to post a full year's worth of events in advance avoiding holidays and other days when you do not want your subscriptions to run.

Another alternative is to have the system generate events for you. Here's an example of a view substitution for the ASN.IBMSNAP_SUBS_EVENT table, which generates the WEEKDAY_EVENT event beginning at 2 AM on Mondays through Fridays. When queried throughout the day, the view returns the same 2 AM event, so that if Apply was delayed in getting started, it would still see the event whenever it queried ASN.IBMSNAP_SUBS_EVENT throughout the day. Also, by making the time-string portion of EVENT_TIME a constant, the event is generated, so that it will drive the subscription only once per day. The SUBSTR() function is used to change the data type of the string constant WEEKDAY_EVENT from VARCHAR to CHAR(18):

```
CREATE VIEW EVENT_TEST
 (EVENT_NAME,EVENT_TIME,END_OF_PERIOD)
 AS SELECT
 SUBSTR('WEEKDAY_EVENT      ',1),
 TIMESTAMP(DATE(CURRENT TIMESTAMP),'02.00.00'),
 NULLIF(1,1)
FROM SYSDUMMY1
WHERE((DAYS(CURRENT TIMESTAMP)-((DAYS(CURRENT TIMESTAMP)/7)*7))+1)
BETWEEN 2 AND 6

B20000I  The SQL command completed successfully.

SELECT * FROM EVENT_TEST

EVENT_NAME         EVENT_TIME                 END_OF_PERIOD
------------------ -------------------------- -------------
WEEKDAY_EVENT      1998-12-01-02.00.00.000000             -

  1 record(s) selected.
```

The SYSDUMMY1 table shown above is a user-defined dummy table that has only one row. DB2 for OS/390 has such a one-row table called SYSIBM.SYSDUMMY1.

4.10.11 Before and After SQL

Another powerful feature of the DB2 Replication product is the ability to associate SQL or stored procedures with your subscription. You can define SQL statements and stored procedures to be run before or after the Apply program copies the data from the source to the target table. This feature is useful for pruning CCD tables and controlling the sequence in which replication subscriptions are processed.

We can use this function for a variety of purposes. You can use this for the maintenance of the APPLYTRAIL table for instance. At the end of a subscription cycle, Apply inserts a row into ASN.IBMSNAP_APPLYTRAIL at the control server. These rows need to be deleted regularly to keep the table from growing too large, and while Apply writes to this table, it never reads from it. The subscription statistics and error diagnostics are written to this table for your benefit, and when you delete these rows is up to you. An easy way to manage the growth of this table is to add a before or after SQL statement to a subscription. For example:

```
DELETE FROM ASN.IBMSNAP_APPLYTRAIL WHERE LASTRUN < (CURRENT
TIMESTAMP - 7 DAYS);
```

This SQL statement will be stored in the ASN.IBMSNAP_SUBS_STMTS table. This table contains statements that are executed immediately or stored procedures that can be executed at the source server or the target server. If you do not specify any statements or stored procedures, this table contains no rows.

4.10.11.1 Change Subscription - Add Before/After SQL

To add before/after SQL to a subscription that has already been defined:

1. Select the **Replication Subscriptions** folder from the object tree. The replication subscriptions appear in the contents pane:

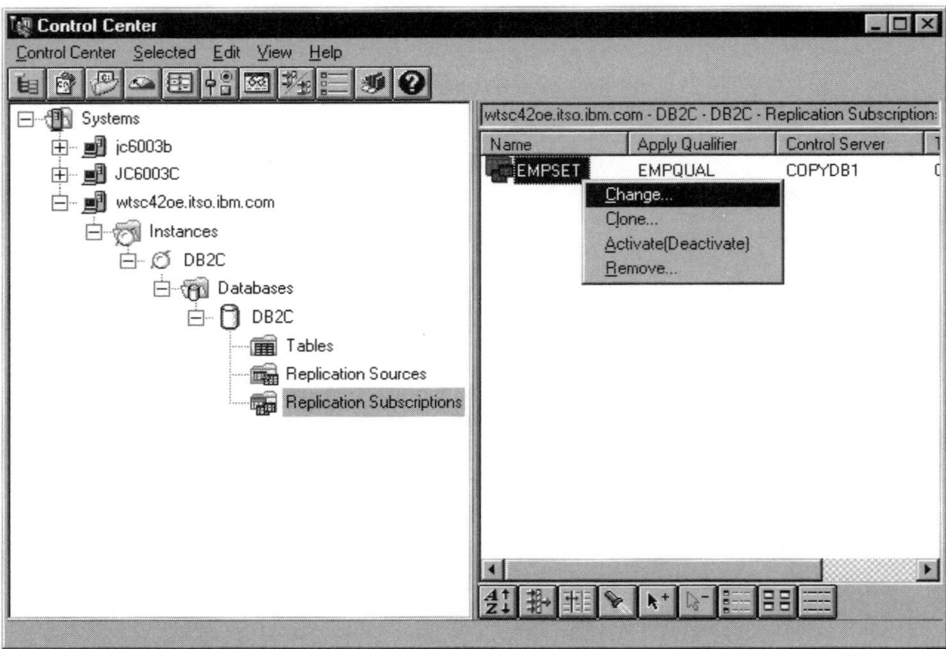

Figure 78. Change Subscription - Add Before/After SQL

2. Right-click on the replication subscription that you want to modify and select **Change** from the pop-up menu. The Change Replication Subscription panel is displayed:

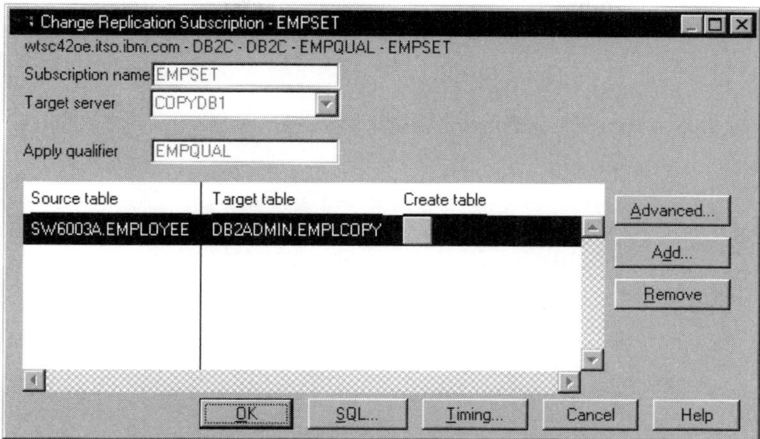

Figure 79. Change Replication Subscription

Click on **SQL** to display the following panel:

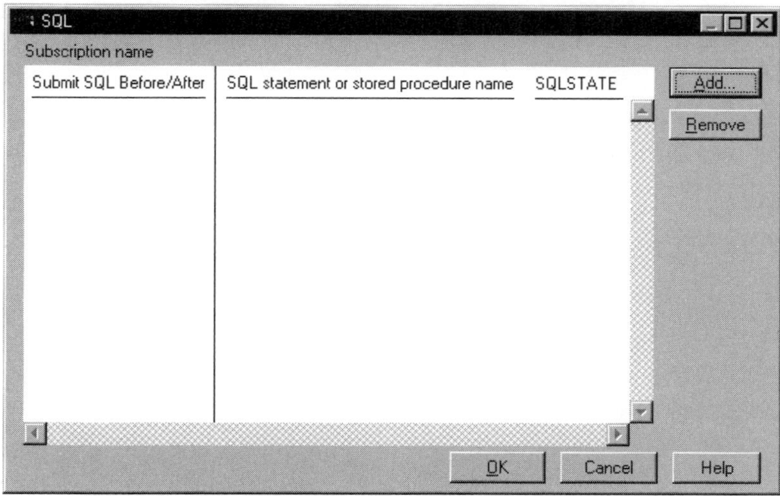

Figure 80. Change Subscription - Before/After SQL

3. You can enter (or remove) before and after SQL statements or stored procedures in this panel. Click on **Add** to display the Add SQL panel:

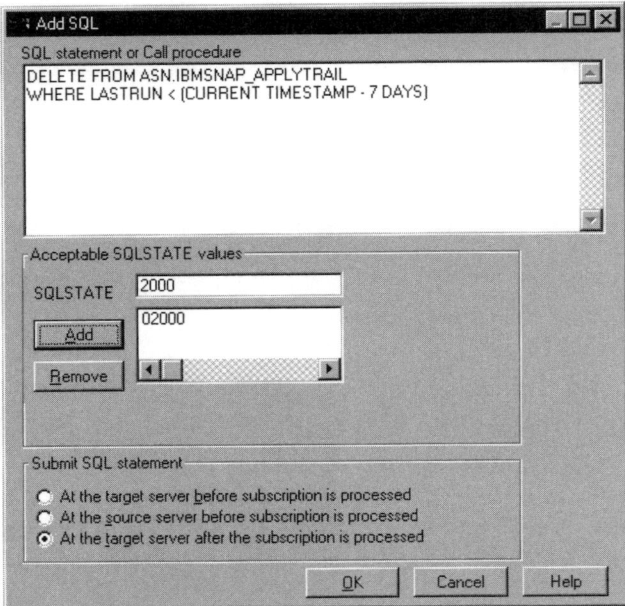

Figure 81. Change Subscription - Before/After SQL

4. Enter the SQL statement or stored procedure name in the SQL statement or Call procedure field. The stored procedure name must begin with CALL. This field can contain ordinary or delimited identifiers.

   The Apply program interprets any values specified in the 'Acceptable SQLSTATE values' field as a successful execution. For example, we have entered 2000 in the SQLSTATE field and clicked on **Add**.

   You can also specify whether you want to submit the SQL statement or CALL statement at the target or source server before or after the replication subscription is processed. Click on the appropriate radio button then click on **OK**.

5. Click **OK** again. This takes you back to the Change Replication Subscription screen. Click **OK** again.

6. The Save SQL file window is displayed. Save the file as addstmt.sql. Click **OK** to save this file.

Open the SQL file with a text editor to examine its contents:

```
CONNECT TO COPYDB1;

DELETE FROM ASN.IBMSNAP_SUBS_SET
WHERE APPLY_QUAL = 'EMPQUAL'
```

```
  AND SET_NAME = 'EMPSET';

DELETE FROM ASN.IBMSNAP_SUBS_STMTS
WHERE APPLY_QUAL = 'EMPQUAL'
  AND SET_NAME = 'EMPSET';

UPDATE ASN.IBMSNAP_SUBS_MEMBR SET
PREDICATES = NULL
WHERE APPLY_QUAL = 'EMPQUAL'
  AND SET_NAME = 'EMPSET'
  AND SOURCE_OWNER = 'SW6003A'
  AND SOURCE_TABLE = 'EMPLOYEE'
  AND TARGET_OWNER = 'DB2ADMIN'
  AND TARGET_TABLE = 'EMPLCOPY'
  AND WHOS_ON_FIRST = 'S';

INSERT INTO ASN.IBMSNAP_SUBS_SET (
ACTIVATE, APPLY_QUAL, SET_NAME, WHOS_ON_FIRST, SOURCE_SERVER,
TARGET_SERVER, STATUS, LASTRUN, REFRESH_TIMING, SLEEP_MINUTES,
EVENT_NAME, LASTSUCCESS, SYNCHPOINT, SYNCHTIME, MAX_SYNCH_MINUTES,
AUX_STMTS, ARCH_LEVEL, SOURCE_ALIAS, TARGET_ALIAS ) VALUES (
1, 'EMPQUAL', 'EMPSET', 'S', 'DB2C', 'COPYDB1', ,
'1998-11-30-11.28.39.000000', 'E', NULL, 'EMPEVENT',
'1998-11-30-11.28.39.000000',
X'00000000539358b40000', '1998-11-30-11.27.04.000280', NULL,
1, '0201', 'DB2C', 'COPYDB1' );

INSERT INTO ASN.IBMSNAP_SUBS_STMTS (
APPLY_QUAL, SET_NAME, WHOS_ON_FIRST, BEFORE_OR_AFTER, STMT_NUMBER,
EI_OR_CALL, SQL_STMT, ACCEPT_SQLSTATES ) VALUES (
'EMPQUAL', 'EMPSET', 'S', 'A', 100, 'E', 'DELETE FROM
ASN.IBMSNAP_APPLYTRAIL WHERE LASTRUN <= (CURRENT TIMESTAMP - 7 DAYS)',
'02000' );
```

Note that the insert statement contains the previous SYNCHPOINT and SYNCHTIME values, so the next start of the Apply program will perform a differential copy, not a full refresh. The AUX_STMTS value in the insert is 1. A zero value indicates the absence of any subscription statement table rows. AUX_STMTS represents the total number of subscription statement table

(ASN.IBMSNAP_SUBS_STMTS) rows. Here are the important columns from the IBMSNAP_SUBS_SET and IBMSNAP_SUBS_STMTS tables:

Table 17. IBMSNAP_SUBS_SET Table

Column name	Description
AUX_STMTS	0. Absence OF IBMSNAP_SUBS_STMTS rows n. The number of IBMSNAP_SUBS_STMTS rows

Table 18. IBMSNAP_SUBS_STMTS Table

Column name	Description
SET_NAME	From IBMSNAP_SUBS_SET
BEFORE_OR_AFTER	**A**. After SQL statement at Target **B**. Before SQL statement at Target **S**. Before SQL statement at Source **G**. Before SQL statement at Source. Will be performed before opening any cursors and before fetching registration details. This is for non-DB2 source replication.
STMT_NUMBER	Relative order number within the scope of BEFORE_OR_AFTER.
EI_OR_CALL	**E**. SQL_STMT by EXEC SQL IMMEDIATE **C**. SQL_STMT by EXEC SQL CALL.
ACCEPT_SQLSTATES	5 byte SQLSTATEs

The commit scopes of Before- and After-SQL are different. The unit of work of Before-SQL is a separate unit of work from the replication unit of work. After-SQL is performed within the same unit of work as the replication process. Note that the replication process will be rolled back if the After-SQL fails.

4.10.11.2 Stored Procedure Considerations

Stored procedures use the SQL CALL statement. A stored procedure used in this context cannot have any IN/OUT/INOUT parameters (except for AS/400 Apply V5).

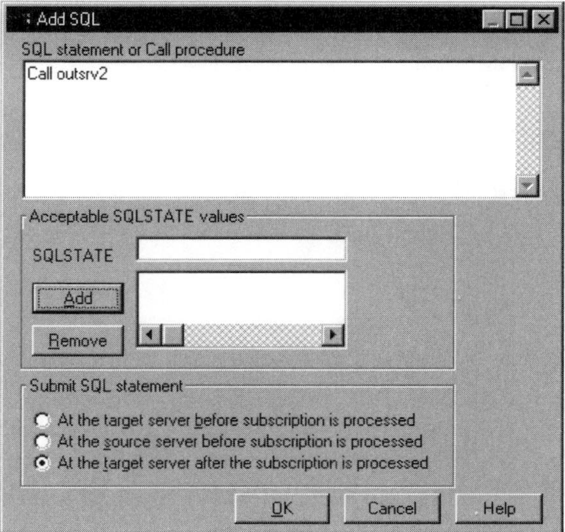

Figure 82. The Add SQL Window

Figure 82 shows an example of using a stored procedure. In this case, the generated SQL statement looks like this:

```
INSERT INTO ASN.IBMSNAP_SUBS_STMTS (
APPLY_QUAL, SET_NAME, WHOS_ON_FIRST, BEFORE_OR_AFTER,
STMT_NUMBER, EI_OR_CALL, SQL_STMT, ACCEPT_SQLSTATES
) VALUES (
'QUAL1', 'SET1', 'S', 'A', 100, 'C', 'outsrv2', '' );
```

The stored procedure name is case sensitive. If you have already created a stored procedure with a lower case name but specify an upper case name in the Add SQL panel, the Apply program will detect the error and will rollback the replication processing when BEFORE_OR_AFTER is set to 'A'. Here is the trace for this case:

```
-------------------------
   stmt_info i = 0
-------------------------
BEFORE_OR_AFTER  = S
STMT_NUMBER      = 10
EI_OR_CALL       = E
SQL_STMT         = UPDATE COUNTER SET COL1=COL1+1
ACCEPT_SQLSTATES = 02000
-------------------------
   stmt_info i = 1
-------------------------
BEFORE_OR_AFTER  = A
STMT_NUMBER      = 100
```

```
  EI_OR_CALL        = C
  SQL_STMT          = Outsrv2
  ACCEPT_SQLSTATES = 02000
..................................
FETSET: The number of rows fetched is 6.
 PSET: Commit3 ok
  CEXPC: connect to V3DB
 -------------------------
 PSET: Commit4 ok
  Compiled(A) at 09:46:34 on Sep 11 1998 (Level 0058)
  EXEI: SQL statement is Outsrv2.
  SQLCA is
       00000000 53514C43 41202020 00000088 FFFFD8E3 SQLCA   ........
       00000010 00232F68 6F6D652F 64623276 332F7371 ...home.db2v3.sq
       00000020 6C6C6962 2F66756E 6374696F 6E2F4F75 llib.function.Ou
       00000030 74737276 32000020 20202020 20202020 tsrv2..
       00000040 20202020 20202020 20202020 20202020
       00000050 20202020 20202020 44415249 4C4F4144         DARILOAD
       00000060 00000000 00000000 00000000 00000000 ................
       00000070 00000000 00000000 20202020 20202020 ........
       00000080 20202020 20202020
  EXEI: Execute sql stmt failed. errcode is 362901. sqlstate is
    . sqlcode is -10013
 PSET: ROLLBACK
```

The name of the stored procedure should be changed to `outsrv2`, instead of `Outsrv2`. The replication transaction was rolled back. Note that an UPDATE statement run as the Before-SQL would be performed against the source server and committed because it is a separate unit of work.

4.10.12 Data Blocking Using MAX_SYNCH_MINUTES

Consider the situation that could occur, if say, due to an operations error, your Apply process had not run for some time. In this case, Capture would, nonetheless, continue running, leaving in its wake a backlog of changes to propagate when the Apply process comes back on line. The backlog of queued transactions could result in any or all of the following system stresses:

- At the source site, a large change data answer set could be generated, in many cases, requiring a large DB2 workfile.
- Transmission of a large answer set all at once might flood the network link, affecting other applications using the same link.
- To hold the large answer set, the number and size of the temporary Apply spill files could grow large.
- At the target site, updating, and thus locking many rows at once, could result in contention for the target tables.

- The logging resources required to support the batched updates could exceed the target's preallocated log space.

Taking control of the backlog of queued transactions is an imprecise activity as there are so many variables.

- The number of transactions is not an exact indicator of work, as a single transaction can change 1 row or perhaps 500,000 rows.
- The number of rows cannot be used directly as a commit boundary, as it is the transaction boundaries that are important. You cannot determine the nearest transaction boundary that would loosely equate to some number of change data rows without first fetching the change data to see how large the transactions are. That's not good, because one of the objectives is to, up front, limit the size of the change data answer sets requested. The boundaries have to be set before the change data cursors are opened.
- A time interval is also an imprecise measurement unit, because the number of transactions committed will vary between two intervals of the same length. Still, it is possible to know the time boundaries of the interval before fetching the queued transaction information.

Given the above, DPropR allows you to control the backlog by prescribing a time interval for your subscription, such that Apply will fetch and propagate at one time only as many transactions that were committed during such a time interval. The control column where the interval is set for the subscription is the MAX_SYNCH_MINUTES column in the ASN.IBMSNAP_SUBS_SET table.

For example, if a given subscription has a value for MAX_SYNCH_MINUTES of 1, then no matter how large the propagation backlog, approximately one minute's worth of committed transactions would be propagated and committed at the target before fetching the next one minute's worth, thus regulating the resources required to process the subscription. Each of these smaller cycles can be termed a mini-subscription cycle.

The MAX_SYNCH_MINUTES default is NULL. This NULL value will copy all committed data available, no matter how big or small. The number of minutes that you set should be enough so that all transactions for the replication subscription that occurred during the interval can be copied without causing the spill file to overflow or a log full condition to occur.

There are some restrictions:

- A unit of work cannot be split.
- Previous mini-subscription cycles cannot be rolled back.

- MAX_SYNCH_MINUTES cannot be used in full refresh, only in update mode.

A large block of changes from one or more CD/UOW/CCD tables will be broken down into subsets of changes by specifying a MAX_SYNCH_MINUTES value. The Apply program converts a single subscription cycle into many mini-cycles. We can examine whether MAX_SYNCH_MINUTES was used or not by looking for STATUS=2 in the IBMSNAP_APPLYTRAIL table.

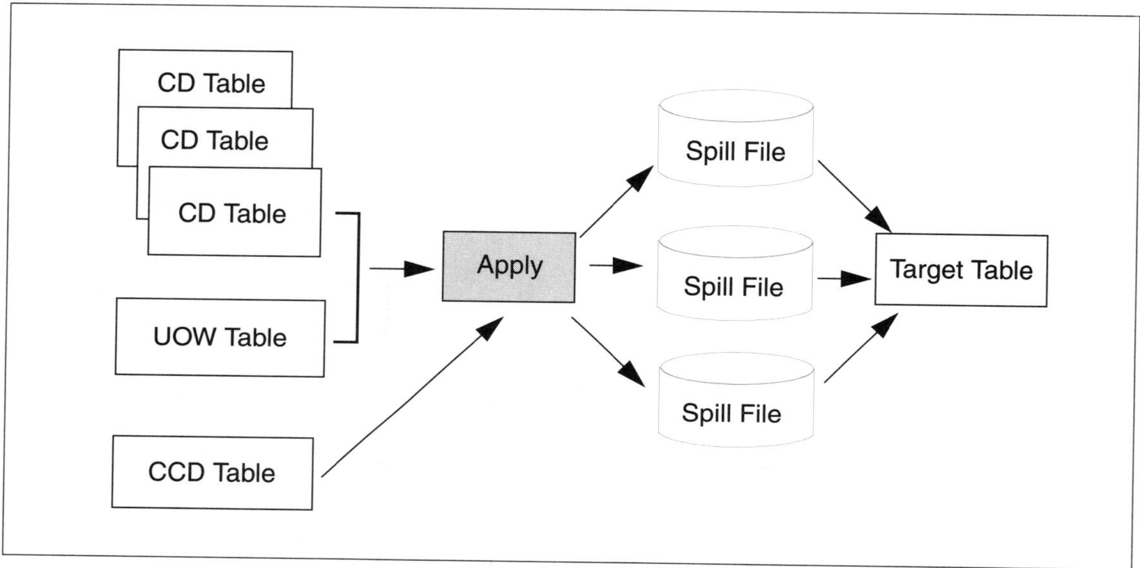

Figure 83. Data Blocking Using MAX_SYNCH_MINUTES

4.10.12.1 Change Subscription - Specify Data Blocking

To change a subscription and set a value for data blocking:

1. Select the **Replication Subscriptions** folder from the object tree. The replication subscriptions appear in the contents pane:

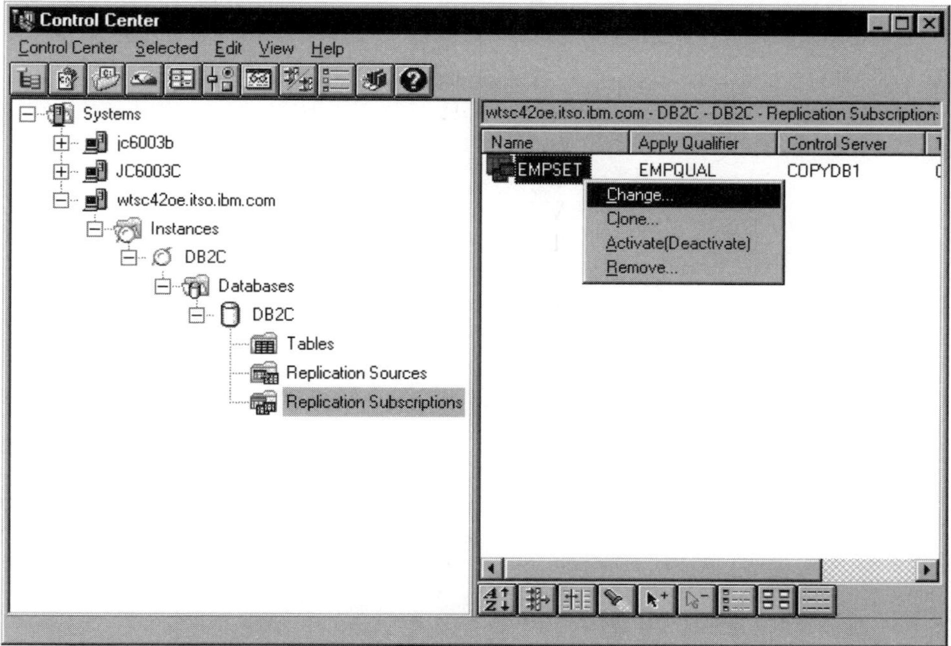

Figure 84. Change Subscription - Specify MAX_SYNCH_MINUTES

2. Right-click on the replication subscription object that you want to modify and select **Change** from pop-up menu. The Change Replication Subscription window is displayed:

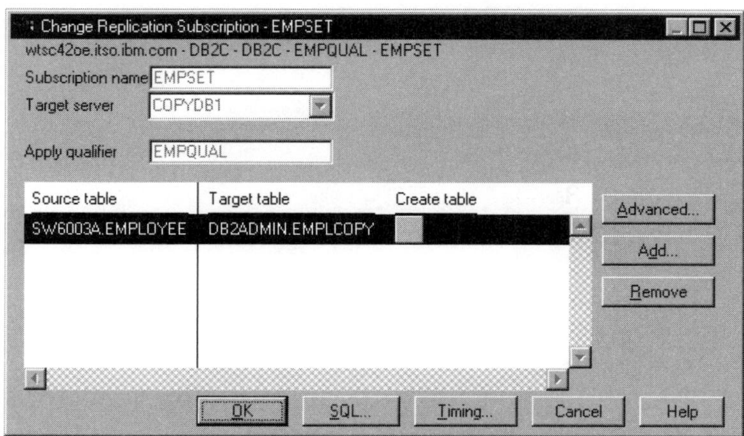

Figure 85. Change Subscription

3. Click on **Timing** and select the **Data Blocking** tab. Enter 1 minute as the value for MAX_SYNCH_MINUTES as shown here:

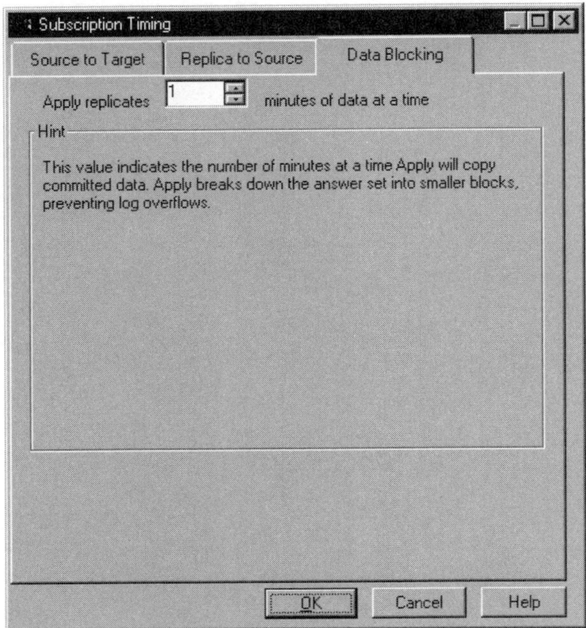

Figure 86. Change Subscription - Specify Data Blocking

4. Click on **OK** to close the panel. This takes you back to the Change Replication Subscription screen. Click on **OK** again.

5. The Save SQL file windows open. Save the file as addmaxs.sql. Click on **OK** to save this file.

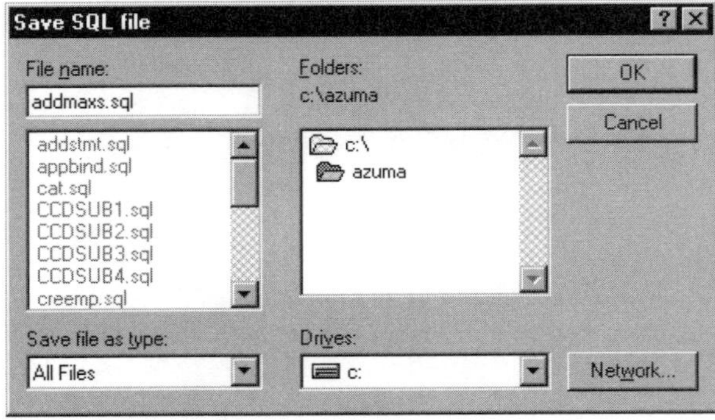

Figure 87. Change Subscription Save SQL File - Specify MAX_SYNCH_MINUTES

Use a text editor to examine this SQL file:

```
CONNECT TO COPYDB1;

DELETE FROM ASN.IBMSNAP_SUBS_SET
WHERE APPLY_QUAL = 'EMPQUAL'
  AND SET_NAME = 'EMPSET';
.........................................................
INSERT INTO ASN.IBMSNAP_SUBS_SET (
ACTIVATE, APPLY_QUAL, SET_NAME, WHOS_ON_FIRST, SOURCE_SERVER,
TARGET_SERVER, STATUS, LASTRUN, REFRESH_TIMING, SLEEP_MINUTES,
EVENT_NAME, LASTSUCCESS, SYNCHPOINT, SYNCHTIME, MAX_SYNCH_MINUTES,
AUX_STMTS, ARCH_LEVEL, SOURCE_ALIAS, TARGET_ALIAS ) VALUES (
1, 'EMPQUAL', 'EMPSET', 'S', 'DB2C', 'COPYDB1', 0,
'1998-12-01-14.43.06.000000', 'E', NULL, 'EMPEVENT',
'1998-12-01-14.43.06.000000', X'00000000539358b40000',
'1998-12-01-15.41.12.000665', 1, 1, '0201', 'DB2C', 'COPYDB1' );
.........................................................
```

Note the value of 1 for MAX_SYNCH_MINUTES. The default value is NULL. If you specify 0 in the Data Blocking panel, the default NULL value will be used for MAX_SYNCH_MINUTES.

6. Run the saved SQL file.
7. Update the source table (EMPLOYEE) at the source server (DB2C) three times:

```
UPDATE SW6003A.EMPLOYEE SET SALARY=SALARY+0.1;
---------+---------+---------+---------+---------+---------+---
DSNE615I NUMBER OF ROWS AFFECTED IS 31
DSNE616I STATEMENT EXECUTION WAS SUCCESSFUL, SQLCODE IS 0
Check the UOW LOGMARKER timestamp value as shown below
SELECT
HEX(IBMSNAP_UOWID),HEX(IBMSNAP_COMMITSEQ)
,IBMSNAP_LOGMARKER
FROM ASN.IBMSNAP_UOW WITH UR
---------+---------+---------+---------+---------+---------+-------
                                                IBMSNAP_LOGMARKER
---------+---------+---------+---------+---------+---------+-------
0000000053B1797B0000  0000000053B190340000
1998-12-02-13.00.37.910487
0000000053B1C7690000  0000000053B1DDEB0000
1998-12-02-13.03.44.173959
0000000053B228480000  0000000053B23F410000
1998-12-02-13.08.05.014167
DSNE610I NUMBER OF ROWS DISPLAYED IS 3
```

8. Start Apply with this command:

```
ASNAPPLY EMPQUAL COPYDB1 TRCFLOW NOSLEEP > MAXS.TRC
```

9. Look at the trace and perform the following SQL query to the Applytrail table. A STATUS value of 2 denotes the execution of a single logical subscription that was divided according to the value of the

MAX_SYNCH_MINUTES control column and is being serviced by multiple subscription cycles.

```
SELECT STATUS,LASTRUN,SET_UPDATED,SYNCHPOINT FROM
ASN.IBMSNAP_APPLYTRAIL ORDER BY LASTRUN;

STATUS LASTRUN                    SET_UPDATED SYNCHPOINT
------ -------------------------- ----------- ------------------
2 1998-12-02-12.57.18.406001               31 x'0000000053B190340000'
2 1998-12-02-12.57.20.796001               31 x'0000000053B1DDEB0000'
0 1998-12-02-12.57.22.843001               31 x'0000000053B23F410000'

  3 record(s) selected
```

If you specify Before/After-SQL statements or stored procedures and also use a value for MAX_SYNCH_MINUTES, these SQL statements or procedures will be run for each mini-cycle much like a regular subscription.

4.11 Summary

In this chapter, we have shown many of the features and functions of basic DB2 Replication. Our example used DB2 for OS/390 as the source server and DB2 for Windows NT as the target server.

We took you through a step by step example of setting up a replication scenario showing the various panels and options available to you. In addition, we explored the options for starting and running Capture on MVS and Apply on Windows NT.

Finally, we discussed a large number of operational considerations for both Apply and Capture that give you a good indication of the power and flexibility of the DB2 Replication product and all you can do with it.

With this information, you should feel comfortable with the DB2 Replication product in general and many of its features.

Chapter 5. Staging Tables

This chapter describes staging tables and why they are needed. An end-to-end staging table example is given, including all the commands used and any hints and tips when using staging tables.

It is important to note that the staging tables discussion in this chapter does not apply to *updateable replicas*. Please see Chapter 6, "Update-Anywhere Replication" on page 211 for a discussion on the update-anywhere scenario that deals with updateable replicas.

The implementation discussion of the various DB2 UDB features in this chapter were current at the time of writing. These may change as the product evolves, and it is important to verify the function on your particular release level of DB2 Universal Database.

5.1 Overview

In a typical replication environment, the Capture program captures changes from the database logs and then inserts the changes into the CD (Change Data) tables and the related transaction information into the UOW (Unit-Of-Work) table. The Apply program determines the committed changes by joining the CD and UOW tables and then propagates these changes to the target tables.

Having CD tables in the replication process is quite efficient because the Capture program needs to capture changes only once even though several Apply programs may be running if data is being replicated to multiple target systems. This is different from traditional message queueing, where the data is redundantly queued for each target system.

It is even more efficient to explicitly define a staging table as the join of the CD and UOW tables. In this case, the Apply program at the target system can read the changed data information from the staging table without needing to join the CD and UOW tables at each subscription cycle (see Figure 88 on page 170):

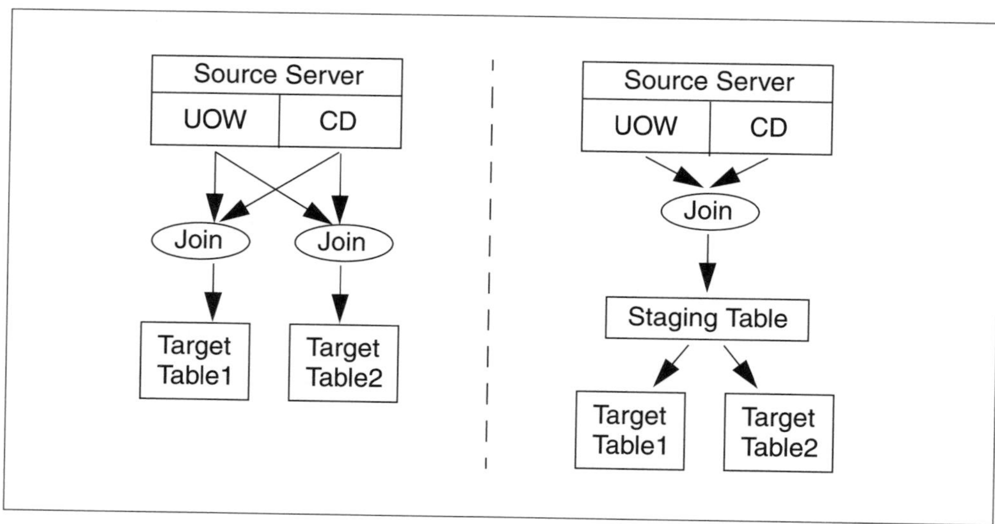

Figure 88. Using a Staging Table

Staging table attributes can differ depending on the application requirements. There are other benefits apart from eliminating the need to join the CD and UOW tables. Before going into the details of staging table configurations and their benefits, let's look at the columns in a staging table:

- IBMSNAP_INTENTSEQ: a unique identifier for the change, indicating the sequence of a change (it provides an overall ordering, not just within one transaction). This column is from the CD table.
- IBMSNAP_OPERATION: a character value of I, U, or D, indicating an insert, update, or delete. This is from the CD table.
- IBMSNAP_COMMITSEQ: a transaction commit sequencing value. This is from the UOW table.
- IBMSNAP_LOGMARKER: the approximate commit time at the source server. This is from the UOW table.
- If the staging table is non-complete, then you can optionally have additional UOW columns included in your staging table. To do this, you should choose to include UOW columns and define a primary key from the Control Center. The columns you have the option of including are:
    - IBMSNAP_UOWID: this is the ID from the log record for this unit of work.
    - IBMSNAP_AUTHTKN: the authentication token associated with the transaction. Useful for auditing purposes.

  - IBMSNAP_AUTHID: the authorization ID associated with the transaction. Also useful for auditing purposes.
  - IBMSNAP_REJ_CODE: a character value of 0, 1, 2, 3, or 4, indicating whether or not a conflict was detected, and if so, the level of conflict.
  - IBMSNAP_APPLY_QUAL: the name of the Apply program if the update was a foreign update. This will be blank if the update was local.
- User data columns: the source table columns you indicated when defining the replication source. These are from the CD table.

The simplest form of staging table is a Consistent Change Data (CCD) table. Like a CD table, a CCD table has changed data information. The difference is that a CD table doesn't have information about the transaction state, which can be committed, rolled back, or not yet decided.

A CD table can have rows from uncommitted or rolled back transactions. So before the Apply program starts to gather change data, it joins the CD and UOW tables first to make sure that only committed data is replicated. Because the CCD table is a join of the CD and UOW tables, it only contains committed changes.

Another difference is that a CCD table can be automatically registered as a replication source and can be used for another subscription if required. As we will see later, the CCD table is only automatically registered if the subscription definition specifies that it is *to be used as a source.*

Note

If Capture is started with the PRUNE option, it periodically prunes change data rows from CD tables after the changes are applied to the target table. However, CCD tables are not automatically pruned. Subscriptions that maintain CCDs can be made to prune the CCDs using SQL-after DELETE statements attached to the subscriptions.

5.1.1 Types of Staging Tables

A staging (CCD) table can be categorized by its location, its contents, and its creation sequence:

1. Its location can be *local* or *remote*:
   - A local CCD table resides in the source database server.
   - A remote CCD table is remote from the source database server.

   You can choose your staging table to be local or remote when you specify the target database in the subscription definition panel.

2. Its contents can be *complete* or *non-complete*:
   - A complete CCD table contains all the rows from the source table. Initially, all the rows from the source table are inserted into a complete CCD table. Afterwards, only the changes from source table rows are replicated.
   - A non-complete CCD table holds only the rows that have been modified in the source table. No initial full refresh is performed for a non-complete CCD table.

   You can make a CCD table complete or non-complete by selecting the **Used as source for future copies** option in the Advanced Subscription Definition panel. If you check this option, then the target table is defined as a complete CCD table and automatically registered as a replication source.

3. Its contents can be *condensed* or *non-condensed*:
   - A condensed CCD table contains only the most current value for the row; therefore it can have only one row with the same key value.
   - A non-condensed CCD table holds a history of all the changes; therefore it can have multiple rows with the same key value.

Note

Since a condensed staging table has only one row per key value, it requires a unique index. If a unique index is not defined on a condensed staging table, Apply will generate an error, and the subscription will fail.

Since a non-condensed staging table has multiple rows for the key, a unique index should not be defined on it. If one is defined, Apply will generate an error, and the subscription will fail.

If a change occurs in the source table, the Apply program replicates the change to a condensed CCD table by updating the existing row and to a non-condensed CCD table by inserting a new row.

There is no option to choose whether a CCD table is condensed or non-condensed from the DB2 UDB Control Center. You have to modify the appropriate control tables to set the condensed option. The IBMSNAP_REGISTER table in the database where the CCD table resides and the IBMSNAP_SUBS_MEMBR table in the control server have the columns that indicate whether the table is condensed or not.

Note

Complete or non-complete can be set by an option in Control Center but there is no option for condensed or non-condensed. If you choose the **Used as source for future copies** option, your staging table is set to complete and also condensed. If you do not choose that option, the staging table is set to non-complete and non-condensed. If you want any other combination, then you must modify the control tables.

4. Its creation sequence determines whether it is an *internal CCD table* or not.

   If a local staging table is the first non-complete CCD table, then it is called an internal CCD table. The second, and any subsequent CCD tables, are just local CCD tables. Only the first one is an internal CCD table.

   When an internal CCD table subscription is defined, the CCD_OWNER and CCD_TABLE columns of the row indicating the source table in the IBMSNAP_REGISTER table are updated. So, the internal CCD table information goes into the IBMSNAP_REGISTER table by updating the rows that have the source table information.

   For a local complete CCD table, information goes into the IBMSNAP_REGISTER table by inserting a new row, not by updating the existing source table row. This makes a local complete CCD table automatically registered (made a replication source), and you can see this table under the Replication Sources folder in the DB2 UDB Control Center.

   You can define another subscription directly from a local CCD table that was automatically registered, but an internal CCD table can not be used as a source explicitly in a subscription. However, the Apply program uses an internal CCD table to replicate changes instead of a CD table if an internal CCD table is defined.

Now, you should have an idea how the staging tables in your replication environment can be defined. Table 19 shows a summary of the possible combinations:

Table 19. CCD Table Attributes

Location	Complete	Condensed	Description
Local	Y	Y	- Local staging table with the same data as a user table - Defined using the Control Center
		N	- Local staging table with a complete history of changes including the original table data - Defined by modifying the control tables
	N	Y	- Local staging table with only the latest change data - Internal staging table if it is the first created - Defined by modifying the control tables
		N	- Local staging table with all change data only - Defined using the Control Center
Remote	Y	Y	- Remote staging table with the same data as a user table - Defined using the Control Center
		N	- Remote staging table with a complete history of changes including the original table data - Defined by modifying the control tables
	N	Y	- Remote staging table with only the latest changed data - Defined by modifying the control tables
		N	- Remote staging table with all changed data only - Defined using the Control Center

If you utilize the correct type of staging tables according to your requirements, your replication environment can be made more efficient and flexible. Staging tables can be used in various ways. Apart from minimizing the effect of joining the CD and UOW tables, which was explained before, here are some other benefits of staging tables:

1. Maintaining a complete history of changes.

   If a CCD table is non-condensed, then it will hold a complete history of changes.

2. Replicating data efficiently to multiple targets.

   If source data is replicated to multiple target tables over a network (a fan-out scenario), then a remote staging table can reduce the network overhead. Without a remote staging table, data has to be replicated over the network multiple times. A remote staging table can read the source table changes over the network once, and then data can be propagated locally to multiple target tables. This can greatly reduce network traffic and allow a consistent copy to be done based on the CCD and not the source table (as the source table could continually be changing). In a more complicated distributed environment, you can balance the workload across multiple databases on multiple platforms with staging tables.

3. Condense *hot-spot* updates.

   If your application performs multiple updates to one row in a short timeframe, a condensed staging table can keep only the latest value for that row and then replicate it to the target instead of replicating all the changes to the target. For example, if updates are made to one row three times within the timeframe of one Apply subscription cycle, without using a condensed staging table, Apply will replicate changed data three times for that one row. By using a condensed staging table, Apply will just replicate the (single) last change for the row. This can also reduce network traffic.

4. Can be used as another source.

   A staging table is auto-registered if it is a complete staging table, so other subscriptions can be defined using the staging table as a source table. It can be used as a source for other copies, which for example, can be used in a data warehouse or general information repository.

5. Serve as a local cache for committed changes.

   An internal CCD table can be used by the Apply program to read the changes to a table. It can be used as a local cache for committed changes.

6. Controlling the time-consistency of transactions propagated to multiple sites.

   As an example, copies at multiple remote sites are maintained using different subscriptions, avoiding the use of a distributed 2-phase-commit transaction, thus avoiding the requirement for 100 per cent network availability. The copies maintained by these independent subscriptions could be inconsistent with one another. A subscription maintaining a staging table in the path between the original source and the final target tables will regulate the transactions available for propagation to the final target tables. During periods when the staging table is stable, the similar copies on the remote sites will converge to consistency with one another even though the original source database is volatile. An infrequently-updated staging table can make a source database appear to be very stable, as new transactions only become visible when changes are propagated to the staging tables.

Examples of some of these uses are provided in "Examples of Staging Table Configurations" on page 194.

5.2 Setting Up Replication Systems Using Staging Tables

In this section, we take you through a step-by-step example of setting up replication systems using the various types of staging tables.

We use two machines in this example, one with AIX, and one with Windows NT. On the AIX server, there is a SAMPLE database that will be used as the replication source. The COPYDB1 and COPYDB2 databases on the Windows NT machine will be used as the target databases. The staging tables can reside either in SAMPLE or COPYDB1. Table 20 shows a summary of the test environment:

Table 20. Staging Table Test Machine Configuration

Machine Name	OS/DB Software	Database (Instance)	Description
jc6003b	AIX 4.3.2 UDB 5.2	SAMPLE (aixinst1)	- Used as replication source - Capture runs here - Apply runs here if Local CCD table is defined.
jc6003c	Windows NT 4.0 UDB 5.2	COPYDB1 (DB2) COPYDB2 (DB2)	- Used as replication target - Remote CCD table in COPYDB1 - Apply runs here

We first installed UDB on the AIX and Windows NT machines, and then configured a remote connection (using TCP/IP) to the SAMPLE database on AIX from the Windows NT machine.

To implement a replication environment using staging tables, we define replication sources and subscriptions as in any other replication configuration. There are some options that are specifically for staging tables that will be explained in this section.

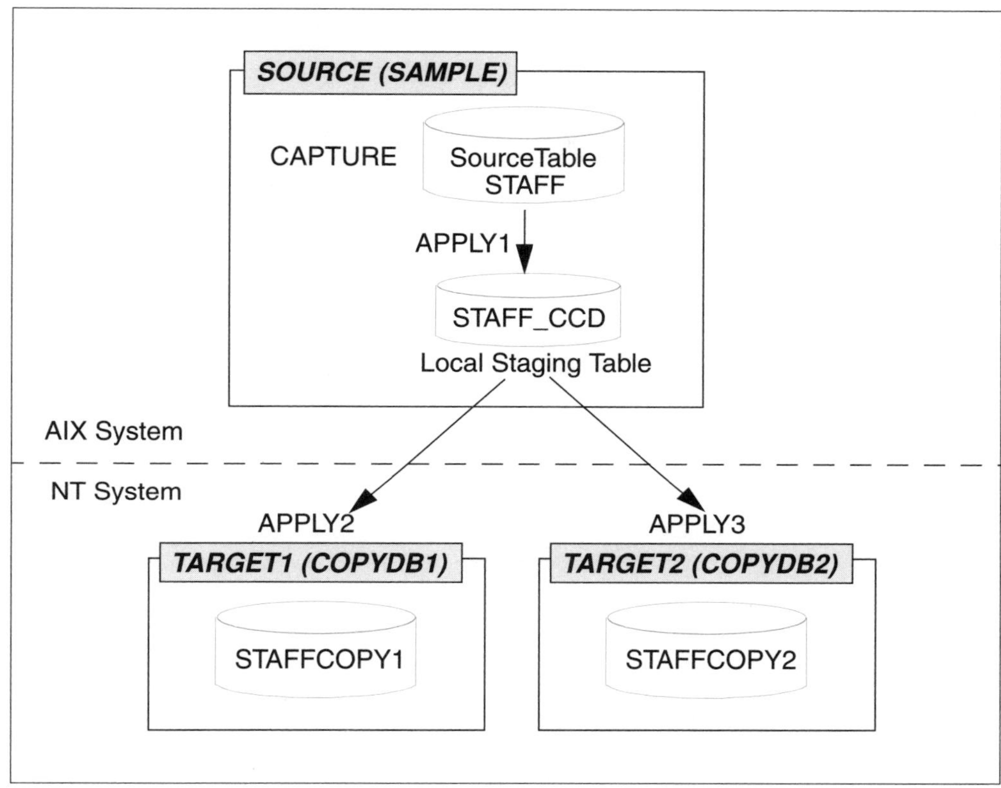

Figure 89. Replication Using a Local Complete Staging Table

As shown in Figure 89, we create a local complete condensed staging table (STAFF_CCD) in the SAMPLE database based on the STAFF table in the SAMPLE database on the AIX machine. STAFF_CCD will be replicated to the STAFFCOPY1 target table in the COPYDB1 database on the Windows NT machine and the STAFFCOPY2 target table in COPYDB2 on the same Windows NT machine.

5.2.1 Defining a Replication Source

We start by defining a replication source using the DB2 UDB Control Center:

1. Start the Control Center on the Windows NT machine and expand the object trees by clicking on **System->jc6003b->SAMPLE**. Click on the tables folder to display the list of tables in the SAMPLE database in the right pane.

2. Find the required source table (STAFF) and click the right mouse button. From the pop-up menu, select **Define as replication source->custom**, as shown in Figure 90:

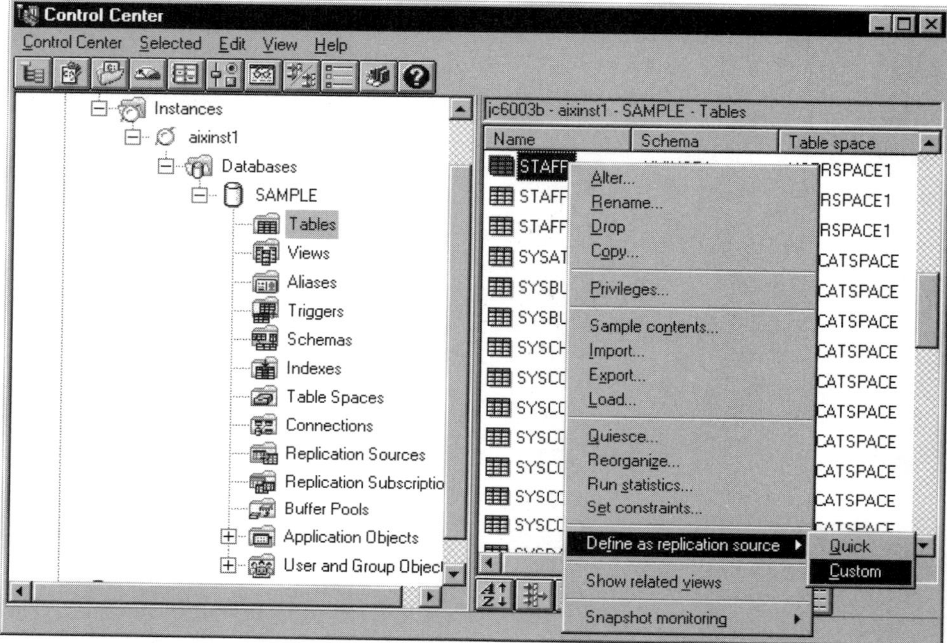

Figure 90. Defining a Custom Replication Source

The Define as a Replication Source panel is displayed:

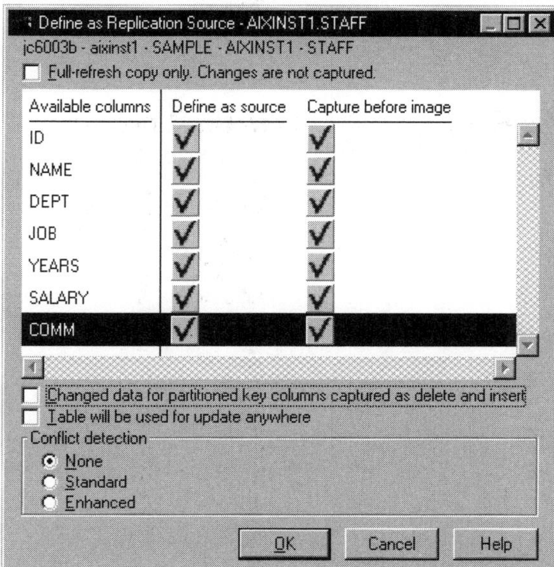

Figure 91. Define as Replication Source Panel

3. Note that, in our example, the **Define as source** and **Capture before image** check boxes are checked for all columns.
4. Make sure the update anywhere option is de-selected.
5. Select **OK** to save the options and close the window. The Run Now or Save SQL window is displayed:

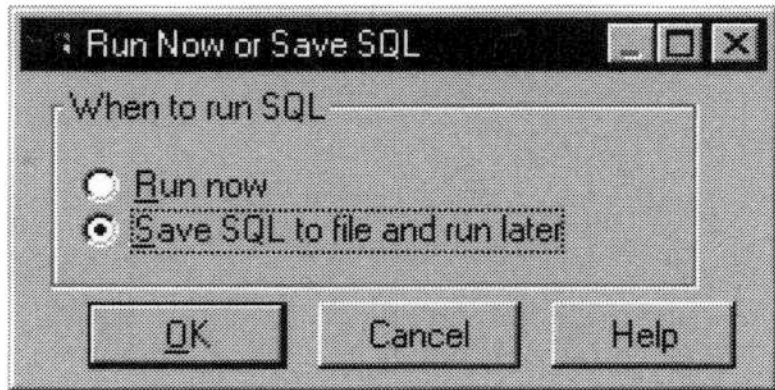

Figure 92. Run Now or Save SQL Pop-up

6. If you choose the Save SQL to file and run later option, the SQL files can be customized to enable you to create multiple copies of the same replication action, customize the CD table name, define the location of the CD table, or create table spaces.

   Select the **Save SQL to file and run later** option and click **OK**. The Save SQL file window is displayed:

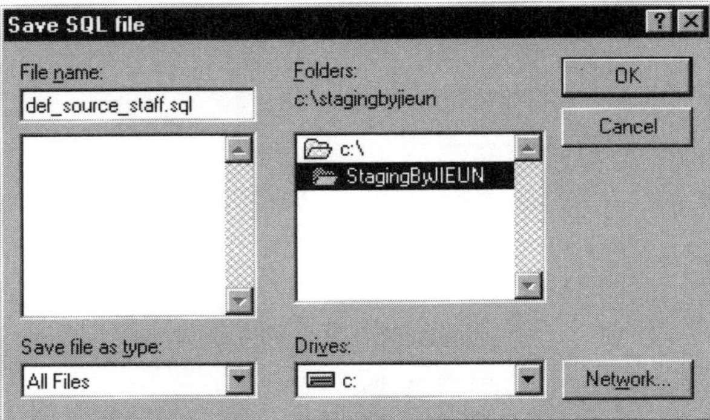

Figure 93. Define Replication Source - Save SQL File

7. Enter a file name (here, def_source_staff.sql). Click **OK** to save the SQL file. You'll get a confirmation message that the SQL file has been saved for later execution.
8. To run the saved SQL file, use the Control Center:

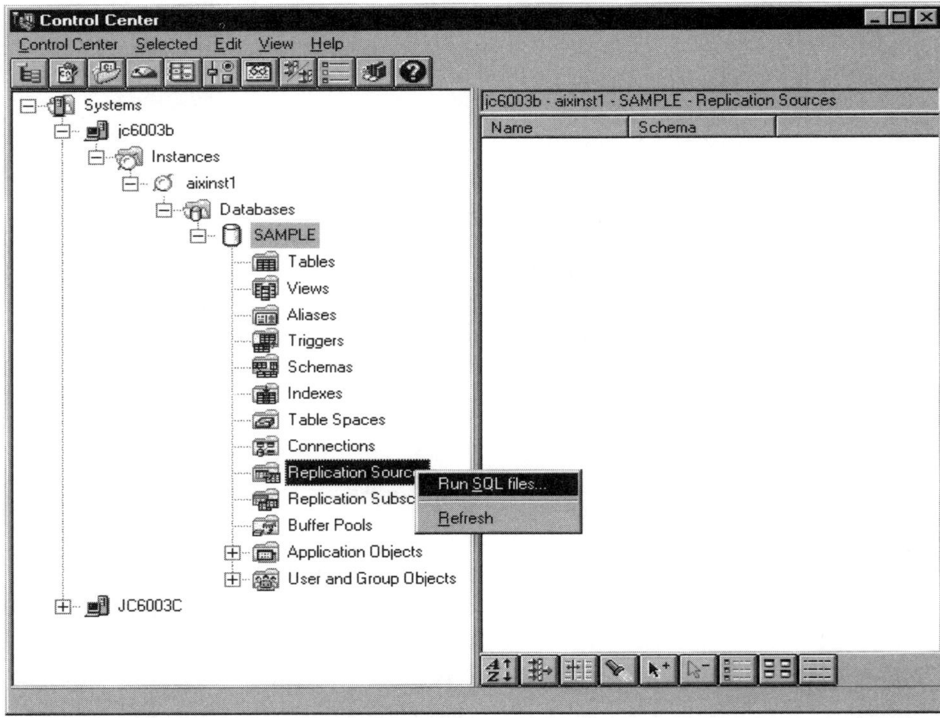

Figure 94. Replication Sources - Run SQL Files

9. As shown in Figure 94 on page 180, select **Replication sources** and click the right mouse button to display the pop-up menu. Select **Run SQL files**.

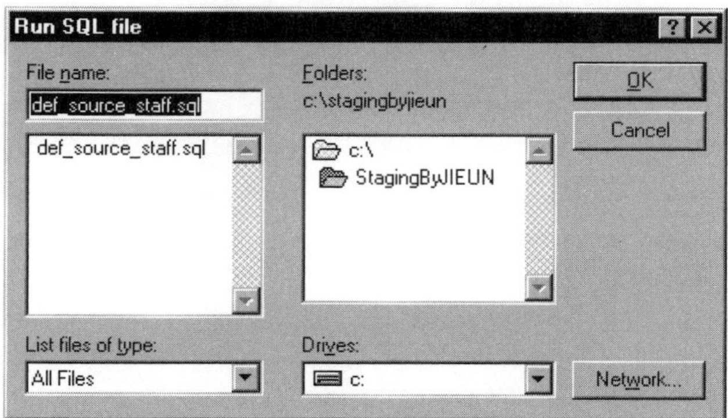

Figure 95. Choose SQL File to Run

10. Select the folder and file name (here, def_source_staff.sql). The default is the last file you saved. Click **OK** to run this file. If the SQL is not successful, then a panel is displayed showing the DB2 error message. There are many SQL statements in the SQL file and processing will stop at the first failure. Unfortunately, the error message does not indicate exactly which line caused the error. You will have to check the SQL statements that were run and correct any problems.

5.2.2 Defining a Subscription

To define a subscription, we again use the DB2 UDB Control Center.

1. Start the Control Center on the Windows NT machine and expand object trees by clicking on **System->jc6003b->SAMPLE**. Click on the **Replication Sources** folder to display the list of replication sources in the right hand pane.

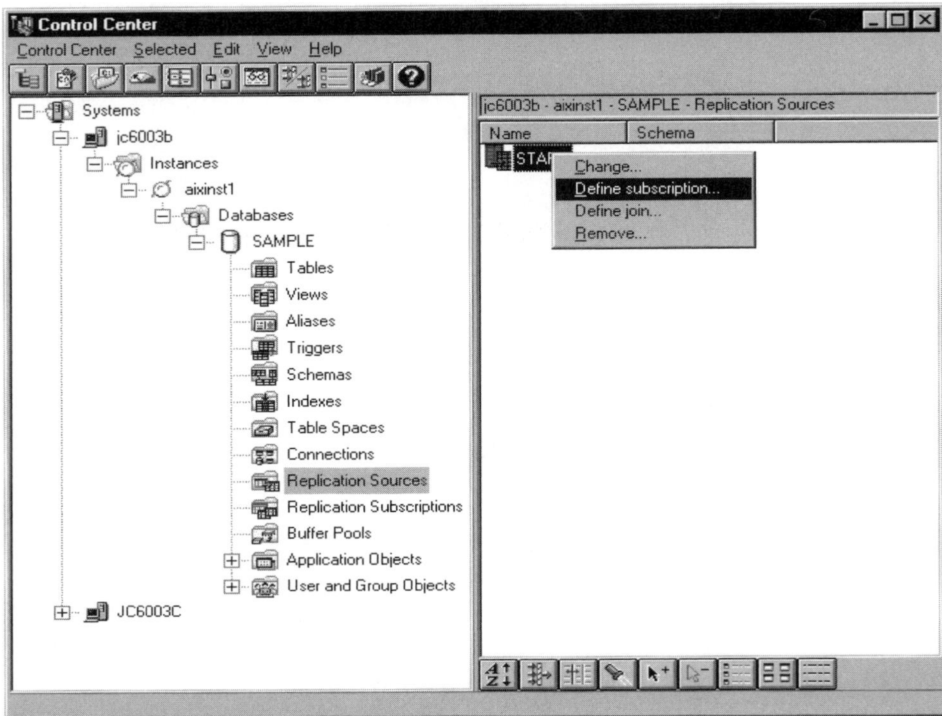

Figure 96. Define Subscription

2. Choose a replication source (here, STAFF) and click the right mouse button. Select **Define Subscription** from the pop-up menu. The Define Subscription panel is displayed:

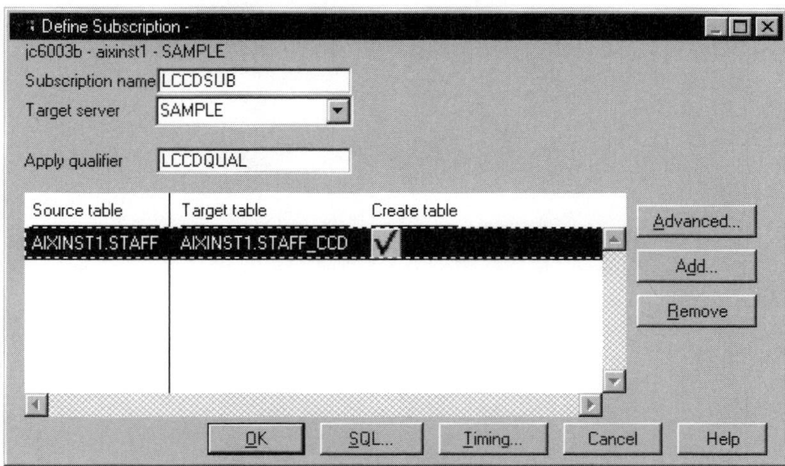

Figure 97. Define Subscription Panel

Enter a subscription name (here, LCCDSUB). This is user defined and can be up to 18 characters long.

Select a target server. In this example, this is the SAMPLE database on the AIX machine (jc6003b). The target table will be local to its source table. If you want your staging table to be remote to its source table, then select the remote database for the target server. Configuring a remote staging table is covered in "Examples of Staging Table Configurations" on page 194.

Enter an apply qualifier (here, LCCDQUAL). The apply qualifier name is always saved in upper case even when entered in lower case. This name will be used later when we run the Apply program and must be unique among all Apply processes sharing a common set of control tables.

Change the name of target table to STAFF_CCD.

Click the **Create table** check box. This will create the STAFF_CCD table in the SAMPLE database when you run this subscription definition.

Select **Advanced** to display the Advanced Subscription Definition panel:

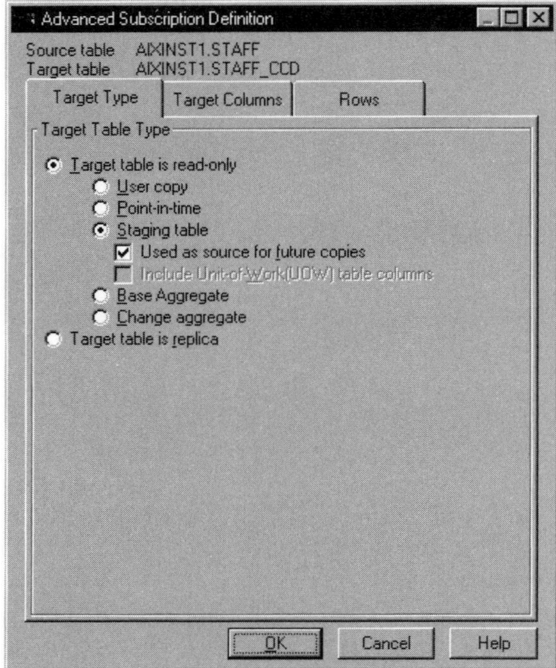

Figure 98. Advanced Subscription Definition Panel

3. Click on **Staging table** and check the **Used as source for future copies** option. This target table will be a complete and condensed staging table.

   Condensed is the default when the **Used as source for future copies** option is chosen.

   If you do not check the **Used as source for future copies** option, then the staging table will be non-complete and non-condensed.

   Non-condensed is the default when the Used as source for future copies is not chosen.

   To explicitly control whether the staging table is condensed or non-condensed, you must modify the control tables directly (rather than using the Control Center panels). Modifying the control tables is covered in "Examples of Staging Table Configurations" on page 194.

   Figure 98 shows an option to include the UOW columns. If you choose this option instead, then the target table will be a non-complete and non-condensed staging table with additional UOW columns included as discussed at the outset of this chapter.

4. Select the Target columns tab:

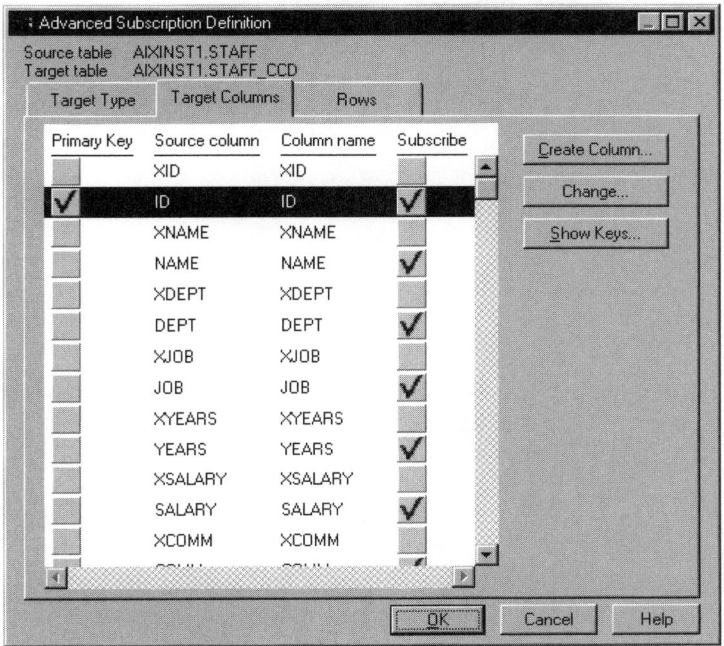

Figure 99. Define Subscription - Primary Key

Click the **Primary key** button against the ID column. Since the target table is condensed, the primary key must be checked. Failure to do this will result in Apply failing to replicate changes. Click **OK**.

If you were defining a non-condensed staging table, then you would not select a primary key in this panel.

5. Click **OK** to return to the Define Subscription panel, and click on the **Timing** button to display the Subscription Timing panel:

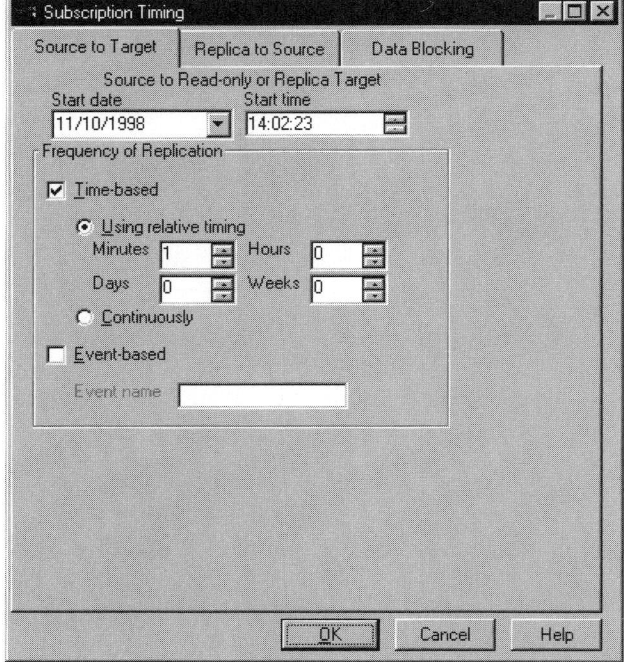

Figure 100. Define Subscription - Timing

6. As this is a test environment, change minutes to one and hours to zero. You can use the spin buttons to change these values or just overtype in the fields. The start date and time defaults to the current date and time. Click **OK**. This takes you back to the Define Subscription screen. Click **OK** again to display this panel:

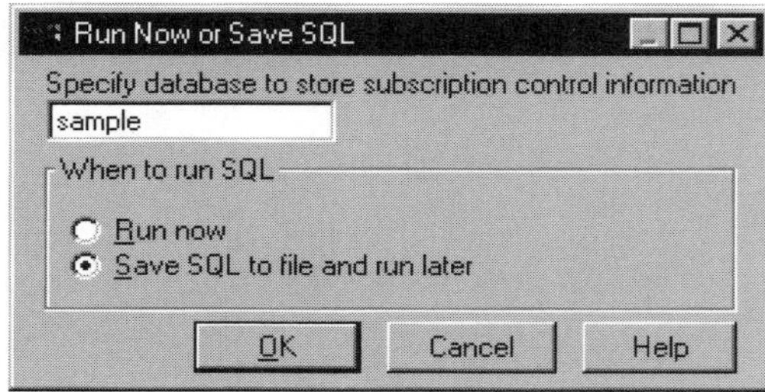

Figure 101. Define Subscription - Run Now or Save SQL

7. Enter the database name you want to use to store the subscription control information. In this example, we chose SAMPLE . In this case, the source

and target databases are both SAMPLE, which is also the control database. Select the **Save SQL to file and run later** option and click **OK**.

8. The Save SQL file window is displayed. Save the file as def_sub_staff.sql.
9. To run this SQL file, go back to the Control Center:

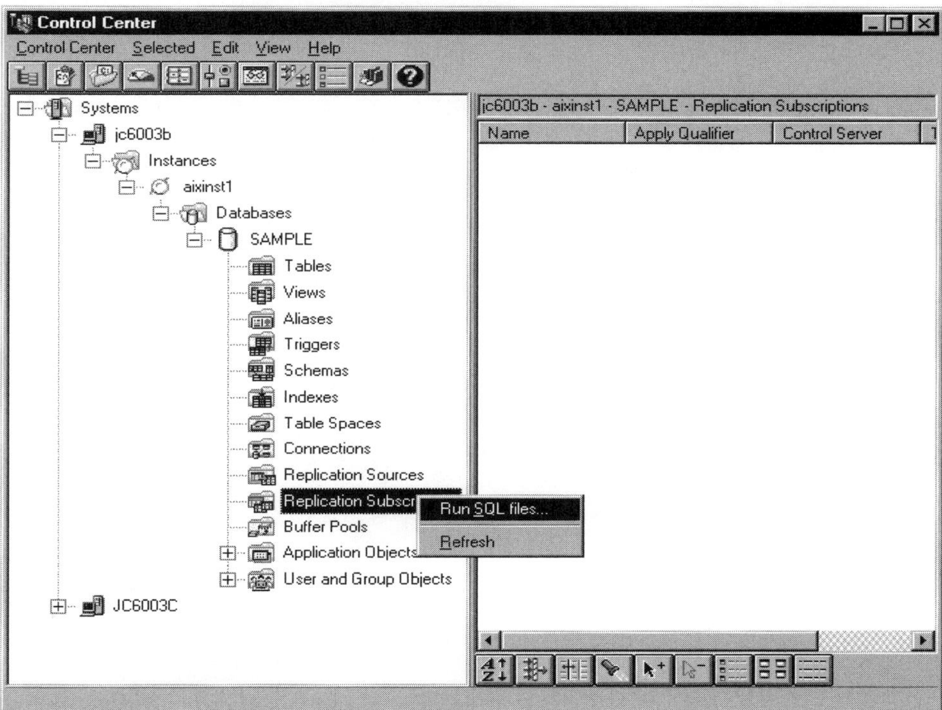

Figure 102. Define Subscription - Run SQL

10. Select **Replication Subscriptions** and click the right mouse button to display the pop-up menu. Select **Run SQL files**.

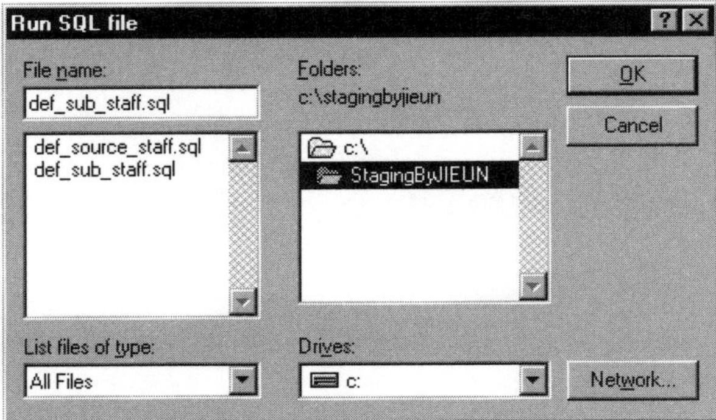

Figure 103. Define Subscription - Run SQL File

11.Select the file name you used (here, def_sub_staff.sql). Click OK to run this file. If you get any errors, check the SQL file.

12.You will find that the STAFF_CCD table is automatically defined as a replication source. Use the Control Center to check this:

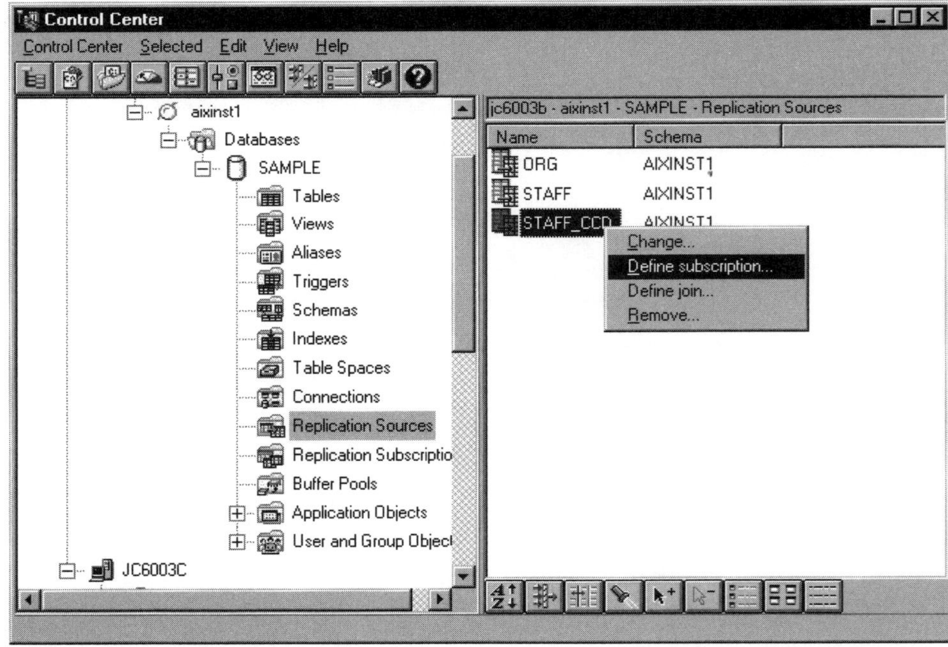

Figure 104. Define Subscription from CCD Table

13.Now we can define another subscription from this CCD table (STAFF_CCD). Select STAFF_CCD, click the right mouse button and from the pop-up menu choose **Define subscription** to display the Define Subscription panel:

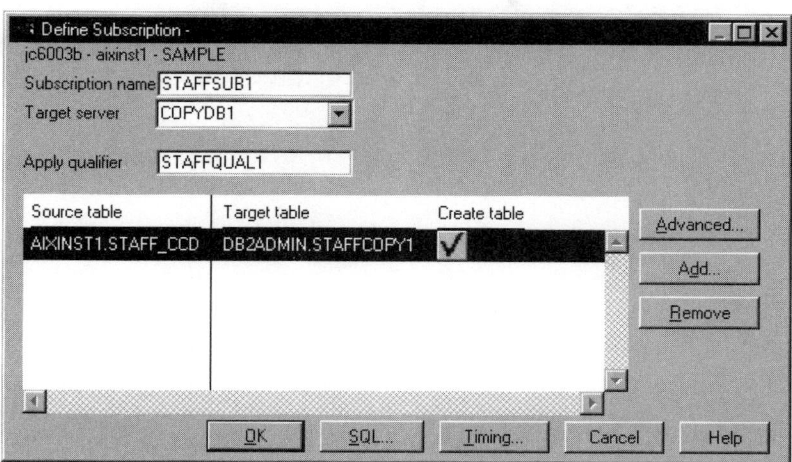

Figure 105. Define Subscription Panel

14.Fill in the values as shown. Notice that the target server is now the COPYDB1 database on the Windows NT machine. Click on **Advanced** to display the next panel:

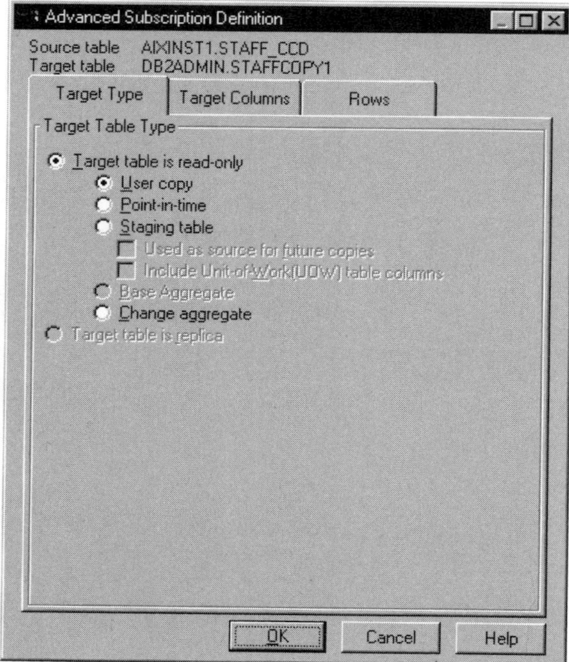

Figure 106. Define Subscription - Advanced Subscription Definition Panel

15.Click on **User copy** as the target table type.

16.In the Target Columns tab, make sure that the primary key is checked. Click **OK** twice to return to the Define Subscription panel.

17.Click on **Timing** and modify the replication interval to two minutes, as this is a test environment. Click **OK** twice to display this panel:

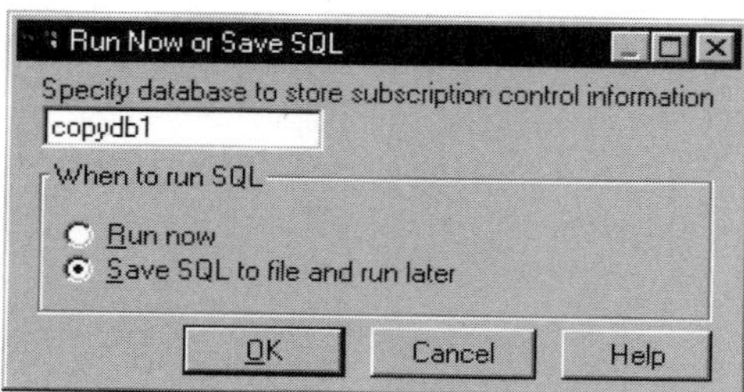

Figure 107. Define Subscription - Run Now or Save SQL

18.Enter COPYDB1 as the database to hold the subscription control information (the control server).

19. Select **OK** and save the SQL as def_sub2_staffcopy1.sql.

20. Run the SQL file as explained previously.

We do not show the steps required for the second target database. They would, however, be similar to those above.

5.2.3 Preparing Apply and Capture

Before starting the Capture and Apply programs, the following steps should be performed:

1. **Capture on the source machine**: For Capture to work, the source database must be enabled for roll-forward recovery. To do this on the master (the AIX machine), set LOGRETAIN on for the SAMPLE database. You are then obliged to perform a backup:

   ```
   $ db2 connect to sample
   $ db2 update db cfg for sample using LOGRETAIN on
   $ db2 backup database sample ...
   ```

   Bind the Capture packages. Change directory to the where the DB2 bind files are stored. On AIX, this is in the sqllib/bnd directory under the instance owner's home directory (in this case, /home/db2inst1):

   ```
   $ db2 connect to sample
   $ db2 bind @capture.lst blocking all
   ```

   If you get errors, check that the replication control tables exist in the database. These are normally created at the first subscription definition.

2. **Apply on the source machine**: Bind the necessary Apply packages to the source server. Make sure you are in the sqllib/bnd directory under the DB2 instance owner's home directory:

   ```
   $ db2 connect to sample user aixinst1 using aixinst1
   $ db2 bind @applycs.lst isolation cs blocking all
   $ db2 bind @applyur.lst isolation ur blocking all
   ```

   In this case, no Apply password file is needed. If a database that Apply needs to connect to (either the source, target, or control database) needs a userid and password, an Apply password file must be created, and the Apply program must be run from the directory in which this password file is stored. This file is used by the Apply program to connect to the databases explicitly. This is the case for the target machine.

3. **Apply on the target machine**: Bind the necessary Apply packages to each server:

   ```
   C:\ db2 connect to sample user aixinst1 using aixinst1
   C:\ db2 bind @applycs.lst isolation cs blocking all
   ```

```
C:\ db2 bind @applyur.lst isolation ur blocking all
C:\ db2 connect to copydb1
C:\ db2 bind @applycs.lst isolation cs blocking all
C:\ db2 bind @applyur.lst isolation ur blocking all
```

If necessary, create an Apply password file. If the Apply program needs a user and password to connect to a remote database, the user and password are stored in this file. The Apply program must be started from the directory in which the password file is stored. In this example, we use C:\RBJ. Use a text editor to create this file or enter the following in a DOS window:

```
copy con STAFFQUAL1DB2COPYDB1.PWD
SERVER=SAMPLE USER=aixinst1 PWD=aixinst1
(ctrl-z)
```

The name of this file is a concatenation of the following:

- Apply qualifier (STAFFQUAL1) in upper case.
- Instance name at the Windows NT (target/replica) machine (DB2).
- Name of the Control database (COPYDB1) in upper case.
- Extension .PWD.

The contents are as follows:

- SERVER=<value>. The name of database for Apply to connect to. In this case, this is SAMPLE, the database at the AIX server, in upper case. If it is not in upper case, Apply will stop with a connection failure error.
- USER=<value>. The user to connect with.
- PWD=<value>. The password to connect with.

5.2.4 Running Capture and Apply

Go to the AIX machine and start the Capture program. First, ensure that you have correctly set the DB2INSTANCE environment variable to the instance containing the source database. You may also optionally choose to set the DB2DBDFT variable to the source database. Then you issue the following command:

```
$ asnccp sample
```

where `sample` is the name of source/master database. Please note that, depending on your situation, you may wish to use the WARM start option when starting Capture.

If you are not returned to the operating system prompt, then Capture is working. If you are returned to the prompt, then you should run Capture with trace activated:

```
$ asnccp sample trace > trace.out
```

At the AIX machine, start the Apply program. Ensure the DB2INSTANCE environment variable is set correctly. Once again you may optionally set the DB2DBDFT variable to point to the database where Apply's control tables are to be found (if you do set this, then the optional positional second parameter is not required). Change directory to the directory that holds the password file (if used) then enter:

```
$ asnapply LCCDQUAL sample
```

This Apply process is for the CCD table replication. If you are not returned to the operating system prompt, then Apply is working. If you are returned to the prompt, then you should run Apply with trace activated:

```
$ asnapply LCCDQUAL sample trcflow > trcflow.out
```

Make sure the Apply qualifier is in upper case. If you type this in lower case, the Apply program will not find any matching subscription definition.

At the Windows NT machine, switch to another MS-DOS Command Window and prepare to start the Apply program for that system. Change directory to the directory that holds the password file and enter this command:

```
C:\RBJ\ asnapply STAFFQUAL1 copydb1
```

This Apply process is for the target table replication. If you are not returned to the operating system prompt, then Apply is working. If you are returned to the prompt, then you should run Apply with trace activated:

```
C:\RBJ\ asnapply STAFFQUAL1 copydb1 trcflow > trcflow.out
```

Make sure that the Apply qualifier is in upper case. If you type this in lower case, the Apply program will not find any matching subscription definition.

Similarly, you will want to start an Apply process for your second database and target table.

5.2.5 Testing the Configuration

Make a change to the source table (STAFF) in SAMPLE. For example, let's update a row in the STAFF table:

```
$ db2 "update staff set comm=300.00 where id=10"
DB20000I  The SQL command completed successfully.
```

Check that the change has been replicated to the staging table (STAFF_CCD) in SAMPLE and also to the target tables (STAFFCOPY1 and STAFFCOPY2) on the Windows NT machine. The STAFF_CCD table and the

STAFFCOPY1 and STAFFCOPY2 tables should have the same data as the source table (STAFF).

5.3 Examples of Staging Table Configurations

Three kinds of staging table configurations are covered here, based on where the staging tables reside and the options selected in the subscription definition. This section describes:

- How these staging tables are defined: using the Control Center or manually.
- What happens when you run a subscription definition.
- How the staging table can be used.

5.3.1 Internal Staging Table (Non-Complete and Condensed)

Since this is the first, local, non-complete staging table, this staging table is called the internal CCD table.

To define a staging table as an internal CCD table, follow the steps described in “Setting Up Replication Systems Using Staging Tables” on page 176. Only the differences will be explained here.

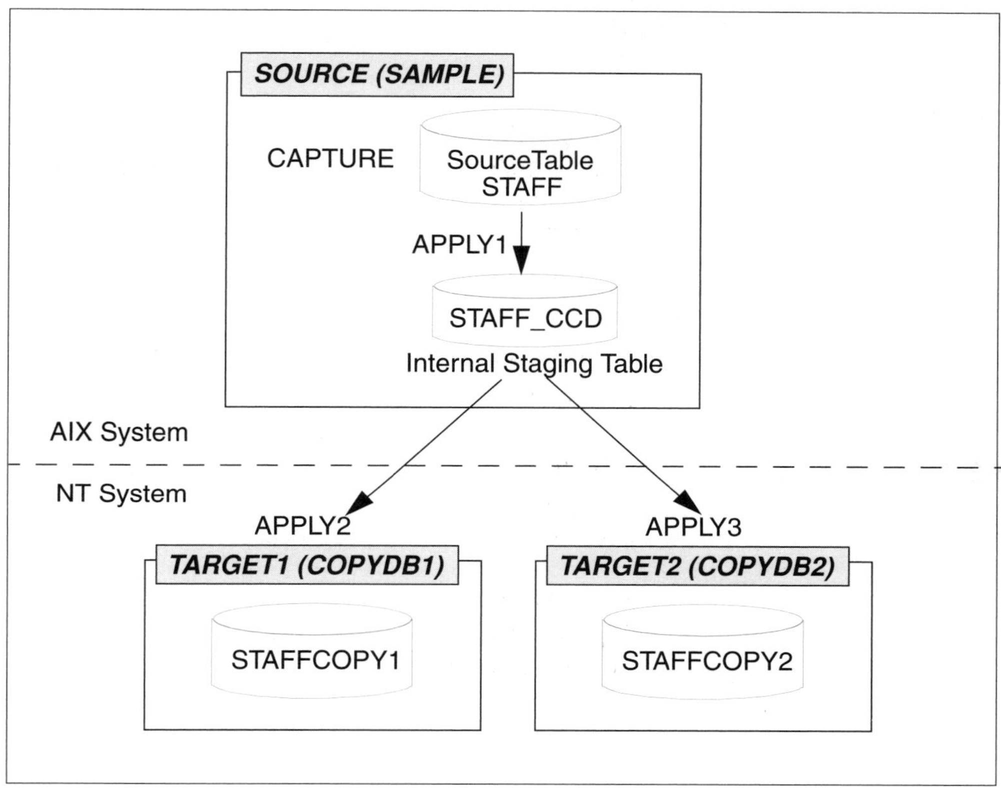

Figure 108. Replication Using an Internal Staging Table

For this example, we only take you through the steps for the first target table on the COPYDB1 database. Similar steps would be used for the second target table on COPYDB2. Here are the steps that are specific to creating an internal CCD table:

1. Once the STAFF table has been defined as a replication source, we must define a subscription using the STAFF table as the source with the following options:

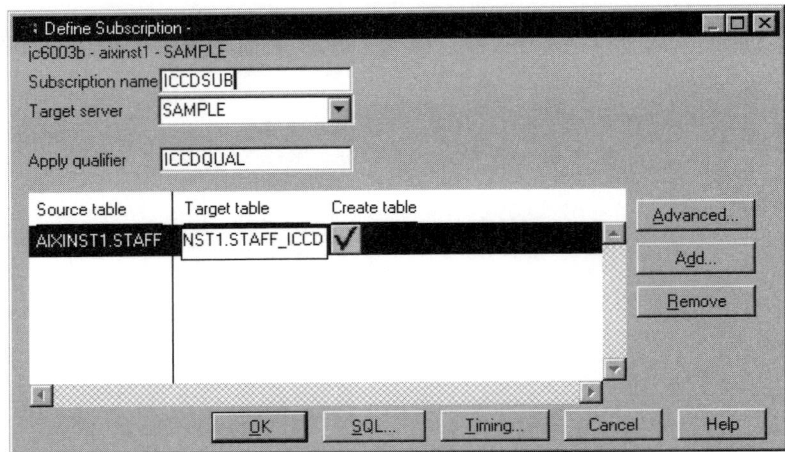

Figure 109. Define Subscription Panel - Internal CCD

2. As this is an internal CCD table, the target server is SAMPLE, which is the database that holds the source table.

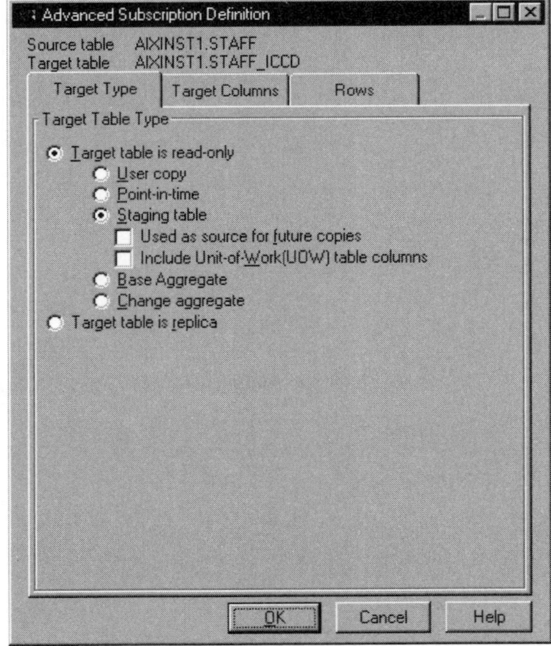

Figure 110. Define Subscription - Advanced for Internal CCD

3. As shown in Figure 110 on page 196, the target table type is **Staging table** and the **Used as source for future copies** option is *not* selected. This target table will be a non-complete staging table.
4. In the Target Columns tab, make sure the primary key is checked. This means that later we can make this table a condensed staging table.
5. Enter SAMPLE for your control database.
6. After you save this subscription definition as an SQL file, open the SQL file with an editor. Let's go through the relevant sections:

- Part One:

```
CONNECT TO SAMPLE;

UPDATE ASN.IBMSNAP_REGISTER
SET CCD_OWNER = 'AIXINST1', CCD_TABLE = 'STAFF_ICCD',
CCD_CONDENSED = 'N', CCD_COMPLETE = 'N'
WHERE SOURCE_OWNER = 'AIXINST1' AND SOURCE_TABLE = 'STAFF';
```

  This shows an update to the IBMSNAP_REGISTER table for the row that holds the source definition for the STAFF table. This is done so that Apply can identify that the STAFF table has an internal CCD table.

  You can see 'N' as the value for the CCD_CONDENSED and CCD_COMPLETE columns. CCD_COMPLETE is 'N' because we did not check the 'Used as source for future copies' option in the subscription definition. CCD_CONDENSED is 'N' because that is the default when CCD_COMPLETE is 'N'.

  Since, in this example, the staging table will be non-complete and condensed, you should modify the value of CCD_CONDENSED from 'N' to 'Y'.

  The staging table in this example is an internal CCD table that is the first, local, non-complete CCD table. However, other local CCD table subscriptions do not generate a statement like this, but insert a new row into the IBMSNAP_REGISTER table.

- Part two:

```
INSERT INTO ASN.IBMSNAP_SUBS_SET (
ACTIVATE, APPLY_QUAL, SET_NAME, WHOS_ON_FIRST,
SOURCE_SERVER, TARGET_SERVER, STATUS, LASTRUN, REFRESH_TIMING,
SLEEP_MINUTES, EVENT_NAME, LASTSUCCESS, SYNCHPOINT,
SYNCHTIME, MAX_SYNCH_MINUTES, AUX_STMTS, ARCH_LEVEL,
SOURCE_ALIAS, TARGET_ALIAS )
) VALUES (
1, 'ICCDQUAL', 'ICCDSUB', 'S', 'SAMPLE', 'SAMPLE',
0, '1998-11-12-15.50.28.000000', 'R', 1, NULL,
'1998-11-12-15.50.28.000000', NULL, NULL, NULL, 0,
'0201', 'SAMPLE', 'SAMPLE' );
```

The above statement inserts a row into the IBMSNAP_SUBS_SET table for the subscription set that was defined using the Control Center.

```
INSERT INTO ASN.IBMSNAP_SUBS_MEMBR (
APPLY_QUAL, SET_NAME, WHOS_ON_FIRST, SOURCE_OWNER,
SOURCE_TABLE, SOURCE_VIEW_QUAL, TARGET_OWNER, TARGET_TABLE,
TARGET_CONDENSED, TARGET_COMPLETE, TARGET_STRUCTURE,
PREDICATES
) VALUES (
'ICCDQUAL', 'ICCDSUB', 'S', 'AIXINST1', 'STAFF', 0,
'AIXINST1', 'STAFF_ICCD', 'N', 'N', 3, NULL);
```

Next, one row is inserted into the IBMSNAP_SUBS_MEMBR table, which holds information about the individual members and target tables defined in the subscription set.

Note the values of the TARGET_COMPLETE and TARGET_CONDENSED columns. Since this staging table is non-complete and condensed, you should change the value of TARGET_CONDENSED from 'N' to 'Y'.

The value of the TARGET_STRUCTURE column is 3, which means a staging table.

```
INSERT INTO ASN.IBMSNAP_SUBS_COLS (
APPLY_QUAL, SET_NAME, WHOS_ON_FIRST, TARGET_OWNER, TARGET_TABLE,
COL_TYPE, TARGET_NAME, IS_KEY, COLNO, EXPRESSION
) VALUES (
'ICCDQUAL', 'ICCDSUB', 'S', 'AIXINST1', 'STAFF_ICCD', 'A',
'ID', 'Y', 0, 'ID');
```

In this statement, one row is inserted into the IBMSNAP_SUBS_COL table, which contains information about a subscription column being copied. There is one row inserted for each column in the STAFF table. In this case, since the STAFF table has seven columns, seven rows are inserted with a total of seven insert statements.

- Part three:

```
INSERT INTO ASN.IBMSNAP_PRUNCNTL (
TARGET_SERVER, TARGET_OWNER, TARGET_TABLE, SYNCHTIME,
SYNCHPOINT, SOURCE_OWNER, SOURCE_TABLE, SOURCE_VIEW_QUAL,
APPLY_QUAL, SET_NAME, CNTL_SERVER, TARGET_STRUCTURE,
CNTL_ALIAS
) VALUES (
'SAMPLE', 'AIXINST1', 'STAFF_ICCD', NULL, NULL, 'AIXINST1',
'STAFF', 0, 'ICCDQUAL', 'ICCDSUB', 'SAMPLE', 3, 'SAMPLE');
```

One row is inserted in the IBMSNAP_PRUNCNTL table, which has a timestamp with a log address. Apply uses this row to trigger Capture and coordinate the CD and UOW table pruning. Here, TARGET_STRUCTURE is again 3, which means staging table.

- Part four:

```
CREATE TABLE AIXINST1.STAFF_ICCD (
IBMSNAP_INTENTSEQ CHAR ( 10 ) FOR BIT DATA NOT NULL,
IBMSNAP_OPERATION CHAR ( 1 ) NOT NULL,
IBMSNAP_COMMITSEQ CHAR ( 10 ) FOR BIT DATA NOT NULL,
IBMSNAP_LOGMARKER TIMESTAMP NOT NULL,
ID SMALLINT NOT NULL, NAME VARCHAR ( 9 ), DEPT SMALLINT,
JOB CHAR ( 5 ), YEARS SMALLINT, SALARY DECIMAL ( 7, 2 ),
COMM DECIMAL ( 7, 2 ) ,PRIMARY KEY ( ID ) );
```

This is the target table (STAFF_ICCD) creation statement.

Look at the table structure. It looks like a normal user table except for the columns whose names start with IBMSNAP.

IBMSNAP_INTENTSEQ is a unique identifier of changes. IBMSNAP_OPERATION can have a value of 'I','U' or 'D' indicating an insert, update or delete operation. IBMSNAP_COMMITSEQ is a transaction commit sequence value. IBMSNAP_LOGMARKER is the approximate commit time at the source server. Data in these columns comes from the join of the CD and UOW tables.

The primary key is defined because we chose this in the subscription definition. If the table does not have a primary key (or unique index), Apply processing will fail as it expects a primary key for a condensed staging table.

7. Since the SQL file is now modified, save the changes and run the saved SQL file from the DB2 UDB Control Center.

You can now see this subscription in the list of replication subscriptions in the Control Center. However, you cannot define another subscription directly using this internal CCD table. It does not appear in the list of replication sources. What you can do is to create another subscription using the STAFF table as the source. Since the IBMSNAP_REGISTER table has a row indicating that an internal CCD table (STAFF_ICCD) exists for the STAFF table, Apply will use it later.

8. Define another subscription using the STAFF table as source and STAFF_COPY1 as target in the COPYDB1 database on the Windows NT machine and run the SQL to generate this subscription.

9. Start Capture on the source machine (AIX):

```
$ asnccp sample
```

   Start Apply on the source machine (AIX):

```
$ asnapply ICCDQUAL sample
```

   Start Apply on the target machine (Windows NT). You may need to create an Apply password file first:

```
c:\ asnapply STAFFICCDQUAL1 copydb1
```

10. Make some changes to the STAFF table (the source table). For example, issue the following update statements:

```
$ db2 "update staff set comm=300.00 where id=30"
$ db2 "update staff set comm=310.00 where id=30"
```

   Make sure that the two statements above are both successfully executed and the STAFF table has value of 310.00 for COMM where ID is 30.

   The following tables show snapshots of some of the important columns in the CD, UOW, and internal CCD tables after the Apply subscription cycle has finished. You can also see the contents of the target table after replication.

Table 21. CD Table in AIX Server

	IBMSNAP_ UOWID	IBMSNAP_ INTENSEQ	IBMSNAP_ OPERATION	ID	XCOMM	COMM
1	x'1029'	x'E344F4'	U	30	-	300.00
2	x'1058'	x'E34798	U	30	300.00	310.00

Table 22. UOW Table in AIX Server

	IBMSNAP_ UOWID	IBMSNAP_ COMMITSEQ	IBMSNAP_ LOGMARKER	IBMSNAP_ REJ_CODE
3	x'1029'	'E34586'	1998-11-12-18.24.30	0
4	x'1058'	'E3482A'	1998-11-12-18.24.37	0

Table 23. CCD Table in AIX server - Internal Staging Table

	IBMSNAP_ INTENTSEQ	IBMSNAP_ OPERATION	IBMSNAP_ COMMITSEQ	IBMSNAP_ LOGMARKER	ID	COMM
5	x'E34798'	U	x'E3482A'	1998-11-12-18.24.37	30	310.00

Table 24. Target table (STAFF_COPY1) in Windows NT Server

	ID	NAME	DEPT	JOB	SALARY	COMM
6	30	Marenghi	38	Mgr	30	310.00

The CD and UOW tables have two rows indicating that two updates have been completed successfully (rows 1, 2, 3, and 4 in Table 21 and Table 22). Let's look at the internal CCD table (STAFF_ICCD) shown in Table 23. You can see that the data in the STAFF_ICCD table comes from the CD and UOW tables. Since this CCD table is a non-complete and condensed staging table, it only contains the last successful update for the source row (row 5 in Table 23). The target table has 310.00 for Marenghi's commission (COMM in row 6 in Table 24). Apply at the target machine does not have to join the CD and UOW tables during each Apply cycle. It can get the changed data from the CCD table.

An internal staging table can be used as a local cache for committed changes. Users cannot define subscriptions directly from an internal CCD table, but the Apply program will use an internal CCD table (if it exists) instead of a CD table in its subscription cycle. Since this table is condensed, our internal CCD table contains only last the successful change for each row of the source table.

5.3.2 Remote Staging Table (Complete and Condensed)

To define a remote staging table that is complete and condensed, follow the basic steps described in “Setting Up Replication Systems Using Staging Tables” on page 176. The only differences are in the target server and control server name. In this example, the ORG table in the SAMPLE database will be used as the replication source.

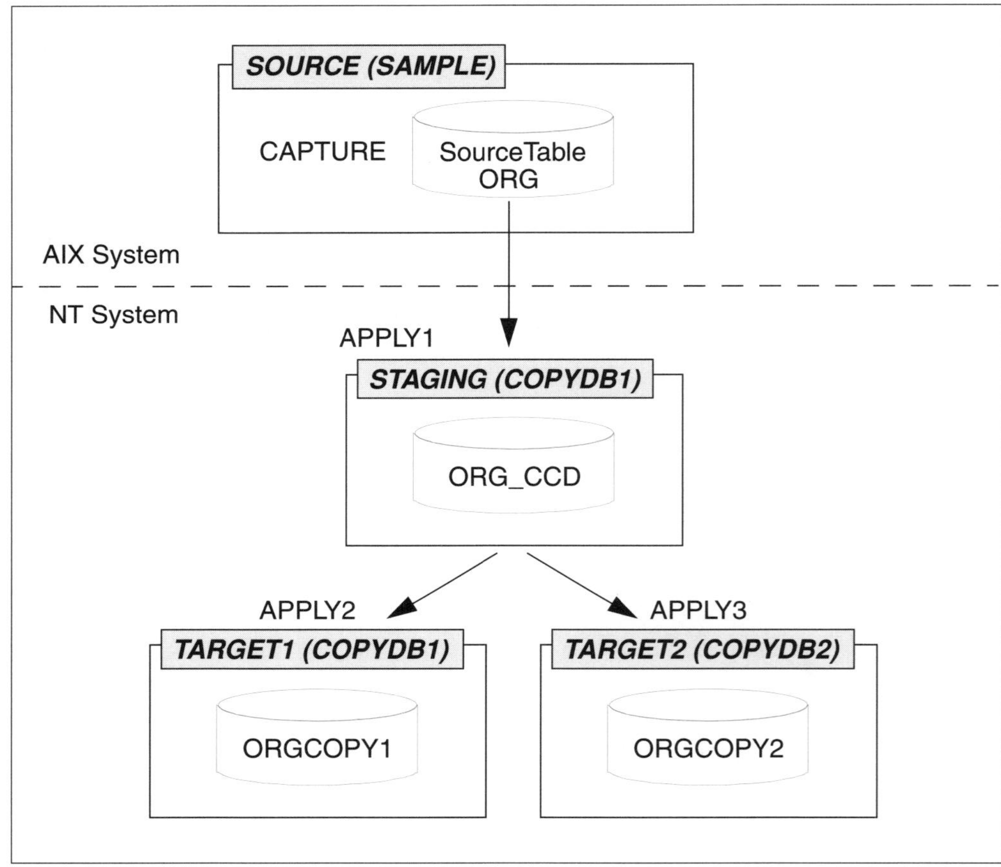

Figure 111. Replication with a Remote Staging Table

1. Define the ORG table as a replication source as previously described.

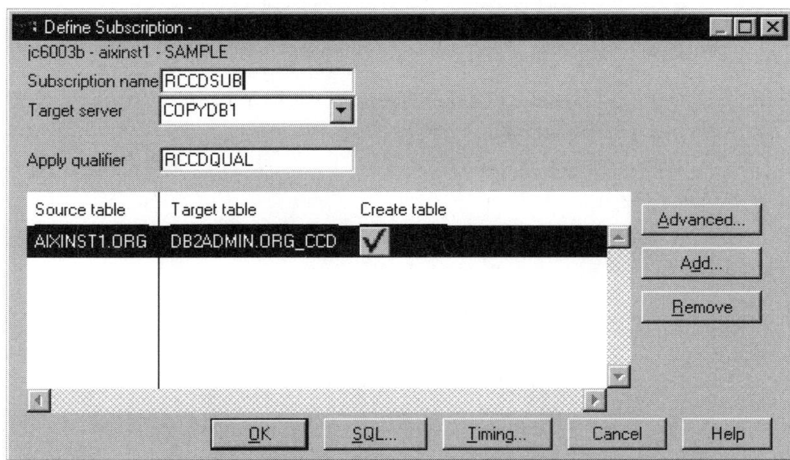

Figure 112. Define Subscription Panel

2. Define a subscription using the values shown in Figure 112. Note that the target server is COPYDB1, which is remote to the source server.

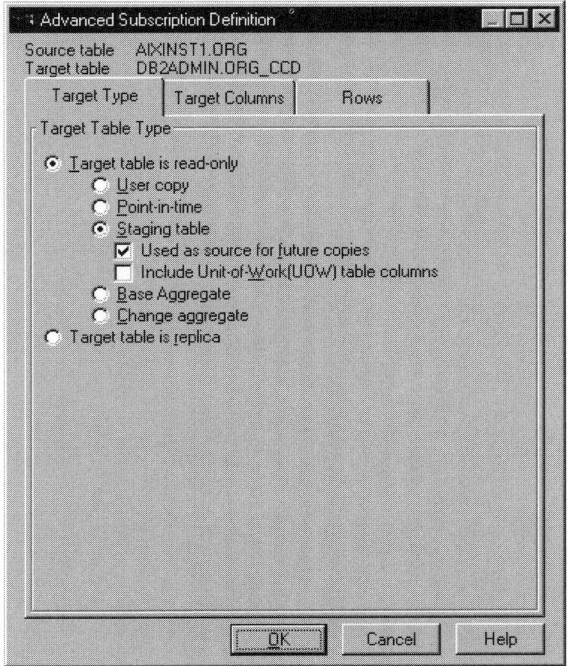

Figure 113. Define Subscription - Advanced

3. The target table type is **Staging table** and **Used as source for future copies** should be checked. This target table is going to be a complete staging table.
4. In the Target Columns tab, make sure the primary key is checked so that the Apply processing will be successful (Apply expects a primary or unique key for a condensed table). This key value will be used when creating the target table and also used by Apply to know which column(s) is the key value.
5. Use COPYDB1 for your control server.

After you save this subscription definition in an SQL file, open the SQL file with an text editor to examine the contents:

- Part one:

```
CONNECT TO COPYDB1;

INSERT INTO ASN.IBMSNAP_SUBS_SET (
ACTIVATE, APPLY_QUAL, SET_NAME, WHOS_ON_FIRST, SOURCE_SERVER,
TARGET_SERVER, STATUS, LASTRUN, REFRESH_TIMING, SLEEP_MINUTES,
EVENT_NAME, LASTSUCCESS, SYNCHPOINT, SYNCHTIME, MAX_SYNCH_MINUTES,
AUX_STMTS, ARCH_LEVEL, SOURCE_ALIAS, TARGET_ALIAS
) VALUES (
1, 'RCCDQUAL', 'RCCDSUB', 'S', 'SAMPLE', 'COPYDB1', 0,
'1998-11-10-18.23.38.000000', 'R', 1, NULL,
'1998-11-10-18.23.38.000000',
NULL, NULL, NULL, 0, '0201', 'SAMPLE', 'COPYDB1' );
```

```
INSERT INTO ASN.IBMSNAP_SUBS_MEMBR (
APPLY_QUAL, SET_NAME, WHOS_ON_FIRST, SOURCE_OWNER, SOURCE_TABLE,
SOURCE_VIEW_QUAL, TARGET_OWNER, TARGET_TABLE, TARGET_CONDENSED,
TARGET_COMPLETE, TARGET_STRUCTURE, PREDICATES
) VALUES (
'RCCDQUAL', 'RCCDSUB', 'S', 'AIXINST1', 'ORG', 0, 'DB2ADMIN',
'ORG_CCD', 'Y', 'Y', 3, NULL);
```

```
INSERT INTO ASN.IBMSNAP_SUBS_COLS (
APPLY_QUAL, SET_NAME, WHOS_ON_FIRST, TARGET_OWNER, TARGET_TABLE,
COL_TYPE, TARGET_NAME, IS_KEY, COLNO, EXPRESSION
) VALUES (
'RCCDQUAL', 'RCCDSUB', 'S', 'DB2ADMIN', 'ORG_CCD',
'A', 'DEPTNUMB', 'Y', 0, 'DEPTNUMB');
```

First, a connection is made to the control database (COPYDB1), which is the target server also.

Next, subscription information is inserted into the control tables. Look at the insert statement for IBMSNAP_SUBS_MEMBR. The TARGET_COMPLETE column has a value 'Y' because we checked the 'Used as source for future copies' option. TARGET_CONDENSED is also 'Y' because this is the default when TARGET_COMPLETE is 'Y'. The value of TARGET_STRUCTURE column is 3, which means a staging table. So, this target table is a complete and condensed staging table.

- Part two:

```
CREATE TABLE DB2ADMIN.ORG_CCD (
IBMSNAP_INTENTSEQ CHAR ( 10 ) FOR BIT DATA NOT NULL,
IBMSNAP_OPERATION CHAR ( 1 ) NOT NULL,
IBMSNAP_COMMITSEQ CHAR ( 10 ) FOR BIT DATA NOT NULL,
IBMSNAP_LOGMARKER TIMESTAMP NOT NULL,
DEPTNUMB SMALLINT NOT NULL, DEPTNAME VARCHAR ( 14 ),
MANAGER SMALLINT, DIVISION VARCHAR ( 10 ), LOCATION VARCHAR ( 13 ) ,
PRIMARY KEY ( DEPTNUMB ) );
```

This is the creation statement for the target staging table, ORG_CCD.

- Part three:

```
INSERT INTO ASN.IBMSNAP_REGISTER (
GLOBAL_RECORD, SOURCE_OWNER, SOURCE_TABLE, SOURCE_VIEW_QUAL,
SOURCE_STRUCTURE, SOURCE_CONDENSED, SOURCE_COMPLETE, CD_OWNER,
CD_TABLE, PHYS_CHANGE_OWNER, PHYS_CHANGE_TABLE, CD_OLD_SYNCHPOINT,
CD_NEW_SYNCHPOINT, DISABLE_REFRESH, CCD_OWNER, CCD_TABLE,
CCD_OLD_SYNCHPOINT, SYNCHPOINT, SYNCHTIME, CCD_CONDENSED,
CCD_COMPLETE, ARCH_LEVEL, DESCRIPTION, BEFORE_IMG_PREFIX,
CONFLICT_LEVEL, PARTITION_KEYS_CHG
) VALUES (
'N', 'DB2ADMIN', 'ORG_CCD', 0, 3, 'Y', 'Y', NULL, NULL, 'DB2ADMIN',
'ORG_CCD', NULL, NULL, 0, NULL, NULL, NULL, NULL, NULL, NULL,
'0201', NULL, 'X', '0', 'N');
```

One row is inserted in the IBMSNAP_REGISTER table. This is the statement for auto-registration. The ORG_CCD table can now be the source for another subscription. The ORG_CCD table will be displayed in the list of replication sources under COPYDB1 in the Control Center.

- Part four:

```
CONNECT TO SAMPLE;

INSERT INTO ASN.IBMSNAP_PRUNCNTL (
TARGET_SERVER, TARGET_OWNER, TARGET_TABLE, SYNCHTIME, SYNCHPOINT,
SOURCE_OWNER, SOURCE_TABLE, SOURCE_VIEW_QUAL, APPLY_QUAL,
SET_NAME, CNTL_SERVER, TARGET_STRUCTURE, CNTL_ALIAS
) VALUES (
'COPYDB1', 'DB2ADMIN', 'ORG_CCD', NULL, NULL, 'AIXINST1', 'ORG',
0, 'RCCDQUAL', 'RCCDSUB', 'COPYDB1', 3, 'COPYDB1');
```

After connecting to the source database, SAMPLE, one row is inserted into the IBMSNAP_PRUNCNTL table. The value of TARGET_STRUCTURE column is 3, which means staging table.

6. Close SQL file and run it.

   Now, you can define another subscription based on the CCD table (ORG_CCD) directly. For our steps below, we assume only the first target table on COPYDB1. You would follow similar steps for the second target table on COPYDB2.

7. From the Control Center, select COPYDB1 and click on **Replication sources**. You can see that ORG_CCD is defined as a replication source. Define a subscription using ORG_CCD as the source, and ORGCOPY1 as the target in COPYDB1.

8. Start Capture on the source machine (AIX):

   ```
   $ asnccp sample
   ```

   Start Apply on the target machine (Windows NT):

   ```
   c:\RBJ\ asnapply RCCDQUAL copydb1
   ```

   Start another Apply on the target machine (Windows NT):

   ```
   c:\RBJ\ asnapply ORGQUAL1 copydb1
   ```

9. Make some changes to the ORG table at the source server.

   ```
   $ db2 update org set location='Austin' where deptnumb=10
   ```

Let's look at the contents of the CCD table. Your ORG_CCD table will look similar to Table 25 (only three rows are shown here):

Table 25. Remote CCD Table in Windows NT - Complete and Condensed

IBMSNAP_ INTENTSEQ	IBMSNAP_ OPERATION	IBMSNAP_ COMMITSEQ	IBMSNAP_ LOGMARKER	DEPTNUMB	LOCATION
x'E4366A'	U	x'E43710'	1998-11-13-13.41.19	10	Austin
x'E3482A'	I	x'E3482A'	1998-11-13-13.19.09	15	Boston

IBMSNAP_ INTENTSEQ	IBMSNAP_ OPERATION	IBMSNAP_ COMMITSEQ	IBMSNAP_ LOGMARKER	DEPTNUMB	LOCATION
x'E3482A'	I	x'E3482A'	1998-11-13-13.19.09	20	Washington

This CCD table is complete, which means it can be used as a replication source. The Apply program will perform an initial refresh first and then replicate the changed data.

Look at the IBMSNAP_OPERATION column. The first row has the value 'U' for IBMSNAP_OPERATION, indicating this row has been updated. The 'I' in the other rows means that these rows are inserted during the initial refresh.

A remote staging table can greatly reduce network traffic when used as a source for replicating to multiple copies that are remote from the source machine.

5.3.3 Remote Staging Table with a Complete History

To hold a complete history of changes in a remote staging table, it should be defined as remote, complete and non-condensed.

Follow the basic steps outlined in "Setting Up Replication Systems Using Staging Tables" on page 176, and use the specific options described here.

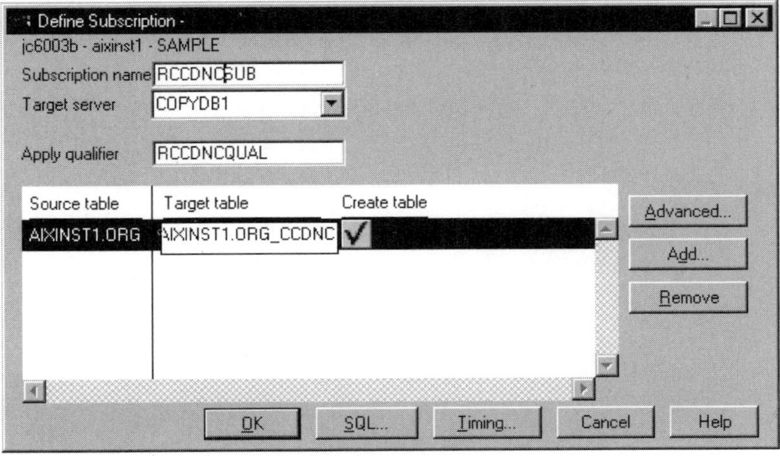

Figure 114. Define Subscription Panel

1. Define a subscription using ORG as the source. Enter the values as shown in Figure 114.

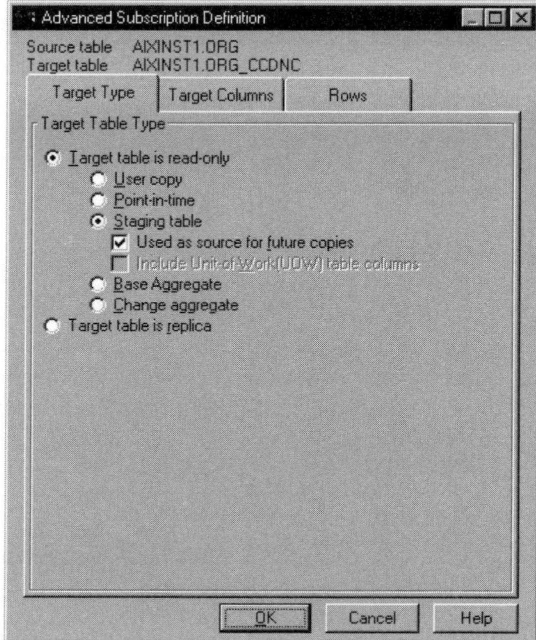

Figure 115. Define Subscription - Advanced

2. The **Used as source for future copies** option should be checked, which makes the CCD table complete (and automatically registered as a replication source).
3. Since this CCD table is non-condensed, do not check the primary key in the Target Columns tab.
4. After you finish the subscription definition, save the SQL for future execution.
5. Look at the saved SQL file before executing it and note the values of the CONDENSED and COMPLETE columns. They should be 'Y' and 'Y'.
6. Modify the 'Y' to 'N' for the TARGET_CONDENSED column in the IBMSNAP_SUBS_MEMBRS table and also for the SOURCE_CONDENSED column in IBMSNAP_REGISTER table.
7. Save the modified SQL file and run it.
8. Start Capture on the source machine (AIX):

```
$ asnccp sample
```

   Start Apply on the target machine (Windows NT):

```
c:\ asnapply RCCDNCQUAL copydb1
```

9. Finally define a subscription using this CCD table as the source to the target database and start the Apply process for this subscription set.

10. Make some changes to the ORG table. For example, update the office location for department number 10 to New York and then update it again to Austin:

```
$ update org set location='New York' where deptnumb=10;
$ update org set location='Austin' where deptnumb=10;
```

Table 26 shows some of the rows in the CCD table after the two updates:

Table 26. Remote Staging (CCD) Table in Windows NT Server - Complete History

IBMSNAP_ INTENTSEQ	IBMSNAP_ OPERATION	IBMSNAP_ COMMITSEQ	IBMSNAP_ LOGMARKER	DEPTNUMB	LOCATION
x'E4C578'	I	x'E4C578'	1998-11-13-15.01.35	10	Austin
x'E51DB4'	U	x'E51DB4'	1998-11-13-15.19.36	10	New York
x'E52351'	U	x'E523F7'	1998-11-13-15.19.50	10	Austin

The IBMSNAP_OPERATION value of the first row in the CCD table is 'I', which means this row was inserted when the data was initially refreshed. So the initial value of LOCATION where DEPTNUMB=10 was Austin. The next two rows represent the two updates we've just issued. You can see that the IBMSNAP_OPERATION values are 'U' for these rows. This shows that this CCD table contains all the changes that occurred in the source table, in this case, from Austin to New York and then from New York to Austin.

Table 27 shows the one row inserted into the target table where DEPTNUMB=10.

Table 27. Target Table in Windows NT - Complete History Scenario

DEPTNUMB	DEPTNAME	MANAGER	DIVISION	LOCATION
10	HeadOffice	160	Corporate	Austin

Remote, complete and non-condensed CCD tables as shown in this example can be used to hold a complete history of changes to the source table.

5.4 Additional Considerations and Uses

As we have demonstrated, staging tables can be used for many different application requirements. In addition to what we have explained above, there are some additional considerations and possible uses for staging tables.

Changes captured within other tools, like DPROPNR (Data Propagator Non-Relational), can also be defined as the source for subscriptions. An external data source should provide a complete CCD table, and this CCD table should be updated by the application. For example, if the source is IMS data, then DPROPNR must provide and maintain the complete CCD table. You can define this CCD table as a replication source in the Control Center.

We call this kind of CCD table an *external CCD table*. An external CCD table is a CCD table that has been populated from an external data source, such as an IMS database. You also can generate and maintain external CCD tables in your own applications.

Some of the things that you should remember when you implement staging tables are:

- CCD tables are not pruned automatically, so you must setup a pruning system manually and maintain the correct values in the control tables if required. Subscriptions that maintain CCDs can be made to prune the CCDs using SQL-after DELETE statements attached to the subscriptions.
- In update-anywhere replication, CCD tables are ignored. This is because update-anywhere requires that every update be replicated in the original order, and the source and target tables are synchronized to detect conflicts. This functionality is not appropriate for CCD tables. It is OK to have CCD tables present, to support read-only copying, in configurations that include replicas.
- Internal CCD tables are ignored by the Apply program when processing a subscription with a replica as a target.
- If a CCD table is condensed, a unique index is required.

Chapter 6. Update-Anywhere Replication

This chapter describes an end-to-end example of update-anywhere replication. The different levels of conflict detection are explained as well as some other additional considerations.

It is important to note that the implementation discussion of the various DB2 UDB features in this chapter were current at time of writing. These may change as the product evolves, and it is important to verify the function on your particular release level of DB2 Universal Database.

6.1 Overview

Update-anywhere replication allows changes to a target table to be replicated to its source table in addition to changes to the source table being replicated to the target. This type of updateable target table is called a *replica target table*.

Without the Data Replication update-anywhere ability, you would define both the source and target tables as ordinary replication sources. However, with this normal replication scenario, any updates to either table will propagate just as if they were unconnected tables. This could cause your table contents to get out of synchronization. Obviously, this is not desirable, and by using the Data Replication update-anywhere functions, this is avoided.

In an update-anywhere configuration, Capture runs on both the source and target machines. Apply runs on the target machine(s) only. When a replica table is updated, Capture at the target machine captures the changes, and Apply at the target machine pushes the changes back to the replication source as shown in Figure 116 on page 212:

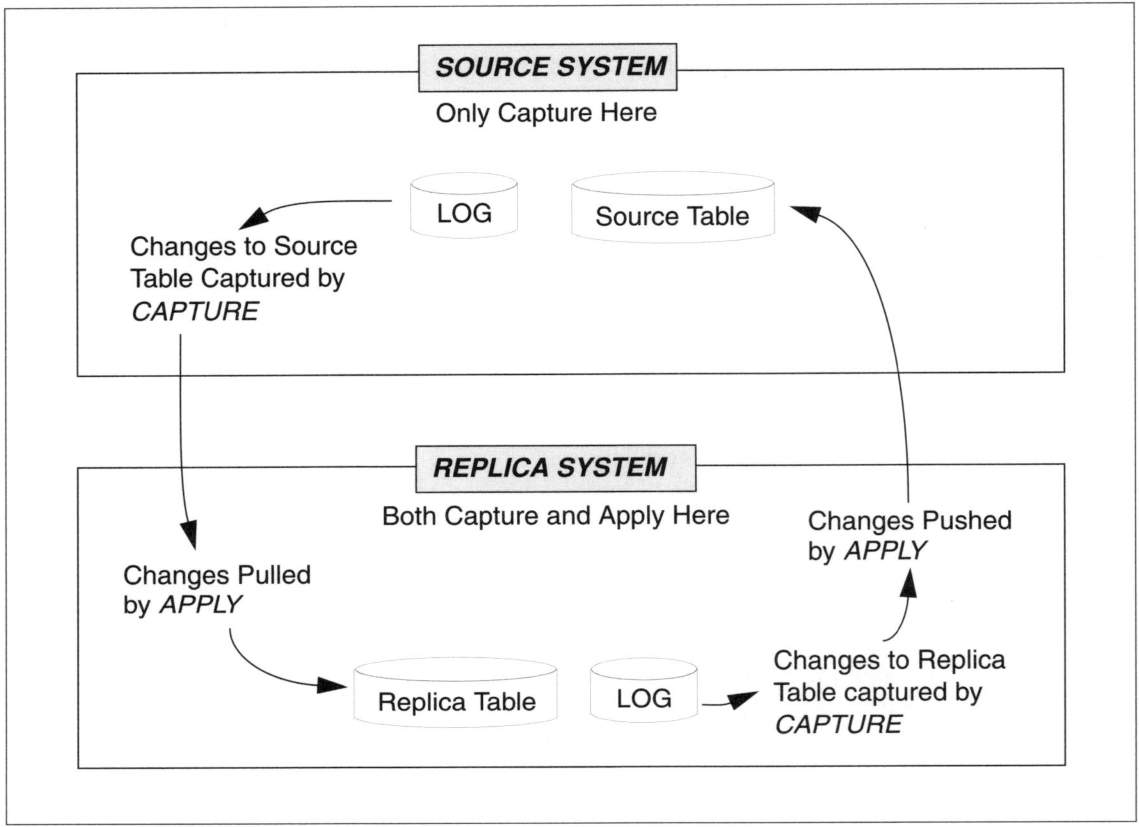

Figure 116. Update-Anywhere Overview

Update-anywhere replication can also be used in a configuration of one replication source and multiple replicas. Changes to any of the target tables (replicas) can be replicated to the replication source table and later to all the other replicas from that source table. Since Capture is running on all machines, changes to the source table and to any of the target table replicas can be captured. Apply then replicates the source table changes to the target tables (in a pull configuration) and the replica target table changes to the source table (in a push configuration). Each replica can be a source of replication back to the source table (and also other replicas through the source table).

There are some issues that should be considered carefully before implementing an update-anywhere replication environment. For example, what if rows with the same primary key value in the source and replica tables are updated at roughly the same time (in the same Apply subscription cycle)? This might cause discrepancies between the source and replica tables.

To handle this kind of issue, you can choose one of three possible levels of conflict detection. Your requirements for data integrity and performance determine which option is best for your environment. The three levels of conflict detection are *None*, *Standard,* and *Enhanced,* and you choose the level you want to use when defining your replication source. Let's take a detailed look at each one of these levels in turn.

6.1.1 No Conflict Detection (None)

With this level of conflict detection, no checking is performed between the source and replica tables. The value of the CONFLICT_LEVEL column in the Register table is set to 0 with this option. Figure 117 on page 214 shows an example of this level of conflict detection. It demonstrates that data in the source and replica tables can end up with different values in the same row. Essentially, this is the same as the update-anywhere functions not having been defined.

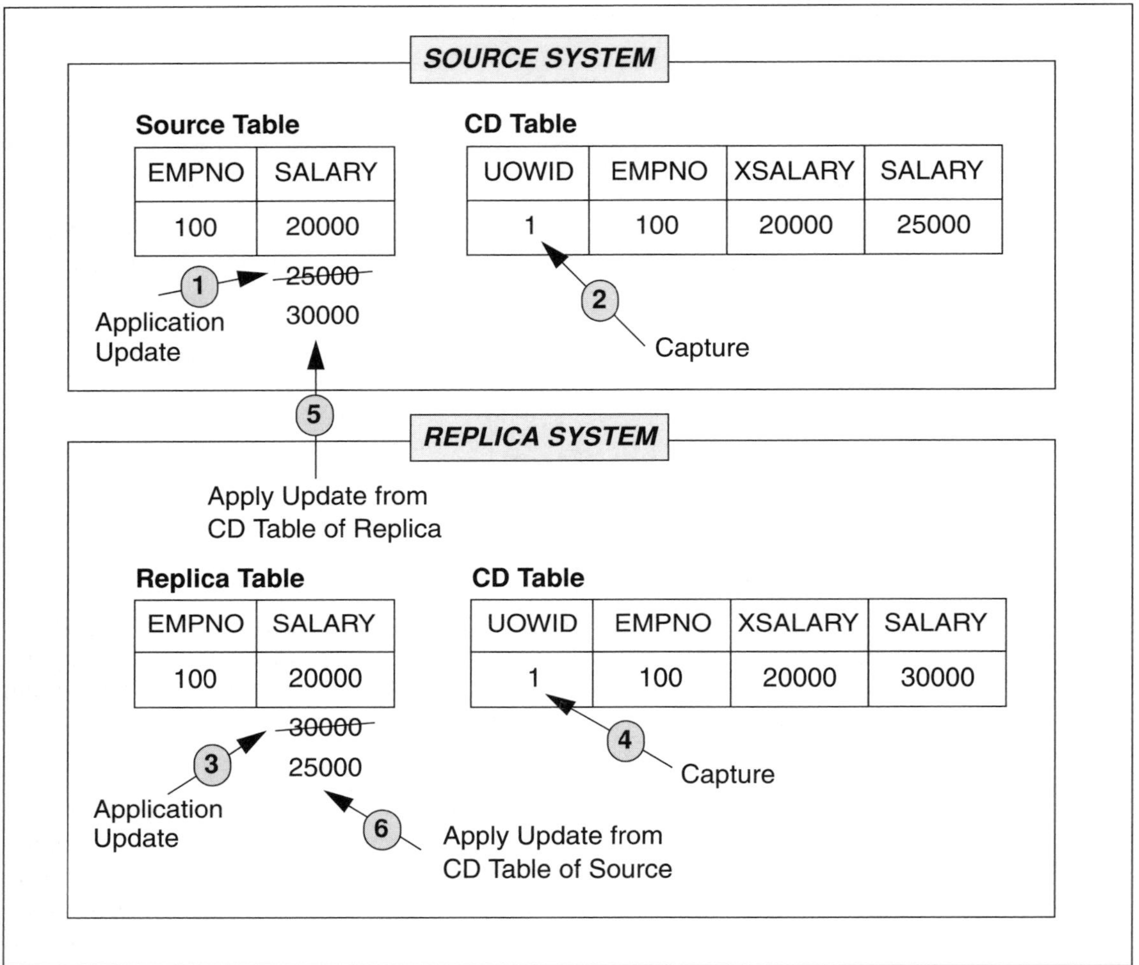

Figure 117. No Conflict Detection

In Figure 117, the following actions take place (in time order):

1. An application updates its local database on the source system:

   ```
   update 'source table' set salary=25000 where empno=100
   ```

2. Capture on the Source system captures this change and inserts a row into the CD table.

3. An application updates its local database on the Replica system:

   ```
   update 'replica table' set salary=30000 where empno=100
   ```

4. Capture on the Replica system captures this change and inserts a row into the CD table on the Replica system.
5. Apply on the Replica system pushes the replica table changes back to source table.
6. Apply on the Replica system pulls the source table changes to the replica table.

There is now data discrepancy between the source and replica tables. For empno=100, the salary is 30000 at the source and 25000 at the replica.

Note

No Conflict detection could be the right option when the replication environment doesn't allow conflicts to occur. For example, if each machine updates a different set of rows within the same table. It saves processing cycles to avoid conflict detection processing.

6.1.2 Standard Conflict Detection

With this level of conflict detection, the Apply program will check for update conflicts using the rows stored in the CD table; however, log entries not yet processed are not checked with this level of detection. Apply always attempts to process the replication from target to source first. In this way, it is able to determine conflicts and what to compensate.

The CONFLICT_LEVEL column in the Register table has the value 1. If any conflict is detected, the unit-or-work that includes the conflicting changes to the replica table (the local update) is first compensated (reversed), then the changes to the source table are applied in the normal propagation fashion. The changes to the replication source (or Master) *always* override the replica changes when conflict occurs. To see which units of work have been compensated, you can look in the UOW table at the target (replica) server. Figure 118 on page 216 shows an example of Standard Conflict Detection:

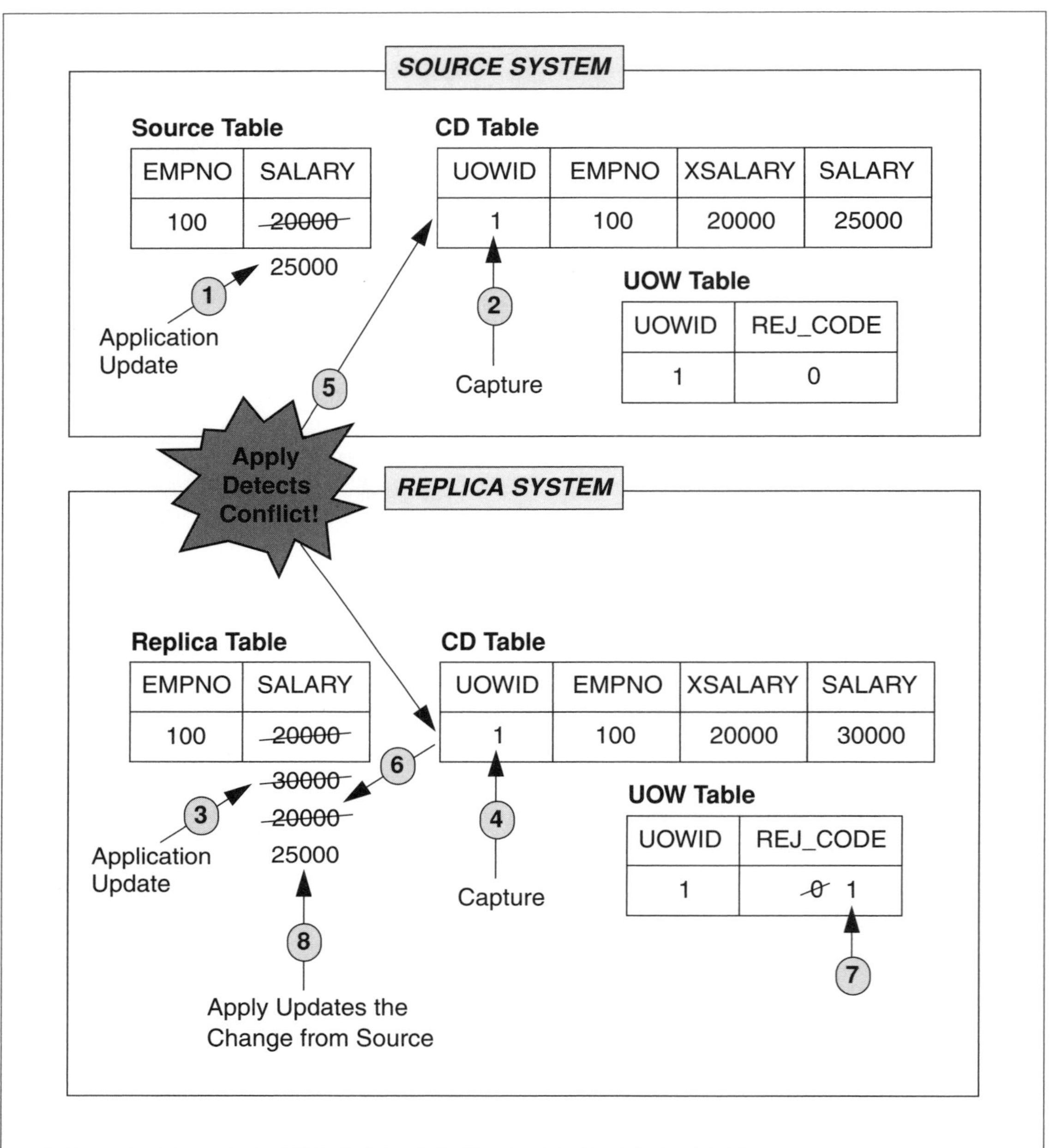

Figure 118. Standard Conflict Detection

In Figure 118, the following actions take place (in time order):

1. An application updates its local database on the Source system:

   ```
   update 'source table' set salary=25000 where empno=100
   ```

2. Capture on the Source system captures this change and inserts a row into the CD table.
3. An application updates its local database on the Replica system:

   ```
   update 'replica table' set salary=30000 where empno=100
   ```

4. Capture on the Replica system captures this change and inserts a row into the CD table.
5. Apply compares the key values in the CD table at the target with the values in the source server CD table. If there are any matching rows with same key values, then a conflict is detected. In our example, Apply detects a conflict because both CD tables have changes for the row with the same primary key value (EMPNO=100), and these changes have not yet been applied by the Apply process.
6. The unit of work in the replica table that caused the conflict is compensated (reversed).
7. The IBMSNAP_REJ_CODE column value in the UOW table for the row corresponding to the reversed unit of work on the Replica system is updated to 1. This means that the unit of work contains at least one same-row update conflict. (Please note that other values for this column are possible; however, we do not cover them here.)
8. Apply on the Replica system pulls the source table changes to the replica table.

This option does not guarantee total data integrity between the source and replica tables as some conflicts can go undetected. Apply can only detect conflicts based on the information that has been captured and inserted into the CD table. Updates recorded in the database logs, but not yet captured, are not checked in standard conflict detection. Figure 119 on page 218 shows the potential for data integrity problems with standard conflict detection:

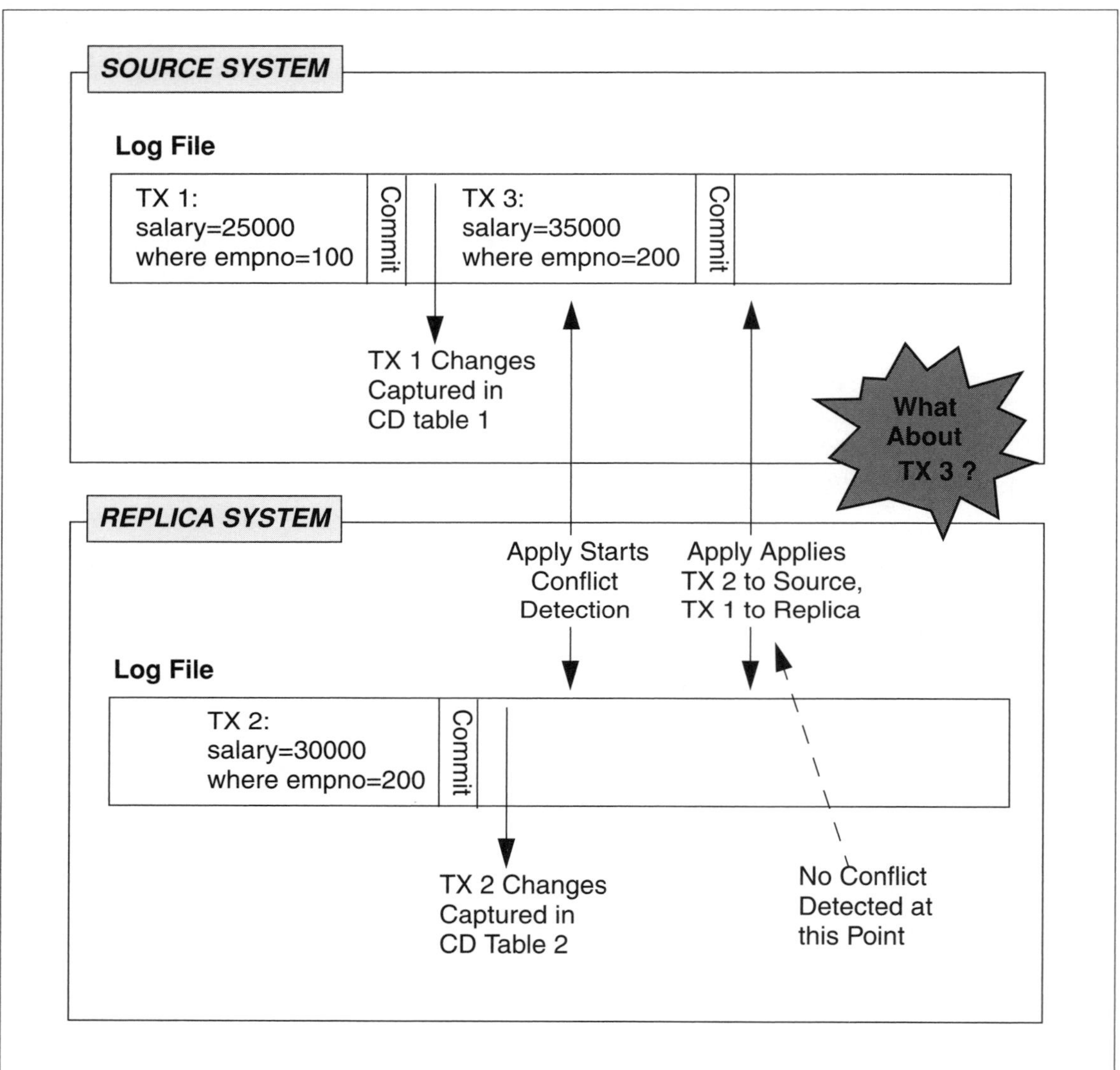

Figure 119. What is Missing in Standard Detection

In Figure 119, the following actions take place (in time order):

- Transaction 1 is committed successfully in the source system:

```
update source table set salary=25000 where empno=100
```

- Transaction 2 is committed in Replica system:

```
update source table set salary=30000 where empno=200
```

- Capture in the Source system captures the changes and inserts a row into the CD table in the Source system.
- Capture in the Replica system captures the changes and inserts a row into the CD table in the Replica system.
- Meanwhile, Transaction 3 is issued:

  ```
  update source table set salary=35000 where empno=200
  ```

  This change is not yet captured, so no information about this change is stored in the CD table.
- Apply starts conflict detection by comparing the two CD tables.
- No conflicts are found at this time.
- Apply pulls Transaction 1's changes from the source table to the replica table.
- Apply pushes Transaction 2's changes back to the source table.

What about Transaction 3, which conflicts with Transaction 2 in the replica system? These two transactions try to update the row with the same primary key value (empno=200). In this example, Standard conflict detection missed this conflict, and the changes to the source (master) table are lost.

6.1.3 Enhanced Conflict Detection

This level of conflict detection is the same as Standard, except that Apply will take a **share** table lock on the tables involved in the subscription set. This lock is held on all tables at both the source and target servers during the conflict detection process. Any application updates will be forced to wait until all the changes remaining in the database log are captured to the CD tables. Conflict detection proceeds in the same manner as with Standard Conflict Detection.

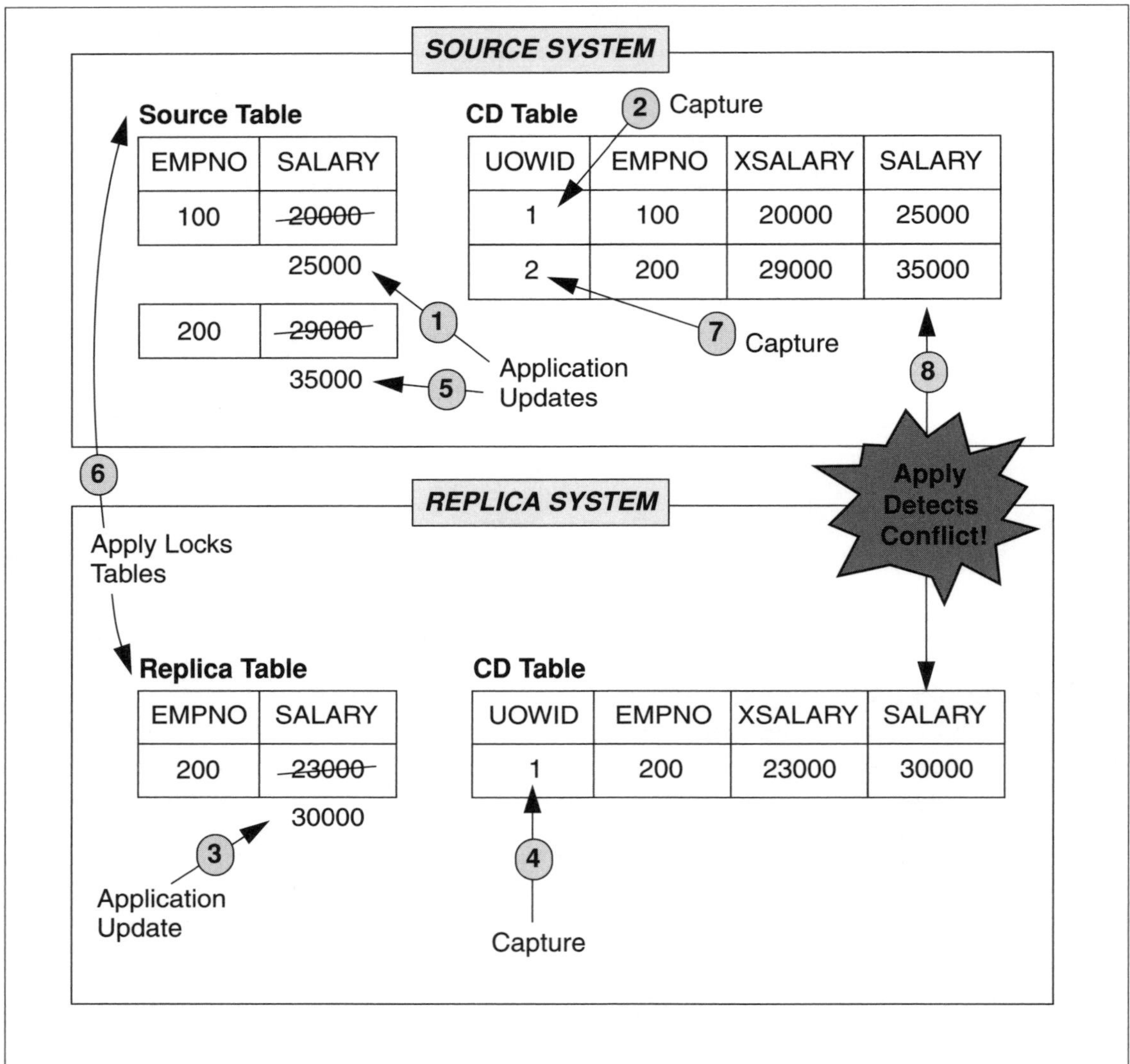

Figure 120. Enhanced Conflict Detection

In Figure 120, the following actions take place (in time order):

1. An application updates its local database on the Source system:

   ```
   update 'source table' set salary=25000 where empno=100"
   ```

2. Capture on the Source system captures this change and inserts a row into the CD table.

3. An application updates its local database on the Replica system:

```
update 'replica table' set salary=30000 where empno=200
```

4. Capture on the Replica system captures this change and inserts a row into the CD table.
5. An application updates its local database on the Source system:

```
update 'source table' set salary=35000 where empno=200
```

6. Before Apply compares the two CD tables on each system to check for conflicts, it gets **share** locks on the tables to ensure that no other application can update these tables during the conflict detection process. Apply then waits for the Capture process to complete its processing of the entries in the log files.
7. Capture captures any changes left in the database logs that are not yet in the CD table and inserts the rows into the CD table.
8. Apply detects the conflict and performs conflict resolution as shown in Figure 118 on page 216 (the example of Standard Conflict Detection).

Note

Standard detection can be implemented with better performance compared to Enhanced detection, but some conflicts are possible. While Enhanced detection provides a higher level of data integrity, it can have a very serious impact on performance. The source system is often a production OLTP system, and locking tables can greatly increase response times - something you would normally try to avoid.

This discussion of the different levels of conflict detection demonstrates the *performance versus data integrity* issue behind implementing an update-anywhere replication environment. Your application requirements will determine which conflict detection option you use. We'll discuss additional considerations and recommendations regarding update-anywhere in "Additional Considerations and Recommendations" on page 245.

6.2 Setting Up an Update-Anywhere Environment

In this section, we take you through a step-by-step example of setting up an update-anywhere environment.

We use two machines in this example, one running AIX and the other Windows NT. On the AIX server, there is a database called SAMPLE which will be used as the replication source. The COPYTEST database on the Windows NT machine will be used as the target database (this is also known as the target replica in update-anywhere configurations). The EMPLOYEE table in the SAMPLE database on the AIX server (jc6003b) will be replicated to the EMPLCOPY table in the COPYTEST database on the Windows NT machine (jc6003c). Table 28 shows the summary of the test environment.

Table 28. Test Configuration for Update Anywhere

Machine Name	OS/DB Software	Database (Instance)	Description
jc6003b	AIX 4.3.2/UDB 5.2	SAMPLE (aixinst1)	Used as replication source. Capture runs here.
jc6003c	NT 4.0/UDB 5.2	COPYTEST (DB2)	Used as target replica. Capture & Apply here.

We first installed UDB on the AIX and Windows NT machines and then configured a remote connection (using TCP/IP) to the SAMPLE database on AIX from the Windows NT machine.

To configure the update-anywhere replication environment, we define a replication source and a subscription just as in a normal replication configuration apart from some options specific to update-anywhere.

6.2.1 Defining a Replication Source

We start by defining a replication source using the DB2 UDB Control Center:

1. Start the Control Center on the Windows NT machine and expand object trees by clicking on **System->jc6003b->SAMPLE**. Click on the tables folder to display the list of tables in the SAMPLE database in the right hand pane.
2. Find the desired source table (EMPLOYEE) and click the right mouse button. From the pop-up menu, select **Define as replication source-> Custom** as shown in Figure 121 on page 223:

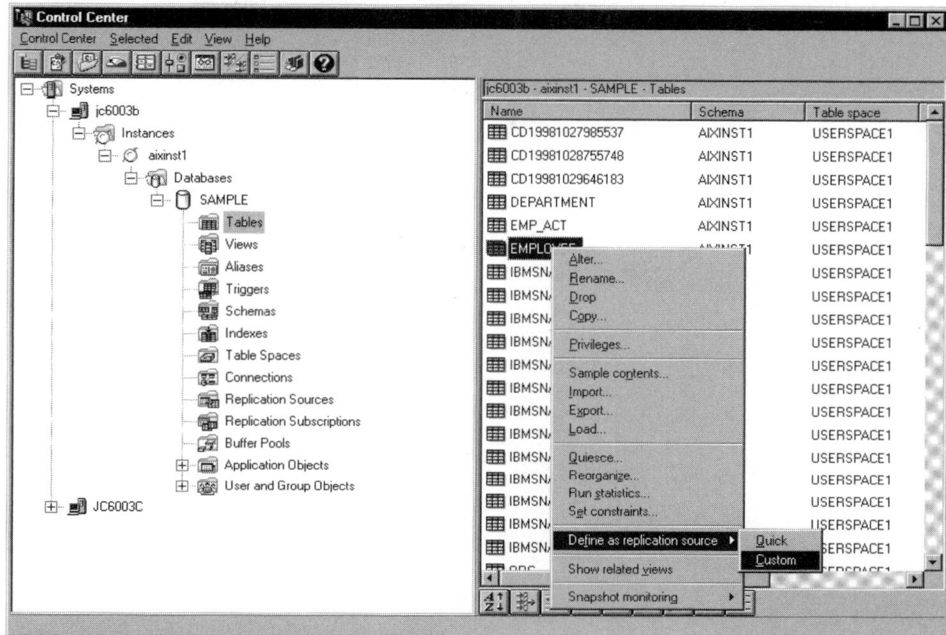

Figure 121. Define Replication Source - Custom

The Define as a Replication Source panel is displayed:

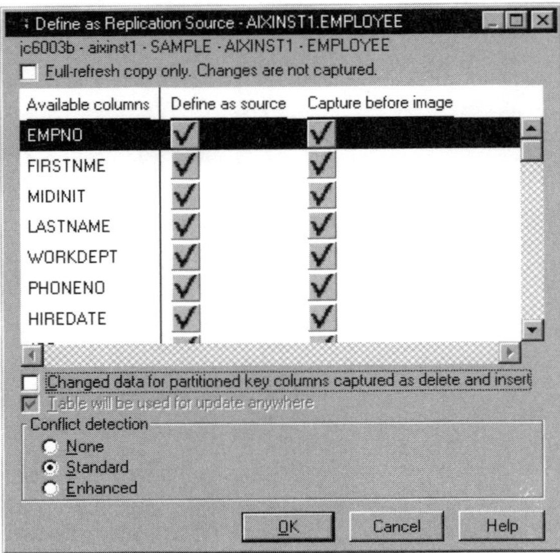

Figure 122. Define Replication Source - Standard Conflict Detection

3. Select the **Table will be used for update-anywhere** check box and **Standard** as the level of conflict detection. This means that the Apply program can search for update conflicts using changes captured in the CD table. The default level of conflict detection is **None**.

   Note that the **Define as source** and **Capture before image** check boxes are selected for all columns. In the current UDB implementation, both sets of check boxes are automatically selected if you select the **Table will be used for update-anywhere** option and the conflict detection level is Standard or Enhanced.

Note

Since the maximum length of a column name in DB2 UDB is 18 characters, and the before image column needs a prefix (usually X) in the CD table, the column name length in update-anywhere should be 17 characters or less in order to capture the before image.

If a column name is 18 characters already, the before image column will be prefixed, and the column name will be truncated to 18 characters.

4. Click **OK** to save the options and close the window. The Run Now or Save SQL window is displayed:

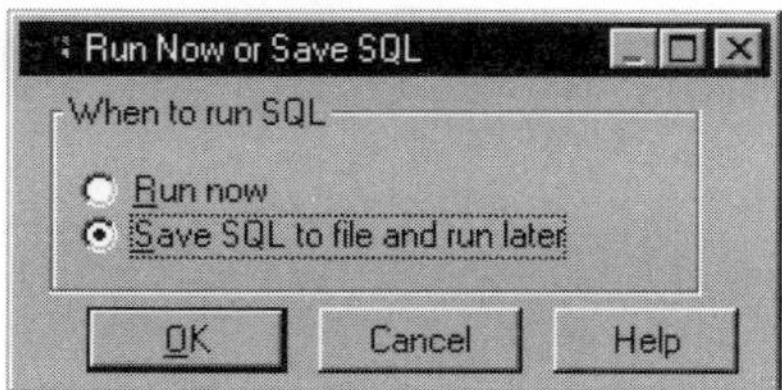

Figure 123. Define Replication Source - Run Now or Save SQL

5. If you choose the Save SQL to file and run later option, the SQL files can be customized to enable you to create multiple copies of the same replication action, customize the CD table name, define the location of the CD table, or create table spaces.

   Select the **Save SQL to file and run later** option and click **OK**. The Save SQL file window is displayed:

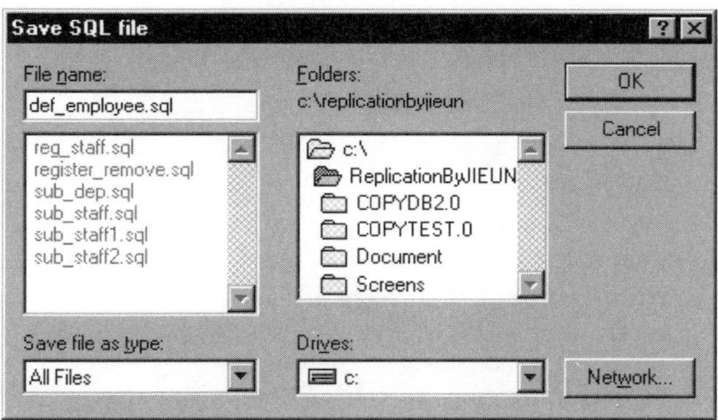

Figure 124. Define as Replication Source - Save SQL File

6. Enter a file name (here, def_employee.sql) and choose a folder to store the file in. Click **OK** to save the SQL file. A message is then displayed confirming that the SQL file has been saved for later execution.
7. To run the saved SQL file, use the Control Center:

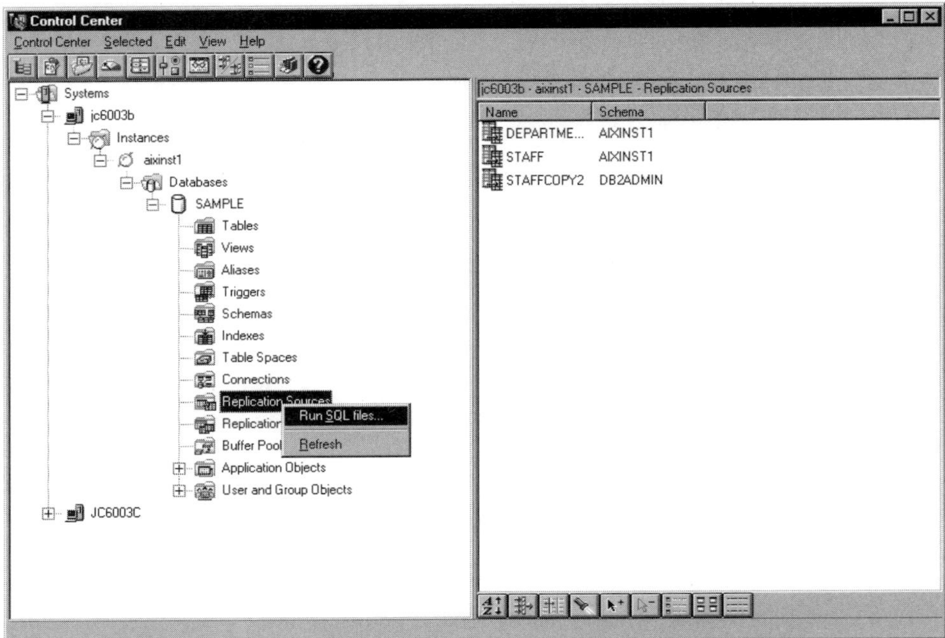

Figure 125. Run SQL Files

8. Select **Replication Sources** and click the right mouse button to display the pop-up menu. Select **Run SQL files**.

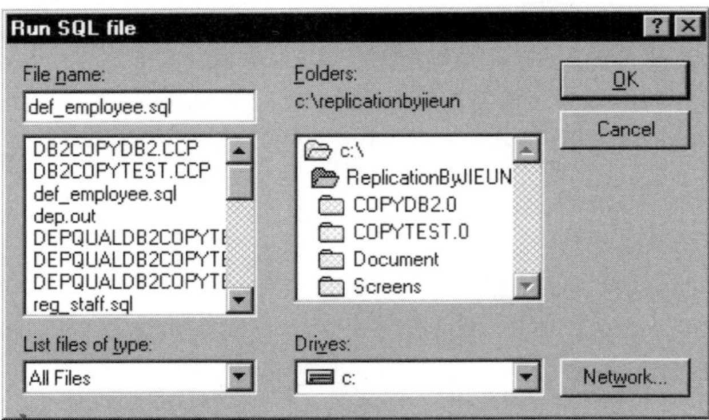

Figure 126. Defining Replication Source - Run SQL File

9. Select the folder and file name (here, def_employee.sql). The default is the last file you saved. Click **OK** to run this file. If the SQL is not successful, then a panel is displayed showing the DB2 error message. There are many SQL statements in the SQL file, and processing will stop

at the first failure. Unfortunately, the error message does not indicate exactly which line caused the error. You will have to check the SQL statements that were run and correct any problems.

Generated SQL

Let's look in detail at the generated SQL. Open the SQL file (def_employee.sql) with your editor. It has these SQL statements:

- Part one:

```
CONNECT TO SAMPLE;
ALTER TABLE AIXINST1.EMPLOYEE DATA CAPTURE CHANGES;
```

  First, we connect to the source server database in which the replication source table (EMPLOYEE) resides, which, in this case, is the SAMPLE database on AIX.

  Next, the replication source table is *altered* so that data capture changes are enabled. This means that extra information regarding changes to this table will be written to the log for use by the Capture program.

- Part two:

```
CREATE TABLE AIXINST1.CD19981030805941 (
IBMSNAP_UOWID CHAR ( 10 ) FOR BIT DATA NOT NULL,
IBMSNAP_INTENTSEQ CHAR ( 10 ) FOR BIT DATA NOT NULL,
IBMSNAP_OPERATION CHAR ( 1 ) NOT NULL,
XEMPNO CHAR ( 6 ),
EMPNO CHAR ( 6 ) NOT NULL,
XFIRSTNME VARCHAR ( 12 ),
FIRSTNME VARCHAR ( 12 ) NOT NULL, and so on .....
```

  Here we see the create table statement for the CD table for the replication source table, EMPLOYEE. A CD table stores changed data information relating to the source table rows.

  There is one CD table per one source table. The timestamp in the table name is from the source server. While this is the default table name, it is important to understand that both the qualifier and name of the table can be changed to suit your needs by modifying the SQL file before running it.

  IBMSNAP_UOWID is the unit of work ID, and IBMSNAP_INTENTSEQ is a unique identifier describing the sequence of changes (it provides a total ordering, not just within one transaction). IBMSNAP_OPERATION can have a value of 'I', 'U', or 'D' indicating an insert, update, or delete operation. There are columns that have the same name as user columns from the source table (for example, EMPNO). For each source column, there is a column with the same name but prefixed with an X (for example, XEMPNO). This column is used to keep the before image. Since standard conflict detection is used here, all before image and after image column values are captured.

- Part three:

```
CREATE UNIQUE INDEX AIXINST1.IX19981030832180
ON AIXINST1.CD19981030805941
( IBMSNAP_UOWID ASC, IBMSNAP_INTENTSEQ ASC );
```

A unique ascending index created on the CD table for the EMPLOYEE table.

- Part four:

```
INSERT INTO ASN.IBMSNAP_REGISTER (
GLOBAL_RECORD, SOURCE_OWNER, SOURCE_TABLE, SOURCE_VIEW_QUAL,
SOURCE_STRUCTURE, SOURCE_CONDENSED, SOURCE_COMPLETE, CD_OWNER,
CD_TABLE, PHYS_CHANGE_OWNER, PHYS_CHANGE_TABLE,
CD_OLD_SYNCHPOINT, CD_NEW_SYNCHPOINT, DISABLE_REFRESH, CCD_OWNER,
CCD_TABLE, CCD_OLD_SYNCHPOINT, SYNCHPOINT, SYNCHTIME, CCD_CONDENSED,
CCD_COMPLETE, ARCH_LEVEL, DESCRIPTION,BEFORE_IMG_PREFIX,
CONFLICT_LEVEL, PARTITION_KEYS_CHG )
VALUES ( 'N', 'AIXINST1', 'EMPLOYEE', 0, 1, 'Y', 'Y', 'AIXINST1',
'CD19981030805941', 'AIXINST1', 'CD19981030805941', NULL, NULL, 0,
NULL, NULL, NULL, NULL, NULL, NULL, NULL, '0201', NULL, 'X', '1',
'N');
```

A row is inserted into the Register table (ASN.IBMSNAP_REGISTER) that contains information about replication source objects at the source server. Note that CONFLICT_LEVEL is set to 1 (standard).

6.2.2 Defining a Subscription

To define a subscription, we again use the DB2 UDB Control Center.

1. Start the Control Center on the Windows NT machine and expand object trees by clicking on **System->jc6003b->SAMPLE**. Click on the **Replication Sources** folder to display the list of replication sources in the right hand pane.

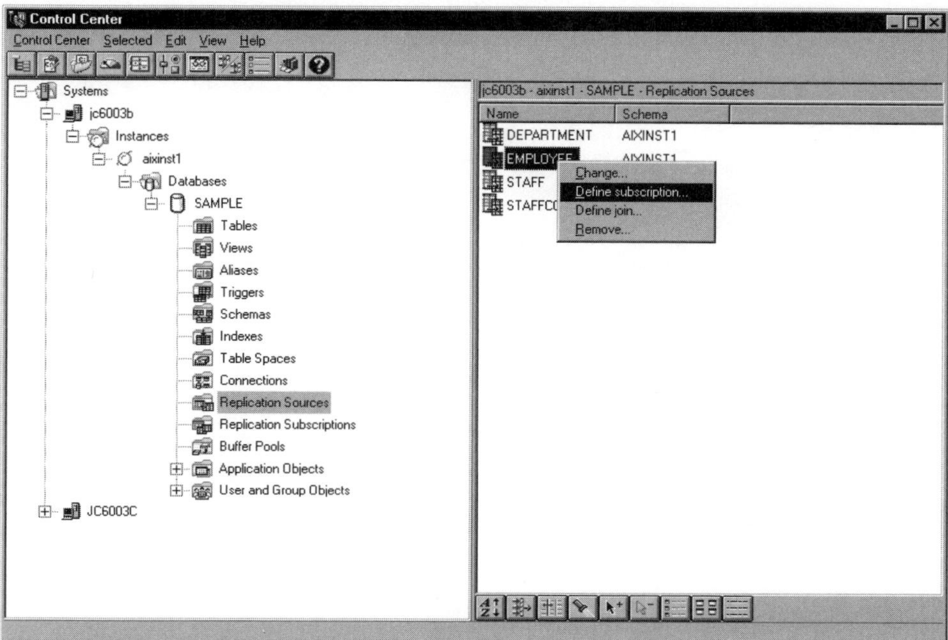

Figure 127. Define Subscription

2. Choose a replication source (here, EMPLOYEE) and click the right mouse button. Select **Define Subscription** from the pop-up menu. The Define Subscription panel is displayed:

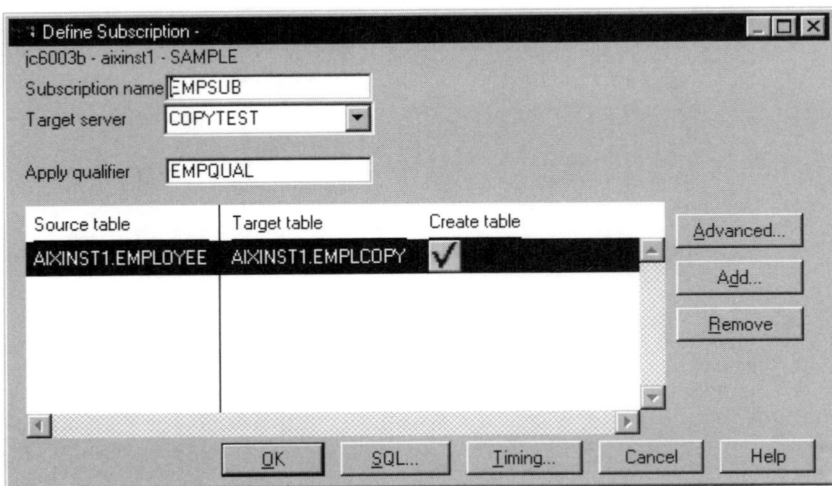

Figure 128. Define Subscription Panel

Enter a subscription name (here, EMPSUB). This is user defined and can be up to 18 characters long.

Select a target server. In this example, this is the COPYTEST database on the Windows NT machine (jc6003c).

Enter an Apply qualifier (here, EMPQUAL). The Apply qualifier name is always saved in upper case even when entered in lower case. This name will be used later when we run the Apply program and must be unique among all Apply processes sharing a common set of control tables.

If you don't want to change the target table name, you can use the displayed default that is same as the source table name. In this example, we have changed the name of the target table to EMPLCOPY for clarity.

Click the **Create table** check box. This will create the EMPLCOPY table in the target database when you run this subscription definition.

Select **Advanced** to display the Advanced Subscription Definition panel:

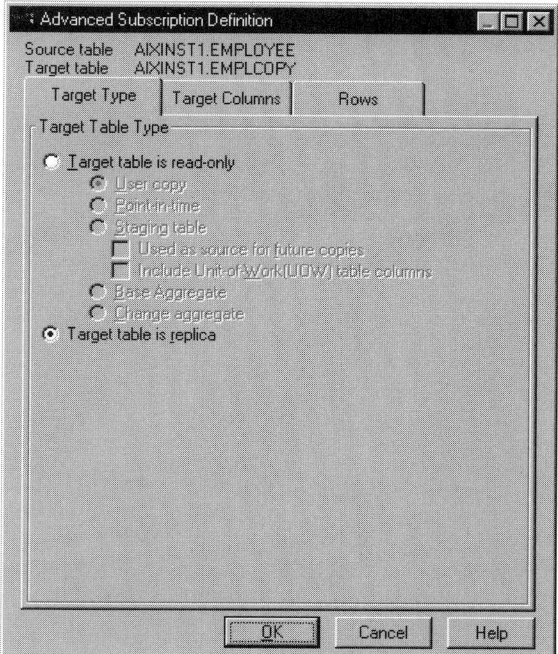

Figure 129. Advanced Subscription Definition

3. Select the **Target table is replica** target table type. In an update-anywhere environment, this target table will be the source for replication in the other direction (replica to source).

   Now select the **Target Columns** tab:

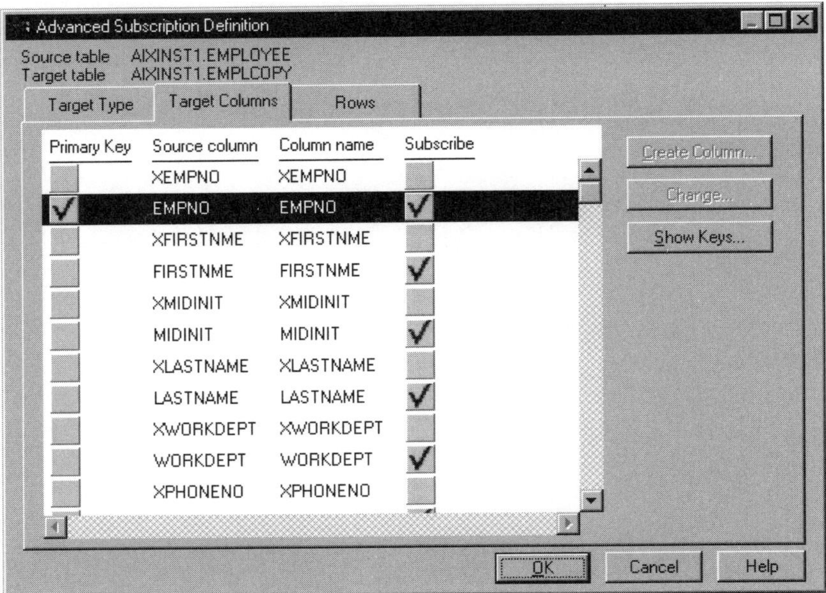

Figure 130. Advanced Subscription Definition - Target Columns

4. Click the primary key button against the primary key of the employee table (EMPNO). Since the target table type is a replica, it must have the same primary key as the source table. By default, if you don't check any of the columns as the primary key, the target table will use the same primary key as the source table. If no primary key is defined on the source table, then the subscription will fail during Apply processing.

   Since the replica table can have only user data columns, the option to create extra columns is disabled.

   There are actually three things that occur when you define a replica subscription. The SQL for the steps listed below can be found later in "Generated SQL" on page 237:

   - A subscription from the user table to the replica (with no before image columns) is defined.
   - Registration of the replica (including all the before image columns).
   - A subscription from the replica to the user table (with no before image columns) is defined.

   The before image columns are required in the implicit replica registration as these values will be used during compensation of rejected transactions.

The CD table created for the replica will include a full complement of before image columns.

Click **OK**, then from the Definition Subscription panel, select the **Timing** button:

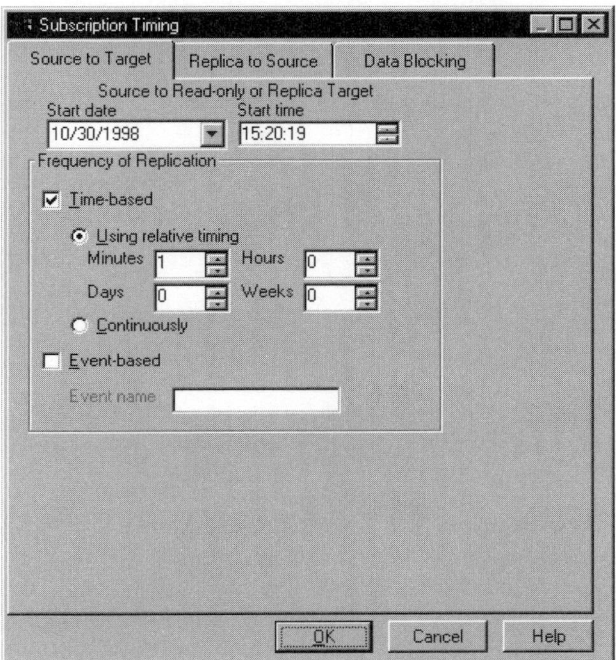

Figure 131. Define Subscription - Subscription Timing

5. As this is a test environment, change minutes to one and hours to zero. You can use the spin buttons to change these values or just overtype in the fields. The start date and time defaults to the current date and time.

   Click on the **Replica to Source** tab:

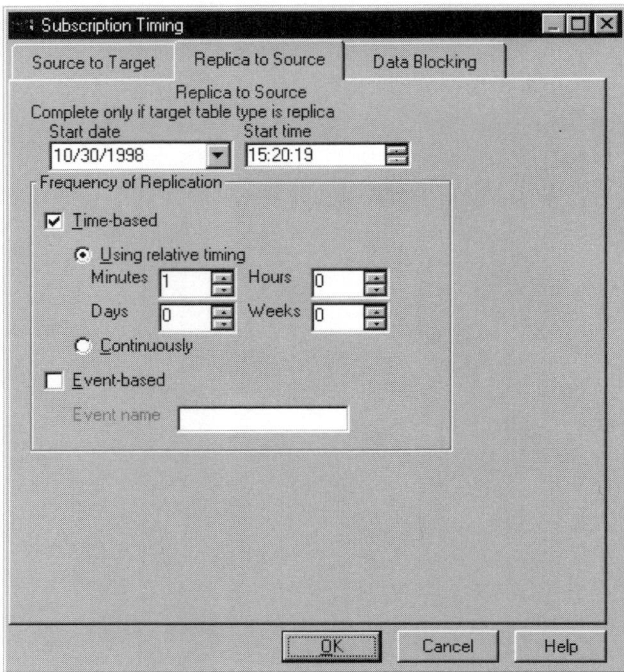

Figure 132. Define Subscription - Replica to SourceTiming

6. Enter similar values for the timing as in the previous panel. This is for the replication in the reverse direction (replica to source).

   Click **OK** to take you back to Define Subscription screen.

   Click **OK** again to display this panel:

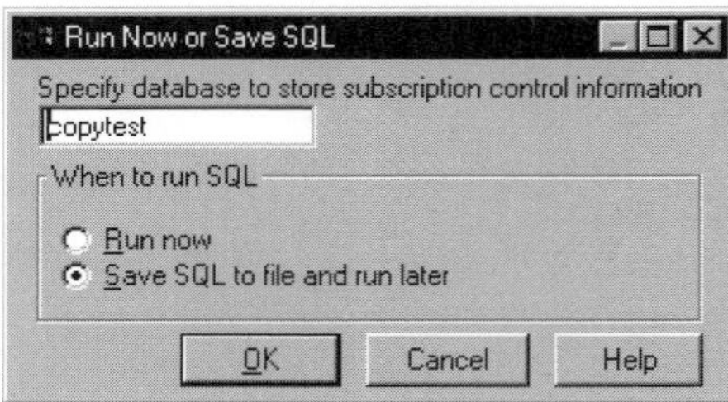

Figure 133. Define Subscription - Run Now or Save SQL

7. Enter the database name to store the subscription control information. In this case, we chose COPYTEST, which is the database at the target system (Windows NT machine).

In this configuration, where Apply is running on the target server, source to target replication is a pull configuration, and the other direction is a push configuration.

Select the **Save SQL to file and run later** option and click **OK**. The Save SQL file window is displayed:

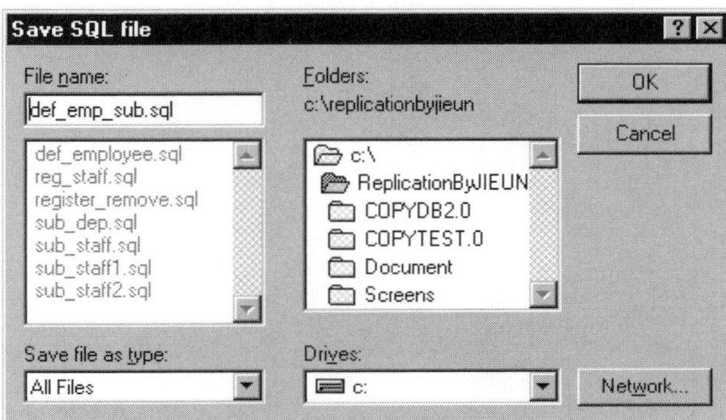

Figure 134. Save SQL File

8. We named this file def_emp_sub.sql. Click **OK** and you should next see the message stating that the SQL has been saved in this file for future execution.
9. To run this SQL file, go back to the Control Center:

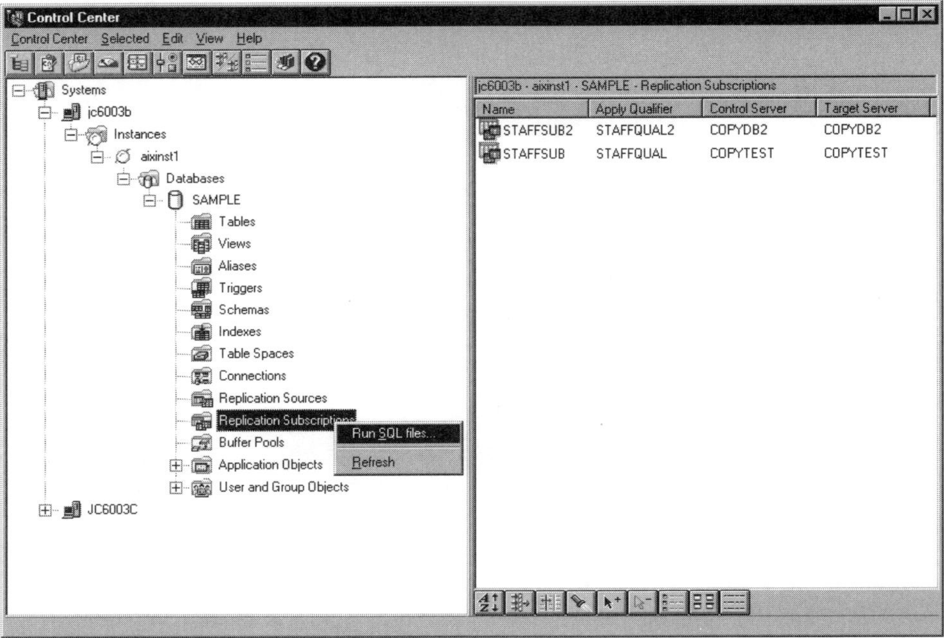

Figure 135. Define Subscription - Run SQL File

10.Select **Replication Subscriptions** and click the right mouse button to display the pop-up menu. Select **Run SQL files**.

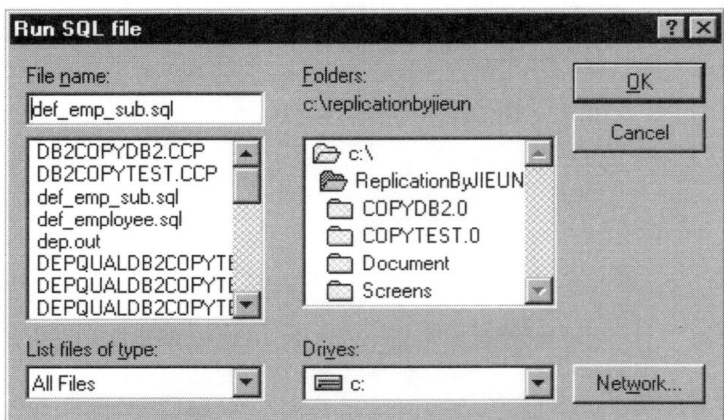

Figure 136. Define Subscription - Run SQL File Panel

11.Select the directory and file name (def_emp_sub.sql). Click **OK** to run this file. If a failure occurs, check the SQL statements in the file.

Generated SQL

The SQL which was run is described below. We highlight the parts that are related to update-anywhere. Please note that the first eight parts are all against the COPYTEST database at the Control server.

- Part one:

```
CONNECT TO COPYTEST;

INSERT INTO ASN.IBMSNAP_SUBS_SET (
ACTIVATE, APPLY_QUAL, SET_NAME, WHOS_ON_FIRST,
SOURCE_SERVER, TARGET_SERVER, STATUS, LASTRUN, REFRESH_TIMING,
SLEEP_MINUTES, EVENT_NAME, LASTSUCCESS, SYNCHPOINT,
SYNCHTIME, MAX_SYNCH_MINUTES, AUX_STMTS, ARCH_LEVEL,
SOURCE_ALIAS, TARGET_ALIAS
) VALUES (
1, 'EMPQUAL', 'EMPSUB', 'F', 'COPYTEST', 'SAMPLE',
0,'1998-10-30-15.20.19.000000', 'R', 1, NULL,
'1998-10-30-15.20.19.000000', NULL, NULL, NULL, 0, '0201',
'COPYTEST', 'SAMPLE' );

INSERT INTO ASN.IBMSNAP_SUBS_SET (<same columns as above>)
VALUES(
1, 'EMPQUAL', 'EMPSUB', 'S', 'SAMPLE', 'COPYTEST',
0,'1998-10-30-15.20.19.000000', 'R', 1, NULL,
'1998-10-30-15.20.19.000000', NULL, NULL, NULL, 0, '0201',
'SAMPLE', 'COPYTEST' );
```

First, a connection is made to the control server database, COPYTEST.

Next, a row is inserted into the Subscription Set table that defines characteristics of replication subscriptions (IBMSNAP_SUBS_SET). You can see EMPQUAL and EMPSUB as the values of the columns named APPLY_QUAL and SET_NAME respectively. Those are the values we defined at the subscription definition stage.

Since we are defining an update-anywhere scenario, there is a second row inserted into the IBMSNAP_SUBS_SET table. Compare the WHOS_ON_FIRST, SOURCE_SERVER and TARGET_SERVER columns between the two insert statements.

The WHOS_ON_FIRST column can have the value 'F' or 'S'. In this situation, 'F' means that the target table is the parent replica, and the source table is the dependent replica. 'S' means that the source table is the parent replica, and the target table is the dependent replica. The value 'F' tells us that Apply does the target -> source direction first.This is done to allow Apply to detect conflicts as we discussed earlier in this chapter. The value 'S' tells us that Apply does the source -> target direction second as part of the subscription processing.

The first insert statement represents the subscription set from replica (COPYTEST) to source (SAMPLE), and the second insert statement is for the subscription set from source (SAMPLE) to replica (COPYTEST).

- Part two:

```
INSERT INTO ASN.IBMSNAP_SUBS_MEMBR (
APPLY_QUAL, SET_NAME, WHOS_ON_FIRST, SOURCE_OWNER,
SOURCE_TABLE, SOURCE_VIEW_QUAL, TARGET_OWNER, TARGET_TABLE,
TARGET_CONDENSED, TARGET_COMPLETE, TARGET_STRUCTURE,
PREDICATES
) VALUES ( 'EMPQUAL', 'EMPSUB', 'F', 'AIXINST1', 'EMPLCOPY',
0, 'AIXINST1', 'EMPLOYEE', 'Y', 'Y', 1, NULL);

INSERT INTO ASN.IBMSNAP_SUBS_MEMBR (<same columns as above>)
VALUES ( 'EMPQUAL', 'EMPSUB', 'S', 'AIXINST1', 'EMPLOYEE',
0, 'AIXINST1', 'EMPLCOPY', 'Y', 'Y', 7, NULL););
```

One row is inserted into the Subscription Targets Member table (IBMSNAP_SUBS_MEMBR) with information about the subscription member and target tables defined for the subscription set. This table also has rows for each direction of replication, so there is a second row inserted in this table. Note the values of the WHOS_ON_FIRST, SOURCE_TABLE, TARGET_TABLE and TARGET_STRUCTURE columns between the two rows. For the TARGET_STRUCTURE column, 1 means source table, and 7 means replica.

- Part three:

```
INSERT INTO ASN.IBMSNAP_SUBS_COLS (
APPLY_QUAL, SET_NAME, WHOS_ON_FIRST, TARGET_OWNER,
TARGET_TABLE, COL_TYPE, TARGET_NAME, IS_KEY, COLNO,
EXPRESSION
) VALUES ( 'EMPQUAL', 'EMPSUB', 'S', 'AIXINST1', 'EMPLCOPY',
'A', 'EMPNO', 'Y', 0, 'EMPNO');

INSERT INTO ASN.IBMSNAP_SUBS_COLS (<same columns as above>)
VALUES ( 'EMPQUAL', 'EMPSUB', 'F', 'AIXINST1', 'EMPLOYEE',
'A', 'EMPNO', 'Y', 0, 'EMPNO');
```

Rows are inserted into the Subscription Columns table (IBMSNAP_SUBS_COLS) with information about the subscription columns being copied. There are two rows inserted for each column in the EMPLOYEE table (the source table), one for each direction of replication. Since the EMPLOYEE table has 14 columns, 28 rows are inserted in this case.

- Part four:

```
INSERT INTO ASN.IBMSNAP_PRUNCNTL (
TARGET_SERVER, TARGET_OWNER, TARGET_TABLE, SYNCHTIME,
SYNCHPOINT, SOURCE_OWNER, SOURCE_TABLE, SOURCE_VIEW_QUAL,
APPLY_QUAL, SET_NAME, CNTL_SERVER, TARGET_STRUCTURE,
CNTL_ALIAS
) VALUES ( 'SAMPLE', 'AIXINST1', 'EMPLOYEE', NULL,
NULL, 'AIXINST1', 'EMPLCOPY', 0,
'EMPQUAL', 'EMPSUB', 'COPYTEST', 1, 'COPYTEST');
```

One row is inserted in the Prune Control table per subscription member. This is used for coordinating the pruning of the CD and UOW tables. Here the TARGET_TABLE is EMPLOYEE (reverse replication) and TARGET_STRUCTURE is 1, which means source table.

- Part five:

```
CREATE TABLE AIXINST1.EMPLCOPY (
EMPNO CHAR ( 6 ) NOT NULL, FIRSTNME VARCHAR ( 12 ) NOT NULL,
MIDINIT CHAR ( 1 ) NOT NULL, LASTNAME VARCHAR ( 15 ) NOT NULL,
WORKDEPT CHAR ( 3 ), PHONENO CHAR ( 4 ),
HIREDATE DATE, JOB CHAR ( 8 ), EDLEVEL SMALLINT NOT NULL,
SEX CHAR ( 1 ), BIRTHDATE DATE, SALARY DECIMAL ( 9, 2 ),
BONUS DECIMAL ( 9, 2 ), COMM DECIMAL ( 9, 2 ) ,
PRIMARY KEY ( EMPNO ) )
DATA CAPTURE CHANGES;
```

This is the creation of the EMPLCOPY target table. This target table is defined as a replica, so the CREATE TABLE statement uses the DATA CAPTURE CHANGES option. We need this for the reverse replication from the target server back to the source server.

- Part six:

```
CREATE TABLE DB2ADMIN.CD19981030796001 (
IBMSNAP_UOWID CHAR ( 10 ) FOR BIT DATA NOT NULL,
IBMSNAP_INTENTSEQ CHAR ( 10 ) FOR BIT DATA NOT NULL,
IBMSNAP_OPERATION CHAR ( 1 ) NOT NULL,
XEMPNO CHAR ( 6 ), EMPNO CHAR ( 6 ) NOT NULL,
XFIRSTNME VARCHAR ( 12 ), FIRSTNME VARCHAR ( 12 ) NOT NULL,
....... more cols ....
```

This is the creation of the CD table for the reverse replication. The default owner of the CD table is the current login userid. It is important to understand that the qualifier and name of the change data table can be anything you want. If you wish to change the name or qualifier to something more relevant to your installation, you can make the changes in the SQL file here before you run it.

• Part seven:

```
CREATE UNIQUE INDEX DB2ADMIN.IX19981030234000
ON DB2ADMIN.CD19981030796001
( IBMSNAP_UOWID ASC, IBMSNAP_INTENTSEQ ASC );
```

This is the index on the CD table for the EMPLCOPY table.

• Part eight:

```
INSERT INTO ASN.IBMSNAP_REGISTER (
GLOBAL_RECORD, SOURCE_OWNER, SOURCE_TABLE,
SOURCE_VIEW_QUAL, SOURCE_STRUCTURE, SOURCE_CONDENSED,
SOURCE_COMPLETE, CD_OWNER, CD_TABLE, PHYS_CHANGE_OWNER,
PHYS_CHANGE_TABLE, CD_OLD_SYNCHPOINT, CD_NEW_SYNCHPOINT,
DISABLE_REFRESH, CCD_OWNER, CCD_TABLE,
CCD_OLD_SYNCHPOINT, SYNCHPOINT, SYNCHTIME, CCD_CONDENSED,
CCD_COMPLETE, ARCH_LEVEL, DESCRIPTION, BEFORE_IMG_PREFIX,
CONFLICT_LEVEL, PARTITION_KEYS_CHG
) VALUES ( 'N', 'AIXINST1', 'EMPLCOPY', 0, 7, 'Y', 'Y',
'DB2ADMIN', 'CD19981030796001', 'DB2ADMIN',
'CD19981030796001', NULL, NULL, 0, NULL, NULL, NULL, NULL,
NULL, NULL, NULL, '0201', NULL, 'X', '1', 'N');
```

One row is inserted in the Register table (IBMSNAP_REGISTER) to define EMPLCOPY (the replica table) as the source of reverse replication. The SOURCE_STRUCTURE is 7 (replica), and CONFLICT_LEVEL is 1 (standard).

• Part nine:

It is important to note that this is now being carried out against the source database at the source server. We have already seen a similar SQL statement above being executed against the control server/target server.

```
CONNECT TO SAMPLE;

INSERT INTO ASN.IBMSNAP_PRUNCNTL (
TARGET_SERVER, TARGET_OWNER, TARGET_TABLE, SYNCHTIME,
SYNCHPOINT, SOURCE_OWNER, SOURCE_TABLE, SOURCE_VIEW_QUAL,
APPLY_QUAL, SET_NAME, CNTL_SERVER, TARGET_STRUCTURE,
CNTL_ALIAS
) VALUES ( 'COPYTEST', 'AIXINST1', 'EMPLCOPY', NULL,
NULL, 'AIXINST1', 'EMPLOYEE', 0, 'EMPQUAL', 'EMPSUB',
'COPYTEST', 7, 'COPYTEST');
```

One row is inserted in the Prune Control table (IBMSNAP_PRUNCNTL) in the SAMPLE database at the AIX machine, the replication source, or master. In this case, the target table is EMPLCOPY, and the

TARGET_STRUCTURE is 7 (replica). This entry allows coordination of the pruning of the CD and UOW tables at the source server.

6.3 Preparing for Capture and Apply

Before starting the Capture and Apply programs, the following steps should be performed:

1. **Capture on source server**: For Capture to work, the source database must be enabled for roll-forward recovery. To do this on the source (the AIX machine), set LOGRETAIN on for the SAMPLE database. You are then obliged to perform a backup:

   ```
   $ db2 connect to sample
   $ db2 update database configuration for sample using
   LOGRETAIN on
   $ db2 backup database sample ...
   ```

   Bind the Capture packages. Change directory to where the DB2 bind files are stored. On AIX, this is in the sqllib/bnd directory under the instance owner's home directory (in this case, /home/db2inst1):

   ```
   $ db2 connect to sample
   $ db2 bind @capture.lst blocking all
   ```

   If you get errors, check that the replication control tables exist in the database. This normally happens at the first subscription definition.

2. **Capture on replica**: As Capture will also run on the Windows NT machine (where the replica table is stored), the COPYTEST database must also be enabled for roll-forward recovery:

   ```
   $ db2 connect to copytest
   $ db2 update database configuration for copytest using
   LOGRETAIN on
   $ db2 backup database copytest ...
   ```

   Bind the Capture packages. Change directory to the where the DB2 bind files are stored. On Windows NT, this is in the SQLLIB\BND directory under the installation drive (here, C:\).

   ```
   $ db2 connect to copytest
   $ db2 bind @capture.lst blocking all
   ```

3. **Apply on replica**: Before starting Apply on the Windows NT machine (the target or replica system), bind the Apply packages to the source and target servers:

   ```
   C:\ db2 connect to sample user aixinst1 using aixinst1
   C:\ db2 bind @applycs.lst isolation cs blocking all
   ```

```
C:\ db2 bind @applyur.lst isolation ur blocking all

C:\ db2 connect to copytest
C:\ db2 bind @applycs.lst isolation cs blocking all
C:\ db2 bind @applyur.lst isolation ur blocking all
```

Create an Apply password file, which is required in a Windows environment (a password file is required to allow end-user authentication to occur at the source server). If the Apply program needs a user and password to connect to a remote database, the user and password are stored in this file. The Apply program must be started from the directory in which the password file is stored. In this example, we use C:\RBJ. Use a text editor to create this file or enter the following in a DOS window:

```
copy con EMPQUALDB2COPYTEST.PWD
SERVER=SAMPLE USER=aixinst1 PWD=aixinst1
(ctrl-z)
```

The name of this file is a concatenation of the following:

- Apply qualifier (`EMPQUAL`).
- Instance name at the Windows NT (target/replica) machine (`DB2`).
- Name of the Control database (`COPYTEST`).
- Extension `.PWD`.

The contents are as follows:

- `SERVER=<value>`. The name of the database for Apply to connect to. In this case, this is `SAMPLE`, the database at the AIX server, in upper case. If it is not in upper case, Apply will stop with a connection failure error.
- `USER=<value>`. The user-id to connect with.
- `PWD=<value>`. The password to connect with.

6.3.1 Running Capture and Apply

Go to the AIX machine and start the Capture program. First ensure that you have correctly set the DB2INSTANCE environment variable to the instance containing the source database. Then you issue the following command:

```
$ asnccp sample
```

where `sample` is the name of source/master database. Please note that depending on your situation, you may wish to start Capture with a WARM start.

If you are not returned to the operating system prompt, then Capture is working. If you are returned to the prompt, then you should run Capture with trace active:

```
$ asnccp sample trace > capture.trc
```

Go to the Windows NT machine and start the Capture program. Recall that, in an update-anywhere environment, we can have Capture running at more than one server. Before you issue the command below, you must ensure that your environment variable DB2INSTANCE is set to the instance containing the database whose changes are to be captured:

```
C:\ asnccp copytest
```

where `copytest` is the target/replica database. If you are not returned to the operating system prompt, then Capture is working. If you are returned to the prompt, then you should run Capture with trace:

```
C:\ asnccp copytest trace > capture.trc
```

At the Windows NT machine, switch to another MS-DOS Command Window and prepare to start the Apply program. Ensure the DB2INSTANCE environment variable is set correctly. Change directory to the directory that holds the password file created in preparation step three (above) and enter this command:

```
C:\RBJ\ asnapply EMPQUAL copytest
```

If you are not returned to the operating system prompt, then Apply is working. If you are returned to the prompt, then you should run Apply with trace:

```
C:\RBJ\ asnapply EMPQUAL copytest trcflow > applyflw.trc
```

Make sure that the Apply qualifier is in upper case. If you type this in lower case, the Apply program will not find any matching subscription definition.

6.3.2 Testing the Configuration

To test that replication is working, make a change to the source table.

For example, let's delete a row from the EMPLOYEE table:

```
$ db2 "delete from employee where EMPNO = '000010'"
DB20000I  The SQL command completed successfully.
```

Check that this change has been replicated to the Windows NT machine:

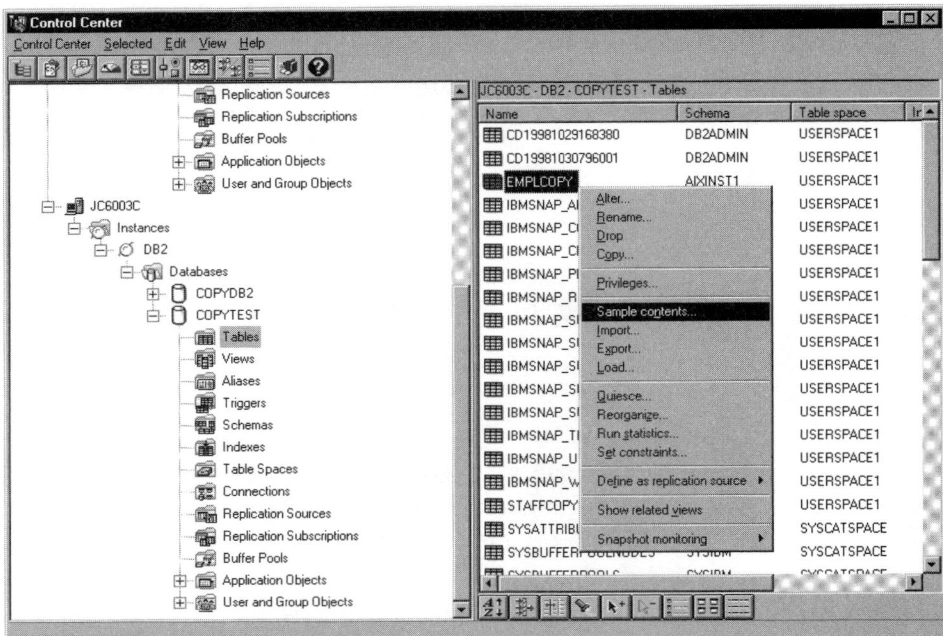

Figure 137. Sample Query from Control Center

Right-click on the **EMPLCOPY** table, and from the pop-up menu choose **Sample contents**. This displays the following rows from the EMPLCOPY table:

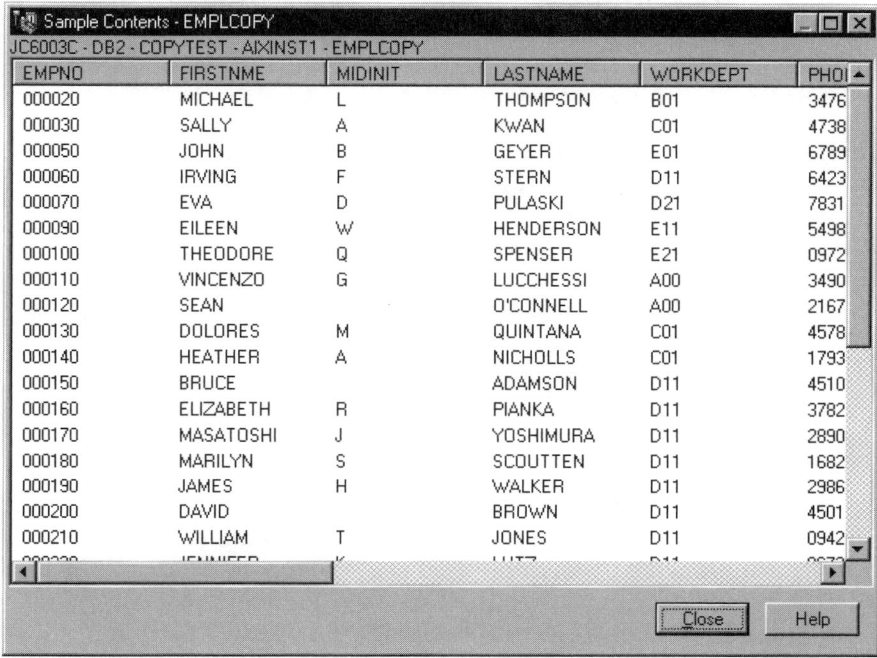
Sample Contents - EMPLCOPY

JC6003C - DB2 - COPYTEST - AIXINST1 - EMPLCOPY

EMPNO	FIRSTNME	MIDINIT	LASTNAME	WORKDEPT	PHO
000020	MICHAEL	L	THOMPSON	B01	3476
000030	SALLY	A	KWAN	C01	4738
000050	JOHN	B	GEYER	E01	6789
000060	IRVING	F	STERN	D11	6423
000070	EVA	D	PULASKI	D21	7831
000090	EILEEN	W	HENDERSON	E11	5498
000100	THEODORE	Q	SPENSER	E21	0972
000110	VINCENZO	G	LUCCHESSI	A00	3490
000120	SEAN		O'CONNELL	A00	2167
000130	DOLORES	M	QUINTANA	C01	4578
000140	HEATHER	A	NICHOLLS	C01	1793
000150	BRUCE		ADAMSON	D11	4510
000160	ELIZABETH	R	PIANKA	D11	3782
000170	MASATOSHI	J	YOSHIMURA	D11	2890
000180	MARILYN	S	SCOUTTEN	D11	1682
000190	JAMES	H	WALKER	D11	2986
000200	DAVID		BROWN	D11	4501
000210	WILLIAM	T	JONES	D11	0942

Figure 138. EMPLCOPY Query Output

Here we can see that the row with EMPNO=00010 is not displayed. This shows that the deletion was successfully replicated.

You can try another update from the replica table (EMPLCOPY) and check that the changes are replicated back to source table (EMPLOYEE).

6.4 Additional Considerations and Recommendations

When you implement update-anywhere replication, the data concurrency and consistency requirements of your system are the most important issues you should consider first. Apply can perform conflict detection to manage data consistency but still has some limitations. Even if you use Enhanced Conflict Detection, there is still the following case to consider: What if an application has read updated information that is later reversed as the result of a conflict being detected? In addition, there are other items to consider when designing your update-anywhere installation that are not covered here. These include the potential conflicts from constraints and triggers.

Another point to bear in mind is that if Referential Integrity (RI) constraints are defined on the source table, then you should explicitly declare the same RI constraints on the replica table. If this is not done, then Apply will not detect an RI violation as a conflict.

6.4.1 Rejected Transactions

When conflict occurs, the transaction at the replica is selected to be rejected and reversed. There is some cost for handling rejected transactions. Even though a transaction is rejected, it has already been committed in the replica system, and the users are not notified automatically when a transaction is rejected. Since the transaction rejection code is in the UOW table, and the before and after image values of each rejected transaction are available in the CD tables, all the details about rejected transactions are available in these tables.

ASNDONE can be used to report or perform a user-defined action after conflict is detected. If Apply was started with the NOTIFY option, it will invoke the ASNDONE user exit program directly after a subscription set is processed regardless of whether there are conflicts or not. You can make a process for handling rejected transactions and implement this using the ASNDONE user exit. A sample user exit program, ASNDONE.SMP, is provided with the installation in SQLLIB\SAMPLES\REPL (on Windows NT for example). You can customize this sample to include any action you want.

The rows in the change data table and unit of work table for rejected transactions will not be pruned in the normal pruning cycle. You can search the CD and UOW tables for rejected transactions periodically, and then, for example, re-run the rejected transactions in the appropriate sequence.

6.5 Summary

To summarize, update-anywhere replication is useful when you wish to have changes performed at the target server on the target table, and yet, you must have data consistency between source and target.

To define your update-anywhere environment, you define a replication source and a subscription with these characteristics:

Replication Source

- Table will be used for update-anywhere.
- Set the appropriate level of conflict detection.

Replication Subscription

- Target table type is replica.
- All after image columns.
- Primary key same as source table.
- Setup the source to replica table.
- Setup the replica to source table.

Considering the risk of compromising data consistency, and the costs of detecting and resolving conflicts, update-anywhere works best if you design your replication environment to eliminate any conflicts before they have a chance to occur.

One possible scenario is to logically partition data so that each application updates only certain ranges of data in tables. Another recommendation is that updates are scheduled so applications are allowed to update data during certain time periods in each site. In this case, there should be enough time allotted so that any uncaptured changes are not left in the database logs when the Apply cycle starts. When you implement update-anywhere, you should identify the users' requirements for data consistency and performance first and plan how to deal with possible conflicts.

Chapter 7. Mobile Replication

This chapter describes mobile replication, gives examples of why you might want to use it, and explains how the facilities provided with DB2 UDB Replication assist you in implementing it. An end-to-end example is provided, including all commands used, and any hints and tips.

7.1 Overview

The term *Mobile Replication* describes the mode of replication in which a mobile client (or portable computer), normally operating disconnected from a network, has a requirement to periodically replicate data to or from a server. More importantly, the mobile client has to be able to initiate and control the replication process.

For example, consider a mobile work force of sales agents working for an insurance company. Their applications running on laptops need to be updated before the start of each day's business with current rating data from the server, and at the end of each day, they need to update the server database with any new or amended policy details.

Without specific support for mobile replication, the end user would need to know a lot of detail about the function included in IBM Data Replication, and would need to take many more steps to accomplish the same end result.

DB2 UDB Replication provides you with the facilities to automate and customize the replication process to meet your requirements in the mobile environment. Mobile replication is accomplished through the use of the mobile replication enabler, and its functionality is provided by the ASNCOPY program. The command line interface of the enabler allows you to control:

- The calling of your telephone dialer software for connection and hang-up.
- The execution of the Capture and Apply processes.
- Which subscriptions to process.

There are a number of ways in which ASNCOPY can be invoked, giving you both *out-of-the-box* simplicity and the flexibility to integrate it into your own environment:

- From a graphical user interface called ASNMOBIL.
- From a command line.
- From your own application code.

Mobile Replication can also be integrated and mixed with non-mobile replication, since the same control tables, Capture and Apply components, and subscription definitions are used as in a standard replication environment. The principal difference when operating in mobile mode is that instead of processing its normal subscription processing cycle, Apply will only process those subscriptions that ASNCOPY specifies, and will only do this once per invocation from ASNCOPY. Normal subscription timing is ignored in mobile mode. This enables a mobile user who sometimes works *docked* in an office to operate in a mix of mobile and non-mobile modes as required.

The switching between mobile and normal modes is done as follows: ASNCOPY enables subscription selection and *process once* capability by altering the value of the ACTIVATE column in the ASN.IBMSNAP_SUBS_SET table at the control server. It sets ACTIVATE=2 for those subscriptions specified in the list to ASNCOPY, which means *process immediately*, and ACTIVATE=0 for those not required, meaning *deactivate*. ASNCOPY will reset the values back to 1 after Apply has completed processing.

Note

Operating in mobile mode reduces the amount of time that the mobile user needs to be connected by telephone, thus reducing costs.

Mobile Replication can also be used to provide a solution to the problem of *occasionally connected* systems. Using the insurance company example, there could be small satellite branches or agency offices where a stand-alone desktop or application server periodically connects to the central server to replicate data.

7.2 Planning for Mobile Replication

The pre-requisites for a mobile replication system are as follows:

7.2.1 Hardware and Software Requirements

In addition to the usual hardware and software requirements for a non-mobile environment detailed in "IBM Data Replication Products" on page 29, you may require some or all of the following depending on your particular needs:

- Modem and telephone line.
- Cellular Phone and interface software.
- Telephonic Dialer Software.
- Other communication software depending on the protocol used.

7.2.2 Security Requirements

For communications, security must be provided by the Dialer software and underlying communications software.

For database security, the same considerations and requirements apply as for non-mobile replication. Typically, the Capture/Apply programs require DBADM on the client database, the usual list of privileges against the source database, and EXECUTE for the Capture and Apply packages on the client database. See Chapter 3, "Capture and Apply" on page 59 for more details.

7.3 Setting Up a Mobile Replication Example

This section describes the steps required to set up an example environment demonstrating mobile replication. For the purposes of this exercise a Windows NT system was used. Where there are potential differences with other operating system environments, these are noted.

We will be using two databases, which will be located on the same machine to simplify the example. We will also be using the ASNMOBIL GUI in this example and providing stub .BAT files to simulate the calls to dialer and hang-up software.

Figure 139 on page 252 shows the example configuration:

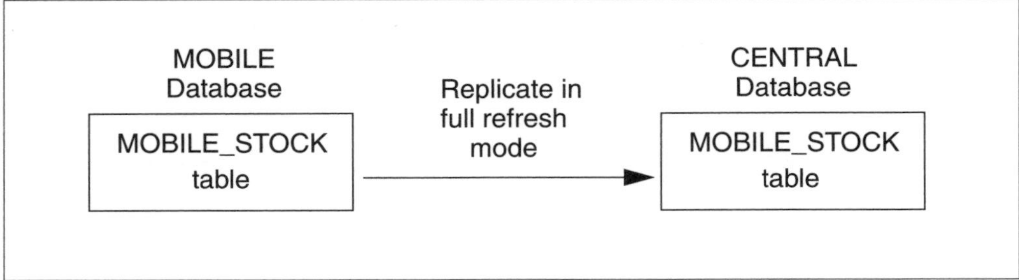

Figure 139. Example Configuration

The MOBILE_STOCK table in the MOBILE database will be replicated using full refresh to the MOBILE_STOCK table in the CENTRAL database.

7.3.1 Creating the Example Databases

First, ensure that you are logged on with a userid with SYSADM or DBADM authority. In this example, you will see userid IEU00045 being used - your userid may well be different, but it's recommended that it have SYSADM authority.

From the DB2 UDB Control Center, create two databases called CENTRAL and MOBILE in your local instance. A single click with the right mouse button on the **Databases** icon will open a pop-up menu, where you can select **Create** and **New**:

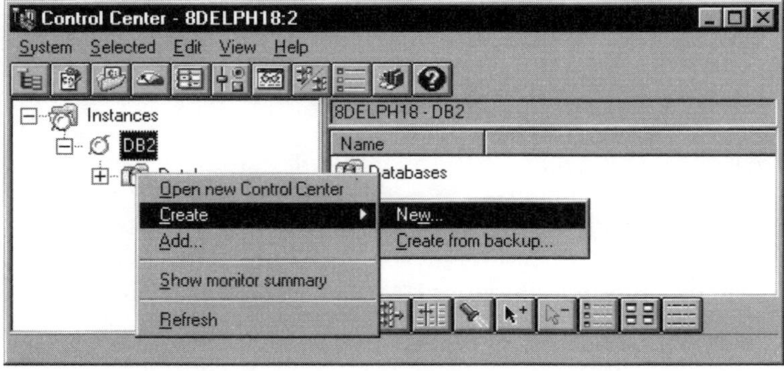

Figure 140. Creating the Example Databases

The Create Database SmartGuide is displayed:

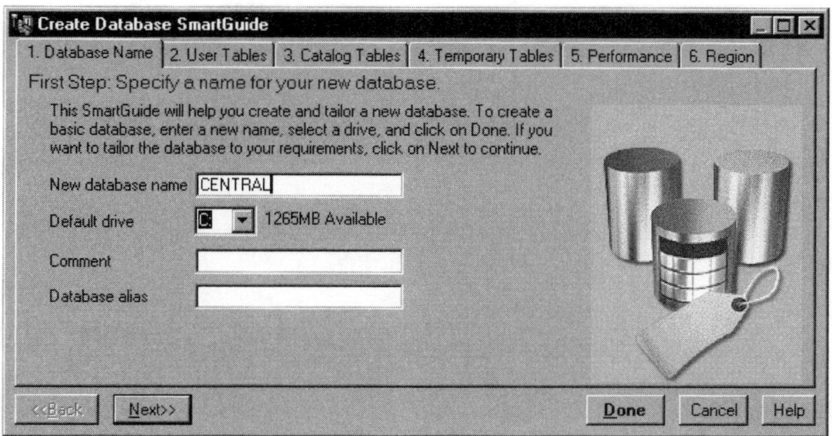

Figure 141. Create Database SmartGuide

Enter CENTRAL as the name of the database, and then specify the drive on which you want it to be created. The other values can be left at their defaults.

Repeat these steps to create the second database, MOBILE. After creating both databases, they are displayed as follows in the Control Center:

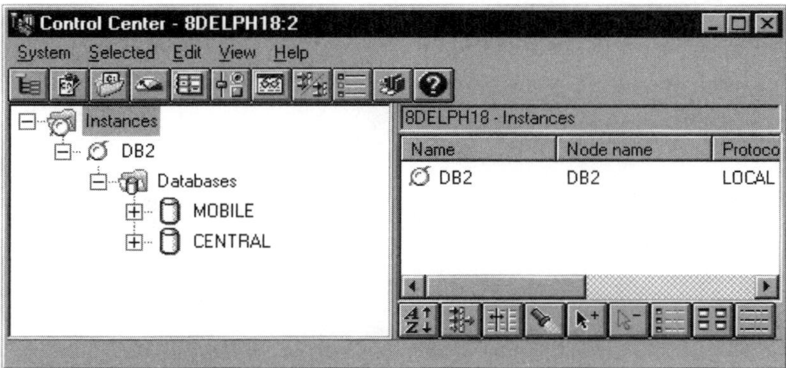

Figure 142. Displaying Example Databases

7.3.2 Creating the Example Tables

Using a text editor, create an SQL script file called mobile_stock.sql and save it in a suitable directory. In this example, we use c:\asn\sql:

```
create table MOBILE_STOCK (
ITEM_NO DECIMAL (5,0) NOT NULL PRIMARY KEY,
QUANTITY_HELD DECIMAL (7,0),
ITEM_DESC CHAR (100),
SALES_ID INTEGER NOT NULL WITH DEFAULT 9999 )
DATA CAPTURE CHANGES;
```

From a DB2 Command Window, connect to the MOBILE database and run the SQL script to create the source table:

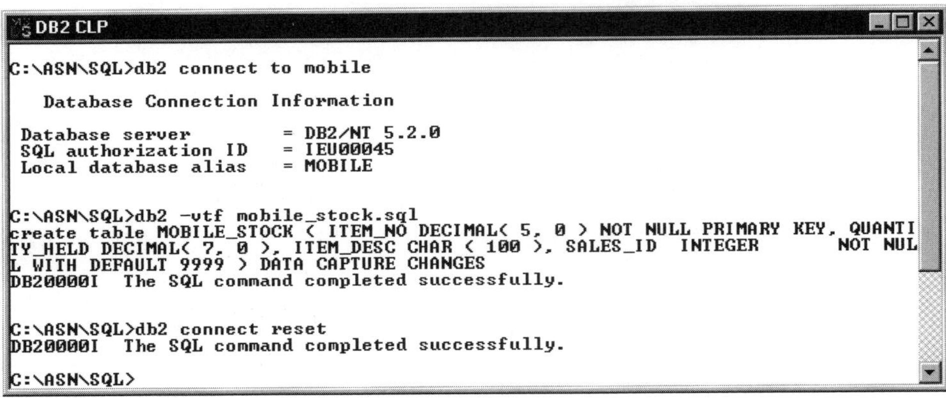

Figure 143. Creating the Source Table in MOBILE

From a DB2 Command Window, connect to the CENTRAL database and run the SQL script to create the target table:

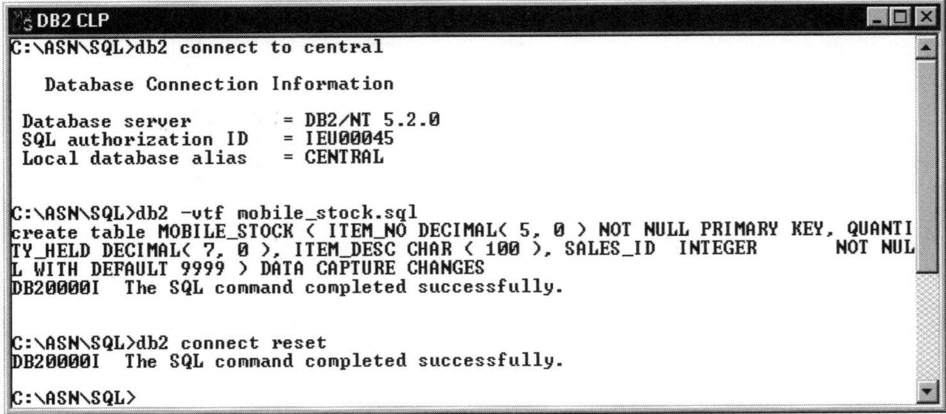

Figure 144. Creating the Target Table in CENTRAL

7.3.3 Defining the Replication Source

In this example, we will setup one-way replication from the MOBILE database to the CENTRAL database.

> **Note**
>
> You can also define your replication subscription to be not only MOBILE->CENTRAL, but also CENTRAL->MOBILE. In this case, it would be an update-anywhere configuration.

From the DB2 Control Center, navigate to the Tables view of the MOBILE database and then right-click on MOBILE_STOCK. Select **Define as a replication source** and **Custom** from the pop-up menus:

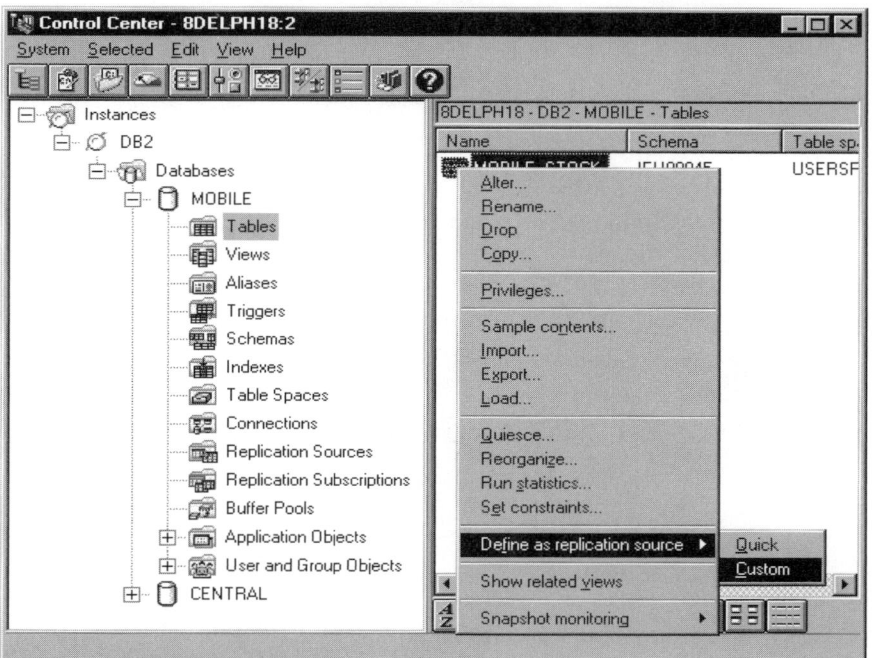

Figure 145. Defining a Replication Source

The Define as a Replication Source panel is displayed:

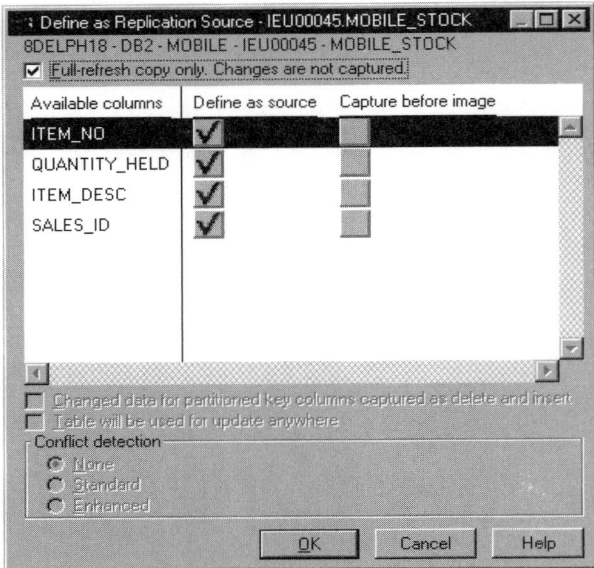

Figure 146. Define as a Replication Source

Select the **Full-refresh copy only** option and click on **OK**. In this example, the volumes of data don't warrant running change capture on the source table. Note also that the 'Capture before image' tick-boxes are deselected and greyed out. The following panel is displayed:

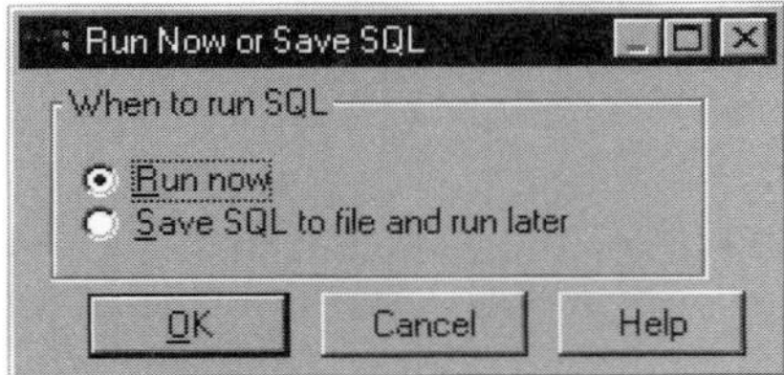

Figure 147. Run Now or Save SQL

Select the **Run now** radio-button and click on **OK**.

You may notice that if you have not already created the Replication Control Tables (those with the schema ASN and names prefixed with IBMSNAP_), that they are created automatically for you by the Control Center. Refreshing the Tables list by right clicking on **Tables** icon and selecting **Refresh** from the popup view will enable you to see these tables:

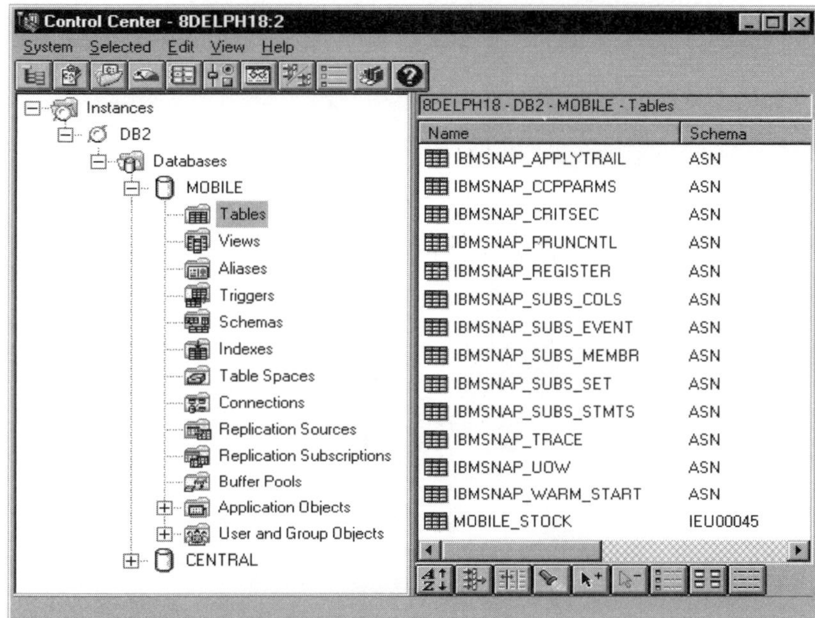

Figure 148. Replication Control Tables

Click on **Replication Sources**, and you should now see that the MOBILE_STOCK table is defined as a replication source:

Figure 149. Replication Sources

7.3.4 Defining the Subscription

We will create one subscription to replicate in full-refresh mode the contents of the MOBILE_STOCK table from the MOBILE database to the CENTRAL database.

From the Replication Sources view, right click on the MOBILE_STOCK replication source icon and select **Define subscription**:

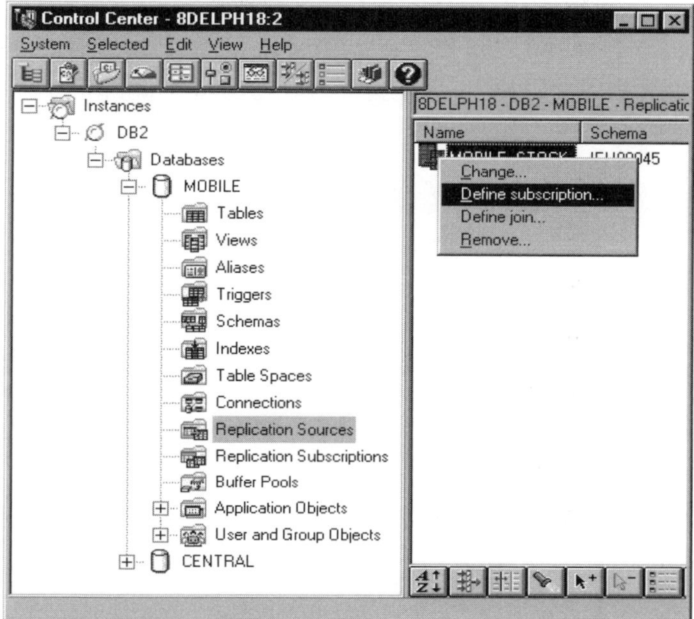

Figure 150. Define Subscription

This will display the Define Subscription panel:

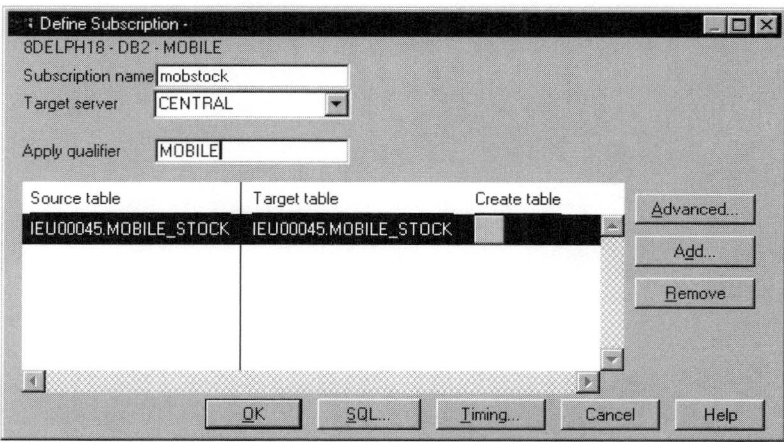

Figure 151. Define Subscription

De-select the **Create table** tick-box as we've already created the target table ourselves. Enter mobstock as the Subscription name.

Select database CENTRAL from the Target database pull-down. Enter MOBILE as the Apply qualifier and click on **OK**. We can leave all the other settings to their defaults for the purposes of this exercise, including the Timing options that are over-ridden in mobile replication. The following panel is displayed:

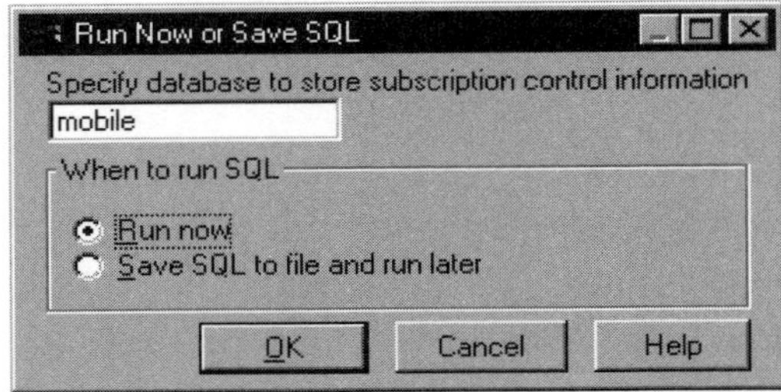

Figure 152. Run Now or Save SQL

At the 'Specify database to store subscription control information' prompt, enter MOBILE. This identifies the database which acts as the Control Server. Select the **Run now** radio-button and click on **OK**.

After a short delay, during which the Control Center generates and runs the SQL to create the subscription entries in the control tables, you should see the following informational message:

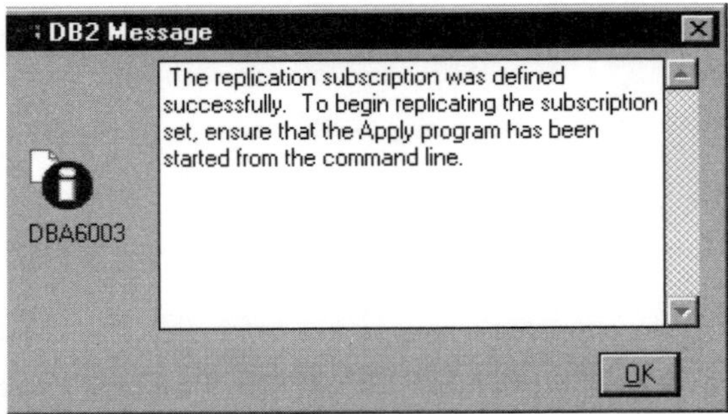

Figure 153. Subscription Defined Successfully

Click on **OK** to return to the Replication Sources view. You can confirm the creation of your subscription by selecting the **Replication Subscriptions** icon. You should see:

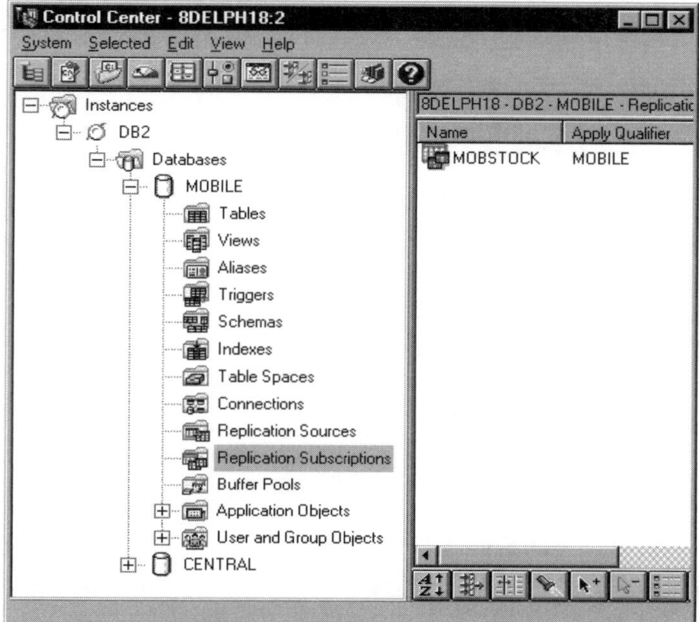

Figure 154. Replication Subscriptions

7.3.5 Binding the Apply Program to the Example Databases

The next step is binding the Apply program to the MOBILE and CENTRAL databases.

Ensure that you are logged on with a userid with DBADM or SYSADM privileges on the two databases. You should already be if you're still logged on as the user who created them.

From a DB2 Command Window, change directory to the path where the .BND files are installed. This is usually c:\sqllib\bnd, but if you have UDB installed on a different drive, substitute your drive accordingly.

Connect to the MOBILE database and enter the BIND commands as shown below, then issue a CONNECT RESET:

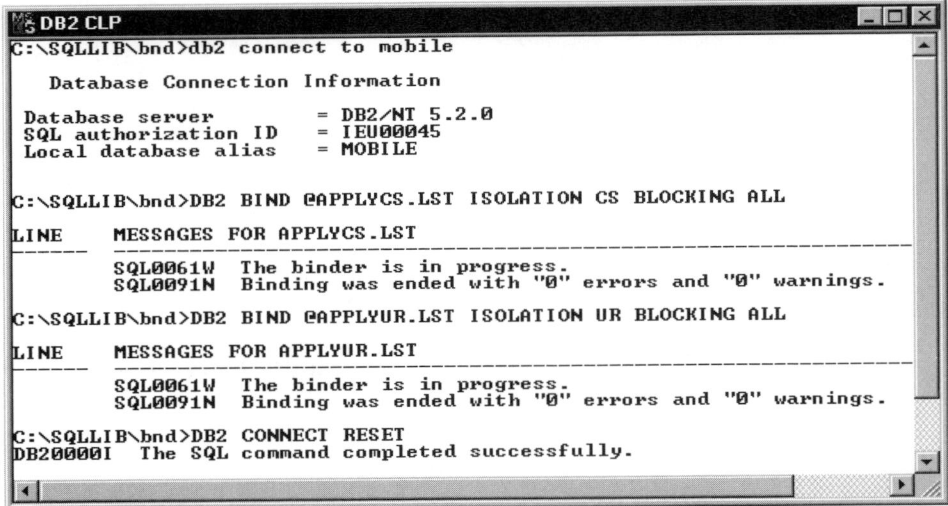
DB2 CLP
C:\SQLLIB\bnd>db2 connect to mobile
Database Connection Information
Database server = DB2/NT 5.2.0
SQL authorization ID = IEU00045
Local database alias = MOBILE
C:\SQLLIB\bnd>DB2 BIND @APPLYCS.LST ISOLATION CS BLOCKING ALL
LINE MESSAGES FOR APPLYCS.LST
SQL0061W The binder is in progress.
SQL0091N Binding was ended with "0" errors and "0" warnings.
C:\SQLLIB\bnd>DB2 BIND @APPLYUR.LST ISOLATION UR BLOCKING ALL
LINE MESSAGES FOR APPLYUR.LST
SQL0061W The binder is in progress.
SQL0091N Binding was ended with "0" errors and "0" warnings.
C:\SQLLIB\bnd>DB2 CONNECT RESET
DB20000I The SQL command completed successfully.

Figure 155. Binding the Apply Program to the Mobile Database

Repeat these steps for the CENTRAL database. Note that the Control Center will have created all of the required Control Tables in the CENTRAL database when you defined the subscription with CENTRAL as the target server. These tables are required in order to bind the Apply program to a database:

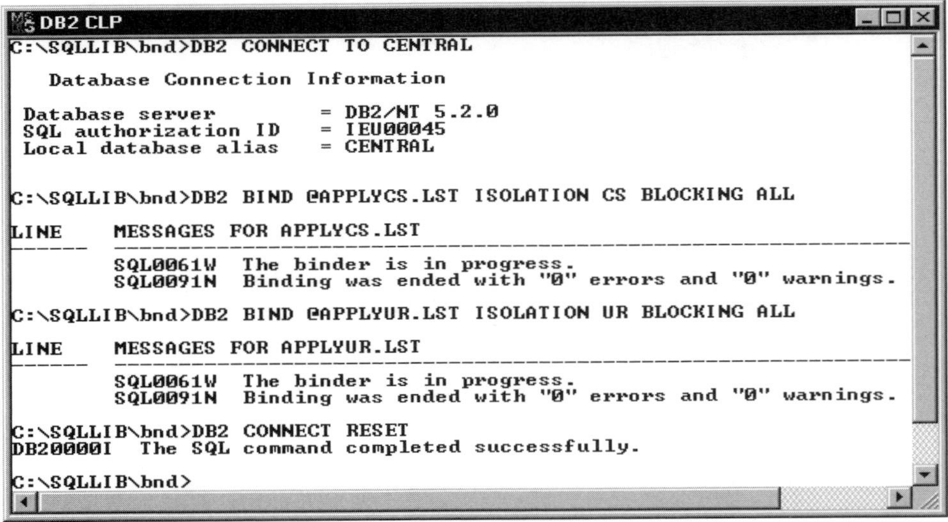
DB2 CLP
C:\SQLLIB\bnd>DB2 CONNECT TO CENTRAL
Database Connection Information
Database server = DB2/NT 5.2.0
SQL authorization ID = IEU00045
Local database alias = CENTRAL
C:\SQLLIB\bnd>DB2 BIND @APPLYCS.LST ISOLATION CS BLOCKING ALL
LINE MESSAGES FOR APPLYCS.LST
SQL0061W The binder is in progress.
SQL0091N Binding was ended with "0" errors and "0" warnings.
C:\SQLLIB\bnd>DB2 BIND @APPLYUR.LST ISOLATION UR BLOCKING ALL
LINE MESSAGES FOR APPLYUR.LST
SQL0061W The binder is in progress.
SQL0091N Binding was ended with "0" errors and "0" warnings.
C:\SQLLIB\bnd>DB2 CONNECT RESET
DB20000I The SQL command completed successfully.
C:\SQLLIB\bnd>

Figure 156. Binding the Apply Program to the Central Database

7.3.6 Binding the Mobile Client GUI

In addition to the usual binds required for setting up non-mobile replication, the ASNMOBIL GUI program needs to be bound to the database where the control server is located. Ensure that you are logged on with a userid with DBADM or SYSADM privileges on the control server database.

Open a DB2 Command Window and change directory to the directory containing the bind files, which is usually C:\SQLLIB\BND. Connect to the control server database and run these BIND commands to create the required packages for ASNMOBIL:

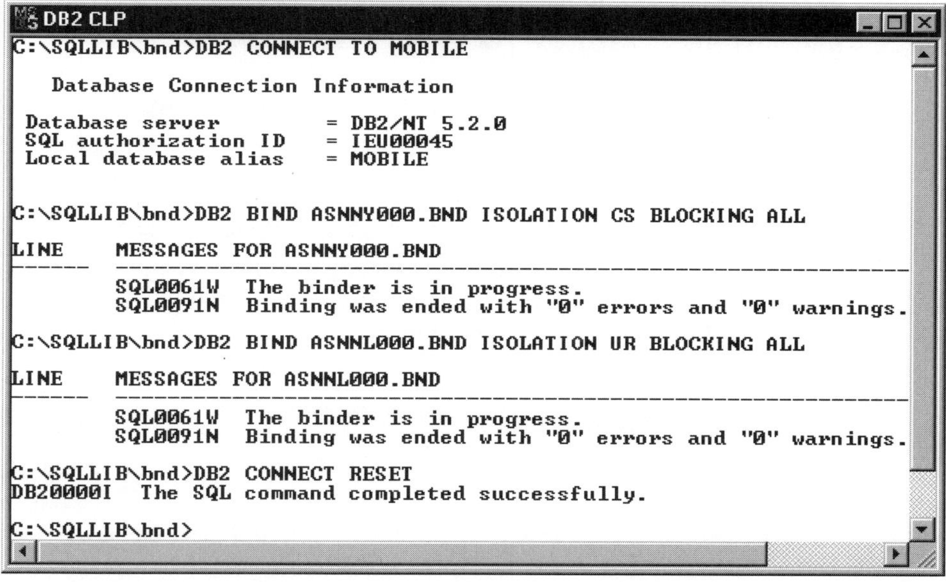
DB2 CLP
C:\SQLLIB\bnd>DB2 CONNECT TO MOBILE
Database Connection Information
Database server = DB2/NT 5.2.0
SQL authorization ID = IEU00045
Local database alias = MOBILE
C:\SQLLIB\bnd>DB2 BIND ASNNY000.BND ISOLATION CS BLOCKING ALL
LINE MESSAGES FOR ASNNY000.BND
SQL0061W The binder is in progress.
SQL0091N Binding was ended with "0" errors and "0" warnings.
C:\SQLLIB\bnd>DB2 BIND ASNNL000.BND ISOLATION UR BLOCKING ALL
LINE MESSAGES FOR ASNNL000.BND
SQL0061W The binder is in progress.
SQL0091N Binding was ended with "0" errors and "0" warnings.
C:\SQLLIB\bnd>DB2 CONNECT RESET
DB20000I The SQL command completed successfully.
C:\SQLLIB\bnd>

Figure 157. Binding the Mobile Client GUI Program

Note that this example applies to Windows NT; for OS/2, the bind files are ASN2Y000.BND and ASN2L000.BND respectively.

7.3.7 Identifying the Control Server Database

The mobile replication enabler requires that the database where the control server is located is identified by the environment variable DB2DBDFT. There are a number of ways of achieving this:

- Windows NT: Set it in Settings/System/Environment.
- OS/2: Set it in CONFIG.SYS using `SET DB2DBDFT=control_server.`

- Windows 95/98: Set it in AUTOEXEC.BAT using
  `SET DB2DBDFT=control_server.`

In this example, the control server is MOBILE.

Ensure that you are using the correct instance by checking that the environment variable DB2INSTANCE is set correctly. In this example, we are using the default DB2 instance.

7.3.8 Directory for Generated Files

Mobile replication and Apply will generate a number of files during processing, and it is a good idea to keep these in a separate directory. In this example, we are using c:\asn\mobile.

7.3.9 Specifying Stub Code for the Dial and Hang-up Software

IBM Data Replication does not provide auto-dial or auto-disconnect functionality. It calls user provided user exits to do this.

The ASNDIAL and ASNHANGUP environment variables are used to specify the path and parameters for calling the user exits for dialing and hanging up during the replication process. In this example we will use two stub .BAT files to simulate the calls to a dialer:

- `SET ASNDIAL=C:\ASN\APPLY\DIAL.BAT` - used for auto-dial
- `SET ASNHANGUP=C:\ASN\APPLY\HANGUP.BAT` - used for auto-disconnect

Each .BAT file simply displays a message to say it has been called to prove that the environment variable setting has worked. If ASNDIAL is null, a connection must be made before invoking ASNCOPY. If ASNHANGUP is null, the connected will not be ended when ASNCOPY completes.

Here are examples of what the two .BAT files should look like for our environment:

- DIAL.BAT:

```
echo This is where your own Dialer gets called to establish a
connection
```

- HANGUP.BAT:

```
echo This is where your own Dialer gets called to hang-up the
connection
```

7.3.10 Creating a Password File

On Windows 95/98 and Windows NT, you need to create a password file for the Apply program. This contains the user IDs and passwords to be used by Apply in order to connect to the Control, Source, and Target server databases.

In the directory that you created earlier to hold the files generated by Mobile Replication and Apply (here, c:\asn\mobile), create a password file with the following format:

```
<APPLYQUAL><instname><CNTLSRVR>.PWD
```

Following this naming convention, in this example, the file is called MOBILEDB2MOBILE.PWD.

Use an editor to create an entry for each of the servers to be connected to by Apply with the following format:

```
SERVER=server_name PWD=password USER=userid
```

So, our example requires two records, one for MOBILE, and one for CENTRAL:

```
SERVER=MOBILE PWD=password USER=IEU00045
SERVER=CENTRAL PWD=password USER=IEU00045
```

If required, substitute your own userid and passwords.

7.3.11 Inserting Test Data

To be able to test that replication is taking place, we need first to insert some test data into the source table. From a DB2 Command Window, connect to the MOBILE database and execute some INSERT statements as shown in Figure 158 on page 266:

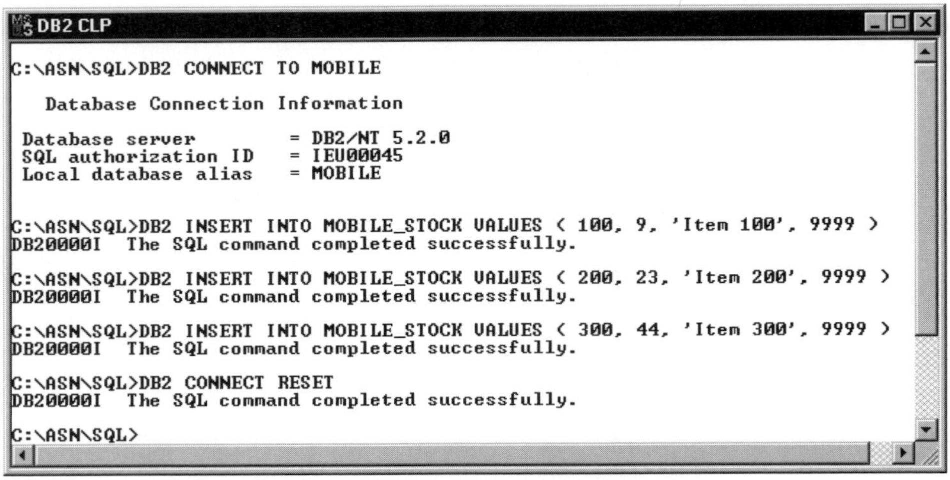

```
C:\ASN\SQL>DB2 CONNECT TO MOBILE

   Database Connection Information

 Database server        = DB2/NT 5.2.0
 SQL authorization ID   = IEU00045
 Local database alias   = MOBILE


C:\ASN\SQL>DB2 INSERT INTO MOBILE_STOCK VALUES ( 100, 9, 'Item 100', 9999 )
DB20000I  The SQL command completed successfully.

C:\ASN\SQL>DB2 INSERT INTO MOBILE_STOCK VALUES ( 200, 23, 'Item 200', 9999 )
DB20000I  The SQL command completed successfully.

C:\ASN\SQL>DB2 INSERT INTO MOBILE_STOCK VALUES ( 300, 44, 'Item 300', 9999 )
DB20000I  The SQL command completed successfully.

C:\ASN\SQL>DB2 CONNECT RESET
DB20000I  The SQL command completed successfully.

C:\ASN\SQL>
```

Figure 158. Inserting Test Data

7.3.12 Invoking the Mobile Replication GUI

From a DB2 Command Window, change directory to the one created earlier (here, c:\asn\mobile). Enter the command ASNMOBIL to start the Mobile Replication GUI:

Mobile Replication Enabler

Apply qualifier: MOBILE

Subscription: U MOBSTOCK

- [ ] Hold the communication line
- [ ] Call ASNLOAD for full-refresh
- [x] Use fast path. Do not call Capture
- [ ] Cold start Capture
- [x] Set trace on
- [ ] Notify completion

OK | Cancel | Help

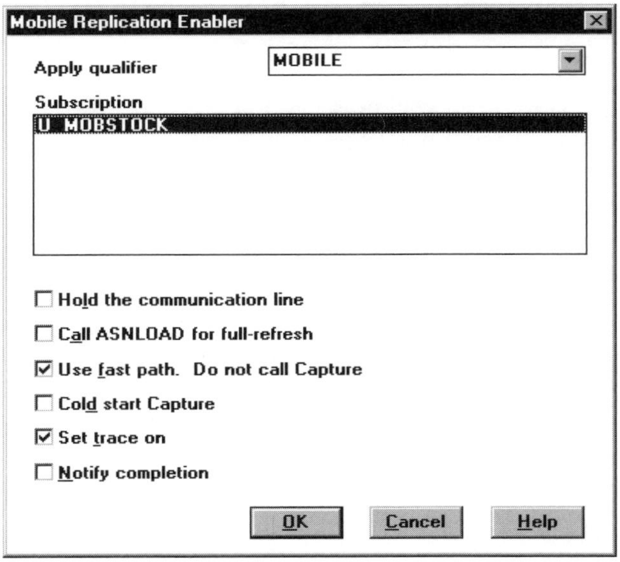

Figure 159. Mobile Replication Enabler

In the Mobile Replication Enabler panel, the **Apply Qualifier** MOBILE should be the only one available and should be selected.

The **Subscription** MOBSTOCK should be the only one available and also should be selected. If you omit to select a subscription, then Apply will execute but not process anything.

Select the **Use fast path. Do not call Capture** option, as we are only doing full-refresh replication.

Select the **Set trace on** tick-box so we can see what gets called.

Click on **OK**. At this point, you may see a window open briefly displaying the echo messages from the calls to the stub Dial and Hang-up .BAT files. After this, you should see an informational popup message:

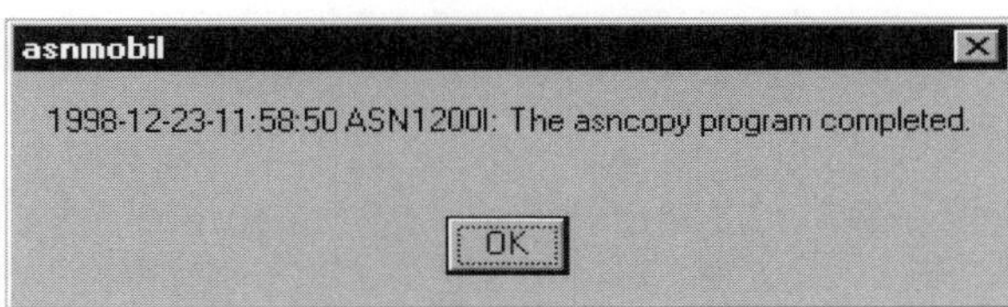

Figure 160. Asnmobil Message

This message indicates that the ASNCOPY program has initiated the processing of the subscription by Apply.

7.3.13 Verifying that Replication Occurred

There are a number of ways to verify that the subscription was processed by Apply:

Check the contents of the MOBILE_STOCK table in the CENTRAL database. From the Control Center, select the **Tables** view for the CENTRAL database, then right click on the MOBILE_STOCK table and select **Sample contents**:

Sample Contents - MOBILE_STOCK

8DELPH18 - DB2 - CENTRAL - IEU00045 - MOBILE_STOCK

ITEM_NO	QUANTITY_HELD	ITEM_DESC	SALES_ID
100	9	Item 100 ...	9999
200	23	Item 200 ...	9999
300	44	Item 300 ...	9999

Figure 161. MOBILE_STOCK in CENTRAL - Sample Contents

You can also examine the contents of the working directory from which ASNMOBIL was invoked. You should see files similar to the following:

```
DB2 CLP
C:\ASN\mobile>dir
 Volume in drive C has no label.
 Volume Serial Number is 58A6-E039

 Directory of C:\ASN\mobile

98/12/23  09:31p        <DIR>          .
98/12/23  09:31p        <DIR>          ..
98/12/23  09:31p                 7,044 APPLY19981223213056.TRC
98/12/23  09:31p                   211 ASNCOPY.LOG
98/12/23  09:31p                 1,268 ASNCOPY.TRC
98/12/23  09:31p                   357 MOBILEDB2MOBILE.000
98/12/23  09:31p                    87 MOBILEDB2MOBILE.LOG
98/12/23  01:35p                    81 MOBILEDB2MOBILE.PWD
               8 File(s)          9,048 bytes
                          1,326,439,424 bytes free

C:\ASN\mobile>
```

Figure 162. ASNMOBIL - Logs and Trace Files

The APPLYtimestamp.TRC file contains a verbose trace from Apply. The MOBILEDB2MOBILE.LOG file is the log created by Apply. The MOBILEDB2MOBILE.000 file is a spill file created by Apply and contains images of rows replicated. The ASNCOPY.LOG file contains informational messages and should look similar to this:

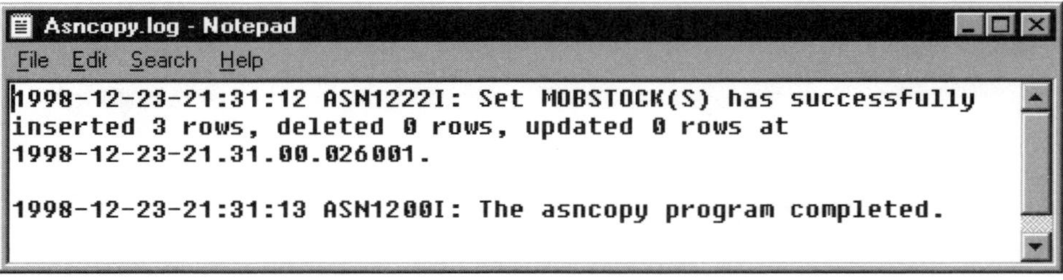

Asncopy.log - Notepad

File Edit Search Help

1998-12-23-21:31:12 ASN1222I: Set MOBSTOCK(S) has successfully inserted 3 rows, deleted 0 rows, updated 0 rows at 1998-12-23-21.31.00.026001.

1998-12-23-21:31:13 ASN1200I: The asncopy program completed.

Figure 163. Asncopy.log File

The ASNCOPY.TRC file contains a trace of the execution of ASNCOPY that is invoked by ASNMOBIL, and which in turn, invokes Apply. It should look similar to this (we show this file in two parts):

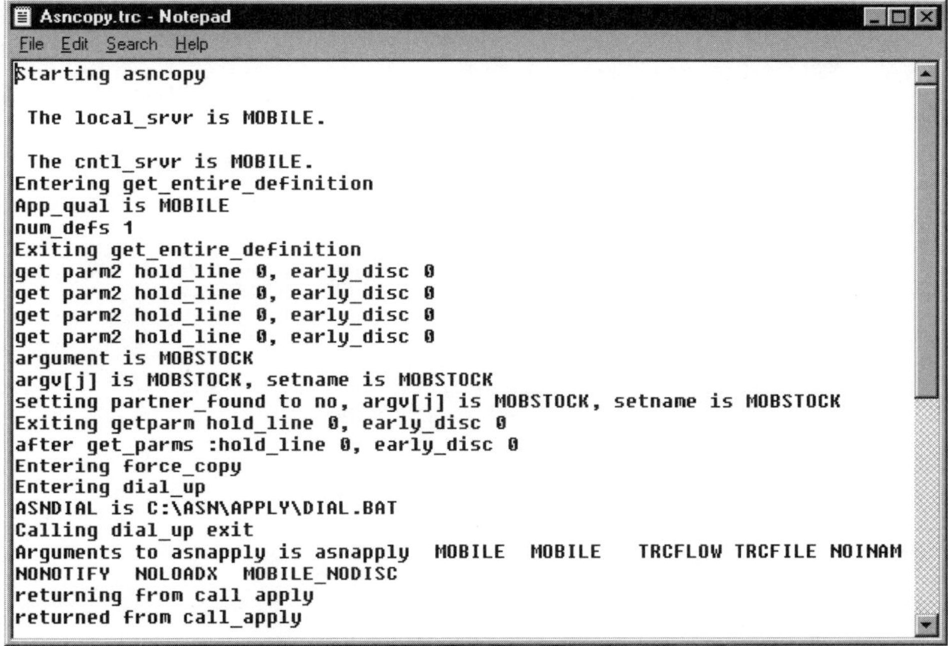

```
Asncopy.trc - Notepad
File Edit Search Help
Starting asncopy

 The local_srvr is MOBILE.

 The cntl_srvr is MOBILE.
Entering get_entire_definition
App_qual is MOBILE
num_defs 1
Exiting get_entire_definition
get parm2 hold_line 0, early_disc 0
get parm2 hold_line 0, early_disc 0
get parm2 hold_line 0, early_disc 0
get parm2 hold_line 0, early_disc 0
argument is MOBSTOCK
argv[j] is MOBSTOCK, setname is MOBSTOCK
setting partner_found to no, argv[j] is MOBSTOCK, setname is MOBSTOCK
Exiting getparm hold_line 0, early_disc 0
after get_parms :hold_line 0, early_disc 0
Entering force_copy
Entering dial_up
ASNDIAL is C:\ASN\APPLY\DIAL.BAT
Calling dial_up exit
Arguments to asnapply is asnapply  MOBILE  MOBILE   TRCFLOW TRCFILE NOINAM
NONOTIFY  NOLOADX  MOBILE_NODISC
returning from call apply
returned from call_apply
```

Figure 164. Asncopy.trc File (Part 1)

In Figure 164, you can see that we enter a dial-up mode and invoke the user-supplied user exit to dial to the source server from our mobile client. You can also see the call to Apply and the parameters provided to Apply for this replication.

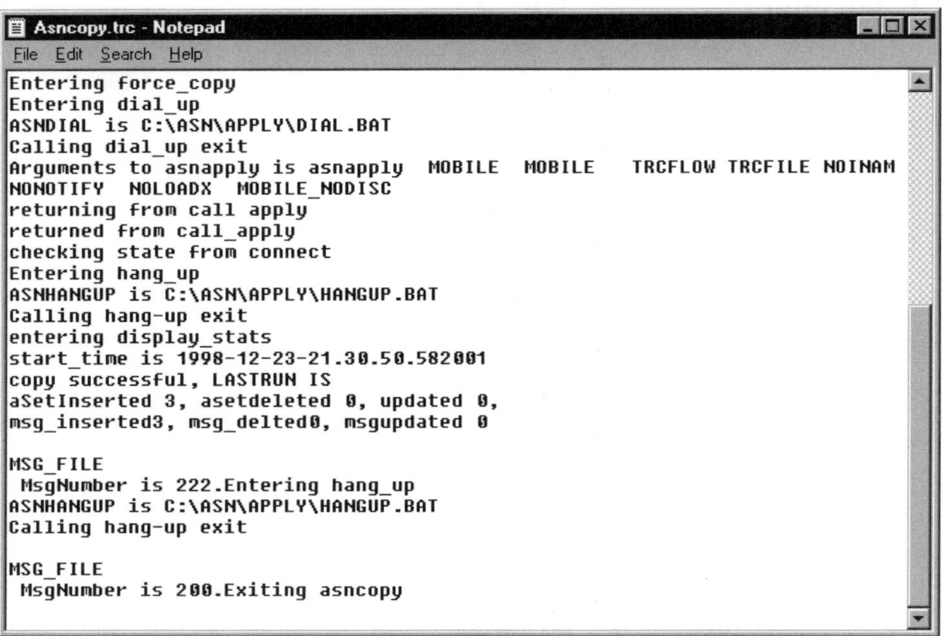
```
Entering force_copy
Entering dial_up
ASNDIAL is C:\ASN\APPLY\DIAL.BAT
Calling dial_up exit
Arguments to asnapply is asnapply  MOBILE  MOBILE   TRCFLOW TRCFILE NOINAM
NONOTIFY  NOLOADX  MOBILE_NODISC
returning from call apply
returned from call_apply
checking state from connect
Entering hang_up
ASNHANGUP is C:\ASN\APPLY\HANGUP.BAT
Calling hang-up exit
entering display_stats
start_time is 1998-12-23-21.30.50.582001
copy successful, LASTRUN IS
aSetInserted 3, asetdeleted 0, updated 0,
msg_inserted3, msg_delted0, msgupdated 0

MSG_FILE
 MsgNumber is 222.Entering hang_up
ASNHANGUP is C:\ASN\APPLY\HANGUP.BAT
Calling hang-up exit

MSG_FILE
 MsgNumber is 200.Exiting asncopy
```

Figure 165. Asncopy.trc File (Part 2)

Figure 165 continues the same trace file, and we see further down in this trace file that after Apply has completed, we invoke the user-supplied user exit to disconnect our connection to the source server from the mobile client.

7.4 Summary

In this chapter, we demonstarted how the mobile replication functionality in IBM Data Replication can be used to support *occasionally connected* users who need to connect on demand, complete the replication required, and disconnect. This is accomplished through the ASNCOPY program.

When Data Replication is invoked in mobile mode, copies are done as soon as possible for the selected subscription sets. Timing settings are ignored.

To summarize the overall procedure:

1. These steps should be performed once during the initial setup:
   - Define the replication sources.
   - Define the replication subscriptions.
   - Bind the Capture and Apply program bind files against the appropriate databases.
   - Bind the ASNMOBIL GUI bind files against the control server database.
   - Identify the control server database on the mobile machine by setting DB2DBDFT.
2. These steps should be performed when you want to trigger replication:
   - Start DB2 on your mobile system.
   - Ensure that the DB2DBDFT, ASNDIAL and ASNHANGUP variables are set.
   - Invoke ASNCOPY, either through the GUI or through the command line.

The steps in your environment will vary depending on whether you wish to setup one-way replication or an update-anywhere configuration.

Chapter 8. Advanced Replication Techniques

In this chapter we take the opportunity to present to you some of the more advanced IBM Data Replication features. In some discussions, knowledge of the DB2 Replication products is assumed. We present these discussions to give you a flavor of some of these more advanced topics, and how they can be used in your replication environment to resolve specific application requirements.

The material covered in this chapter is not strictly required for the Data Replication certification exam #508; however it will help you better understand DB2 Replication, and this will provide you with a more solid foundation for certification.

Specifically, the issues we cover here are:

- “Join Replication” on page 273.
- “Replicating From Oracle to DB2 UDB” on page 288.
- “CCD Table Considerations” on page 314.
- “DB2 ODBC Catalog” on page 333.
- “DB2 UDB Enterprise-Extended Edition Considerations” on page 349.
- “DB2 UDB Long Varchar Support” on page 352.

8.1 Join Replication

When a target table needs to contain columns from multiple tables in the source database, you need to use the ability to define a replication source which is actually a DB2 view of the multiple source tables. In this section we discuss this ability and take you through an example, including a discussion of some issues that need to be addressed with Join views.

Join views can be very useful in replication configurations. They can be used to denormalize (or restructure) copies in data warehouse scenarios, to enable easier querying of copied data, and also to address the routing problem (sometimes called the database partitioning problem) in distributed computing scenarios. For example, knowing where to send a bank account update may require a join of the account table with the customer table in order to know which branch of the bank the customer deals with. Typically, production databases are normalized so that the geographic details, such as branch number, are not stored redundantly throughout the production database.

Joins are used in a variety of replication scenarios and are specified in views, and the views are then registered as replication sources. Joins themselves are defined in source registrations, not subscriptions.

8.1.1 Join Scenario Overview

To illustrate an example of using join replication sources, we will use the EMPLOYEE and DEPARTMENT tables in the DB2 for OS/390 system. The target table in the DB2 UDB for Windows NT system is called DEPTEMP.

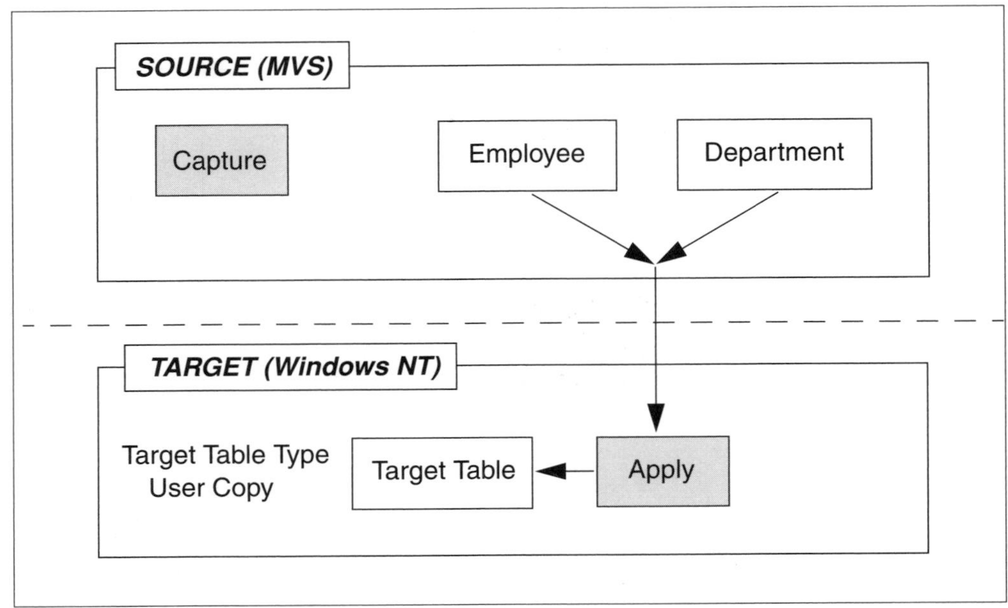

Figure 166. Join Replication Scenario Overview

For reference, here is the DDL for the two source tables:

```
CONNECT TO DB2C USER SW6003A USING AZUMA;
------------------------------------------------
-- DDL Statements for table "SW6003A"."DEPARTMENT"
------------------------------------------------
DROP TABLE DEPARTMENT;
CREATE TABLE "SW6003A"."DEPARTMENT"  (
 "DEPTNO" CHAR(3) NOT NULL , "DEPTNAME" VARCHAR(29) NOT NULL ,
 "MGRNO" CHAR(6) , "ADMRDEPT" CHAR(3) NOT NULL ,
 "LOCATION" CHAR(16) ) ;
------------------------------------------------
-- DDL Statements for table "SW6003A"."EMPLOYEE"
------------------------------------------------
```

```
DROP TABLE EMPLOYEE;
CREATE TABLE "SW6003A"."EMPLOYEE"  (
"EMPNO" CHAR(6) NOT NULL , "FIRSTNME" VARCHAR(12) NOT NULL ,
"MIDINIT" CHAR(1) NOT NULL , "LASTNAME" VARCHAR(15) NOT NULL ,
"WORKDEPT" CHAR(3) , "PHONENO" CHAR(4) ,
"HIREDATE" DATE , "JOB" CHAR(8) , "EDLEVEL" SMALLINT NOT NULL ,
"SEX" CHAR(1) , "BIRTHDATE" DATE , "SALARY" DECIMAL(9,2) ,
"BONUS" DECIMAL(9,2) , "COMM" DECIMAL(9,2) );
```

8.1.2 Defining a Join Replication Source

Once the two source tables exist, you can create a view replication source based on these tables. The view source is then available to be copied to a target table.

1. From the Control Center, select **Replication Sources** to display the replication sources in the contents pane. Hold the **Ctrl** key and click on each replication source desired to highlight each one, then right-click and select **Define join**:

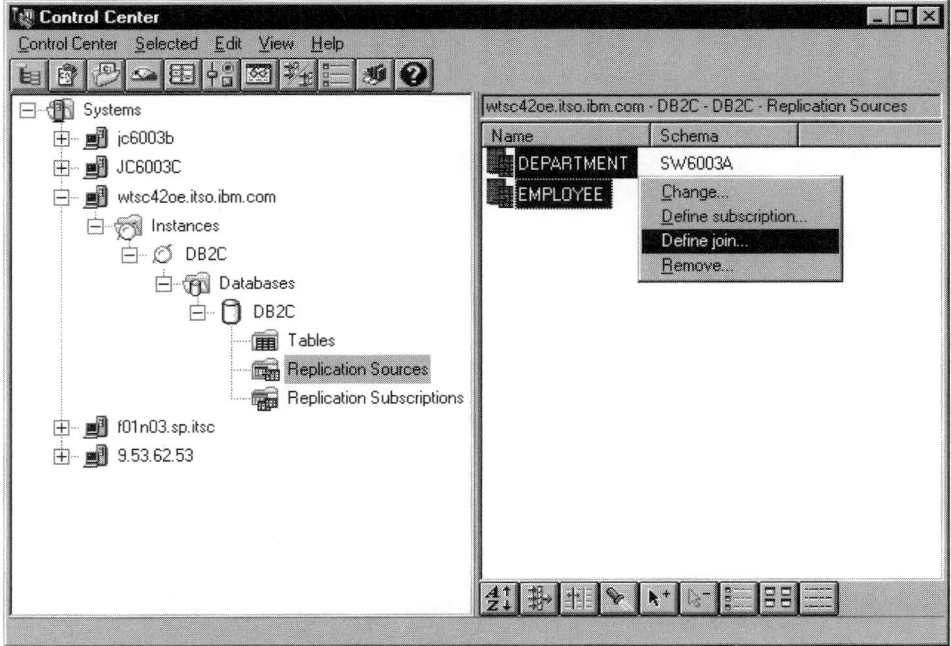

Figure 167. Define Join Replication Source

We will join these two tables in the following way:

```
CREATE VIEW DEPTEMP (DEPTNO,LASTNAME,SALARY,BONUS) AS SELECT
A.DEPTNO,B.LASTNAME,B.SALARY,B.BONUS FROM DEPARTMENT A,EMPLOYEE
B WHERE A.DEPTNO=B.WORKDEPT AND DEPTNO LIKE 'E%'
DB20000I  The SQL command completed successfully.
SELECT * FROM DEPTEMP
DEPTNO FIRSTNME        SALARY      BONUS
------ --------------- ----------- -----------
E01    GEYER              40175.00      800.00
E11    HENDERSON          29750.00      600.00
E11    SCHNEIDER          26250.00      500.00
E11    SMITH              17750.00      400.00
E11    PARKER             15340.00      300.00
E11    SETRIGHT           15900.00      300.00
E21    MEHTA              19950.00      400.00
E21    GOUNOT             23840.00      500.00
E21    LEE                25370.00      500.00
E21    SPENSER            26150.00      500.00
10 record(s) selected.
```

2. In the Define Join panel, enter the view definition, as shown here:

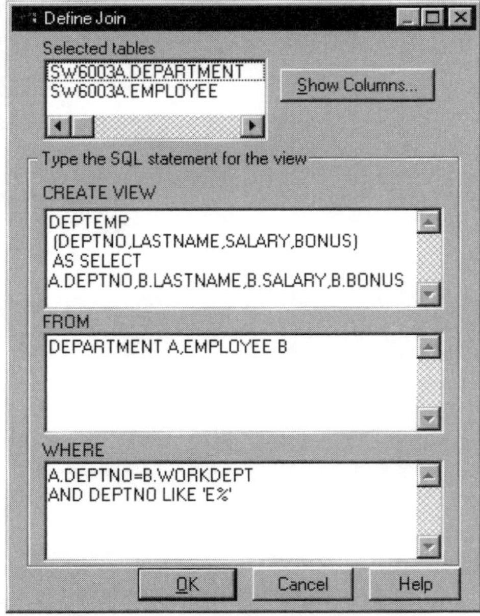

Figure 168. The Define Join Window

The generated SQL file should be as follows:

```
CONNECT TO DB2C;
CREATE VIEW DEPTEMP
```

```
(DEPTNO,LASTNAME,SALARY,BONUS)
AS SELECT
A.DEPTNO,B.LASTNAME,B.SALARY,B.BONUS
FROM DEPARTMENT A,EMPLOYEE B
WHERE A.DEPTNO=B.WORKDEPT
AND DEPTNO LIKE 'E%';

CREATE VIEW SW6003A.EMPDEPCD (IBMSNAP_UOWID, IBMSNAP_INTENTSEQ,
IBMSNAP_OPERATION, DEPTNO,LASTNAME,SALARY,BONUS)
AS SELECT A.IBMSNAP_UOWID, A.IBMSNAP_INTENTSEQ, A.IBMSNAP_OPERATION,
A.DEPTNO,B.LASTNAME,B.SALARY,B.BONUS
FROM SW6003A.DEPCD A,EMPLOYEE B
WHERE A.DEPTNO=B.WORKDEPT
AND DEPTNO LIKE 'E%';

INSERT INTO ASN.IBMSNAP_REGISTER ( GLOBAL_RECORD, SOURCE_OWNER,
SOURCE_TABLE, SOURCE_VIEW_QUAL, SOURCE_STRUCTURE, SOURCE_CONDENSED,
SOURCE_COMPLETE, CD_OWNER, CD_TABLE, PHYS_CHANGE_OWNER,
PHYS_CHANGE_TABLE,
CD_OLD_SYNCHPOINT, CD_NEW_SYNCHPOINT, DISABLE_REFRESH, CCD_OWNER,
CCD_TABLE, CCD_OLD_SYNCHPOINT, SYNCHPOINT, SYNCHTIME, CCD_CONDENSED,
CCD_COMPLETE, ARCH_LEVEL, DESCRIPTION, BEFORE_IMG_PREFIX,
CONFLICT_LEVEL, PARTITION_KEYS_CHG
) VALUES (
'N', 'SW6003A', 'DEPTEMP', 1, 1, 'Y', 'Y', 'SW6003A', 'EMPDEPCD',
'SW6003A', 'DEPCD', NULL, NULL,0, NULL, NULL, NULL, NULL, NULL,
NULL, NULL, '0201', NULL, 'X', '0', 'N');

CREATE VIEW SW6003A.DEPEMPCD (IBMSNAP_UOWID, IBMSNAP_INTENTSEQ,
IBMSNAP_OPERATION, DEPTNO,LASTNAME,SALARY,BONUS)
AS SELECT B.IBMSNAP_UOWID, B.IBMSNAP_INTENTSEQ, B.IBMSNAP_OPERATION,
A.DEPTNO,B.LASTNAME,B.SALARY,B.BONUS
FROM DEPARTMENT A,SW6003A.EMPCD B
WHERE A.DEPTNO=B.WORKDEPT
AND DEPTNO LIKE 'E%';

INSERT INTO ASN.IBMSNAP_REGISTER ( GLOBAL_RECORD, SOURCE_OWNER,
SOURCE_TABLE, SOURCE_VIEW_QUAL, SOURCE_STRUCTURE, SOURCE_CONDENSED,
SOURCE_COMPLETE, CD_OWNER, CD_TABLE, PHYS_CHANGE_OWNER,
PHYS_CHANGE_TABLE,
CD_OLD_SYNCHPOINT, CD_NEW_SYNCHPOINT, DISABLE_REFRESH, CCD_OWNER,
CCD_TABLE, CCD_OLD_SYNCHPOINT, SYNCHPOINT, SYNCHTIME, CCD_CONDENSED,
CCD_COMPLETE, ARCH_LEVEL, DESCRIPTION, BEFORE_IMG_PREFIX,
CONFLICT_LEVEL, PARTITION_KEYS_CHG
) VALUES (
'N', 'SW6003A', 'DEPTEMP', 2, 1, 'Y', 'Y', 'SW6003A', 'DEPEMPCD',
'SW6003A', 'EMPCD', NULL, NULL, 0, NULL, NULL, NULL, NULL, NULL,
NULL, NULL, '0201', NULL, 'X', '0', 'N');
```

Since there is a view which describes a join between the two source tables DEPARTMENT and EMPLOYEE, and there is a change data table (CD) for each source table, two rows will be inserted for the view registration into the

ASN.IBMSNAP_REGISTER table. Each of these rows will refer to a different change data view:

1. A view of DEPARTMENT's CD table (DEPCD) joined with EMPLOYEE
2. A view of EMPLOYEE's CD table (EMPCD) joined with DEPARTMENT

Figure 169 illustrates the view registration:

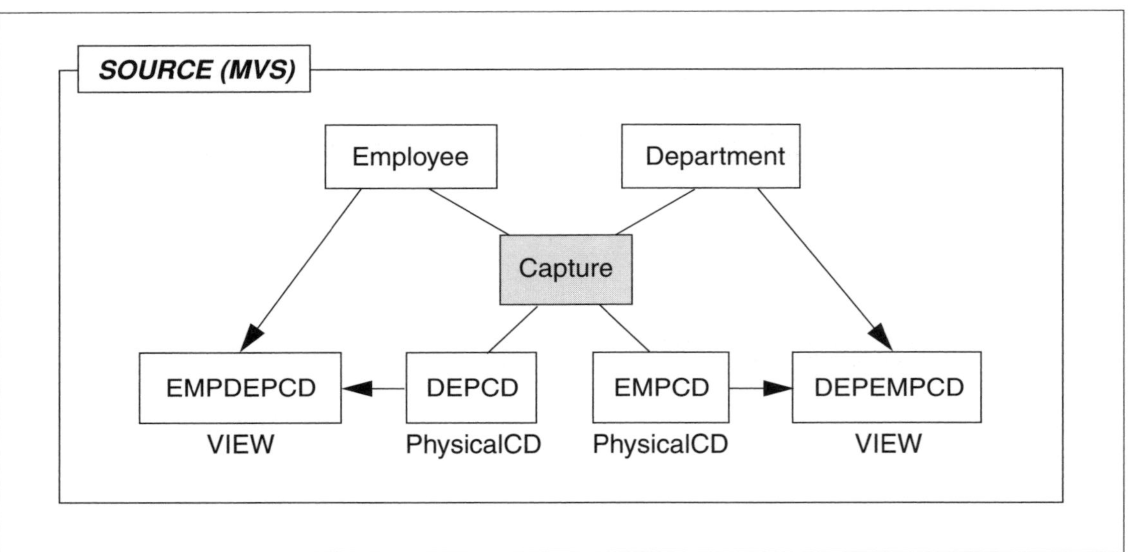

Figure 169. Join Replication Scenario

If we assume that your applications always insert or update B when they update or insert into A, and vice versa, then the changes will propagate through the views as duplicates, being driven by both updates to A and updates to B. In this case, just one change table is sufficient to drive propagation through the view. This can only be determined, however, with the knowledge that the applications always insert or update these tables together.

If you determine that it is not necessary for every view components' change table to drive propagation, then you might leave out one (or more, in more complex view scenarios) of the ASN.IBMSNAP_REGISTER table entries and refrain from creating the change data view corresponding with that entry. The resulting subscriptions will each cut down on the work to maintain their copies. Make this adjustment before defining any subscription members referring to the source view.

8.1.3 Defining the Subscription

After you define your join source and register the related views at the source server, you can define a subscription using the Control Center. In this example, we specify a DB2 UDB for Windows NT database called COPYDB1 as the target server and control server with following subscription conditions:

- SET_NAME=JOINSET
- APPLY_QUAL=JOINQUAL
- TARGET_TABLE=AZUMA.DEPTEMP
- TARGET TYPE=User Copy
- SLEEP_MINUTES=1

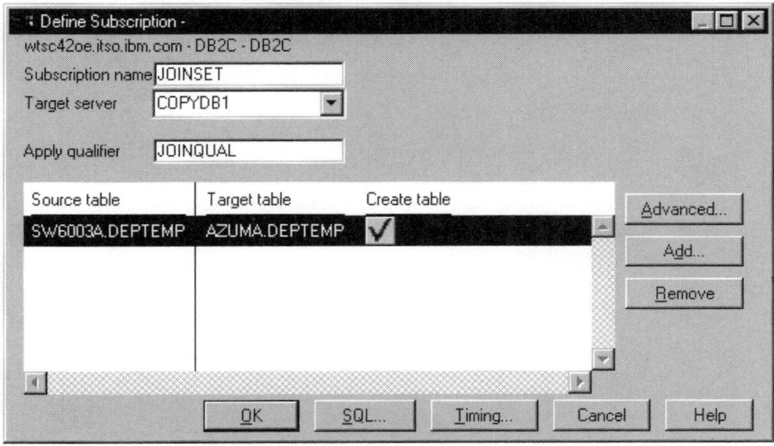

Figure 170. Join Replication - Define Subscription

The subscription definition process is the same as for a normal (single table) replication source, but the generated SQL statements differ slightly. Note that two subscription members will be generated as part of the one subscription set (JOINSET). For details on these two members refer to the SQL generated below and to the discussion following Figure 171 on page 282. In particular note the SOURCE_TABLE column and the SOURCE_VIEW_QUAL column in the IBMSNAP_SUBS_MEMBR table. The SOURCE_TABLE value is the view source we created earlier in “Defining a Join Replication Source” on page 275. The SOURCE_VIEW_QUAL value will match up with the similar column in the register table, for this SOURCE_TABLE. Here is the generated SQL:

```
CONNECT TO COPYDB1;

INSERT INTO ASN.IBMSNAP_SUBS_SET ( ACTIVATE, APPLY_QUAL, SET_NAME,
WHOS_ON_FIRST, SOURCE_SERVER, TARGET_SERVER, STATUS, LASTRUN,
```

```
REFRESH_TIMING, SLEEP_MINUTES, EVENT_NAME, LASTSUCCESS, SYNCHPOINT,
SYNCHTIME, MAX_SYNCH_MINUTES, AUX_STMTS, ARCH_LEVEL, SOURCE_ALIAS,
TARGET_ALIAS
) VALUES (
1, 'JOINQUAL', 'JOINSET', 'S', 'DB2C', 'COPYDB1', 0,
'1998-12-08-16.15.09.000000', 'R', 1, NULL,
'1998-12-08-16.15.09.000000',
NULL, NULL, NULL, 0, '0201', 'DB2C', 'COPYDB1' );

INSERT INTO ASN.IBMSNAP_SUBS_MEMBR ( APPLY_QUAL, SET_NAME,
WHOS_ON_FIRST,
SOURCE_OWNER, SOURCE_TABLE, SOURCE_VIEW_QUAL, TARGET_OWNER,
TARGET_TABLE, TARGET_CONDENSED, TARGET_COMPLETE, TARGET_STRUCTURE,
PREDICATES
) VALUES (
'JOINQUAL', 'JOINSET', 'S', 'SW6003A', 'DEPTEMP', 2, 'AZUMA',
'DEPTEMP', 'Y', 'Y', 8, NULL);

INSERT INTO ASN.IBMSNAP_SUBS_MEMBR ( APPLY_QUAL, SET_NAME,
WHOS_ON_FIRST, SOURCE_OWNER, SOURCE_TABLE, SOURCE_VIEW_QUAL,
TARGET_OWNER, TARGET_TABLE, TARGET_CONDENSED, TARGET_COMPLETE,
TARGET_STRUCTURE, PREDICATES
) VALUES (
'JOINQUAL', 'JOINSET', 'S', 'SW6003A', 'DEPTEMP', 1, 'AZUMA',
'DEPTEMP', 'Y', 'Y', 8, NULL);

INSERT INTO ASN.IBMSNAP_SUBS_COLS ( APPLY_QUAL, SET_NAME, WHOS_ON_FIRST,
TARGET_OWNER, TARGET_TABLE, COL_TYPE, TARGET_NAME, IS_KEY, COLNO,
EXPRESSION ) VALUES ( 'JOINQUAL', 'JOINSET', 'S', 'AZUMA', 'DEPTEMP',
'A', 'DEPTNO', 'N', 0, 'DEPTNO');

INSERT INTO ASN.IBMSNAP_SUBS_COLS ( APPLY_QUAL, SET_NAME, WHOS_ON_FIRST,
TARGET_OWNER, TARGET_TABLE, COL_TYPE, TARGET_NAME, IS_KEY, COLNO,
EXPRESSION ) VALUES ( 'JOINQUAL', 'JOINSET', 'S', 'AZUMA', 'DEPTEMP',
'A', 'LASTNAME', 'Y', 1, 'LASTNAME');

INSERT INTO ASN.IBMSNAP_SUBS_COLS ( APPLY_QUAL, SET_NAME, WHOS_ON_FIRST,
TARGET_OWNER, TARGET_TABLE, COL_TYPE, TARGET_NAME, IS_KEY, COLNO,
EXPRESSION ) VALUES ( 'JOINQUAL', 'JOINSET', 'S', 'AZUMA', 'DEPTEMP',
'A', 'SALARY', 'N', 2, 'SALARY');

INSERT INTO ASN.IBMSNAP_SUBS_COLS ( APPLY_QUAL, SET_NAME, WHOS_ON_FIRST,
TARGET_OWNER, TARGET_TABLE, COL_TYPE, TARGET_NAME, IS_KEY, COLNO,
EXPRESSION ) VALUES ( 'JOINQUAL', 'JOINSET', 'S', 'AZUMA', 'DEPTEMP',
'A', 'BONUS', 'N', 3, 'BONUS');

CREATE TABLE AZUMA.DEPTEMP (
```

```
DEPTNO CHAR ( 3 ) NOT NULL,
LASTNAME VARCHAR ( 15 ) NOT NULL,
SALARY DECIMAL ( 9, 2 ),
BONUS DECIMAL ( 9, 2 ) ,
PRIMARY KEY ( LASTNAME ) );

CONNECT TO DB2C;

INSERT INTO ASN.IBMSNAP_PRUNCNTL ( TARGET_SERVER, TARGET_OWNER,
TARGET_TABLE, SYNCHTIME, SYNCHPOINT, SOURCE_OWNER, SOURCE_TABLE,
SOURCE_VIEW_QUAL, APPLY_QUAL, SET_NAME, CNTL_SERVER, TARGET_STRUCTURE,
CNTL_ALIAS ) VALUES ( 'COPYDB1', 'AZUMA', 'DEPTEMP', NULL, NULL,
'SW6003A', 'DEPTEMP', 2, 'JOINQUAL', 'JOINSET', 'COPYDB1', 8, 'COPYDB1'
);

INSERT INTO ASN.IBMSNAP_PRUNCNTL ( TARGET_SERVER, TARGET_OWNER,
TARGET_TABLE, SYNCHTIME, SYNCHPOINT, SOURCE_OWNER, SOURCE_TABLE,
SOURCE_VIEW_QUAL, APPLY_QUAL, SET_NAME, CNTL_SERVER, TARGET_STRUCTURE,
CNTL_ALIAS ) VALUES ( 'COPYDB1', 'AZUMA', 'DEPTEMP', NULL, NULL,
'SW6003A', 'DEPTEMP', 1, 'JOINQUAL', 'JOINSET', 'COPYDB1', 8,
'COPYDB1');
```

Figure 171 illustrates the subscription that has been created:

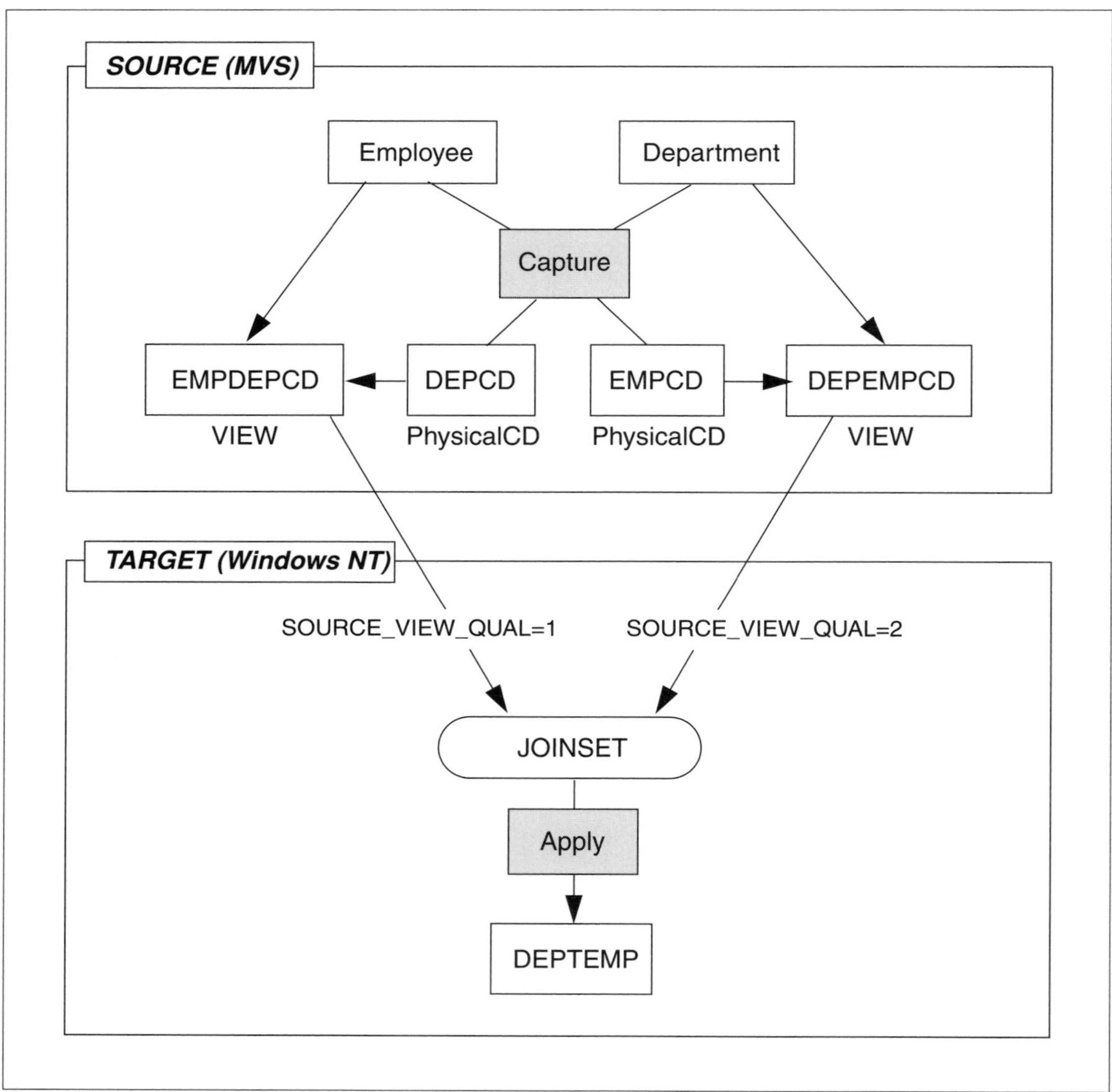

Figure 171. Join Replication - Subscription

A subscription member defines a relationship between a source table and a target table. The member also defines the structure of the target table and specifies what is to be replicated to the target table. A subscription set contains the set's attributes and zero or more subscription members. Subscription members that are associated with a particular source server and a particular target server can be grouped in together in subscription sets. As a result of this grouping, the changed data for all the subscription members in a subscription set are replicated from their source tables to the specified target tables in one database unit-of-work.

In this case, two members are defined with different SOURCE_VIEW_QUAL values. Both map the source table view SW6003A.DEPTEMP to the target table AZUMA.DEPTEMP. However, the CD table that is associated with the source table is different:

- SOURCE_VIEW_QUAL=1: maps view EMPDEPCD to DEPTEMP
- SOURCE_VIEW_QUAL=2: maps view DEPEMPCD to DEPTEMP

Note

SOURCE_VIEW_QUAL=0 for registered physical tables. Other values greater than 0 are for view registrations.

8.1.4 Full Refresh

Even though two members have been defined, the Apply program only performs the full refresh once through a view (DEPTEMP) defined at the source server. When this happens, you can see the following GOCAPT messages in the TRACE table at the source server:

```
ASN0104I Change Capture started for owner SW6003A ; the table name is
DEPARTMENT          at log sequence number (LSN) 000000006ABFF8E20000.
ASN0104I Change Capture started for owner SW6003A ; the table name is
EMPLOYEE            at log sequence number (LSN) 000000006ABFF9EE0000.
```

After the full refresh, the target table has the following rows:

```
connect to copydb1

   Database Connection Information
Database server         = DB2/NT 5.2.0
SQL authorization ID    = AZUMA
Local database alias    = COPYDB1

select * from deptemp

DEPTNO FIRSTNME        SALARY      BONUS
------ --------------- ----------- -----------
E01    GEYER              40175.00      800.00
E11    HENDERSON          29750.00      600.00
E11    SCHNEIDER          26250.00      500.00
E11    SMITH              17750.00      400.00
```

```
E11     PARKER                 15340.00          300.00
E11     SETRIGHT               15900.00          300.00
E21     MEHTA                  19950.00          400.00
E21     GOUNOT                 23840.00          500.00
E21     LEE                    25370.00          500.00
E21     SPENSER                26150.00          500.00

10 record(s) selected.
```

8.1.5 Differential Copy

Using replication through the 2-table join views, UPDATE and DELETE transactions on the source table will be replicated as the same UPDATE and DELETE. However, INSERT transactions at about same time will be replicated as an INSERT and UPDATE pair in the APPLYTRAIL table (the SET_REWORKED message flags this action). The reason for this behavior is the following: the Apply program performs an INSERT from one of the views into the target table with IBMSNAP_OPERATION='I' first. The second INSERT attempt from another view fails due to the unique constraint of the key, and so this INSERT is converted to an UPDATE automatically by Apply.

For example, you run the following INSERTs at the source server.

```
CONNECT TO DB2C USER SW6003A USING xxxx

   Database Connection Information

 Database server        = DB2 OS/390 5.1.1
 SQL authorization ID   = SW6003A
 Local database alias   = DB2C

INSERT INTO DEPARTMENT
(DEPTNO,DEPTNAME,MGRNO,ADMRDEPT,LOCATION) VALUES ('E99','
DPROPR TECHNICAL SUPPORT','000900','E99','TOKYO')
DB20000I  The SQL command completed successfully.

INSERT INTO EMPLOYEE (EMPNO,FIRSTNME,MIDINIT,LASTNAME,WORKDEPT,
PHONENO,HIREDATE
,JOB,EDLEVEL,SEX,BIRTHDATE, SALARY,BONUS,COMM) VALUES
('080598','TADAKATSU','T',
'AZUMA','E99', '6152','1986-04-01', 'SE',18,'M','1933-08-24',
12750.00,1000.00,1220.00)
DB20000I  The SQL command completed successfully.
```

The Apply program replication trace was :

```
PSET: Fetch answer set for member 0
```

```
 Compiled(F) at 14:49:09 on Aug 12 1998 (Level 0053)
  CDSET: spill_file(0) = JOINQUALDB2COPYDB1.000
 FETSET: The number of rows fetched is 1.
PSET: Fetch answer set for member 1
 Compiled(F) at 14:49:09 on Aug 12 1998 (Level 0053)
  CDSET: spill_file(1) = JOINQUALDB2COPYDB1.001
 FETSET: The number of rows fetched is 1.
 UP1SYT: Synchtime is 1998-12-14-20.59.24.364225
PSET: Commit3 ok
 CEXPC: connect to COPYDB1
 CEXPC: CONNECT with USERID/PASSWORD
 CEXPC: serverIsolationUR is 1.
-------------------------
PSET: Commit4 ok
 Compiled(A) at 14:49:19 on Aug 12 1998 (Level 0053)
PSET: Commit6 ok
 CEXPC: connect to COPYDB1
 CLOS: setRepeatCopy is 0
 CLOS: activate = 1
 CLOS: status   = 0
 CLOS: lastrun = 1998-12-14-19.57.15.125001
 CLOS: lastsuccess = 1998-12-14-19.57.09.000000
 CLOS: Synchpoint is  000000006ad8cf1f0000
 CLOS: synchtime = 1998-12-14-20.59.24.364225
 CLOS: apply_qual = JOINQUAL
 CLOS: set_name = JOINSET
 CLOS: sWhosOnFirst = S
 CEXPC: connect to DB2C
 CEXPC: CONNECT with USERID/PASSWORD
 CEXPC: serverIsolationUR is 1.
 CEXPC: connect to COPYDB1
 CEXPC: CONNECT with USERID/PASSWORD
 CEXPC: serverIsolationUR is 1.
 SAT: ASNLOAD = N, EFFECT_MEMBERS = 2
 SAT: MASS_DELETE = N
 SAT: SET_INSERTED = 1
 SAT: SET_DELETED = 0
 SAT: SET_UPDATED = 1
 SAT: SET_REWORKED = 1
 SAT: SET_REJECTED_TRXS = 0
 SAT: STATUS = 0
 SAT: LASTRUN = 1998-12-14-19.57.15.125001
 SAT: LASTSUCCESS = 1998-12-14-19.57.09.000000
 SAT: SYNCHPOINT is 000000006ad8cf1f0000
 SAT: SYNCHTIME is 1998-12-14-20.59.24.364225
 SAT: SOURCE_ALIAS is DB2C
 SAT: SOURCE_SERVER is DB2C
```

```
SAT: SOURCE_OWNER is
SAT: SOURCE_TABLE is
SAT: TARGET_ALIAS is COPYDB1
SAT: TARGET_SERVER is COPYDB1
```

Note the SET_INSERTED, SET_UPDATED and SET_REWORKED entries in the trace. The target table (DEPTEMP) at the target server then shows the single additional row:

```
DEPTNO FIRSTNME        SALARY      BONUS
------ --------------- ----------- -----------
E01    GEYER              40175.00      800.00
E11    HENDERSON          29750.00      600.00
E11    SCHNEIDER          26250.00      500.00
E11    SMITH              17750.00      400.00
E11    PARKER             15340.00      300.00
E11    SETRIGHT           15900.00      300.00
E21    MEHTA              19950.00      400.00
E21    GOUNOT             23840.00      500.00
E21    LEE                25370.00      500.00
E21    SPENSER            26150.00      500.00
E99    AZUMA              12750.00     1000.00

  11 record(s) selected.
```

8.1.6 Double Delete

Let's consider the case where your application deletes the matching rows from the DEPARTMENT and EMPLOYEE tables at the same time (or within the same subscription cycle). When Apply opens a cursor against the view describing the join of DEPARTMENT's change data table (DEPCD) joined with EMPLOYEE, there will be no row in EMPLOYEE table to match with the captured delete to the DEPARTMENT table. Also, when Apply opens a cursor against the view describing the join of EMPLOYEE's change data table (EMPCD) joined with DEPARTMENT, there will be no row in DEPARTMENT to match with the captured delete to the EMPLOYEE table.

If you encounter this situation, and it is important to propagate the captured deletes, you'll need to customize the view registration generated by the Control Center by defining additional views and inserting additional rows into the ASN.IBMSNAP_REGISTER table. The objective is to join one change data table with another change data table so that each of the captured deletes will always find a matching row.

Figure 172 illustrates another view registration designed to solve the "double delete" issue described above.

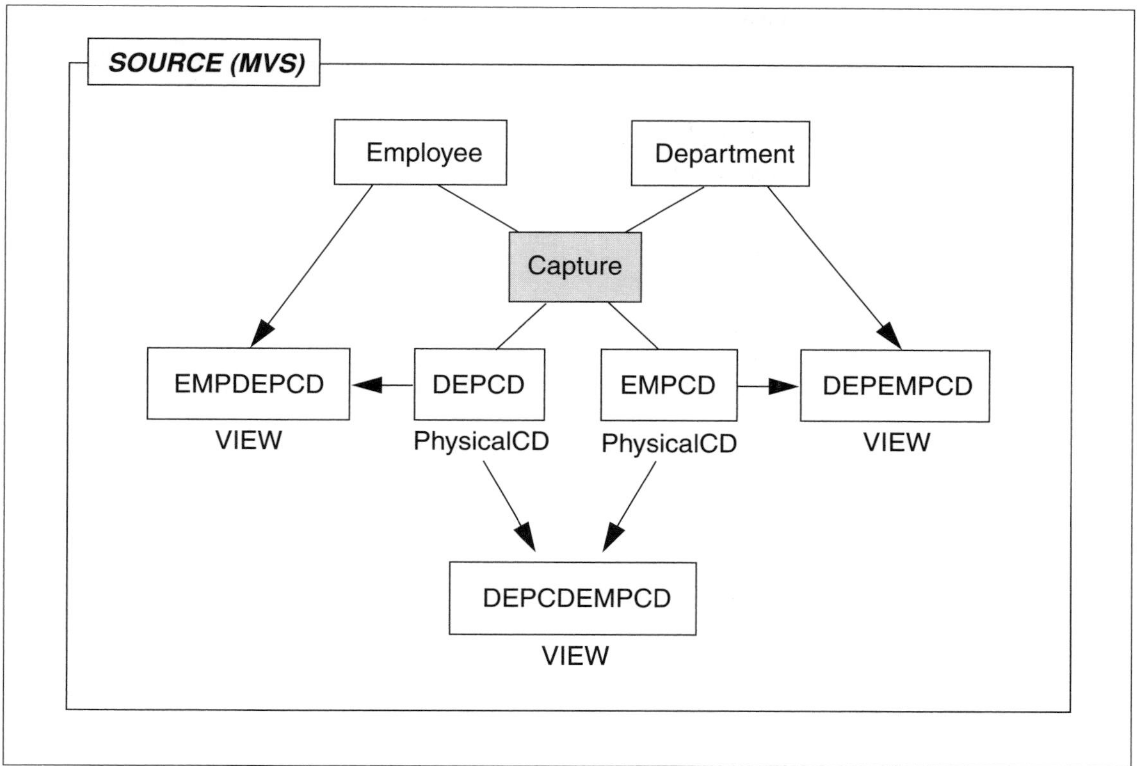

Figure 172. Join Replication - Double Deletes

In this example scenario, the following SQL should be added to the registration information with SOURCE_VIEW_QUAL=3. This must be done manually:

```
--View Registration (DEPCD & EMPCD)

CREATE VIEW DEPCDEMPCD
(IBMSNAP_UOWID, IBMSNAP_INTENTSEQ, IBMSNAP_OPERATION,
DEPTNO,LASTNAME,SALARY,BONUS)
AS SELECT
 A.IBMSNAP_UOWID,A.IBMSNAP_INTENTSEQ,A.IBMSNAP_OPERATION,
 A.DEPTNO,B.LASTNAME,B.SALARY,B.BONUS
FROM DEPCD A,EMPCD B
WHERE A.DEPTNO=B.WORKDEPT
AND A.DEPTNO LIKE 'E%'
AND   A.IBMSNAP_OPERATION='D'
AND   B.IBMSNAP_OPERATION='D'
;

INSERT INTO ASN.IBMSNAP_REGISTER(GLOBAL_RECORD,SOURCE_OWNER,
```

```
SOURCE_TABLE,SOURCE_VIEW_QUAL,SOURCE_STRUCTURE,SOURCE_CONDENSED,
SOURCE_COMPLETE,CD_OWNER,CD_TABLE,PHYS_CHANGE_OWNER,PHYS_CHANGE_TABLE,
DISABLE_REFRESH,ARCH_LEVEL,BEFORE_IMG_PREFIX,CONFLICT_LEVEL,
PARTITION_KEYS_CHG) VALUES('N','SW6003A','DEPTEMP', 3 , 1 ,'Y','Y',
'SW6003A','DEPCDEMPCD','SW6003A','DEPCD', 0 ,'0201','X',
'0','N');
```

You also need to add the following entries to the subscription information. These rows are manually inserted into the SUBS_MEMBR table at the control server and the Pruning Control table at the source server:

```
--connect to the control server
CONNECT TO COPYDB1;

INSERT INTO ASN.IBMSNAP_SUBS_MEMBR ( APPLY_QUAL, SET_NAME,
WHOS_ON_FIRST, SOURCE_OWNER, SOURCE_TABLE, SOURCE_VIEW_QUAL,
TARGET_OWNER, TARGET_TABLE, TARGET_CONDENSED, TARGET_COMPLETE,
TARGET_STRUCTURE, PREDICATES
VALUES (
'JOINQUAL', 'JOINSET', 'S', 'SW6003A', 'DEPTEMP', 3, 'AZUMA',
'DEPTEMP', 'Y', 'Y', 8, NULL);

--connect to the source server
CONNECT TO DB2C USER SW6003A USING

INSERT INTO ASN.IBMSNAP_PRUNCNTL (
TARGET_SERVER, TARGET_OWNER, TARGET_TABLE, SYNCHTIME, SYNCHPOINT,
SOURCE_OWNER, SOURCE_TABLE, SOURCE_VIEW_QUAL, APPLY_QUAL, SET_NAME,
CNTL_SERVER, TARGET_STRUCTURE, CNTL_ALIAS
) VALUES (
'COPYDB1', 'AZUMA', 'DEPTEMP', NULL, NULL, 'SW6003A', 'DEPTEMP',
3, 'JOINQUAL', 'JOINSET', 'COPYDB1', 8, 'COPYDB1');
```

8.2 Replicating From Oracle to DB2 UDB

DataJoiner complements IBM's Data Replication products. DataJoiner provides access to a wide variety of data sources: the DB2 family, Oracle, Sybase, Microsoft SQL Server, Informix, and SQL Anywhere. From the viewpoint of the Apply program, all data sources look as if they are DB2 databases. The Apply program does not need to know the physical location of the data source.

In this example, we show you how to replicate Oracle/AIX V8 data to DB2 UDB for AIX using the DB2 DataJoiner Replication Administration (DJRA) GUI tool instead of the DB2 UDB Control Center.

Information about administering DataJoiner is contained in the *DataJoiner for AIX Planning, Installation, and Configuration Guide* (SC26-9145) and the *DataJoiner for Windows NT Systems Planning, Installation, and Configuration*

Guide (SC26-9150) books. These two books are provided with DataJoiner or can be ordered separately.

We assume that the following configurations have already been completed:

- **Linking**: To enable access to data source types, the DataJoiner server must be link-edited to the client libraries using **djxlink**. The link-edit process creates a data access module for each data source. If you use SLQ*NET to access Oracle, you must create the sqlnet or Net8 data access module. If the data source is DB2, we do not need to create it.
- **Server mapping**: DataJoiner databases differ from normal DB2 UDB databases in that they have virtual entries which are not tied to any particular server address and described in the SYSTEM views. You must use the CREATE SERVER MAPPING DDL statement to update the SYSCAT.SERVERS view.
- **User mapping**: You must use the CREATE USER MAPPING DDL statement to update the SYSCAT.REMOTEUSERS view. This DDL statement is used to map information about authorization IDs and passwords that are used to access a data source.

8.2.1 Overview of the Replication Configuration

Figure 173 illustrates this replication configuration. The objective is to replicate changes to data stored in Oracle tables to a DB2 UDB database using Oracle Triggers. Triggers are automatically generated by DJRA when you define the registration information.

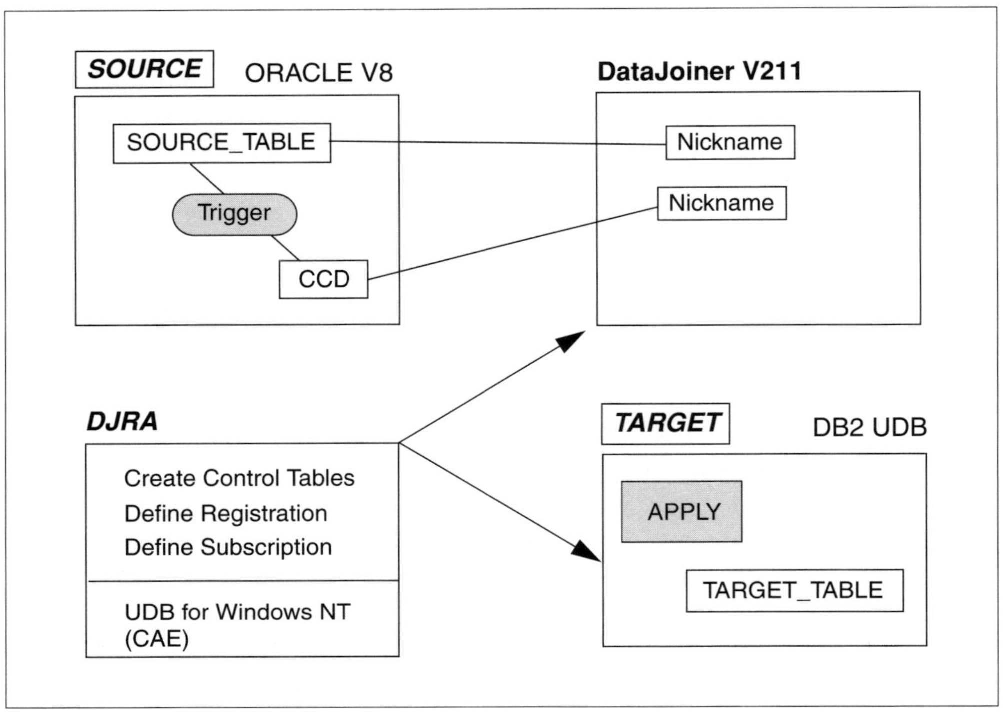

Figure 173. Oracle to DB2 UDB Replication Overview

8.2.2 Placement of the Control Tables and Data Tables

The control tables and data tables are distributed among the Oracle source database, the DataJoiner database, and the DB2 UDB target database. Figure 174 shows where the control tables and data tables are located:

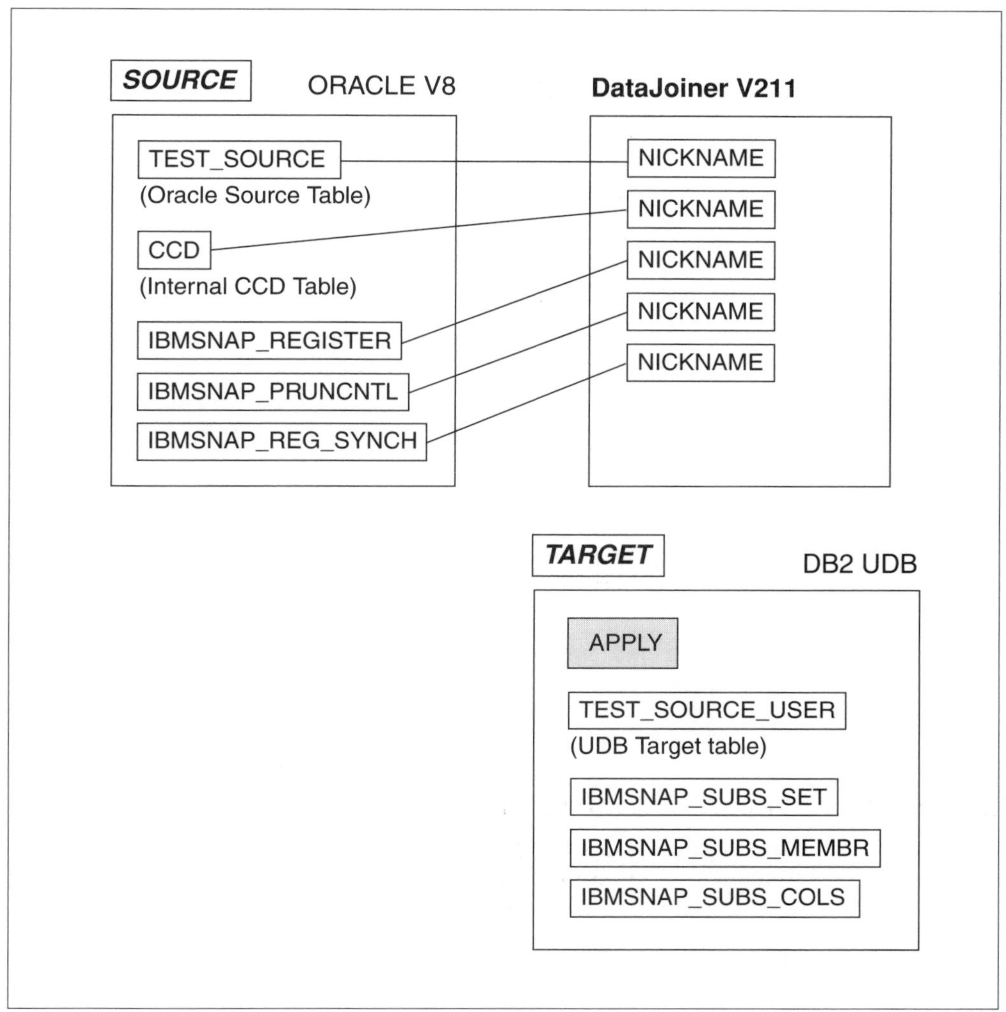

Figure 174. Oracle to UDB Control and Data Tables

8.2.3 Configuring the Source Table - Nickname Definition

DataJoiner uses nicknames to access tables in other data sources. We must define a nickname to the source table in the Oracle database before we start to define a registration using DJRA.

```
set passthru ora80;

create table test_source
(row_number number(5,0) not null,
test_data number(5,0),
```

```
 description char(20));

create unique index test_source_x on test_source (row_number);

insert into test_source values (1,1,'ROW1');
insert into test_source values (2,2,'ROW1');
insert into test_source values (3,3,'ROW1');

set passthru reset;
create nickname test_source for ora80.scott.test_source;
```

8.2.4 Defining the Control Tables

When DJRA recognizes that DataJoiner is configured to use a non-DB2 source, such as Oracle, it creates the IBMSNAP_REGISTER and IBMSNAP_PRUNCNTL tables at the source server using the SET PASSTHRU function of DataJoiner. It then creates the nicknames with the ASN qualifier for these replication control tables in the DataJoiner database.

To generate the control table scripts:

1. From the DJRA main panel, select **Create Replication Control Tables**:

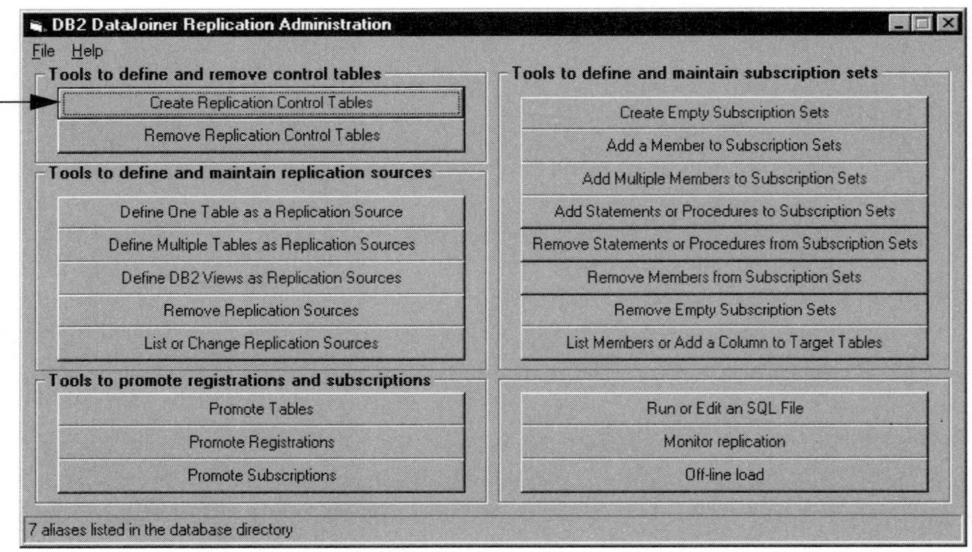

Figure 175. DJRA - Create Replication Control Tables

The following panel is displayed:

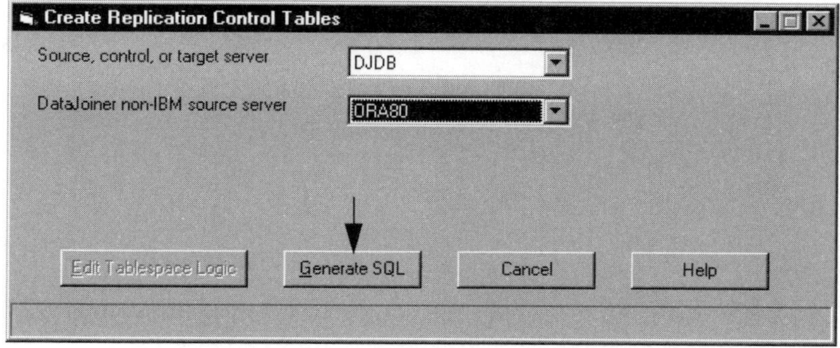

Figure 176. DJRA - Select Non-IBM Source Server

2. Select the DataJoiner database (here, DJDB) and the remote server name (here, ORA80), then click on **Generate SQL**. This is the SQL generated in this example:

```
--* echo input: CRTABLES DJDB ORA80
--*
-- using REXX password file PASSWORD.REX

-- If you don't see: '-- now done interpreting...' then check your PASSWORD.REX
code
-- now done interpreting REXX password file PASSWORD.REX
--* Checking for non-DB2 system
--* CONNECTING TO DJDB USER djv2 USING djv2;
--*
--* Oracle is a supported database through DataJoiner
--* CONNECTING TO DJDB USER djv2 USING djv2;
--*
--* SYSREMOTEUSERS.REMOTE_AUTHID is SCOTT
--* for remote server ORA80
-- About connect to alias  DJDB
COMMIT;
CONNECT TO DJDB USER djv2 USING djv2;

-- Connect OK
-- USERID=DJV2     SOURCE_ALIAS alias=DJDB     PRDID=SQL0201 16 Dec 1998 8:08am
VERSION=0201
-- Creating Register and Pruncontrol tables on ORACLE
SET SERVER OPTION TWO_PHASE_COMMIT TO 'N' FOR SERVER ORA80;
SET PASSTHRU ORA80;
--* Create the IBMSNAP_REGISTER table for holding registration information in
Oracle database
CREATE TABLE IBMSNAP_REGISTER (  SOURCE_OWNER CHAR(18) NOT NULL,
SOURCE_TABLE CHAR(18) NOT NULL, SOURCE_VIEW_QUAL NUMBER(4 , 0) NOT
NULL, GLOBAL_RECORD CHAR(1) NOT NULL, SOURCE_STRUCTURE NUMBER(4 , 0)
NOT NULL, SOURCE_CONDENSED CHAR(1) NOT NULL, SOURCE_COMPLETE   CHAR(1)
NOT NULL, CD_OWNER CHAR(18), CD_TABLE CHAR(18), PHYS_CHANGE_OWNER CHAR(
18), PHYS_CHANGE_TABLE CHAR(18), CD_OLD_SYNCHPOINT RAW(10),
CD_NEW_SYNCHPOINT RAW(10), DISABLE_REFRESH NUMBER(4 , 0) NOT NULL,
CCD_OWNER CHAR(18), CCD_TABLE CHAR(18), CCD_OLD_SYNCHPOINT RAW(10),
SYNCHPOINT RAW(10), SYNCHTIME DATE, CCD_CONDENSED CHAR(1),
CCD_COMPLETE   CHAR(1), ARCH_LEVEL CHAR(4) NOT NULL, DESCRIPTION CHAR(
254), BEFORE_IMG_PREFIX VARCHAR(4), CONFLICT_LEVEL CHAR(1),
PARTITION_KEYS_CHG CHAR(1));

--* Create an index for IBMSNAP_REGISTER
```

```
CREATE UNIQUE INDEX IBMSNAP_REGISTERX ON IBMSNAP_REGISTER(SOURCE_OWNER,
SOURCE_TABLE, SOURCE_VIEW_QUAL);

--* Create the IBMSNAP_PRUNCNTL table for holding registration information
CREATE TABLE IBMSNAP_PRUNCNTL (  TARGET_SERVER CHAR (18) NOT NULL,
TARGET_OWNER CHAR (18) NOT NULL,TARGET_TABLE CHAR(18) NOT NULL,
SYNCHTIME DATE,SYNCHPOINT RAW(10),SOURCE_OWNER CHAR (18) NOT NULL,
SOURCE_TABLE CHAR (18) NOT NULL,SOURCE_VIEW_QUAL NUMBER(4 , 0) NOT
NULL,APPLY_QUAL CHAR (18) NOT NULL,SET_NAME CHAR (18) NOT NULL,
CNTL_SERVER CHAR(18) NOT NULL,TARGET_STRUCTURE NUMBER(4 , 0) NOT NULL,
CNTL_ALIAS CHAR(8));

--* Create an index for IBMSNAP_PRUNCNTL
CREATE UNIQUE INDEX IBMSNAP_PRUNCNTLX ON IBMSNAP_PRUNCNTL (
SOURCE_OWNER, SOURCE_TABLE, SOURCE_VIEW_QUAL, SET_NAME, TARGET_SERVER,
TARGET_TABLE, TARGET_OWNER);

-- Creating register synchpoint trigger on ORACLE
--* Create the IBMSNAP_REG_SYNCH TABLE
CREATE TABLE IBMSNAP_REG_SYNCH (TRIGGER_ME CHAR(1));

INSERT INTO IBMSNAP_REG_SYNCH VALUES ('Y');

CREATE TRIGGER SCOTT.REG_SYNCH_TRIGGER AFTER UPDATE ON
SCOTT.IBMSNAP_REG_SYNCH BEGIN UPDATE SCOTT.IBMSNAP_REGISTER SET
SYNCHPOINT=LPAD(TO_CHAR(SCOTT.SGENERATOR001.NEXTVAL), 20 , '0'),
SYNCHTIME=SYSDATE;END;

--:ENDOFTRIGGER:

--* Create the Oracle sequence number generator
CREATE SEQUENCE SCOTT.SGENERATOR001 MINVALUE 100 INCREMENT BY 1;

COMMIT;
SET PASSTHRU RESET;
--* create a DataJoiner nickname for the REGISTER table in ORA80
--*
CREATE NICKNAME ASN.IBMSNAP_REGISTER FOR ORA80.SCOTT.IBMSNAP_REGISTER;

--* create a DataJoiner nickname for the Pruning Control table in ORA80
--*
CREATE NICKNAME ASN.IBMSNAP_PRUNCNTL FOR ORA80.SCOTT.IBMSNAP_PRUNCNTL;

--* create a DataJoiner nickname for the Reg_Synch table in ORA80
--*
CREATE NICKNAME ASN.IBMSNAP_REG_SYNCH FOR
ORA80.SCOTT.IBMSNAP_REG_SYNCH;

--* Create the ASN.IBMSNAP_APPLYTRAIL table for holding subscription statistics
CREATE TABLE ASN.IBMSNAP_APPLYTRAIL (  APPLY_QUAL CHAR(18) NOT NULL,
SET_NAME CHAR (18) NOT NULL,WHOS_ON_FIRST CHAR(1) NOT NULL,ASNLOAD
CHAR(1),MASS_DELETE CHAR(1),EFFECTIVE_MEMBERS INT,SET_INSERTED INT NOT
NULL,SET_DELETED INT NOT NULL,SET_UPDATED INT NOT NULL,SET_REWORKED
INT NOT NULL,SET_REJECTED_TRXS INT NOT NULL,STATUS SMALLINT NOT NULL,
LASTRUN TIMESTAMP NOT NULL,LASTSUCCESS TIMESTAMP,SYNCHPOINT CHAR(10)
FOR BIT DATA,SYNCHTIME TIMESTAMP,SOURCE_SERVER CHAR(18) NOT NULL,
SOURCE_ALIAS CHAR(8),SOURCE_OWNER CHAR (18),SOURCE_TABLE CHAR(18),
SOURCE_VIEW_QUAL SMALLINT,TARGET_SERVER CHAR(18) NOT NULL,TARGET_ALIAS
CHAR(8),TARGET_OWNER CHAR (18) NOT NULL,TARGET_TABLE CHAR(18) NOT NULL,
SQLSTATE CHAR(5),SQLCODE INTEGER,SQLERRP CHAR(8),SQLERRM VARCHAR(70),
APPERRM VARCHAR(760));

--* Create the ASN.IBMSNAP_CCPPARMS table for holding subscription statistics
CREATE TABLE ASN.IBMSNAP_CCPPARMS (  RETENTION_LIMIT INT,LAG_LIMIT INT,
COMMIT_INTERVAL INT,PRUNE_INTERVAL INT);

--* insert the default values
```

```
INSERT INTO ASN.IBMSNAP_CCPPARMS (RETENTION_LIMIT,LAG_LIMIT,
COMMIT_INTERVAL,PRUNE_INTERVAL)VALUES (10800 , 10800 , 30 , 300);

--* Create the ASN.IBMSNAP_CRITSEC table for holding subscription statistics
CREATE TABLE ASN.IBMSNAP_CRITSEC (  APPLY_QUAL CHAR(18) NOT NULL) DATA
CAPTURE CHANGES;

--* Create the index for the ASN.IBMSNAP_CRITSEC table  subscription statistics
CREATE UNIQUE INDEX ASN.IBMSNAP_CRITSECX ON ASN.IBMSNAP_CRITSEC (
APPLY_QUAL);

--* Create the ASN.IBMSNAP_SUBS_COLS table for holding subscription information
CREATE TABLE ASN.IBMSNAP_SUBS_COLS (  APPLY_QUAL CHAR(18) NOT NULL,
SET_NAME CHAR (18) NOT NULL,WHOS_ON_FIRST CHAR (1) NOT NULL,
TARGET_OWNER CHAR(18) NOT NULL,TARGET_TABLE CHAR(18) NOT NULL,COL_TYPE
CHAR(1) NOT NULL,TARGET_NAME CHAR(18) NOT NULL,IS_KEY CHAR(1) NOT NULL,
COLNO SMALLINT NOT NULL,EXPRESSION VARCHAR(254) NOT NULL);

--* Create an index for ASN.IBMSNAP_SUBS_COLS
CREATE UNIQUE INDEX ASN.IBMSNAP_SUBS_COLSX ON ASN.IBMSNAP_SUBS_COLS (
APPLY_QUAL, SET_NAME, WHOS_ON_FIRST, TARGET_OWNER,TARGET_TABLE,
TARGET_NAME);

--* Create the ASN.IBMSNAP_SUBS_EVENT table for holding subscription information
CREATE TABLE ASN.IBMSNAP_SUBS_EVENT (  EVENT_NAME CHAR(18) NOT NULL,
EVENT_TIME TIMESTAMP NOT NULL,END_OF_PERIOD TIMESTAMP);

--* Create an index for ASN.IBMSNAP_SUBS_EVENT
CREATE UNIQUE INDEX ASN.IBMSNAP_SUBS_EVENX ON ASN.IBMSNAP_SUBS_EVENT (
EVENT_NAME, EVENT_TIME);

--* Create the ASN.IBMSNAP_SUBS_MEMBR table for holding subscription information
CREATE TABLE ASN.IBMSNAP_SUBS_MEMBR (  APPLY_QUAL CHAR(18) NOT NULL,
SET_NAME CHAR (18) NOT NULL,WHOS_ON_FIRST CHAR(1) NOT NULL,
SOURCE_OWNER CHAR(18) NOT NULL,SOURCE_TABLE CHAR(18) NOT NULL,
SOURCE_VIEW_QUAL SMALLINT NOT NULL,TARGET_OWNER CHAR(18) NOT NULL,
TARGET_TABLE CHAR(18) NOT NULL,TARGET_CONDENSED CHAR(1) NOT NULL,
TARGET_COMPLETE CHAR(1) NOT NULL,TARGET_STRUCTURE SMALLINT NOT NULL,
PREDICATES VARCHAR(512));

--* Create an index for ASN.IBMSNAP_SUBS_MEMBR
CREATE UNIQUE INDEX ASN.IBMSNAP_SUBS_MEMBX ON ASN.IBMSNAP_SUBS_MEMBR (
APPLY_QUAL, SET_NAME,WHOS_ON_FIRST,SOURCE_OWNER,SOURCE_TABLE,
SOURCE_VIEW_QUAL,TARGET_OWNER,TARGET_TABLE);

--* Create the ASN.IBMSNAP_SUBS_SET table for holding subscription information
CREATE TABLE ASN.IBMSNAP_SUBS_SET (  APPLY_QUAL CHAR(18) NOT NULL,
SET_NAME CHAR (18) NOT NULL,WHOS_ON_FIRST CHAR(1) NOT NULL,ACTIVATE
SMALLINT NOT NULL,SOURCE_SERVER CHAR(18) NOT NULL,SOURCE_ALIAS CHAR(8),
TARGET_SERVER CHAR(18) NOT NULL,TARGET_ALIAS CHAR(8),STATUS SMALLINT
NOT NULL,LASTRUN TIMESTAMP NOT NULL,REFRESH_TIMING CHAR(1) NOT NULL,
SLEEP_MINUTES INT,EVENT_NAME CHAR(18),LASTSUCCESS TIMESTAMP,SYNCHPOINT
CHAR(10) FOR BIT DATA,SYNCHTIME TIMESTAMP,MAX_SYNCH_MINUTES INT,
AUX_STMTS SMALLINT NOT NULL,ARCH_LEVEL CHAR(4) NOT NULL);

--* Create an index for ASN.IBMSNAP_SUBS_SET
CREATE UNIQUE INDEX ASN.IBMSNAP_SUBS_SETX ON ASN.IBMSNAP_SUBS_SET (
APPLY_QUAL, SET_NAME, WHOS_ON_FIRST);

--* Create the ASN.IBMSNAP_SUBS_STMTS table for holding subscription information
CREATE TABLE ASN.IBMSNAP_SUBS_STMTS (  APPLY_QUAL CHAR(18) NOT NULL,
SET_NAME CHAR (18) NOT NULL,WHOS_ON_FIRST CHAR(1) NOT NULL,
BEFORE_OR_AFTER CHAR(1) NOT NULL,STMT_NUMBER SMALLINT NOT NULL,
EI_OR_CALL CHAR(1) NOT NULL,SQL_STMT VARCHAR(1024),ACCEPT_SQLSTATES
VARCHAR(50));

--* Create an index for ASN.IBMSNAP_SUBS_STMTS
```

```
CREATE UNIQUE INDEX ASN.IBMSNAP_SUBS_STMTX ON ASN.IBMSNAP_SUBS_STMTS (
APPLY_QUAL, SET_NAME,WHOS_ON_FIRST,BEFORE_OR_AFTER,STMT_NUMBER);

--* Create the ASN.IBMSNAP_TRACE table for holding CAPTURE diagnostics
CREATE TABLE ASN.IBMSNAP_TRACE (  OPERATION CHAR(8) NOT NULL,
TRACE_TIME TIMESTAMP NOT NULL,DESCRIPTION VARCHAR(254) NOT NULL);

--* Create the ASN.IBMSNAP_UOW table for holding transaction information
CREATE TABLE ASN.IBMSNAP_UOW (  IBMSNAP_UOWID CHAR(10) FOR BIT DATA
NOT NULL,IBMSNAP_COMMITSEQ CHAR(10) FOR BIT DATA  NOT NULL,
IBMSNAP_LOGMARKER TIMESTAMP NOT NULL,IBMSNAP_AUTHTKN CHAR(12) NOT NULL,
IBMSNAP_AUTHID CHAR(18) NOT NULL,IBMSNAP_REJ_CODE CHAR(1) NOT NULL
WITH DEFAULT,IBMSNAP_APPLY_QUAL CHAR(18) NOT NULL WITH DEFAULT );

--* Create index for ASN.IBMSNAP_UOW
CREATE UNIQUE INDEX ASN.IBMSNAP_UOW_IDX ON ASN.IBMSNAP_UOW(
IBMSNAP_COMMITSEQ ASC, IBMSNAP_UOWID ASC, IBMSNAP_LOGMARKER ASC);

--* Create the ASN.IBMSNAP_WARM_START table for holding
--* CAPTURE restart information
CREATE TABLE ASN.IBMSNAP_WARM_START (  SEQ CHAR(10) FOR BIT DATA,
AUTHTKN CHAR(12),AUTHID CHAR(18),CAPTURED CHAR(1),UOWTIME INT);

--* Generate IBMSNAP_SCHEMA_CHG
--*
--* Create the ASN.IBMSNAP_SCHEMA_CHG
CREATE TABLE ASN.IBMSNAP_SCHEMA_CHG (  APPLY_QUAL CHAR(18) NOT NULL,
SET_NAME CHAR (18) NOT NULL,LAST_CHANGED TIMESTAMP NOT NULL);

--* Generate IBMSNAP_SUBS_TGTS
--*
--* Create the ASN.IBMSNAP_SUBS_TGTS
CREATE TABLE ASN.IBMSNAP_SUBS_TGTS (  APPLY_QUAL CHAR(18) NOT NULL,
SET_NAME CHAR (18) NOT NULL,WHOS_ON_FIRST CHAR(1) NOT NULL,
TARGET_OWNER CHAR (18) NOT NULL,TARGET_TABLE CHAR(18) NOT NULL,
LAST_POSTED TIMESTAMP);

--* Create an index for ASN.IBMSNAP_SUBS_TGTS
CREATE UNIQUE INDEX ASN.IBMSNAP_SUBS_TGTSX ON ASN.IBMSNAP_SUBS_TGTS (
APPLY_QUAL ASC, SET_NAME ASC, WHOS_ON_FIRST ASC, TARGET_OWNER,
TARGET_TABLE);

COMMIT;

-- Satisfactory completion at 8:08am
```

In this script, we are creating the following objects in the Oracle database:

- ASN.IBMSNAP_REGISTER
- ASN.IBMSNAP_PRUNCNTL
- ASN.IBMSNAP_REG_SYNCH with a trigger
- SEQUENCE

The IBMSNAP_REG_SYNCH table is a special table to improve the trigger performance. It will be updated by the Apply program as a Before-SQL statement during replication processing. To simulate log sequencing, we are using the Oracle sequence number function. Apply uses this generated sequence number as if it was the log sequence number that would be supplied by a log-based change Capture program.

Other control tables will be created on the local DataJoiner database.

3. Run the SQL script.

   To run the generated SQL, we need to use **Run or Edit an SQL file** from the DJRA main panel:

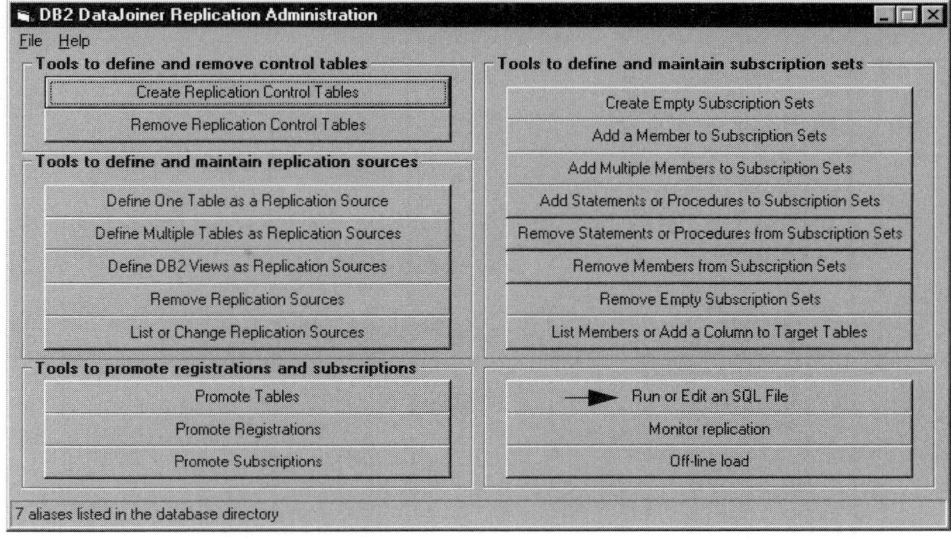

Figure 177. Run or Edit an SQL File

Don't run it from a DB2 command window using `db2 -vtf xxx.sql`, since the trigger definition contains a semicolon that might be treated as a statement termination character.

8.2.5 Defining a Registration

In this example, we have chosen the TEST_SOURCE table as the source table. This is really a DataJoiner nickname that points to a physical Oracle source table. During the registration definition, the triggers and CCD table are created. After this, the nickname for the CCD table is created in the DataJoiner database.

To define a registration:

1. From the DJRA main panel, select **Define One Table as a Replication Source**:

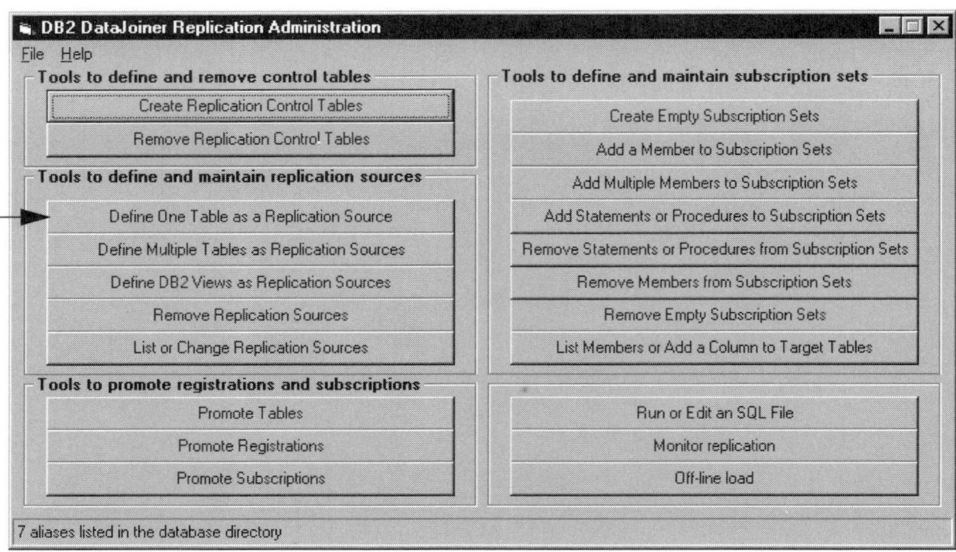

Figure 178. DJRA - Define One Table as a Replication Source

The following panel is displayed:

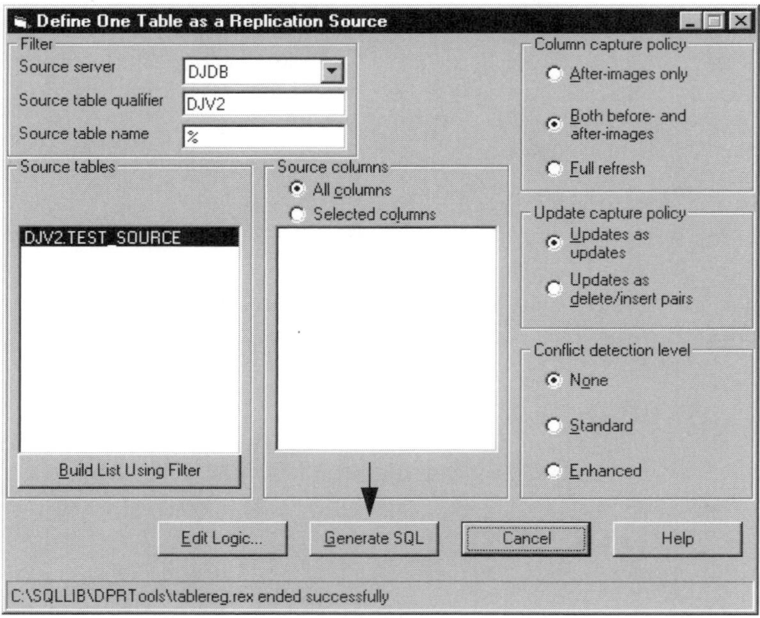

Figure 179. Define One Table as a Replication Source

2. Select the DataJoiner database (here, DJDB) as the Source Server, enter DJV2 as the Source Table qualifier and click on **Build List using filter**. From the list, select DJV2.TEST_SOURCE as the Source Table, then click on **Generate SQL**.

In this example, the following SQL script was generated:

```
--* echo input: TABLEREG DJDB DJV2 TEST_SOURCE BOTH NONEEXCLUDED
--* DELETEINSERTUPDATE NONE
--*
-- using SRCESVR.REX as the  REXX logic filename
-- using REXX password file PASSWORD.REX
-- If you don't see: '-- now done interpreting...'
-- then check your REXX code.
-- now done interpreting REXX password file PASSWORD.REX
-- connect to the source-server
CONNECT TO DJDB USER djv2 USING djv2;

-- USERID=DJV2     SOURCE_ALIAS alias=DJDB
--  PRDID=SQL0201     16 Dec 1998 9:09am

-- source server DJDB     is a DataJoiner server
-- no existing registrations, all candidates eligible
-- the remote server for DJDB     is ORA80
-- Oracle is a supported source through DataJoiner
-- SYSREMOTEUSERS.REMOTE_AUTHID is SCOTT
-- for remote server ORA80
-- 1 candidate registrations for Oracle server found
-- 0 tables already known to be registered
-- The following tables are candidates for registration:
--    1 table               DJV2.TEST_SOURCE

SET SERVER OPTION TWO_PHASE_COMMIT TO 'N' FOR SERVER ORA80;

-- registration candidate #1 DJV2.TEST_SOURCE
-- DJV2.TEST_SOURCE is assumed a USER table
-- reading REXX logic file SRCESVR.REX
-- If you don't see: '-- now done interpreting...'
-- then check your REXX code.
-- now done interpreting REXX logic file SRCESVR.REX
--* Source table DJV2.TEST_SOURCE is on a remote server, no need to
--* create an alter statement, proceeding to ccd table.
--*
COMMIT;

SET PASSTHRU ORA80;

-- SOURCE.REMOTE_AUTHID is SCOTT
-- for remote source table TEST_SOURCE
-- selecting 'X' as the before-image prefix character
CREATE TABLE SCOTT.CCD(IBMSNAP_COMMITSEQ RAW(10) NOT
NULL,IBMSNAP_INTENTSEQ RAW(10) NOT NULL,IBMSNAP_OPERATION CHAR(1) NOT
NULL,IBMSNAP_LOGMARKER DATE NOT NULL,ROW_NUMBER NUMBER(5 , 0) NOT NULL,
XROW_NUMBER NUMBER(5 , 0),TEST_DATA NUMBER(5 , 0),XTEST_DATA NUMBER(5 ,
0),DESCRIPTION CHAR(20),XDESCRIPTION CHAR(20));

-- no index is necessary for the consistent change data table
-- when the remote server is Oracle Server

-- create the insert trigger for DJV2.TEST_SOURCE
CREATE TRIGGER SCOTT.ICCD AFTER INSERT ON
SCOTT.TEST_SOURCE FOR EACH ROW BEGIN INSERT INTO
SCOTT.CCD(ROW_NUMBER,TEST_DATA,DESCRIPTION,XROW_NUMBER,
XTEST_DATA,XDESCRIPTION,IBMSNAP_COMMITSEQ,IBMSNAP_INTENTSEQ,
```

```
IBMSNAP_OPERATION,IBMSNAP_LOGMARKER) VALUES(:NEW.ROW_NUMBER,
:NEW.TEST_DATA,:NEW.DESCRIPTION,NULL,NULL,NULL,LPAD(TO_CHAR(
SCOTT.SGENERATOR001.NEXTVAL), 20 ,'0'),LPAD(TO_CHAR(
SCOTT.SGENERATOR001.NEXTVAL), 20 ,'0'),'I',SYSDATE);END;

--:ENDOFTRIGGER:

-- create the update trigger for DJV2.TEST_SOURCE
CREATE TRIGGER SCOTT.UCCD AFTER UPDATE ON
SCOTT.TEST_SOURCE FOR EACH ROW BEGIN INSERT INTO
SCOTT.CCD(ROW_NUMBER,TEST_DATA,DESCRIPTION,XROW_NUMBER,
XTEST_DATA,XDESCRIPTION,IBMSNAP_COMMITSEQ,IBMSNAP_INTENTSEQ,
IBMSNAP_OPERATION,IBMSNAP_LOGMARKER) VALUES(:NEW.ROW_NUMBER,
:NEW.TEST_DATA,:NEW.DESCRIPTION,:OLD.ROW_NUMBER,:OLD.TEST_DATA,
:OLD.DESCRIPTION,LPAD(TO_CHAR(SCOTT.SGENERATOR001.NEXTVAL), 20 ,'0'),
LPAD(TO_CHAR(SCOTT.SGENERATOR001.NEXTVAL), 20 ,'0'),'U',SYSDATE);END;

--:ENDOFTRIGGER:

-- create the AFTER delete trigger for DJV2.TEST_SOURCE
CREATE TRIGGER SCOTT.DCCD AFTER DELETE ON
SCOTT.TEST_SOURCE FOR EACH ROW BEGIN INSERT INTO
SCOTT.CCD(ROW_NUMBER,TEST_DATA,DESCRIPTION,XROW_NUMBER,
XTEST_DATA,XDESCRIPTION,IBMSNAP_COMMITSEQ,IBMSNAP_INTENTSEQ,
IBMSNAP_OPERATION,IBMSNAP_LOGMARKER) VALUES(:OLD.ROW_NUMBER,
:OLD.TEST_DATA,:OLD.DESCRIPTION,:OLD.ROW_NUMBER,:OLD.TEST_DATA,
:OLD.DESCRIPTION,LPAD(TO_CHAR(SCOTT.SGENERATOR001.NEXTVAL), 20 ,'0'),
LPAD(TO_CHAR(SCOTT.SGENERATOR001.NEXTVAL), 20 ,'0'),'D',SYSDATE);END;

--:ENDOFTRIGGER:

COMMIT;
SET PASSTHRU RESET;
--* create a DataJoiner nickname for the table in ORA80
--*
CREATE NICKNAME DJV2.CCD FOR
ORA80.SCOTT."CCD";

--* Oracle source and ccd ALTER nickname procedure.
--* When propagating an Oracle NUMBER column, DataJoiner requires
--* some fixup, as in most cases DataJoiner will assume the Oracle
--* NUMBER column is a FLOAT. If no fixup is required system will
--* proceed to registration.
--*

COMMIT;
-- begining of Alter statement for DataJoiner
ALTER NICKNAME DJV2.TEST_SOURCE SET COLUMN ROW_NUMBER LOCAL TYPE
DECIMAL(5 , 0);

ALTER NICKNAME DJV2.CCD SET COLUMN ROW_NUMBER LOCAL
TYPE DECIMAL(5 , 0);

ALTER NICKNAME DJV2.CCD SET COLUMN XROW_NUMBER LOCAL
TYPE DECIMAL(5 , 0);

ALTER NICKNAME DJV2.TEST_SOURCE SET COLUMN TEST_DATA LOCAL TYPE
DECIMAL(5 , 0);

ALTER NICKNAME DJV2.CCD SET COLUMN TEST_DATA LOCAL TYPE
DECIMAL(5 , 0);

ALTER NICKNAME DJV2.CCD SET COLUMN XTEST_DATA LOCAL
TYPE DECIMAL(5 , 0);

COMMIT;
-- insert a registration record into ASN.IBMSNAP_REGISTER
```

```
INSERT INTO ASN.IBMSNAP_REGISTER(GLOBAL_RECORD,CD_OWNER,CD_TABLE,
CCD_CONDENSED,CCD_COMPLETE,SOURCE_OWNER,SOURCE_TABLE,SOURCE_VIEW_QUAL,
SOURCE_STRUCTURE,SOURCE_CONDENSED,SOURCE_COMPLETE,CCD_OWNER,CCD_TABLE,
PHYS_CHANGE_OWNER,PHYS_CHANGE_TABLE,DISABLE_REFRESH,ARCH_LEVEL,
BEFORE_IMG_PREFIX,CONFLICT_LEVEL,PARTITION_KEYS_CHG,CCD_OLD_SYNCHPOINT)
VALUES('N','NONE','000000000000000001','N','N','DJV2','TEST_SOURCE',
0 , 1 ,'Y','Y','DJV2','CCD','DJV2','CCD',
0 ,'0201','X','0','N',X'00000000000000000001');

-- 1 ccd table(s) available for additional inclusion into
-- the prunning control trigger

COMMIT;
SET PASSTHRU ORA80;

-- proceeding to create the trigger for the IBMSNAP_PRUNCNTL table in Oracle
CREATE TRIGGER SCOTT.PRUNCNTL_TRIGGER AFTER UPDATE ON
SCOTT.IBMSNAP_PRUNCNTL DECLARE MIN_SYNCHPOINT RAW (10); CHANGE_OWNER
CHAR (18); CHANGE_TABLE CHAR (18); CURSOR C1 IS SELECT DISTINCT
SOURCE_OWNER, SOURCE_TABLE, SOURCE_VIEW_QUAL FROM
SCOTT.IBMSNAP_PRUNCNTL WHERE SYNCHPOINT IS NOT NULL; C1_REC C1%ROWTYPE;
MUTATING EXCEPTION; PRAGMA EXCEPTION_INIT(MUTATING, -4091); BEGIN
OPEN C1; LOOP FETCH C1 INTO C1_REC; EXIT WHEN C1%NOTFOUND; BEGIN
SELECT MIN(SYNCHPOINT)INTO MIN_SYNCHPOINT FROM SCOTT.IBMSNAP_PRUNCNTL
WHERE SOURCE_OWNER=C1_REC.SOURCE_OWNER AND
SOURCE_TABLE=C1_REC.SOURCE_TABLE; SELECT PHYS_CHANGE_OWNER INTO
CHANGE_OWNER FROM SCOTT.IBMSNAP_REGISTER WHERE
SOURCE_OWNER=C1_REC.SOURCE_OWNER AND SOURCE_TABLE=C1_REC.SOURCE_TABLE
AND SOURCE_VIEW_QUAL=C1_REC.SOURCE_VIEW_QUAL; SELECT PHYS_CHANGE_TABLE
INTO CHANGE_TABLE FROM SCOTT.IBMSNAP_REGISTER WHERE
SOURCE_OWNER=C1_REC.SOURCE_OWNER AND SOURCE_TABLE=C1_REC.SOURCE_TABLE
AND SOURCE_VIEW_QUAL=C1_REC.SOURCE_VIEW_QUAL; EXCEPTION WHEN
NO_DATA_FOUND THEN NULL; END; BEGIN IF CHANGE_OWNER IS NULL AND
CHANGE_TABLE IS NULL THEN CHANGE_TABLE:=NULL;ELSIF
CHANGE_TABLE='CCD' AND CHANGE_OWNER='DJV2' THEN DELETE
FROM SCOTT.CCD WHERE IBMSNAP_COMMITSEQ < MIN_SYNCHPOINT;
END IF; END; IF MIN_SYNCHPOINT=HEXTORAW('00000000000000000000') THEN
UPDATE SCOTT.IBMSNAP_PRUNCNTL SET SYNCHPOINT=LPAD(TO_CHAR(
SCOTT.SGENERATOR001.NEXTVAL), 20 , '0'), SYNCHTIME=SYSDATE WHERE
SYNCHPOINT=HEXTORAW('00000000000000000000'); END IF; END LOOP; CLOSE
C1; EXCEPTION WHEN MUTATING THEN NULL;END;

--:ENDOFTRIGGER:

COMMIT;
SET PASSTHRU RESET;
COMMIT;
```

In this script, we are creating the following objects in the Oracle Database:

- Internal CCD table.
- Insert/update/delete triggers on the TEST_SOURCE source table.

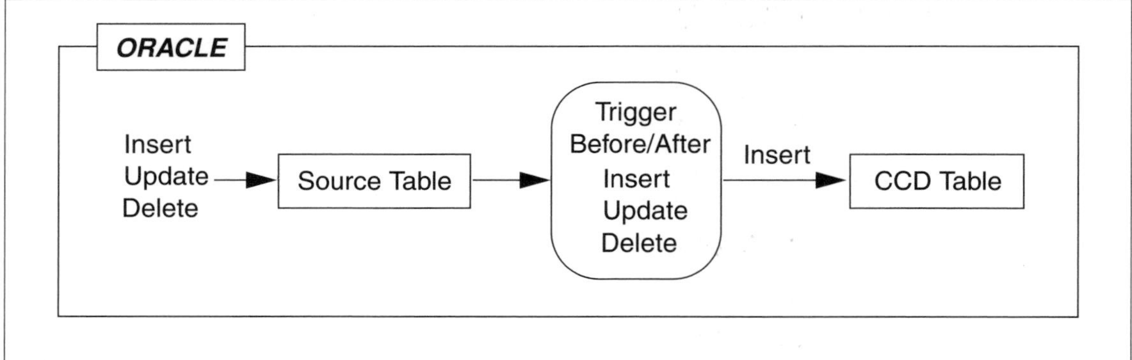

Figure 180. Oracle Triggers

There are update, insert, and delete triggers on every registered source table. These triggers insert changed data into the CCD table (as shown in Figure 180). There is one CCD table per source table.

- Update trigger on ASN.IBMSNAP_PRUNCNTL.
- CCD table registration as an internal CCD for TEST_SOURCE.

  This internal CCD table is condensed and non-complete.

3. Run the SQL script from DJRA.

8.2.6 Defining a Subscription Set

During the subscription definition, if the target server is a non-DB2 database, a target table is created using the SET PASSTHRU function and a nickname is created in the DataJoiner database. In this example, the target database is a DB2 UDB database, therefore no PASSTHRU statement is necessary nor is a nickname required.

Using DJRA, the definition of a subscription consists of several steps. First, you need to define a subscription set:

1. From the DJRA main panel, select **Create Empty Subscription Sets** to display the following panel:

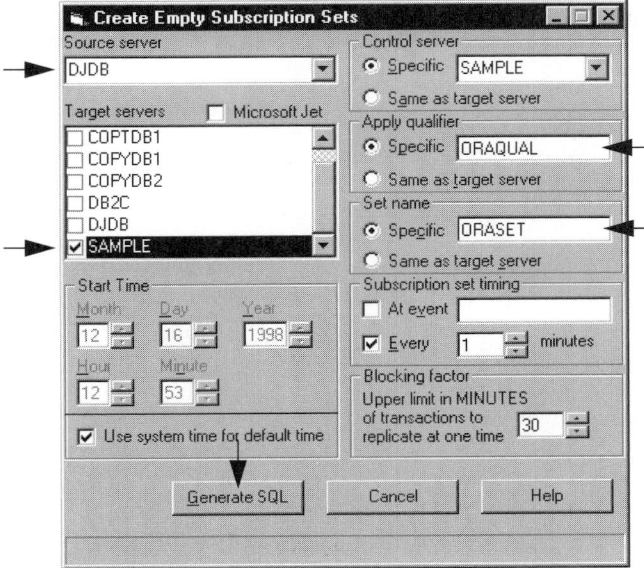

Figure 181. Create Empty Subscription Set

2. Enter the following information in this panel:
   - Source server=DJDB
   - Target server=SAMPLE
   - Control server=SAMPLE
   - Apply qualifier=ORAQUAL
   - Set name=ORASET
   - Subscription set timing: Every 1 minutes
3. Click on the **Generate SQL** button.

In this example the following SQL script was generated:

```
--*
--* Calling ADDSET for set 1 : ORAQUAL/ORASET
--*
--* echo input: ADDSET SAMPLE ORAQUAL ORASET DJDB SAMPLE 19981216141600 R 20
--* NULL 30
--*
-- using REXX password file PASSWORD.REX

-- If you don't see: '-- now done interpreting...' then check your REXX code
-- now done interpreting REXX password file PASSWORD.REX
--* CONNECTing TO DJDB USER djv2 USING djv2;
--*
--* The ALIAS name 'DJDB' matches the RDBNAM 'DJDB'
--*
-- the remote server for DJDB is ORA80
--* CONNECTing TO SAMPLE;
```

```
--*
--* The ALIAS name 'SAMPLE' matches the RDBNAM 'SAMPLE'
--*
--* connect to the CNTL_ALIAS
--*
CONNECT TO SAMPLE user db2inst1 using db2inst1;

-- current USERID=DB2ADMIN CNTL_ALIAS alias=SAMPLE   16 Dec 1998 2:36pm
-- create a new row in IBMSNAP_SUBS_SET
INSERT INTO ASN.IBMSNAP_SUBS_SET( ACTIVATE,APPLY_QUAL,SET_NAME,
WHOS_ON_FIRST,SOURCE_SERVER,SOURCE_ALIAS,TARGET_SERVER,TARGET_ALIAS,
STATUS,LASTRUN,REFRESH_TIMING,SLEEP_MINUTES,EVENT_NAME,
MAX_SYNCH_MINUTES,AUX_STMTS,ARCH_LEVEL) VALUES (0  , 'ORAQUAL' , 'ORASET' , 'S'
, 'DJDB' , 'DJDB' , 'SAMPLE' , 'SAMPLE' , 0 , '1998-12-16-14.16.00' ,
'R' , 1 ,NULL , 30 , 0 ,'0201');

-- create a new row in IBMSNAP_SUBS_SET
INSERT INTO ASN.IBMSNAP_SUBS_SET( ACTIVATE,APPLY_QUAL,SET_NAME,
WHOS_ON_FIRST,SOURCE_SERVER,SOURCE_ALIAS,TARGET_SERVER,TARGET_ALIAS,
STATUS,LASTRUN,REFRESH_TIMING,SLEEP_MINUTES,EVENT_NAME,
MAX_SYNCH_MINUTES,AUX_STMTS,ARCH_LEVEL) VALUES (0  , 'ORAQUAL' , 'ORASET' , 'F'
, 'SAMPLE' , 'SAMPLE' , 'DJDB' , 'DJDB' , 0 , '1998-12-16-14.16.00' ,
'R' , 1 ,NULL , 30 , 0 ,'0201');

-- create a new row in IBMSNAP_SUBS_STMTS
INSERT INTO ASN.IBMSNAP_SUBS_STMTS(APPLY_QUAL,SET_NAME,WHOS_ON_FIRST,
BEFORE_OR_AFTER,STMT_NUMBER,EI_OR_CALL,SQL_STMT,ACCEPT_SQLSTATES)
VALUES('ORAQUAL','ORASET','S','G', 1 ,'E','UPDATE ASN.IBMSNAP_REG_SYNCH SET
TRIGGER_ME=''Y''','02000');

-- increment the AUX_STMTS counter in IBMSNAP_SUBS_SET
UPDATE ASN.IBMSNAP_SUBS_SET SET AUX_STMTS=AUX_STMTS + 1 WHERE
APPLY_QUAL='ORAQUAL' AND SET_NAME='ORASET' AND WHOS_ON_FIRST='S';

--* commit work at SAMPLE
--*
COMMIT;

-- Satisfactory completion of ADDSET at 2:36pm
```

The generated SQL has one Before-SQL statement with BEFORE_OR_AFTER='G'. This SQL will fire the trigger on the REG_SYNCH table. This trigger action performs an update to the ASN.IBMSNAP_REGISTER table's SYNCHPOINT and SYNCHTIME values before the Apply program starts the replication process. It is required to enable the Apply program to fetch new changed data from the internal CCD table.

8.2.7 Defining a Subscription Member

The next step is to add a member to the subscription set:

1. From the DJRA main panel, select **Add a Member to Subscription Sets** to display the following panel:

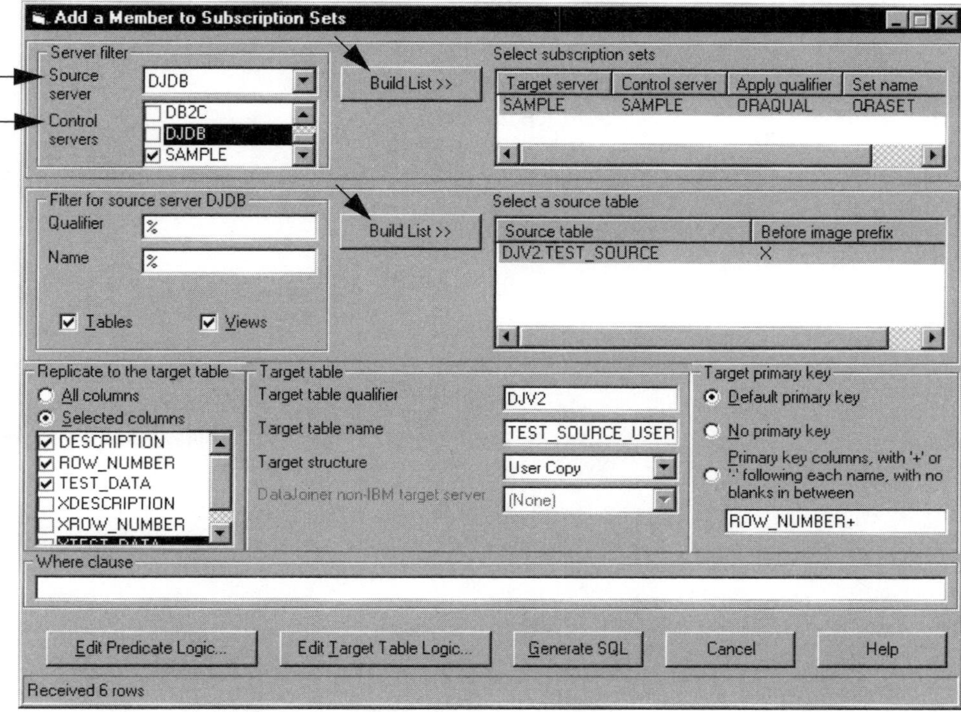

Figure 182. Add a Member to a Subscription Set

2. Enter the following information in this panel:
   - Source server=DJDB
   - Target server=SAMPLE
   - Subscription set=ORASET
   - Source table=DJV2.TEST_SOURCE

In this example, the following SQL script was generated:

```
--*
--* Calling C:\sqllib\DPRTools\addmembr.rex for ORAQUAL/ORASET pair # 1
--*
--* Echo input: ADDMEMBR SAMPLE ORAQUAL ORASET DJV2 TEST_SOURCE
--* XDESCRIPTION,XROW_NUMBER,XTEST_DATA UCOPY DEFAULT DJV2
--* TEST_SOURCE_USER NODATAJOINER U
--*
-- using REXX password file PASSWORD.REX

-- If you don't see: '-- now done interpreting...' then check your REXX code
-- now done interpreting REXX password file PASSWORD.REX
--* Connect to the CNTL_ALIAS
--*
CONNECT TO SAMPLE USER db2inst1 USING db2inst1;
```

```
--* The ALIAS name 'SAMPLE   ' matches the RDBNAM 'SAMPLE'
--*
--* Current USERID=DB2INST1 CNTL_ALIAS alias=         16 Dec 1998 4:24pm
--* Fetching from the ASN.IBMSNAP_SUBS_SET table at SAMPLE
--*
--* CONNECTing TO DJDB     USER djv2 USING djv2;
--*
--* The ALIAS name 'DJDB    ' matches the RDBNAM 'DJDB'
--*
--* Fetching from the ASN.IBMSNAP_REGISTER table at DJDB
--*
-- using REXX logic file CNTLSVR.REX

--* If you don't see: '--* now done interpreting REXX logic file
--* CNTLSVR.REX', then check your REXX code
--*
--* The subscription predicate was not changed by the user logic in
--* CNTLSVR.REX
--* now done interpreting REXX logic file CNTLSVR.REX

-- create a new row in IBMSNAP_SUBS_MEMBR
INSERT INTO ASN.IBMSNAP_SUBS_MEMBR( APPLY_QUAL,SET_NAME,WHOS_ON_FIRST,
SOURCE_OWNER,SOURCE_TABLE,SOURCE_VIEW_QUAL,TARGET_OWNER,TARGET_TABLE,
TARGET_CONDENSED,TARGET_COMPLETE,TARGET_STRUCTURE,PREDICATES) VALUES (
'ORAQUAL' , 'ORASET' , 'S' , 'DJV2' , 'TEST_SOURCE' , 0 ,'DJV2',
'TEST_SOURCE_USER','Y','Y', 8 ,NULL);

-- Create a new row in IBMSNAP_SUBS_COLS
INSERT INTO ASN.IBMSNAP_SUBS_COLS(APPLY_QUAL,SET_NAME,WHOS_ON_FIRST,
TARGET_OWNER,TARGET_TABLE,COL_TYPE,TARGET_NAME,IS_KEY,COLNO,EXPRESSION)
VALUES('ORAQUAL','ORASET' , 'S','DJV2','TEST_SOURCE_USER' ,'A',
'ROW_NUMBER','Y', 1 ,'ROW_NUMBER');

-- Create a new row in IBMSNAP_SUBS_COLS
INSERT INTO ASN.IBMSNAP_SUBS_COLS(APPLY_QUAL,SET_NAME,WHOS_ON_FIRST,
TARGET_OWNER,TARGET_TABLE,COL_TYPE,TARGET_NAME,IS_KEY,COLNO,EXPRESSION)
VALUES('ORAQUAL','ORASET' , 'S','DJV2','TEST_SOURCE_USER' ,'A',
'TEST_DATA','N', 2 ,'TEST_DATA');

-- Create a new row in IBMSNAP_SUBS_COLS
INSERT INTO ASN.IBMSNAP_SUBS_COLS(APPLY_QUAL,SET_NAME,WHOS_ON_FIRST,
TARGET_OWNER,TARGET_TABLE,COL_TYPE,TARGET_NAME,IS_KEY,COLNO,EXPRESSION)
VALUES('ORAQUAL','ORASET' , 'S','DJV2','TEST_SOURCE_USER' ,'A',
'DESCRIPTION','N', 3 ,'DESCRIPTION');

--* I noticed the set subscription is inactive
--*
UPDATE  ASN.IBMSNAP_SUBS_SET SET ACTIVATE=1 WHERE APPLY_QUAL='ORAQUAL'
AND SET_NAME='ORASET' AND WHOS_ON_FIRST='S';

--* Commit work at cntl_ALIAS SAMPLE
--*
COMMIT;

--* Connect to the SOURCE_ALIAS
--*
CONNECT TO DJDB     USER djv2 USING djv2;

--* The ALIAS name 'DJDB    ' matches the RDBNAM 'DJDB'
--*
--* record the subscription in the pruning control table at the
--* source server
--*
```

```
INSERT INTO ASN.IBMSNAP_PRUNCNTL( TARGET_SERVER,TARGET_OWNER,
TARGET_TABLE,SOURCE_OWNER,SOURCE_TABLE,SOURCE_VIEW_QUAL,APPLY_QUAL,
SET_NAME,CNTL_SERVER,TARGET_STRUCTURE,CNTL_ALIAS)VALUES('SAMPLE',
'DJV2','TEST_SOURCE_USER','DJV2','TEST_SOURCE', 0 ,'ORAQUAL','ORASET',
'SAMPLE', 8 ,'SAMPLE');

--* Commit work at source_ALIAS DJDB
--*
COMMIT;

--* Connect to the TARGET_ALIAS
CONNECT TO SAMPLE   USER db2inst1 USING db2inst1;

--* The ALIAS name 'SAMPLE   ' matches the RDBNAM 'SAMPLE'
--*
-- using REXX logic file TARGSVR.REX

--* If you don't see: -- now done interpreting REXX logic file
--* TARGSVR.REX, then check your REXX code
--*
-- in TARGSVR.REX
-- now done interpreting REXX logic file TARGSVR.REX

-- The target table does not yet exist
-- Not remote to DataJoiner target
-- Create the target table DJV2.TEST_SOURCE_USER
CREATE TABLE DJV2.TEST_SOURCE_USER(ROW_NUMBER DECIMAL(5 , 0) NOT NULL,
TEST_DATA DECIMAL(5 , 0),DESCRIPTION CHAR(20));

-- Create an index for the TARGET DJV2.TEST_SOURCE_USER
CREATE UNIQUE INDEX DJV2.TEST_SOURCE_USER ON DJV2.TEST_SOURCE_USER(
ROW_NUMBER ASC);

--* Commit work at target server SAMPLE
--*
COMMIT;

--* Satisfactory completion of ADDMEMBR at 4:24pm
```

3. Run this SQL script from DJRA.

8.2.8 Trigger to Coordinate Capture and Apply

The Apply program reads the ASN.IBMSNAP_SUBS_SET table to identify which subscription sets belong to the current Apply Qualifier. It also reads the ASN.IBMSNAP_REGISTER table to identify the source table that it needs to copy data from. Before it does the full refresh, the Apply program puts hex zeros in the SYNCHPOINT column of the ASN.IBMSNAP_PRUNCNTL table. The Capture program translates the hex zeros to the sequence number of the log read.

When the data source is non-DB2, there is no Capture program. Instead, this function is built in the trigger on the IBMSNAP_PRUNCNTL table. You can find the following logic in the trigger:

```
IF MIN_SYNCHPOINT=HEXTORAW('00000000000000000000') THEN
UPDATE SCOTT.IBMSNAP_PRUNCNTL SET SYNCHPOINT=LPAD(TO_CHAR(
SCOTT.SGENERATOR001.NEXTVAL), 20 , '0'), SYNCHTIME=SYSDATE WHERE
```

```
SYNCHPOINT=HEXTORAW('00000000000000000000'); END IF;
```

This trigger is created during the registration process, as described in "Defining a Registration" on page 297.

8.2.9 Upper Limit of the Apply Program

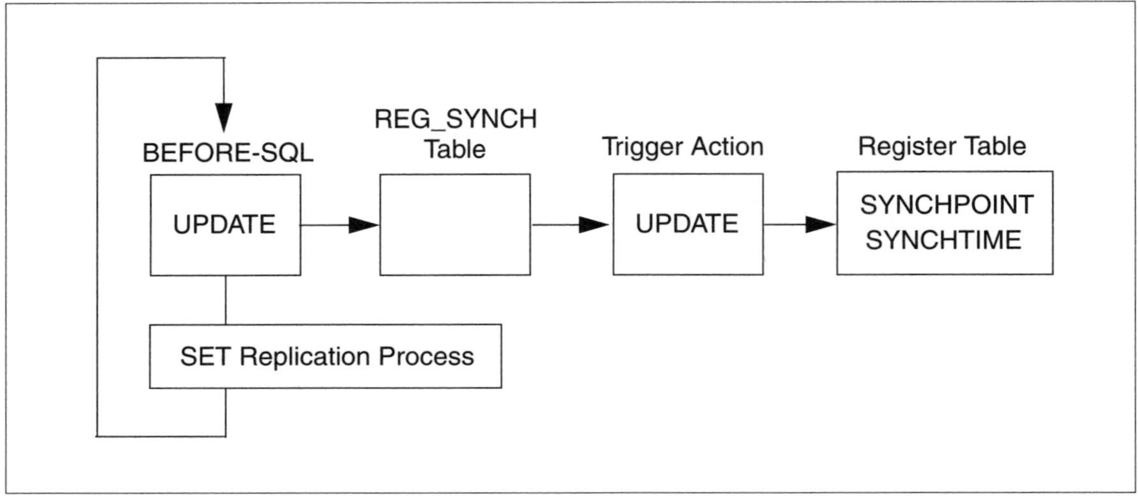

Figure 183. Set Upper Limit Logic

The Apply program needs to know the upper limit of the data captured at the source server (the lower limit is in the PRUNCNTL table). The upper limit should be given by the SYNCHPOINT value of the IBMSNAP_REGISTER table. This is done via the update trigger on the IBMSNAP_REG_SYNCH table. Note that this table is used only for non-DB2 sources. The update trigger will update SYNCHPOINT in the REGISTER table with the next sequence number. During the subscription phase, when DJRA becomes aware that the source is non-DB2, then it stores an update statement against the IBMSNAP_REG_SYNCH table. This table has only one column, TRIGGER-ME. This statement is executed by the Apply program before it opens its cursor to read the IBMSNAP_REGISTER table. The timing of the firing this trigger is controlled by the value of 'G' in the BEFORE_OR_AFTER column in the SUBS_STMTS table. In this way, the Apply program can get the upper limit of the CCD table from the Register table. If the SYNCHPOINT value in the register table is less than the IBMSNAP_COMMITSEQ value in the CCD table, the captured change is never copied by the Apply program.

Table 18 on page 160 shows the SUBS_STMTS table, including the possible values that the BEFORE_OR_AFTER can take.

You can find the following DDL in the creating control tables phase as seen in "Defining the Control Tables" on page 292.

```
-- Creating register synchpoint trigger on ORACLE
--* Create the IBMSNAP_REG_SYNCH TABLE
CREATE TABLE IBMSNAP_REG_SYNCH (TRIGGER_ME CHAR(1));

INSERT INTO IBMSNAP_REG_SYNCH VALUES ('Y');

CREATE TRIGGER SCOTT.REG_SYNCH_TRIGGER AFTER UPDATE ON
SCOTT.IBMSNAP_REG_SYNCH BEGIN UPDATE SCOTT.IBMSNAP_REGISTER SET
SYNCHPOINT=LPAD(TO_CHAR(SCOTT.SGENERATOR001.NEXTVAL), 20 , '0'),
SYNCHTIME=SYSDATE;END;
```

You can see the creation of the Before-SQL statement in the SQL generated when the subscription set is created (see "Defining a Subscription Set" on page 302):

```
-- create a new row in IBMSNAP_SUBS_STMTS
INSERT INTO ASN.IBMSNAP_SUBS_STMTS(APPLY_QUAL,SET_NAME,WHOS_ON_FIRST,
BEFORE_OR_AFTER,STMT_NUMBER,EI_OR_CALL,SQL_STMT,ACCEPT_SQLSTATES)
VALUES('ORAQUAL','ORASET','S','G', 1 ,'E','UPDATE ASN.IBMSNAP_REG_SYNCH
SET
TRIGGER_ME=''Y''','02000');

-- increment the AUX_STMTS counter in IBMSNAP_SUBS_SET
UPDATE ASN.IBMSNAP_SUBS_SET SET AUX_STMTS=AUX_STMTS + 1 WHERE
APPLY_QUAL='ORAQUAL' AND SET_NAME='ORASET' AND WHOS_ON_FIRST='S';
```

8.2.10 Pruning the CCD Table

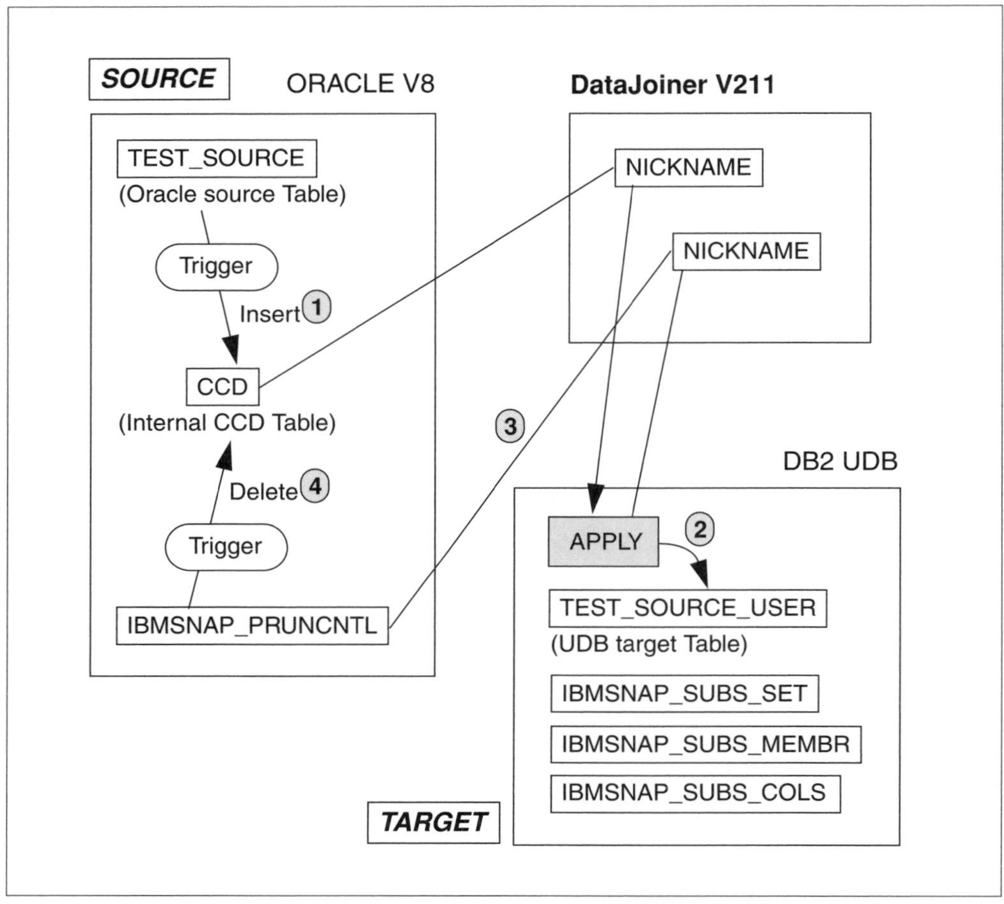

Figure 184. ORACLE to UDB Replication - CCD Pruning

In a DB2 to DB2 replication environment, the CD and UOW tables (but not CCD tables) are pruned by the Capture program. In some cases, pruning is also advisable against the CCD tables. A condensed CCD table does not grow without bound; however, a non-condensed CCD table contains a history of all changes. In this Oracle to DB2 replication example, we are using a condensed, non-complete CCD table used as an internal CCD table at the source server. This table will grow (with enough update activity) to approach the size of a complete CCD table. There is no value in letting this table grow, since the most recent changes will always be fetched from it. The update trigger on the IBMSNAP_PRUNCNTL table can prune the CCD table by deleting rows after they have been copied.After the subscription set is processed, the Apply program updates the SYNCHTIME and SYNCHPOINT columns of the ASN.IBMSNAP_PRUNCNTL table if the source table has been updated. If the source table has not had changes against it, then Apply only updates the SYNCHTIME column. This then makes the trigger prune the data that has been copied.

This process can be summarized in Figure 184 on page 310:

1. The change made to the source will be populated into the CCD table by the trigger on the source.
2. Apply will propagate the changed data to the target.
3. Apply marks the processing point in the Pruning Control table.
4. The trigger on the Pruning Control table will be fired and the pruning will be done by the DELETE SQL statement in the trigger body.

You can find the following DELETE SQL statement in the trigger action section in the SQL for defining the trigger on the Pruning Control table in "Defining a Registration" on page 297:

```
.............................
SELECT MIN(SYNCHPOINT)INTO MIN_SYNCHPOINT FROM SCOTT.IBMSNAP_PRUNCNTL
WHERE SOURCE_OWNER=C1_REC.SOURCE_OWNER AND
SOURCE_TABLE=C1_REC.SOURCE_TABLE;
.............................
DELETE FROM SCOTT.CCD WHERE IBMSNAP_COMMITSEQ < MIN_SYNCHPOINT;
```

This will prune behind the oldest of all subscriptions that refer to the source table.

8.2.11 Logical Partitioning Key Support in Triggers

By default, the update trigger generates an update to the source as an UPDATE statement. Sometimes you need to instruct the trigger to generate DELETE and INSERT statements instead of an UPDATE. For example, when:

- Oracle source applications update one or more columns of a target table primary key.
- Oracle source applications update one or more columns of a target partitioning key, and the target database is managed by DB2 UDB EEE or a DB2 for MVS partitioned table space.
- Oracle source applications update one or more columns referenced in a subscription predicate.

From the DJRA registration panel, you can specify that UPDATES are captured as DELETE and INSERT pairs:

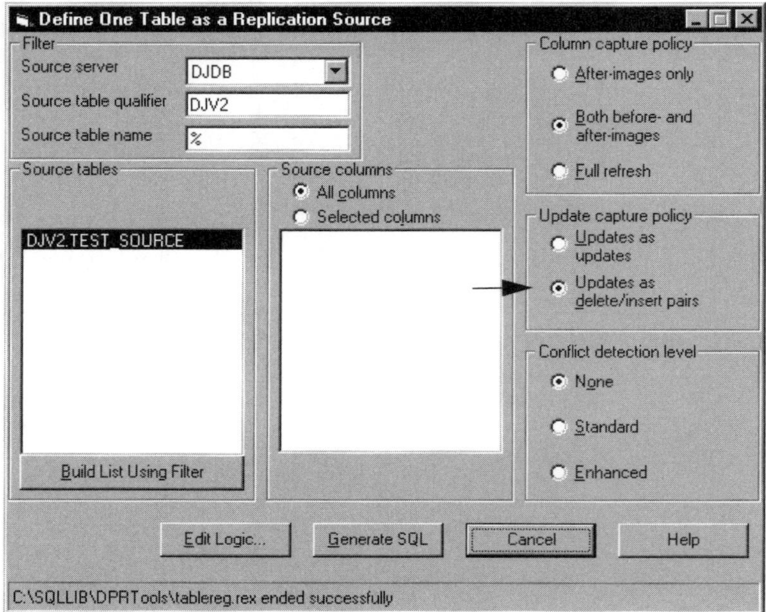

Figure 185. Logical Partitioning Key Support

The generated update trigger action on the source table contains two SQL inserts into the CCD table, one each for the DELETE and INSERT operations:

```
-- create the update trigger for DJV2.TEST_SOURCE
CREATE TRIGGER SCOTT.UCCD AFTER UPDATE ON
SCOTT.TEST_SOURCE FOR EACH ROW BEGIN INSERT INTO
SCOTT.CCD(ROW_NUMBER,TEST_DATA,DESCRIPTION,XROW_NUMBER,
XTEST_DATA,XDESCRIPTION,IBMSNAP_COMMITSEQ,IBMSNAP_INTENTSEQ,
IBMSNAP_OPERATION,IBMSNAP_LOGMARKER) VALUES(:OLD.ROW_NUMBER,
:OLD.TEST_DATA,:OLD.DESCRIPTION,:OLD.ROW_NUMBER,:OLD.TEST_DATA,
:OLD.DESCRIPTION,LPAD(TO_CHAR(SCOTT.SGENERATOR001.NEXTVAL), 20 ,'0'),
LPAD(TO_CHAR(SCOTT.SGENERATOR001.NEXTVAL), 20 ,'0'),'D',SYSDATE);
INSERT INTO SCOTT.CCD(ROW_NUMBER,TEST_DATA,DESCRIPTION,
XROW_NUMBER,XTEST_DATA,XDESCRIPTION,IBMSNAP_COMMITSEQ,
IBMSNAP_INTENTSEQ,IBMSNAP_OPERATION,IBMSNAP_LOGMARKER) VALUES(
:NEW.ROW_NUMBER,:NEW.TEST_DATA,:NEW.DESCRIPTION,:OLD.ROW_NUMBER,
:OLD.TEST_DATA,:OLD.DESCRIPTION,LPAD(TO_CHAR(
SCOTT.SGENERATOR001.NEXTVAL), 20 ,'0'),LPAD(TO_CHAR(
SCOTT.SGENERATOR001.NEXTVAL), 20 ,'0'),'I',SYSDATE);END;
```

8.2.12 Obtaining a Sequence Number from Other Sources

In Oracle, there is a function to generate a sequence number. This is used during the creation of control tables, and triggers use this function to get a unique ascending number. For SQL Server, Sybase, and SQL Anywhere, their GETDATE() function is manipulated to get a unique timestamp. Informix deals with this in another way. While Oracle, SQL Server, and SQL Anywhere have a compatible datatype for CHAR(10) FOR BIT DATA, there is no such compatible data type in Informix. Therefore, a separate table is generated in the Informix database to generate the unique ascending number.

Here is a example of part of the trigger body in Sybase, MS SQL Server, and SQL Anywhere:

```
create trigger TEST_SOURCE_INS
on TEST_SOURCE
for insert
as
insert into TEST_SOURCE_CCD
select
convert(binary(10),getdate()),'I',convert(binary(10),getdate()),getdate
(),ROW_NUMBER,TEST_DATA,
DESCRIPTION from inserted
```

8.2.13 The Trigger Already Exists

Another interesting situation occurs if the source table already has triggers defined on it before they are used in a replication configuration. In Oracle, Informix, and SQL Anywhere, this situation will result in a run-time error indicating that the same event triggers exists. In Microsoft SQL Server and Sybase SQL Server, however, the same event trigger is replaced automatically with the new trigger body. To prevent this action, DJRA checks if the trigger exists on the source table, and the trigger body is generated as comments during the registration phase.

8.2.14 SQL30090N When Dropping Control Tables

If you recreate the control tables in the Oracle database after you run the BIND for the Apply program, you might receive SQLCODE -30090 with Reason Code 18. For example:

```
CEXPC: connect to DJDB
  CEXPC: CONNECT with USERID/PASSWORD
  CEXPC: serverIsolationUR is 1.
  GSST: Source server timestamp is 1998-12-17-08.01.34.254879
  EXEI: SQL statement is UPDATE ASN.IBMSNAP_REG_SYNCH SET TRIGGER_ME='Y'.
  Compiled(I) at 17:13:05 on Nov 17 1998 (Level 0066)
   SQLCA is
        00000000 53514C43 41202020 00000088 FFFF8A76 SQLCA    ....˘˘.v
        00000010 00023138 20202020 20202020 20202020 ..18
        00000020 20202020 20202020 20202020 20202020
```

```
        00000030 20202020 20202020 20202020 20202020
        00000040 20202020 20202020 20202020 20202020
        00000050 20202020 20202020 53514C52 41445250          SQLRADRP
        00000060 FFFF877E 00000000 00000000 00000000 ˇˇ..............
        00000070 00000000 00000000 20202020 20202020 ........
        00000080 20202032 35303030                             25000
   RGRS: SELECT failed. errcode is 490101. sqlstate is 25000. sqlcode is -30090
   RGRS: SP = 00000000000000000000
   RGRS: ST = |
  DSYL: SELECT1 failed errcode is 910101. sqlstate is 25000. sqlcode is -30090

SQL30090N Operation invalid for application execution
          environment.  Reason code = "<reason-code>"

o   18 - An update request (or, a DDL operation that
    results in the update of a system catalog table) has
    been issued that would result in multiple data sources
    being updated when one or more of the data sources in
    the unit of work only supports one-phase commit.
```

This reason for this negative SQLCODE is that the Apply program packages became invalid when you dropped the control tables. Subsequently, an automatic bind is attempted at Apply execution time. This attempt is treated as a multiple update violation within the same unit of work. This is because the Apply program needs to update the Oracle database and DataJoiner database in the same unit of work, and the DataJoiner two phase commit setting is set to 'N'. Note that DataJoiner itself can support two phase commit processing between a UDB and an Oracle Database.

In this case, you explicitly need to run the bind for the Apply program before you start the Apply program to avoid this problem.

8.3 CCD Table Considerations

In this section, we cover two sample replication cases using CCD tables. First, we describe how to use a CCD table as a change history table. This is typically used for security auditing. Secondly, we describe how to manage a CCD table that a user-defined application maintains.

Chapter 5, "Staging Tables" on page 169 presents a introduction to CCD (or staging) tables.

Let's first review how a CCD table is characterized.

8.3.1 Local or Remote

CCD tables can be located at the source server, in which case, they are *local* CCD tables. When CCD tables are located at the target server, they are *remote* CCD tables.

8.3.2 Complete or Condensed

A *complete* staging table consists of every row of interest from the original source table. All the source table data is inserted initially into a complete CCD table, and then only the data in changed rows is replicated afterwards. A *non-complete* CCD table holds the changes to source table rows. No initial full refresh is performed to a non-complete CCD table.

A *condensed* staging table contains only the most current value for the row. It can have only one row per key value. A *non-condensed* staging table has all the changes, therefore it can have multiple rows for the same key value.

8.3.3 Internal or External CCD

A CCD table is termed *internal* when it is the first CCD table created as the local target of a subscription to a source table and you did not choose the 'to be used as a source' option. Only one internal CCD can be created for one source table. Any additional local CCD tables created will be non-internal CCD tables. Remote CCD tables are always non-internal CCD tables.

When a subscription specifies a CCD target table with the 'to be used as a source' option, the Control Center administration will automatically define the CCD target table as a replication source. This is known as auto-registration.

Internal CCD tables are auto-registered differently than non-internal CCD tables. When internal CCD tables are auto-registered, replication source information is stored in the CCD_OWNER and CCD_TABLE columns of the source row in the Register table. You can not create a replication subscription against internal CCD tables. Instead, the CCD table associated with the defined replication source will be chosen rather than CD table when the Apply program updates a target.

8.3.4 Change History CCD Example

Consider the following CCD table replication scenario, shown in Figure 186 on page 316:

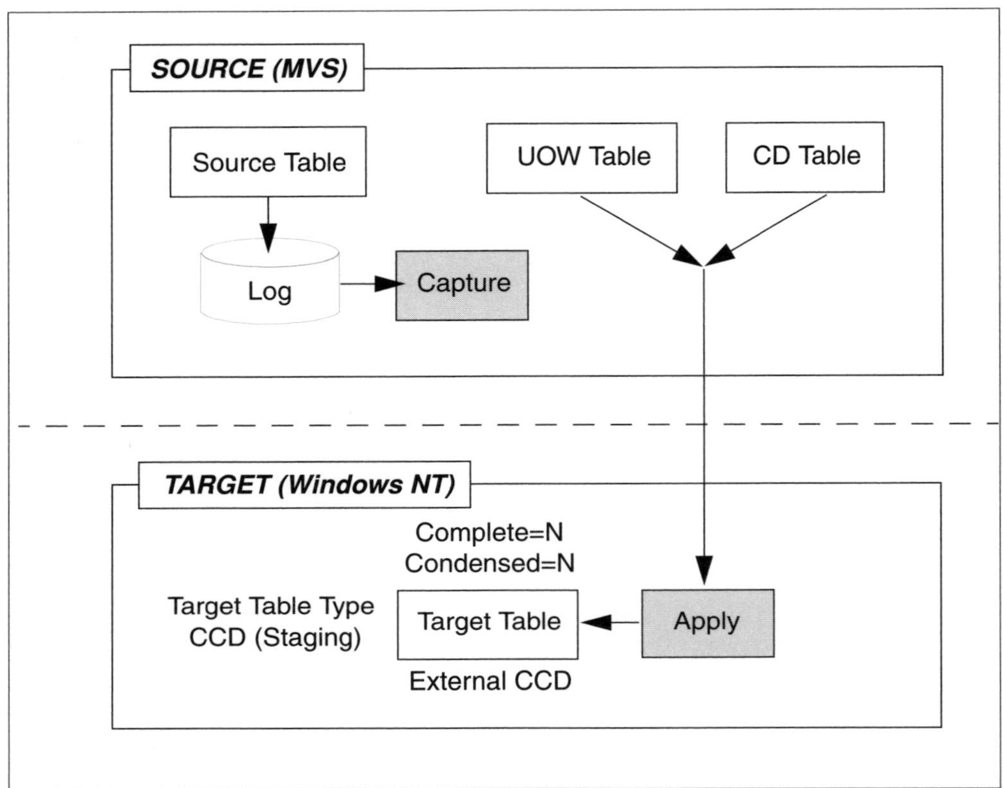

Figure 186. CCD History Table

In this scenario, the target table is non-complete and non-condensed. This means it can be used as a change history table for the source table. It might be useful for auditing purpose because all transactions affecting the source table will be recorded in this change history table.

To define a change history table as described above, add a subscription as shown below. This example uses the configuration described in "Test Environment for OS/390 and Windows NT Replication" on page 95.

1. From the Control Center, expand the object tree until you see the Replication Sources folder (**System->wtsc42oe->DB2C**). Click on the **Replication Sources** folder to display a list of the defined replication sources in the right hand pane:

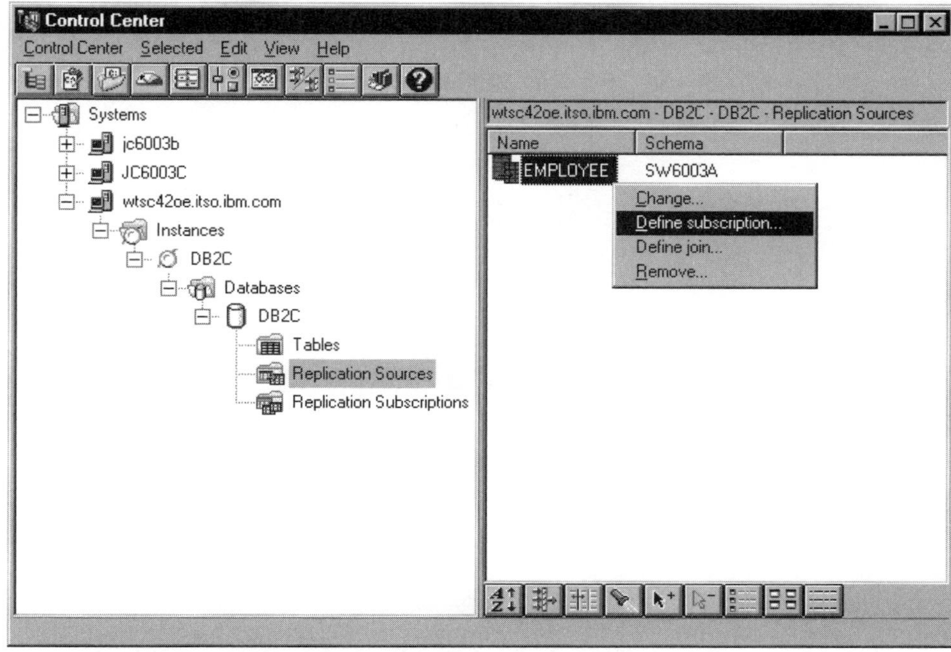

Figure 187. Define Subscription

2. Choose a replication source (here, EMPLOYEE) and click the right mouse button. Choose **Define subscription** to display the following panel:

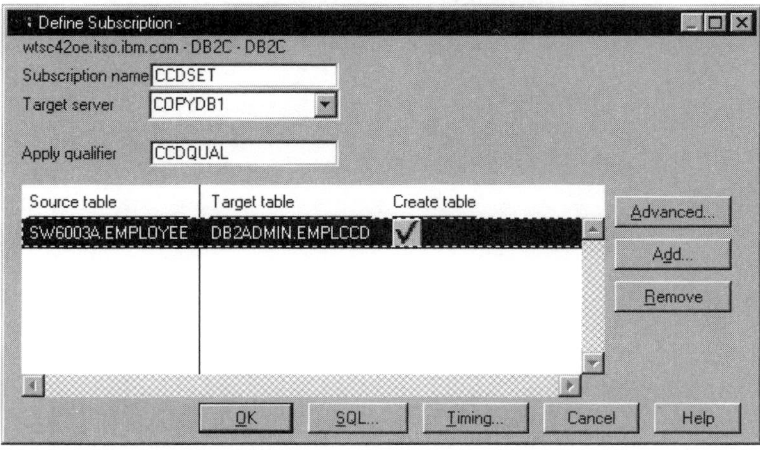

Figure 188. Define Subscription

3. Enter the values as shown in Figure 188:

- SET_NAME =CCDSET
- APPLY_QUAL=CCDQUAL
- TARGET_TABLE=DB2ADMIN.EMPLCCD
- TARGET_SERVER=COPYDB1

4. Select **Advanced** to open the Advanced Subscription Definition panel:

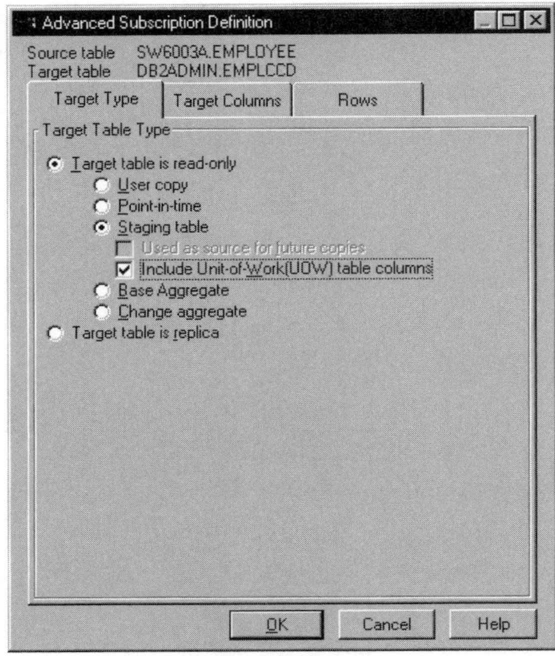

Figure 189. Advanced Subscription Definition - Target Type

5. Click on **Staging table** and **Include Unit of work table columns**. Select the **Target Columns** tab:

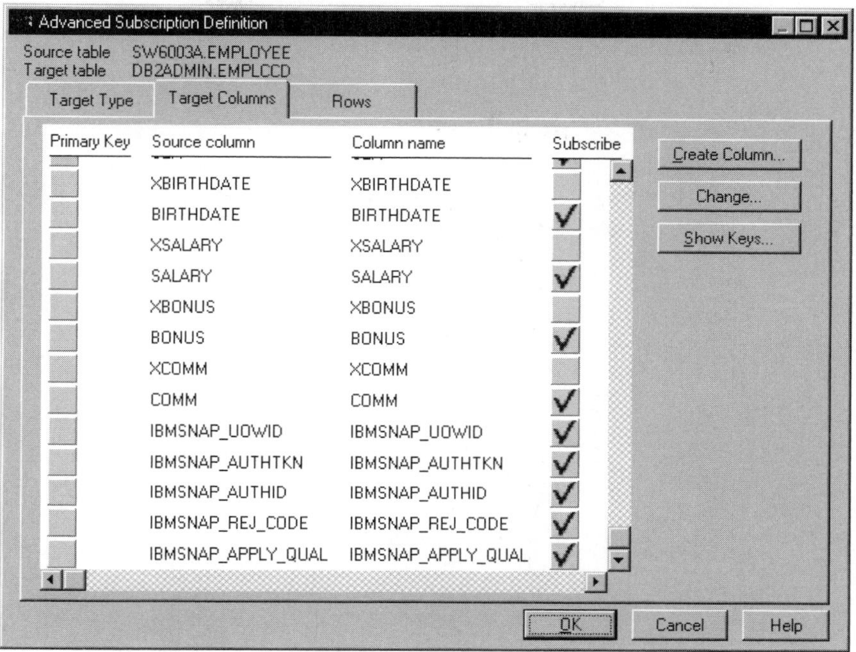

Figure 190. Advanced Subscription - Target Columns

6. This panel shows you which UOW columns will be included in the CCD table. Make sure that no column is defined as the primary key.

Note

A unique index should not be defined because a non-condensed staging table can have multiple rows for one key value. The Apply program will fail if a primary (or unique) key exists on the CCD table.

7. Return to the Define Subscription panel, and select **Timing**:

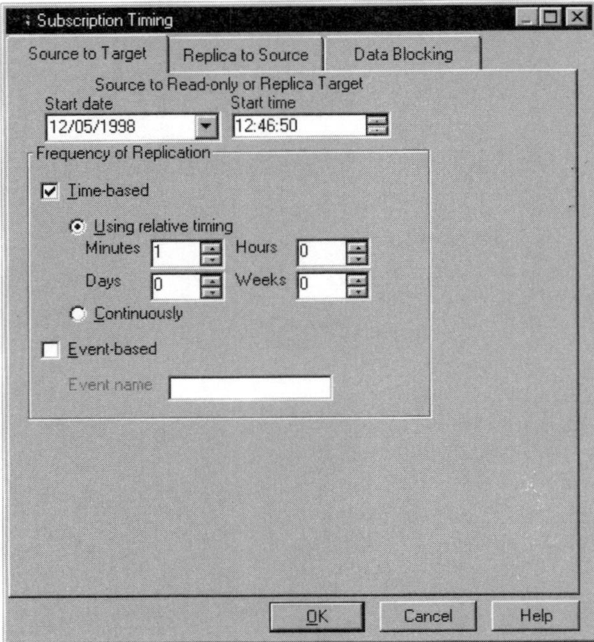

Figure 191. Define subscription - Timing

8. As this is a test environment, change minutes to one, and click on **OK**. Click OK again to complete the definition panels.
9. Enter the database name to store subscription control information (the control server). We chose COPYDB1, which is also the target database.
10. The Save SQL File panel is displayed. Save the file as CCDSUB.SQL.

The generated SQL should contain the following insert statement to the SUBS_MEMBR table with TARGET_CONDENSED=N and TARGET_COMPLETE=N:

```
INSERT INTO ASN.IBMSNAP_SUBS_MEMBR (
APPLY_QUAL, SET_NAME, WHOS_ON_FIRST, SOURCE_OWNER, SOURCE_TABLE,
SOURCE_VIEW_QUAL, TARGET_OWNER, TARGET_TABLE, TARGET_CONDENSED,
TARGET_COMPLETE, TARGET_STRUCTURE, PREDICATES ) VALUES (
'CCDQUAL', 'CCDSET', 'S', 'SW6003A', 'EMPLOYEE', 0, 'DB2ADMIN',
'EMPLCCD', 'N', 'N', 3, NULL);
```

The target CCD table contains these extra columns: IBMSNAP_UOWID, IBMSNAP_AUTHTKN, IBMSNAP_AUTHID, IBMSNAP_REJ_CODE, and IBMSNAP_APPLY_QUAL. The values for these additional columns come from the UOW Table.

```
CREATE TABLE DB2ADMIN.EMPLCCD (
IBMSNAP_INTENTSEQ CHAR ( 10 ) FOR BIT DATA NOT NULL,
IBMSNAP_OPERATION CHAR ( 1 ) NOT NULL,
IBMSNAP_COMMITSEQ CHAR ( 10 ) FOR BIT DATA NOT NULL,
IBMSNAP_LOGMARKER TIMESTAMP NOT NULL,
IBMSNAP_UOWID CHAR ( 10 ) FOR BIT DATA NOT NULL,
IBMSNAP_AUTHTKN CHAR ( 12 ) NOT NULL,
IBMSNAP_AUTHID CHAR ( 18 ) NOT NULL,
IBMSNAP_REJ_CODE CHAR ( 1 ) NOT NULL,
IBMSNAP_APPLY_QUAL CHAR ( 18 ) NOT NULL,
EMPNO CHAR ( 6 ) NOT NULL,
FIRSTNME VARCHAR ( 12 ) NOT NULL,
.............
```

These columns may be useful, for example, if you want to record the transaction authorization ID for security-auditing purposes.

Even if you cold start the Capture program, and then start the Apply program, a full refresh will never happen since the target table is non-complete. However, a GOCAPT message will be recorded in the Trace table if Capture has not started capturing the source table at that time.

8.3.5 Gap Resolution

When using this kind of change history CCD table, if you shut down the Capture program and then cold start it, it deletes all the rows from the CD table. Between the time you shut down the Capture program and then cold start it, updates might have been made that the Capture program did not capture. Additionally, any updates that were in the CD table were deleted at the cold start before the Apply program could copy them. A *gap* now exists between the target table and the CD table.

8.3.5.1 The Definition of Gap

A gap exists if the SYNCHPOINT in the SUBS_SET table at the target server is lower than the CD_OLD_SYNCHPOINT in the REGISTER table at the source server.

Note

If REGISTER.CD_OLD_SYNCHPOINT > SUBS_SET.SYNCHPOINT, then a gap exists.

When a gap is present, the Apply program attempts to perform a complete refresh of the affected target table unless the target table is non-complete. If the target table is non-complete, since the Apply program does not perform a full refresh, data integrity could be lost. In this case, the Apply trace shows us the following:

```
------------------------------------------
  TARGET_SERVER  = COPYDB1
  TARGET_OWNER   = DB2ADMIN
  TARGET_TABLE   = EMPLCCD
  SYNCHTIME      = 1998-12-06-15.37.00.291285
  SYNCHPOINT is null
  SOURCE_OWNER   = SW6003A
  SOURCE_TABLE   = EMPLOYEE
  SOURCE_VIEW_QUAL = 0
  APPLY_QUAL      = CCDQUAL
  SET_NAME        = CCDSET
  CONTROL_SERVER  = COPYDB1
  TARGET_STRUCTURE = 3
  ------------------------------------------
  Compiled(B) at 14:48:59 on Aug 12 1998 (Level 0053)
   WPNUSR: target_structure is CCD.
       MSGF: MsgNumber is 51.
The NLS msg is ASN1051E: The Apply program detected a gap between the
source table, CD, and the target table. The error code is 4A5102.
PTST: A gap(2) has been detected.
```

The ASN1051E error does not appear in the APPLYTRAIL table if the following APAR fix has been applied to the Apply program:

```
APAR Identifier ...... PQ13460      Last Changed ........
98/04/02
ASN1051E 4A5102 THE ONLY WAY TO EXIT FROM A GAP SITUATION WHEN
USING INTERNAL CCD IS TO MANUALLY UPDATE DPROPR CONTROL TABLES
```

If this fix has been applied, Apply no longer notices the occurrence of a gap as an error and does not stop processing. The Apply program automatically resets the gap between the CD and the target tables and continues processing. A trace shows the following:

```
PSET: Commit6 ok
  CEXPC: connect to COPYDB1
  CLOS: setRepeatCopy is 0
  CLOS: activate = 1
  CLOS: status   = 0
  CLOS: lastrun = 1998-12-06-14.51.34.484001
  CLOS: lastsuccess = 1998-12-06-14.50.50.000000
  CLOS: synchpoint is null
  CLOS: synchtime = 1998-12-06-15.50.31.260709
  CLOS: apply_qual = CCDQUAL
  CLOS: set_name = CCDSET
  CLOS: sWhosOnFirst = S
  CEXPC: connect to DB2C
  CEXPC: CONNECT with USERID/PASSWORD
  CEXPC: serverIsolationUR is 1.
  CEXPC: connect to COPYDB1
```

```
CEXPC: CONNECT without USERID/PASSWORD
CEXPC: serverIsolationUR is 1.
SAT: ASNLOAD = N, EFFECT_MEMBERS = 0
SAT: MASS_DELETE = N
SAT: SET_INSERTED = 0
SAT: SET_DELETED = 0
SAT: SET_UPDATED = 0
SAT: SET_REWORKED = 0
SAT: SET_REJECTED_TRXS = 0
SAT: STATUS = 0
SAT: LASTRUN = 1998-12-06-14.51.34.484001
SAT: LASTSUCCESS = 1998-12-06-14.50.50.000000
SAT: SYNCHPOINT is null
```

As the STATUS is not -1 (a known failed execution), this situation is treated as a normal condition. The gap reset operation is done internally by the Apply program.

8.3.6 External Data Considerations

CCD staging tables usually hold captured changes (inserts, updates, or deletes) to a source table. Changes that are captured by applications or other products, such as DataPropagator NonRelational, Data Difference Utility (DDU), your own developed triggers or other applications, can be defined as the source for replication subscriptions. When using these kinds of external data sources, a complete CCD table must be provided, and this CCD table must be updated by an application.

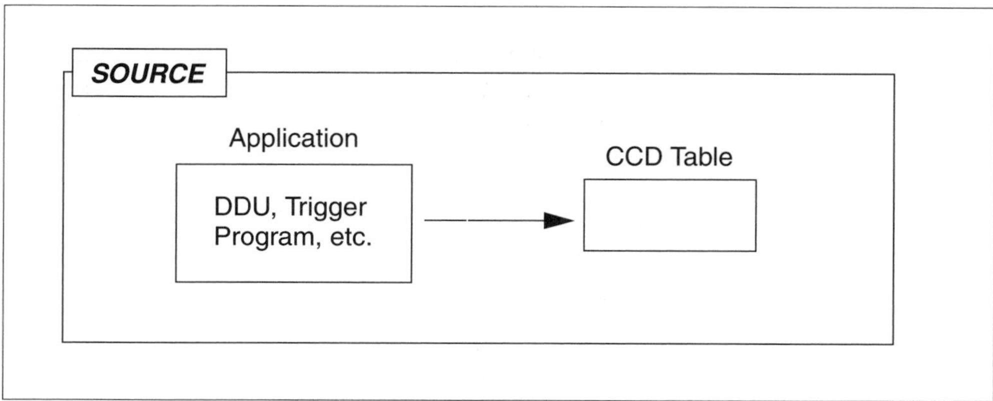

Figure 192. CCD Table Maintained by an Application

You can define replication subscriptions referring to CCD tables that are remotely located from the original source site.

If you want to maintain your own CCD table, you must update three columns in the Register table:

- CCD_OLD_SYNCHPOINT - this is the SYNCHPOINT associated with the oldest row remaining in the CCD table, though this sequence number might be older if the CCD table is condensed and the oldest row was overwritten by a more recent update.
- SYNCHPOINT - this is a sequence value used to maintain the state of CCD copies, subscription states, and for controlling pruning.
- SYNCHTIME - this is the timestamp equivalent of SYNCHPOINT.

Let's look at the rules that external programs should follow when maintaining CCD tables.

8.3.6.1 How External CCD Tables Are Refreshed

When the CCD table is fully refreshed, set the CCD_OLD_SYNCHPOINT to a value greater than the previous value of SYNCHPOINT. This will induce a false gap condition. If SYNCHPOINT has no previous value (such as just after the subscription was defined), set:

- CCD_OLD_SYNCHPOINT to x'00000000000000000001'
- SYNCHPOINT to MAX(IBMSNAP_COMMITSEQ) in CCD
- SYNCHTIME to MAX(IBMSNAPLOGMARKER) in CCD

If the CCD_OLD_SYNCHPOINT remains NULL, the Apply program will repeatedly perform a full refresh.

8.3.6.2 Change Propagation

Update the SYNCHPOINT column in the Register table to MAX(IBMSNAP_COMMITSEQ) in the CCD whenever committing new changes to the CCD. SYNCHTIME should also be set accordingly, since it is the timestamp equivalent of SYNCHPOINT.

- SYNCHPOINT to MAX(IBMSNAP_COMMITSEQ) in CCD
- SYNCHTIME to MAX(IBMSNAP_LOGMARKER) in CCD

If your application does not perform the above SQL against the Register table, the Apply program will never detect any changes from the CCD table even though the CCD table contains the recent changed data.

8.3.6.3 Example of an Application Maintaining a CCD Table

Let's look at an example of an application that uses triggers to maintain a CCD table.

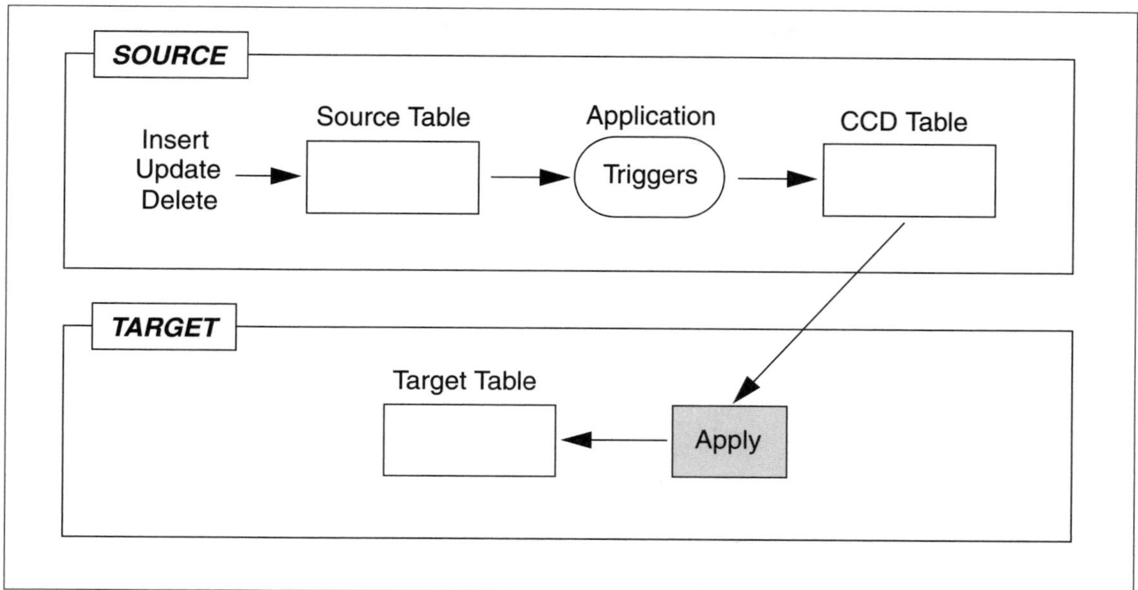

Figure 193. CCD Maintained by an Application

The CCD table is complete and condensed. This example includes insert, update, and delete triggers that are used to maintain this CCD table. The GENERATE_UNIQUE() function is used to generate a unique sequence number. Note that this example will not work in a DB2 UDB EEE environment because we truncate the generated number from CHAR (13) for BIT DATA to CHAR(10) for BIT DATA and these last three truncated bytes indicate the node number information. We are using only the timestamp range of GENERATE_UNIQUE() as the sequence number. In the EEE environment, UDB can't guarantee a unique ascending sequence number since each node's timestamp might differ slightly.

Using GENERATE_UNIQUE() is better than using CURRENT TIMESTAMP since GENERATE_UNIQUE() ensures uniqueness even if two rows have the same timestamp.

1. To create and populate the source table:

```
create table SOURCE
(c1 int not null,
 c2 char(10),
 primary key(c1));

insert into source values (1,'INIT');
```

2. To create and populate the CCD table:

```
create table TARGETCCD
(IBMSNAP_INTENTSEQ CHAR ( 10 ) FOR BIT DATA NOT NULL ,
IBMSNAP_OPERATION CHAR ( 1 ) NOT NULL,
IBMSNAP_COMMITSEQ CHAR ( 10 ) FOR BIT DATA NOT NULL ,
IBMSNAP_LOGMARKER TIMESTAMP NOT NULL,
 c1 int not null,
 c2 char(10)
,primary key(c1));

insert into targetccd values (
x'00000000000000000010',
'I',
x'00000000000000000010',
current timestamp,
1,'INIT');
```

3. To create and populate the target table:

```
CREATE TABLE USERCOPY(
C1 INT NOT NULL,
C2 CHAR(10));

CREATE UNIQUE INDEX USERCOPYX ON USERCOPY(C1);

insert into usercopy values (1,'INIT');
```

4. To define the triggers:

```
-- To run, issue "db2 -td# -vt xxx.sql"

drop trigger TR_I #
create trigger TR_I
after insert on SOURCE
referencing new as N
for each row mode db2sql
begin atomic
delete from TARGETCCD where c1=N.c1;
insert into TARGETCCD values
(SUBSTR(GENERATE_UNIQUE(),1,10),'I',
SUBSTR(GENERATE_UNIQUE(),1,10),CURRENT TIMESTAMP,N.c1,N.c2) ;
end#

drop trigger TR_U #
create trigger TR_U
after update on SOURCE
referencing new as N
for each row mode db2sql
```

```
begin atomic
delete from TARGETCCD where c1=N.c1;
insert into TARGETCCD values
(SUBSTR(GENERATE_UNIQUE(),1,10),'U',
SUBSTR(GENERATE_UNIQUE(),1,10),CURRENT TIMESTAMP,N.c1,N.c2) ;
end#

drop trigger TR_D #
create trigger TR_D
after delete on SOURCE
referencing old as o
for each row mode db2sql
begin atomic
delete from TARGETCCD where c1=o.c1;
insert into TARGETCCD values
(SUBSTR(GENERATE_UNIQUE(),1,10),'D',
SUBSTR(GENERATE_UNIQUE(),1,10),CURRENT TIMESTAMP,o.c1,o.c2) ;
end#
```

8.3.6.4 Defining the Replication Source

We can use the Control Center to define this CCD table as a replication source:

1. In the Tables list, right-click against the TARGETCCD table. Select **Define as replication source** and **Custom**.

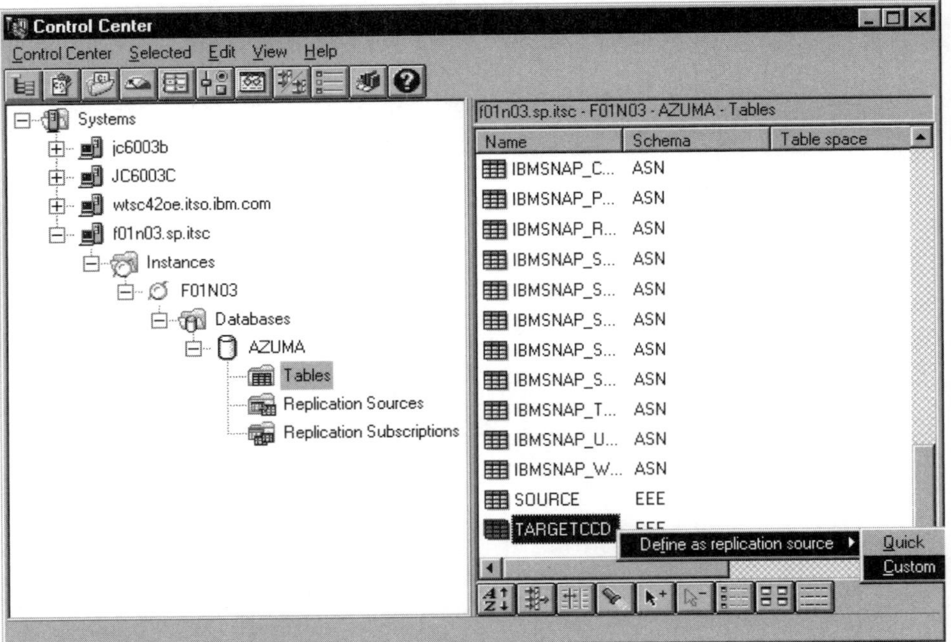

Figure 194. Define Replication Source - External Data Source

2. In this case, no panel is displayed to configure this replication source. Instead, the Run Now or Save SQL window is displayed:

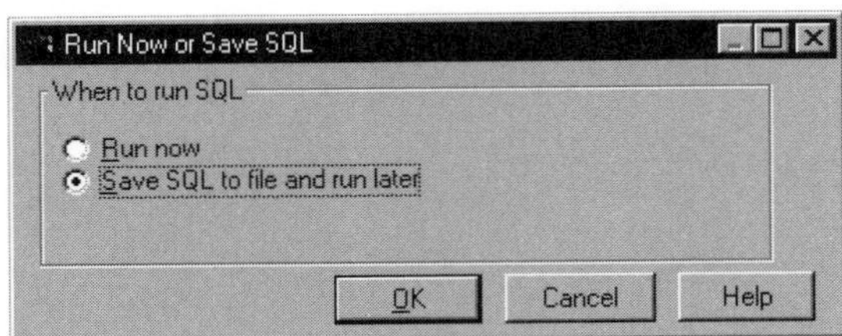

Figure 195. Run Now or Save SQL

Save the SQL in a file, then use a text editor to examine it:

```
INSERT INTO ASN.IBMSNAP_REGISTER (
GLOBAL_RECORD, SOURCE_OWNER, SOURCE_TABLE, SOURCE_VIEW_QUAL,
SOURCE_STRUCTURE, SOURCE_CONDENSED, SOURCE_COMPLETE, CD_OWNER,
CD_TABLE, PHYS_CHANGE_OWNER, PHYS_CHANGE_TABLE, CD_OLD_SYNCHPOINT,
CD_NEW_SYNCHPOINT, DISABLE_REFRESH, CCD_OWNER, CCD_TABLE,
CCD_OLD_SYNCHPOINT, SYNCHPOINT, SYNCHTIME, CCD_CONDENSED,
CCD_COMPLETE, ARCH_LEVEL, DESCRIPTION, BEFORE_IMG_PREFIX,
CONFLICT_LEVEL, PARTITION_KEYS_CHG ) VALUES (
```

```
'N', 'EEE', 'TARGETCCD', 0, 3, 'N', 'Y', NULL, NULL, 'EEE',
'TARGETCCD', NULL, NULL, 0, NULL, NULL, X'00000000000000000010',
X'00000000000000000010', 1998-12-13-13.04.02.000000, NULL, NULL,
'0201', NULL, NULL, '0', 'N');
```

CCD_OLD_SYNCHPOINT is set to MIN(IBMSNAP_COMMITSEQ), SYNCHPOINT to MAX(IBMSNAP_COMMITSEQ), and SYNCHTIME to MAX(IBMSNAP_LOGMARKER) for an non-empty external CCD table. If the CCD table is empty, these three values should be set to NULL.

3. Run the saved SQL file.

8.3.6.5 Defining a Subscription

Use the Control Center to define a subscription. Use the following values:

- Target Table Type : User copy
- Target Table Name: USERCOPY
- SLEEP_MINUTES: 1 (Relative timer was selected)

8.3.6.6 CCD Table Initialization

Since this is a complete CCD table, we must make sure that the Apply program can do the full refresh from CCD.

If the CCD table is initialized, we need to run the following SQL to make sure the Apply program will do the full refresh from the CCD to the target table:

- When CCD_OLD_SYNCHPOINT is set to NULL:

```
update asn.ibmsnap_register set
ccd_old_synchpoint=
(select min(ibmsnap_commitseq) from targetccd);

update asn.ibmsnap_register
set synchpoint=
(select max(ibmsnap_commitseq) from targetccd);

update asn.ibmsnap_register
set synchtime=
(select max(ibmsnap_logmarker) from targetccd);
```

  When we fully refresh the CCD table, we set IBMSNAP_COMMITSEQ to x'00000000000000000001'.

- When CCD_OLD_SYNCHPOINT is NOT set to NULL:

```
update asn.ibmsnap_register set
ccd_old_synchpoint=substr(generate_unique(),1,10)
where source_table='TARGETCCD';
```

The above SQL sets the CCD_OLD_SYNCHPOINT to a value greater than the previous value of SYNCHPOINT in the SUBS_SET table, and also sets it to a value less than MAX(IBMSNAP_COMMITSEQ) in the CCD table.

```
update asn.ibmsnap_register
set synchpoint=
(select max(ibmsnap_commitseq) from targetccd)
where source_table='TARGETCCD';

update asn.ibmsnap_register
set synchtime=
(select max(ibmsnap_logmarker) from targetccd)
where source_table='TARGETCCD';
```

8.3.6.7 Change Replication

The Apply program has upper boundary (SYNCHPOINT) when it does a differential copy.

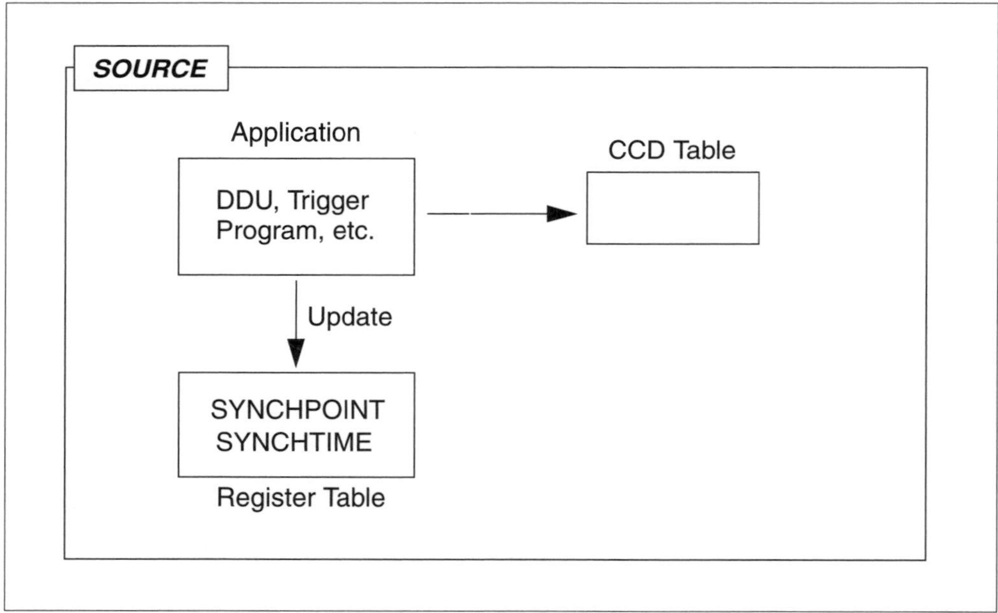

Figure 196. CCD Maintained by the Application

The SYNCHTIME is updated every COMMIT_INTERVAL as specified in the CCPPARMS table. Since there is no Capture program in this case, your application must provide this SYNCHPOINT in the Register table whenever your application commits a new change to the CCD table. Otherwise, the

Apply program will never do the differential copy to the target table. The following SQL is required after you make changes to the CCD table:

```
update asn.ibmsnap_register
set synchpoint=
(select max(ibmsnap_commitseq) from targetccd)
where source_table='TARGETCCD';

update asn.ibmsnap_register
set synchtime=
(select max(ibmsnap_logmarker) from targetccd)
where source_table='TARGETCCD';
```

8.3.6.8 Manual Loading from the CCD to the Target

The Apply program uses mass delete and insert SQL statements when it does a full refresh. You might want to use another method to perform the full refresh. This example shows you how to avoid the Apply full refresh when the source is an external CCD table.

1. Optional: It is recommended that you disable the full refresh capability for the applicable source table as shown in the following SQL statements. The Apply program might issue an error message rather than performing a full refresh if the following procedure is not performed correctly.

```
--Connect to the Source server

UPDATE ASN.IBMSNAP_REGISTER SET DISABLE_REFRESH =1
WHERE SOURCE_OWNER='EEE' AND
SOURCE_TABLE='TARGETCCD';
```

2. Ensure that the Apply program is inactive, or deactivate the applicable replication subscription as shown in the following SQL statement:

```
--Connect to the Control server

UPDATE ASN.IBMSNAP_SUBS_SET SET ACTIVATE=0
WHERE SET_NAME='SET1' AND APPLY_QUAL='QUAL1';
```

3. Update SYNCHPOINT and SYNCHTIME in ASN.IBMSNAP_PRUNCNTL for each row that corresponds to a member of the replication subscription as shown in the following SQL statement:

```
--Connect to the Source server

update asn.ibmsnap_pruncntl
set
synchpoint=substr(generate_unique(),1,10),
synchtime= current timestamp
where apply_qual='QUAL1';
```

4. Verify that Trigger program has emulated *RBA translation*.
5. Run your own unload/load procedure outside DPropR.
6. Update ASN.IBMSNAP_REGISTER as shown in the following SQL statement:

```
--Connect to the Source server

update asn.ibmsnap_register
set ccd_old_synchpoint=
(select min(synchpoint) from asn.ibmsnap_pruncntl)
where source_table='TARGETCCD';
update asn.ibmsnap_register
set synchpoint=
(select min(synchpoint) from asn.ibmsnap_pruncntl)
where source_table='TARGETCCD';
update asn.ibmsnap_register
set synchtime=
(select min(synchtime) from asn.ibmsnap_pruncntl)
where source_table='TARGETCCD';
```

7. Update ASN.IBMSNAP_SUBS_SET as shown in the following SQL statement:

```
--Connect to the control server

update asn.ibmsnap_subs_set
set lastrun=
(select min(synchtime) from asn.ibmsnap_pruncntl)
where apply_qual='QUAL1';
update asn.ibmsnap_subs_set
set lastsuccess=
(select min(synchtime) from asn.ibmsnap_pruncntl)
where apply_qual='QUAL1';
update asn.ibmsnap_subs_set
set synchtime=
(select min(synchtime) from asn.ibmsnap_pruncntl)
where apply_qual='QUAL1';
update asn.ibmsnap_subs_set
set synchpoint=
(select min(synchpoint) from asn.ibmsnap_pruncntl)
where apply_qual='QUAL1';
```

8. Start the Apply program after you set ACTIVATE=1 for the applicable subscription:

```
--Connect to the Control server

UPDATE ASN.IBMSNAP_SUBS_SET SET ACTIVATE=1
```

```
WHERE SET_NAME='SET1' AND APPLY_QUAL='QUAL1';
```

8.4 DB2 ODBC Catalog

This section introduces a replication solution, known as DB2 ODBC Catalog, for users and applications who use ODBC to access data stored in DB2 for OS/390 via DB2 Connect.

Many of today's popular desktop tools use ODBC to access data stored in DB2 for OS/390. These desktop tools often allow end users to construct SQL queries interactively by way of a graphical interface that displays the tables (and their columns) that exist in DB2. Desktop tools collect this information by using the ODBC driver to retrieve data from the DB2 catalog. This kind of interactive access to the DB2 catalog presents several challenges for the DB2 administrator, as illustrated in Figure 197:

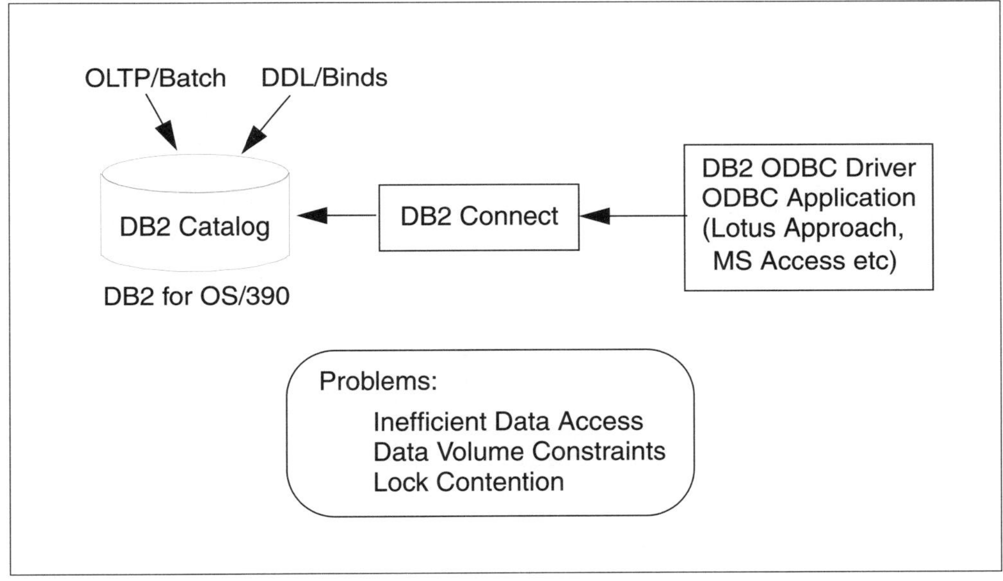

Figure 197. ODBC Access to DB2

The issues the DBA has to address are:

- Inefficient data access

  The DB2 catalog tables are not specifically designed for ODBC. The tables that make up the DB2 catalog contain many columns that are not required by the ODBC driver, causing DB2 to retrieve a lot of extraneous data when reading DB2 catalog data pages. Also, the ODBC driver often has to join multiple DB2 catalog tables to produce the output required by the ODBC driver's callable interfaces.

- Data volume constraints

  Some customers have very large DB2 catalog tables, which define hundreds or even thousands of DB2 tables. Most ODBC end users require access to a very small subset of these tables. Attempts to return the entire contents of the DB2 catalog to the end user can result in slow response times, due to the network delays involved in transmitting such massive amounts of data. End users can also encounter out-of-memory conditions when attempting to display the DB2 catalog data.

- Lock contention

  As the ODBC driver collects data from the catalog, locks are acquired on the pages of the DB2 catalog tables. When large numbers of end users hold such locks, lock timeouts can occur during DDL operations (CREATE, DROP, etc.) and BIND operations. This can create situations where the catalog is largely inaccessible for these types of database operations.

Until recently, IBM's ODBC driver offered only limited relief to DBAs who encountered the issues described above. The ODBC driver provided a DB2CLI.INI setting (SYSSCHEMA) that allowed the customer to direct the ODBC catalog queries to a set of user-defined tables. Using SYSSCHEMA offered two main advantages:

- The DBA was able to create multiple sets of these tables, so that each set of tables contained a subset of the DB2 catalog rows. This capability resolved data volume concerns for the ODBC users, by allowing them to operate with a small subset of the DB2 catalog data.
- These tables also relieved catalog lock contention, since end users were able to issue queries against the user-defined tables rather than the real DB2 catalog tables.

However, this approach did nothing to improve data access efficiency, because the user-defined tables were mirror images of the DB2 catalog tables. The ODBC driver still had to join rows from multiple tables to produce the information required by the ODBC user. While user-defined catalog tables solved some of the problems encountered by ODBC users, this approach introduced a new challenge in the form of maintaining data currency. The DB2 administrator had to manually ensure that the user-defined tables were synchronized with the real DB2 catalog. Failure to do so resulted in situations where the user-defined tables failed to list tables and columns that were added to DB2 after the catalog data was copied into the user-defined tables.

Similarly, the user-defined tables could include tables or indexes that had been subsequently dropped from the real DB2 catalog.

8.4.1 DB2 ODBC Catalog Enhancements

IBM has recently completed a set of product enhancements that customers can use to significantly improve the efficiency of ODBC access to DB2 catalog data. There are two distinct groups of enhancements that make up the solution:

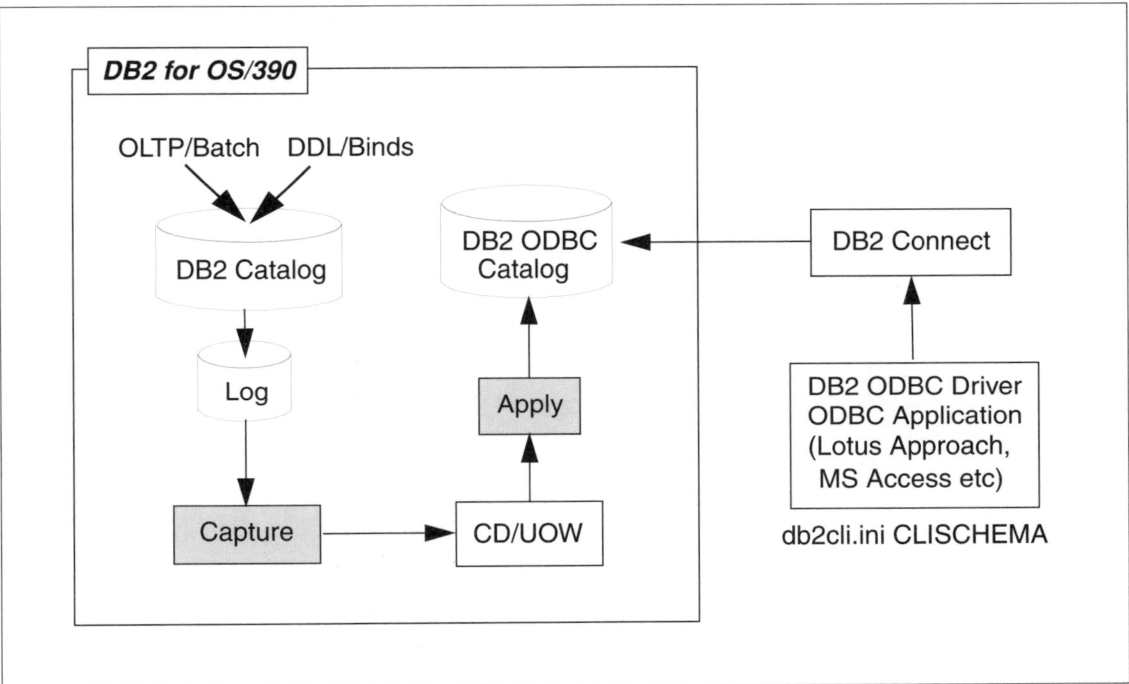

Figure 198. DB2 ODBC Catalog Replication Solution

1. The DB2 ODBC catalog

   The IBM ODBC driver is enhanced to understand a new set of pseudo-catalog tables, called the *DB2 ODBC catalog*, which are designed to improve the performance of ODBC applications. The DB2 ODBC catalog contains rows representing objects defined in the real DB2 catalog, but these rows include only the columns necessary to support ODBC operations. The tables in the DB2 ODBC catalog are pre-joined and specifically indexed to support fast catalog access for ODBC applications. IBM's ODBC driver is also enhanced to support multiple views of the DB2

ODBC catalog. System administrators can create DB2 ODBC catalog views containing only the rows that are needed by a particular segment of the end user community. End users can select the DB2 ODBC catalog view they wish to use with the new CLISCHEMA setting in the DB2CLI.INI file, which must be specified in the DSN or common section of the DB2CLI.INI file. Use of the CLISCHEMA setting is completely transparent to the ODBC application program; so, you can use this option with any of the popular desktop tools.

2. Automatic DB2 ODBC catalog maintenance

   The second group of enhancements enable DB2 and DataPropagator Relational to maintain the DB2 ODBC catalog tables. DB2 is enhanced to support the DATA CAPTURE CHANGES clause on the ALTER statement for use with the DB2 catalog tables. This allows DB2 to specially mark the log records associated with statements that change the DB2 catalog (such as CREATE or DROP statements), so that DataPropagator Relational can detect these changes in the log stream. DataPropagator Relational is enhanced in two areas. The Capture process is now able to identify log records that represent changes to the DB2 catalog and to record these changed data records in a staging table. The Apply process is enhanced to propagate the changed data records to the DB2 ODBC catalog tables. This allows DataPropagator Relational to resolve the management issues associated with keeping the data in the DB2 ODBC catalog tables synchronized with the content of the real DB2 catalog tables. As with other tables managed by DataPropagator Relational, the customer can specify how often the Apply process should run.

8.4.2 Software Requirements

To use the DB2 ODBC catalog function, at the time of writing the following software is required:

- DB2 Connect V5.0 (Enterprise or Personal Edition) plus Fixpack 6 or later.
- DB2 for OS/390 V5.1, plus APARs PQ15661 (PTF UQ17669 SQLCODE -332 From the Remote Client) and PQ13031 (PTF UQ21649 Allow ALTER TABLE xxx DATA CAPTURE CHANGES to DB2 for OS390 catalog table).
- Capture for MVS V5 plus APAR PQ16905 (PTF UQ21491).
- The current level of maintenance for Apply for MVS V5.

8.4.3 Setting up Capture for MVS

This is described in “Setting up Capture for MVS” on page 117.

8.4.4 Setting up Apply for MVS

Apply for MVS is packaged in SMP/E format. The installation sequence is as follows:

1. Use SMP/E to install (RECEIVE/APPLY/ACCEPT).
2. Link-Edit Apply/MVS.
3. Create and load VSAM message files.
4. Bind to the DB2 subsystem.

```
x//ASNABIND JOB (999,POK),'INSTALL ',CLASS=A,MSGCLASS=T,
// NOTIFY=&SYSUID,TIME=1440,REGION=4M
/*JOBPARM L=999,SYSAFF=SC42
//***************************************************************/
//* JOB NAME = ASNA2BD5                                          */
//*                                                              */
//* DESCRIPTIVE NAME = BIND PACKAGE JCL FOR THE IBM              */
//*                    DATAPROPAGATOR RELATIONAL APPLY FOR MVS */
//*                    FOR DB2 V5                                */
//*                                                              */
//* STATUS = VERSION 05  RELEASE 01  MODIFICATION LEVEL 00       */
//*                                                              */
//* FUNCTION = BIND THE DATAPROPAGATOR RELATIONAL                */
//*            APPLY FOR MVS PACKAGE FOR DB2 V5                  */
//*                                                              */
//*       LICENSED MATERIALS - PROPERTY OF IBM                   */
//*       5655-A22 (C) COPYRIGHT IBM CORP 1993, 1997             */
//*       ALL RIGHTS RESERVED.                                   */
//*       US GOVERNMENT USERS RESTRICTED RIGHTS -                */
//*       USE, DUPLICATION OR DISCLOSURE RESTRICTED              */
//*       BY GSA ADP SCHEDULE CONTRACT WITH IBM CORP.            */
//*                                                              */
//* NOTES =                                                      */
//* 1) REVIEW ALL STATEMENTS.                                    */
//* 2) CHANGE THE HLQUAL FIELD(S) TO A VALID HIGH LEVEL          */
//*    QUALIFIER TO COMPLY WITH YOUR SITE'S NAMING STANDARDS.    */
//*    ASNA.V5R1M0 IS RECOMMENDED AS THE HIGH LEVEL QUALIFIER.   */
//* 3) DELETE THE TEXT THAT BEGINS WITH <== AT THE               */
//*    END OF SOME LINES                                         */
//*                                                              */
//***************************************************************/
//*
//***************************************************************/
//*    FOR EXECUTION OF APPLY FOR MVS BIND PROCEDURE             */
//***************************************************************/
//ASNA2BD5 EXEC PGM=IKJEFT01
//SYSPRINT DD  SYSOUT=*
//SYSTSPRT DD  SYSOUT=*
//SYSUDUMP DD  SYSOUT=*
//STEPLIB  DD  DISP=SHR,DSN=DB2V510.SDSNLOAD
//DBRMLIB  DD  DISP=SHR,DSN=ASNA.V5R1M0.SASNADBM
//SYSTSIN  DD  *
```

```
DSN S(DB2C)
BIND PACKAGE(DB2C.ASNA) -
MEMBER(ASNDI000) -
ACTION(REP) -
RELEASE(COMMIT) ISOLATION(UR)

BIND PACKAGE(DB2C.ASNA) -
MEMBER(ASND4000) -
ACTION(REP) -
RELEASE(COMMIT) ISOLATION(UR)

BIND PACKAGE(DB2C.ASNA) -
MEMBER(ASNDP000) -
ACTION(REP) -
RELEASE(COMMIT) ISOLATION(UR)

BIND PACKAGE(DB2C.ASNA) -
MEMBER(ASNDB000) -
ACTION(REP) -
RELEASE(COMMIT) ISOLATION(UR)

BIND PACKAGE(DB2C.ASNA) -
MEMBER(ASNDF000) -
ACTION(REP) -
RELEASE(COMMIT) ISOLATION(CS)

BIND PACKAGE(DB2C.ASNA) -
MEMBER(ASNDA000) -
ACTION(REP) -
RELEASE(COMMIT) ISOLATION(UR)

BIND PACKAGE(DB2C.ASNA) -
MEMBER(ASNDC000) -
ACTION(REP) -
RELEASE(COMMIT) ISOLATION(UR)

BIND PLAN(ASNAP510) -
PKLIST(DB2C.ASNA.*) -
ACTION(REP) ACQUIRE(USE) -
RELEASE(COMMIT)
/*
```

5. Customize and invoke the JCL.

   Prepare the JCL by specifying the appropriate optional parameters in the PARM field of the ASNRUN*nn* command. Tailor the JCL to meet your site's requirements:

   - nn=23 - The Apply for MVS that runs on DB2 for MVS V3.1
   - nn=24 - The Apply for MVS that runs on DB2 for MVS V4.1
   - nn=25 - The Apply for MVS that runs on DB2 for MVS V5.1

   In this example, the invocation JCL is:

```
//ASNARUN  EXEC PGM=ASNAPV25,
//*            PARM='QUAL1 DB2C DB2C DISK TRCFLOW NOSLEEP'
//             PARM='CAT_QUAL DB2C DB2C DISK TRCFLOW '
//*                  <== VERIFY APPLY_QUALIFIER
//*                                  <== VERIFY DB2 SUBSYSTEM ID
//*                                       <== VERIFY  CONTROL_SERVER
```

Table 29 displays a list of the startup parameters for Apply/MVS.

Table 29. Apply/MVS Startup Parameters

Parameter	**Definition**
APPLY_QUAL	- Specify the Apply program qualifier that the Apply program uses to identify the subscription to be served. The name of Apply_QUAL is case-sensitive and must match the value of APPLY_QUAL in the subscription set table. This must be the first parameter.
DB2_subsys_name	- This is a positional parameter that is required as the second parameter
Control_Server	- Specify the name of the server where the replication control tables resides. If you do not specify this optional positional parameter, the default is the current server.
LOADXit **NOLOADXit** (Default)	- Invoke ASNLOAD exit program. This is optional. - Do not invoke ASNLOAD exit program.
Memory (Default) DISK	- Specify that a memory file stores the fetched answer set. This keyword is optional. - Specify that a disk file stores the fetched answer set.This keyword is optional.
INAMsg (Default) NOINAMsg	- Issue a message when the Apply program is inactive. - Do not issue a message when the Apply program is inactive. This keyword is optional.
NOTRC (Default) TRCERR TRCFLOW	- Do not generate a trace. - Generate a trace that contains only error information. This keyword is optional. - Generate a trace that contains error and execution flow information. This keyword is optional.
NOTIFY **NONOTIFY** (Default)	- Invoke the ASNDONE exit program when the Apply program processing ends. This keyword is optional. - Do not invoke the ASNDONE exit program.
SLEEP (Default) NOSLEEP	- The Apply program is to go to sleep if no new subscriptions are eligible for processing. - The Apply program is to stop if no new subscriptions are eligible for processing. This keyword is optional.
DELAY(n) **DELAY(6)** (Default)	- Where n=0,1,2,3,4,5,6. Specify the delay time in seconds at the end of each Apply program cycle when continuous replication is used. This keyword is optional. - Set a delay time to 6 seconds at the end of each Apply program cycle when continuous replication is used.

8.4.5 Defining the Replication Sources and Subscriptions

Capture and Apply for MVS populate and maintain the DB2 ODBC catalog tables for DB2 for OS/390 V5. For this replication scenario, there is no need to define replication sources and subscriptions from the Control Center. Capture for MVS V5 PTF UQ21491 provides the administration files for these tasks. You can run these files from HOST DB2/MVS SPUFI or from a DB2 command prompt on a workstation via DB2 Connect.

There are four administration files:

Table 30. List of Administration Files

File name	Purpose
ASNL2CN5	Creating IBM Replication control tables. (This is optional)
ASNL2SY5	Registering the OS/390 catalog tables
ASNL2RE5	Registering the OS/390 catalog views.
ASNL2SU5	Subscribing to the OS/390 catalog views

1. ASNL2CN5 (Optional)

   This is used to create the control tables. You can skip to step two if the control tables already exist in DB2 for OS/390.

   - Review the header portion of ASNL2CN5 file.
   - Update the table space definitions to fit your site requirements.
   - Either run `db2 -vtf ASNL2CN5.SQL` from the client DB2 Command prompt or run it locally using SPUFI. If you run it remotely, PTF UQ17669 (SQLCODE -332 problem) is required to DB2 for OS/390 to support the CASE expression in the DRDA flow.

2. ASNL2SY5 (Required)

   This contains DB2 ALTER TABLE statements against DB2 catalog tables:

   ```
   ALTER TABLE SYSIBM.SYSINDEXES DATA CAPTURE CHANGES;
   ALTER TABLE SYSIBM.SYSKEYS DATA CAPTURE CHANGES;
   ALTER TABLE SYSIBM.SYSTABAUTH DATA CAPTURE CHANGES;
   ALTER TABLE SYSIBM.SYSCOLUMNS DATA CAPTURE CHANGES;
   ALTER TABLE SYSIBM.SYSFOREIGNKEYS DATA CAPTURE CHANGES;
   ALTER TABLE SYSIBM.SYSRELS DATA CAPTURE CHANGES;
   ALTER TABLE SYSIBM.SYSTABLES DATA CAPTURE CHANGES;
   ALTER TABLE SYSIBM.SYSPROCEDURES DATA CAPTURE CHANGES;
   ALTER TABLE SYSIBM.SYSCOLAUTH DATA CAPTURE CHANGES;
   ALTER TABLE SYSIBM.SYSSYNONYMS DATA CAPTURE CHANGES;
   ```

3. ASNL2RE5 (Required)

   This is used to create views and registration information. To support full and differential refresh, appropriate views (such as CD views) are defined. Inserts are made into the Register table for the subscriptions to use.

4. ASNL2SU5 (Required)

   This is used to create the subscription information. It creates the target ODBC catalog tables and views. The default Apply Qualifier name is CAT_QUAL. There are two sets under this APPLY Qualifier. The SUBS_MEMBER table should contain the following rows:

```
SET_NAME  SOURCE_OWNER SOURCE_TABLE       TARGET_OWNER  TARGET_TABLE
--------  ------------ ------------------ ------------  -----------
CAT_SET   CLISCHEM     COLUMNPRIVILEGES2  CLISCHEM      COLUMNPRIVILEGES
CAT_SET   CLISCHEM     COLUMNPRIVILEGES1  CLISCHEM      COLUMNPRIVILEGES
CAT_SET   CLISCHEM     TABLEPRIVILEGES4   CLISCHEM      TABLEPRIVILEGES
CAT_SET   CLISCHEM     TABLEPRIVILEGES3   CLISCHEM      TABLEPRIVILEGES
CAT_SET   CLISCHEM     TABLEPRIVILEGES2   CLISCHEM      TABLEPRIVILEGES
CAT_SET   CLISCHEM     TABLEPRIVILEGES1   CLISCHEM      TABLEPRIVILEGES
CAT_SET   CLISCHEM     V_SYSTABLES2       CLISCHEM      TABLES_T
CAT_SET   CLISCHEM     V_SYSTABLES        CLISCHEM      TABLES_T
CAT_SET   CLISCHEM     V_SYSSYNONYMS      CLISCHEM      TABLES_T
CAT_SET   CLISCHEM     V_SYSPROCEDURES    CLISCHEM      PROCEDURES
CAT_SET   CLISCHEM     V_SYSPRIMARYKEYS   CLISCHEM      PRIMARYKEYS
CAT_SET   CLISCHEM     V_SYSCOLUMNS       CLISCHEM      COLUMNS
CAT_SET   CLISCHEM     V_COLPRIVILEGES_U  CLISCHEM      COLUMNPRIVILEGES
CAT_SET   CLISCHEM     V_COLPRIVILEGES_U  CLISCHEM      COLUMNPRIVILEGES
CAT_SET   CLISCHEM     V_COLPRIVILEGES_S  CLISCHEM      COLUMNPRIVILEGES
CAT_SET   CLISCHEM     V_COLPRIVILEGES_S  CLISCHEM      COLUMNPRIVILEGES
CAT_SET   CLISCHEM     V_COLPRIVILEGES_I  CLISCHEM      COLUMNPRIVILEGES
CAT_SET   CLISCHEM     V_COLPRIVILEGES_I  CLISCHEM      COLUMNPRIVILEGES
CAT_SET   CLISCHEM     TABLEPRIVILEGES6   CLISCHEM      TABLEPRIVILEGES
CAT_SET   CLISCHEM     TABLEPRIVILEGES5   CLISCHEM      TABLEPRIVILEGES
CAT_SET2  CLISCHEM     SPECIALCOLUMNS2    CLISCHEM      SPECIALCOLUMNS_T
CAT_SET2  CLISCHEM     SPECIALCOLUMNS1    CLISCHEM      SPECIALCOLUMNS_T
CAT_SET2  CLISCHEM     V_TSTATISTICS2     CLISCHEM      TSTATISTICS_T
CAT_SET2  CLISCHEM     V_TSTATISTICS      CLISCHEM      TSTATISTICS_T
CAT_SET2  CLISCHEM     V_FOREIGNKEYS      CLISCHEM      FOREIGNKEYS
```

8.4.6 Setting up the Workstation Client

There are two options you can choose, either specifying the entire DB2 ODBC catalog, or a customized view.

8.4.6.1 Specifying the Entire DB2 ODBC Catalog

You must update the DB2CLI.INI file on each client machine that accesses the DB2 ODBC Catalog. To use the entire DB2 ODBC catalog, add the entry CLISCHEMA=CLISCHEM to your DB2CLI.INI file. CLISCHEM is the only recognized schema name for access to the entire DB2 ODBC catalog. Here is the relevant section in the DB2CLI.INI file:

```
[DB2C]
AUTOCOMMIT=1
CURSORHOLD=1
LOBMAXCOLUMNSIZE=33554431
LONGDATACOMPAT=1
PWD=AZUMA
UID=SW6003A
DBALIAS=DB2C
DESCRIPTION=DB2/MVS
CLISCHEMA=CLISCHEM
```

8.4.6.2 Using a Customized View of the DB2 ODBC Catalog

To use a customized set of views rather than the entire DB2 ODBC catalog, add the entry CLISCHEMA=MYSCHEMA to the DB2CLI.INI file. Substitute any name for MYSCHEMA that is appropriate for your needs. The DB2CLI.INI file used in our example is shown below. We are using userid SW6003A when connecting to DB2 for OS/390 via DB2 Connect.

```
; Comment lines start with a semi-colon.
[DB2C]
AUTOCOMMIT=1
LOBMAXCOLUMNSIZE=33554431
LONGDATACOMPAT=1
PWD=AZUMA
UID=SW6003A
DBALIAS=DB2C
CLISCHEMA=SW6003A
; CLISCHEMA=CLISCHEM
```

In this case, ODBC catalog queries are directed to views on the ODBC catalog. This can be used to restrict catalog information available to a user's ODBC application.

You must define views for all the DB2 ODBC catalog tables when you use your own schema. Table 31 shows the specific DB2 ODBC catalog tables for which you must have a view defined:

Table 31. ODBC Function Calls and List of ODBC Catalog Tables

ODBC Function Call	DB2 ODBC Catalog tables	SET Name
SQLColumns	CLISCHEM.COLUMNS	CAT_SET
SQLColumnPrivilege	CLISCHEM.COLUMNPRIVILEGES	CAT_SET
SQLPrimaryKeys	CLISCHEM.PRIMARYKEYS	CAT_SET
SQLProcedures	CLISCHEM.PROCEDURES	CAT_SET
SQLTablesPrivileges	CLISCHEM.TABLEPRIVILEGES	CAT_SET
SQLTables	CLISCHEM.TABLES	CAT_SET
SQLForegnKeys	CLISCHEM.FOREGNKEYS	CAT_SET2
SQLSpecialColumns	CLISCHEM.SPECIALCOLUMNS	CAT_SET2
SQLStatistics	CLISCHEM.TSTATISTICS	CAT_SET2

You can use the VIEW statements similar to the following to define your own views on the CLISCHEM.*table_name* ODBC tables:

```
CREATE VIEW SW6003A.COLUMNPRIVILEGES
AS SELECT * FROM CLISCHEM.COLUMNPRIVILEGES
WHERE TABLE_SCHEM='SW6003A' ;

CREATE VIEW SW6003A.TABLEPRIVILEGES
AS SELECT * FROM CLISCHEM.TABLEPRIVILEGES
WHERE TABLE_SCHEM='SW6003A' ;

CREATE VIEW SW6003A.TABLES
AS SELECT * FROM CLISCHEM.TABLES
WHERE TABLE_SCHEM='SW6003A' ;

--CREATE VIEW SW6003A.PROCEDURES
--AS SELECT * FROM CLISCHEM.PROCEDURES
--WHERE TABLE_SCHEM='SW6003A' ;

CREATE VIEW SW6003A.PRIMARYKEYS
AS SELECT * FROM CLISCHEM.PRIMARYKEYS
WHERE TABLE_SCHEM='SW6003A' ;

CREATE VIEW SW6003A.COLUMNS
AS SELECT * FROM CLISCHEM.COLUMNS
WHERE TABLE_SCHEM='SW6003A' ;

CREATE VIEW SW6003A.SPECIALCOLUMNS
AS SELECT * FROM CLISCHEM.SPECIALCOLUMNS
WHERE TABLE_SCHEM='SW6003A' ;

CREATE VIEW SW6003A.TSTATISTICS
AS SELECT * FROM CLISCHEM.TSTATISTICS
WHERE TABLE_SCHEM='SW6003A' ;

--CREATE VIEW SW6003A.FOREIGNKEYS
--AS SELECT * FROM CLISCHEM.FOREIGNKEYS
--WHERE TABLE_SCHEM='SW6003A' ;
```

You are now ready to start the Capture and Apply programs on OS/390, which will populate the DB2 ODBC catalog on OS/390.

8.4.7 Starting Capture for MVS

This is described in “Starting Capture for MVS” on page 125.

8.4.8 Starting Apply for MVS

To maintain the DB2 ODBC catalog, it is necessary to run both the Capture and Apply programs on the OS/390 server. Make sure that the Capture program is completely initialized before invoking the Apply program.

The following list shows valid Apply program control table values when using DB2 ODBC catalog:

- APPLY_QUAL=CAT_QUAL for all subscription sets.
- SET_NAME=CAT_SET for all subscriptions that will be *differentially refreshed*.
- SET_NAME=CAT_SET2 for all subscriptions that will be *fully refreshed.*
- SLEEP_MINUTES = 1 HOUR for all CAT_SET subscription sets.
- SLEEP_MINUTES = 1 DAY for all CAT_SET2 subscription sets.

If you want to change these default values, modify the ASNL2SU5 file and run it again.

Here is the JCL we used to start Apply for MVS:

```
//APPLY JOB (999,POK),'INSTALL ',CLASS=A,MSGCLASS=T,
// NOTIFY=&SYSUID,TIME=1440,REGION=4M
/*JOBPARM L=999,SYSAFF=SC42
//*************************************************************/
//* JOB NAME = ASNA2RN5                                       */
//*                                                           */
//* DESCRIPTIVE NAME = INVOCATION JCL FOR THE IBM             */
//*                    DATAPROPAGATOR RELATIONAL APPLY FOR MVS */
//*                                                           */
//* STATUS = VERSION 05  RELEASE 01  MODIFICATION LEVEL 00    */
//*                                                           */
//* FUNCTION = INVOKE THE DATAPROPAGATOR RELATIONAL           */
//*            APPLY FOR MVS PROGRAM                          */
//*                                                           */
//*       LICENSED MATERIALS - PROPERTY OF IBM                */
//*       5655-A22 (C) COPYRIGHT IBM CORP 1993, 1997          */
//*       ALL RIGHTS RESERVED.                                */
//*       US GOVERNMENT USERS RESTRICTED RIGHTS -             */
//*       USE, DUPLICATION OR DISCLOSURE RESTRICTED           */
//*       BY GSA ADP SCHEDULE CONTRACT WITH IBM CORP.         */
//*                                                           */
//* NOTES =                                                   */
//* 1) REVIEW ALL STATEMENTS.                                 */
//* 2) CHANGE THE HLQUAL FIELD(S) TO A VALID HIGH LEVEL       */
//*    QUALIFIER TO COMPLY WITH YOUR SITE'S NAMING STANDARDS.  */
//*    ASNA.V5R1M0 IS RECOMMENDED AS THE HIGH LEVEL QUALIFIER. */
//* 3) MODIFY THE BLKSIZE IN THE ASNASPL DD STATEMENT TO THE  */
//*    ONE THAT IS MOST APPROPRIATE AT YOUR INSTALLATION      */
//* 4) IF YOU ARE RUNNING UNDER LE/370 ENVIRONMENT, ADD       */
//*    REGION=3M IN THE EXEC STATEMENT.                       */
//* 5) DELETE THE TEXT THAT BEGINS WITH <== AT THE            */
//*    END OF SOME LINES                                      */
//* 6) REPLACE D51A WITH YOUR SUBSYSTEM NAME                  */
//*                                                           */
//*************************************************************/
//*
//*
//*************************************************************/
//ASNARUN  EXEC PGM=ASNAPV25,
//*             PARM='QUAL1 DB2C DB2C DISK TRCFLOW NOSLEEP'
//              PARM='CAT_QUAL DB2C DB2C DISK TRCFLOW '
//*                   <== VERIFY APPLY_QUALIFIER
//*                                   <== VERIFY DB2 SUBSYSTEM ID
//*                                        <== VERIFY  CONTROL_SERVER
//SYSTERM  DD  SYSOUT=*
//SYSTSPRT DD  SYSOUT=*
//SYSUDUMP DD  SYSOUT=*
//SYSPRINT DD  SYSOUT=*
//STEPLIB  DD  DISP=SHR,DSN=ASNA.V5R1M0.SASNALNK
//         DD  DISP=SHR,DSN=DB2V510.SDSNLOAD
//         DD  DISP=SHR,DSN=EDC.V2R2M0.SEDCLINK
//         DD  DISP=SHR,DSN=PLI.V2R3M0.SIBMLINK
//MSGS     DD  DISP=SHR,DSN=ASNA.V5R1M0.MSGS
//ASNASPL  DD  DSN=&&ASNASPL,
//             DISP=(NEW,DELETE,DELETE),
//             UNIT=SYSDA,SPACE=(CYL,(15,15)),
//             DCB=(RECFM=VB,BLKSIZE=6404)
//
```

8.4.9 Stopping Apply for MVS

Enter the following command from a TSO or MVS console to stop Apply for MVS:

```
P jobname
```

For example:

```
P APPLY
 ASN1100I A user has stopped the Apply program.
```

8.4.10 Verifying That the DB2 ODBC Catalog Was Used

The easiest way to verify that an ODBC application is issuing queries against the DB2 ODBC catalog, take a DDCS trace at the DB2 Connect workstation by using the `ddcstrc` command.

The syntax of the ddcstrc command is:

```
ddcstrc on  [-i] [-c] [-r] [-s] [-l=LENGTH]
ddcstrc off [-t=TRACEFILE] [-p=PROCESSID]
```

where:

`on`	Turns the DRDA trace on.
`off`	Turns the DRDA trace off.
`-i`	Include timestamps.
`-c`	Trace SQLCAs.
`-r`	Trace DRDA receive buffers.
`-s`	Trace DRDA send buffers.
`-l=LENGTH`	LENGTH is the size of the trace buffer. The default value is one megabyte.
`-t=TRACEFILE`	TRACEFILE is the file name where the captured trace will be stored. The default file name is ddcstrc.dmp. DRDA send buffers.
`-p=PROCESSID`	PROCESSID is the ID of a process to be traced. If PROCESSID is not specified, all process IDs for the DB2 instance are traced.

Let's first look at the case when the DB2 ODBC catalog is not used. The CLISCHEMA parameter in the DB2CLI.INI is not specified:

```
[DB2C]
AUTOCOMMIT=1
LOBMAXCOLUMNSIZE=33554431
LONGDATACOMPAT=1
```

```
PWD=AZUMA
UID=SW6003A
DBALIAS=DB2C
; CLISCHEMA=SW6003A
; CLISCHEMA=CLISCHEM
```

Here is the DDCS trace for this example:

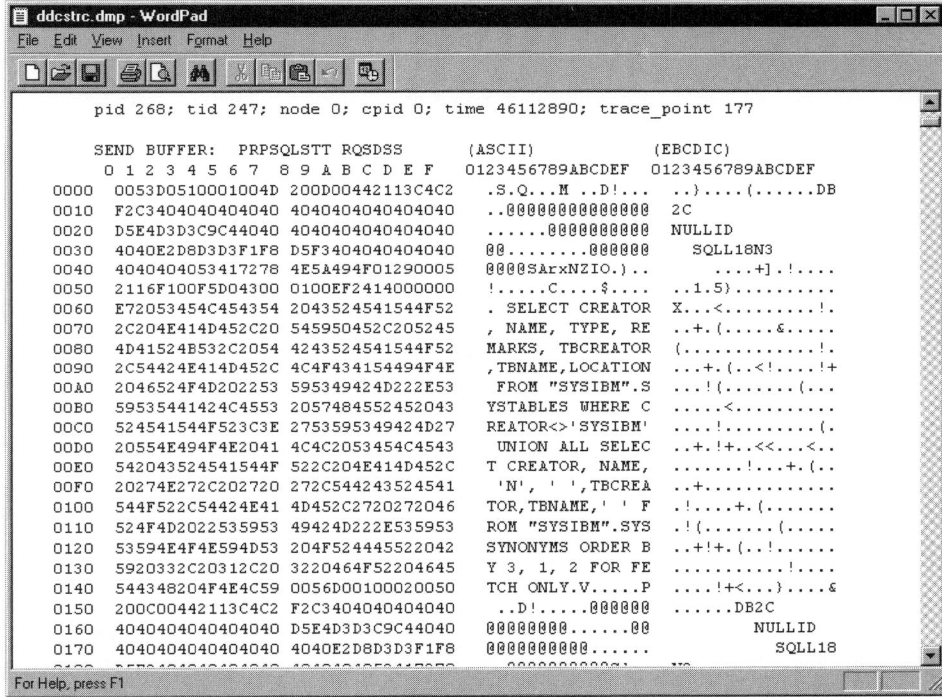

```
pid 268; tid 247; node 0; cpid 0; time 46112890; trace_point 177

SEND BUFFER:  PRPSQLSTT RQSDSS       (ASCII)           (EBCDIC)
 0 1 2 3 4 5 6 7  8 9 A B C D E F   0123456789ABCDEF  0123456789ABCDEF
0000  0053D0510001004D 200D00442113C4C2   .S.Q...M ..D!...  ..}....(......DB
0010  F2C3404040404040 4040404040404040   ..@@@@@@@@@@@@@@  2C
0020  D5E4D3D3C9C44040 4040404040404040   ......@@@@@@@@@@  NULLID
0030  4040E2D8D3D3F1F8 D5F3404040404040   @@........@@@@@@    SQLL18N3
0040  4040404053417278 4E5A494F01290005   @@@@SArxNZIO.)..      ....+].!....
0050  2116F100F5D04300 0100EF2414000000   !.....C....$....  ..1.5)..........
0060  E72053454C454354 2043524541544F52   . SELECT CREATOR  X...<.........!.
0070  2C204E414D452C20 545950452C205245   , NAME, TYPE, RE  ..+.(.....&.....
0080  4D41524B532C2054 4243524541544F52   MARKS, TBCREATOR  (.............!.
0090  2C54424E414D452C 4C4F434154494F4E   ,TBNAME,LOCATION  ...+.(..<!....!+
00A0  2046524F4D202253 595349424D222E53    FROM "SYSIBM".S  ...!(.......(...
00B0  5953544142C4553 2057484552452043   YSTABLES WHERE C  .....<..........
00C0  524541544F523C3E 275359534942D27   REATOR<>'SYSIBM'  ....!.........(.
00D0  20554E494F4E2041 4C4C2053454C4543    UNION ALL SELEC  ..+.!+..<<...<..
00E0  542043524541544F 522C204E414D452C   T CREATOR, NAME,  .......!...+.(..
00F0  20274E272C202720 272C544243524541    'N', ' ',TBCREA  ..+.............
0100  544F522C54424E41 4D452C2720272046   TOR,TBNAME,' ' F  .!....+.(.......
0110  524F4D2022535953 49424D222E535953   ROM "SYSIBM".SYS  .!(.......(.....
0120  53594E4F4E594D53 204F524445522042   SYNONYMS ORDER B  ..+!+.(..!......
0130  5920332C20312C20 3220464F52204645   Y 3, 1, 2 FOR FE  ...........!....
0140  544348204F4E4C59 0056D00100020050   TCH ONLY.V.....P  ....!+<...}....&
0150  200C00442113C4C2 F2C3404040404040    ..D!.....@@@@@@  ......DB2C
0160  4040404040404040 D5E4D3D3C9C44040   @@@@@@@@......@@          NULLID
0170  4040404040404040 4040E2D8D3D3F1F8   @@@@@@@@@@......            SQLL18
```

Figure 199. Example of DDCS Trace

This trace shows an ODBC application retrieving table information from the SYSIBM.SYSTABLES table (the real DB2 catalog table).

Next, we set CLISCHEMA to CLISCHEM in order to specify the entire DB2 ODBC catalog:

```
[DB2C]
AUTOCOMMIT=1
LOBMAXCOLUMNSIZE=33554431
LONGDATACOMPAT=1
PWD=AZUMA
UID=SW6003A
DBALIAS=DB2C
```

```
; CLISCHEMA=SW6003A
CLISCHEMA=CLISCHEM
```

Here is the DDCS trace for this case:

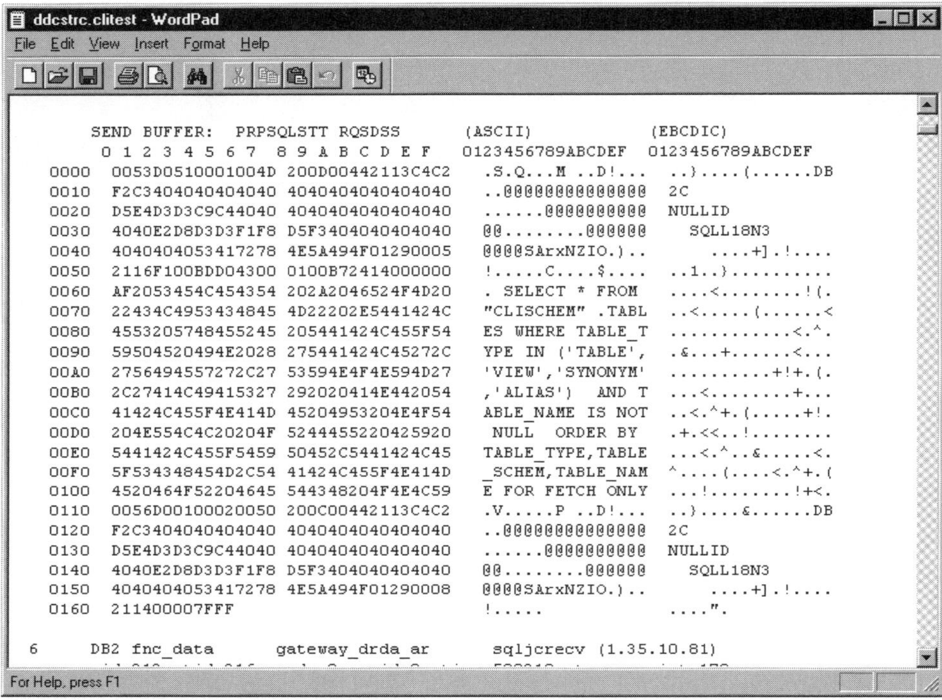

```
ddcstrc.clitest - WordPad
File Edit View Insert Format Help

     SEND BUFFER:  PRPSQLSTT RQSDSS       (ASCII)           (EBCDIC)
      0 1 2 3 4 5 6 7  8 9 A B C D E F   0123456789ABCDEF  0123456789ABCDEF
 0000  0053D0510001004D 200D00442113C4C2   .S.Q...M ..D!...  ..}....(......DB
 0010  F2C3404040404040 4040404040404040   ..@@@@@@@@@@@@@@  2C
 0020  D5E4D3D3C9C44040 4040404040404040   ......@@@@@@@@@@  NULLID
 0030  4040E2D8D3D3F1F8 D5F3404040404040   @@........@@@@@@    SQLL18N3
 0040  4040404053417278 4E5A494F01290005   @@@@SArxNZIO.)..       ....+].!....
 0050  2116F100BDD04300 0100B72414000000   !.....C....$....  ..1..}..........
 0060  AF2053454C454354 202A2046524F4D20   . SELECT * FROM   ....<........!(.
 0070  22434C4953434845 4D22202E5441424C   "CLISCHEM" .TABL  ..<.....(......<
 0080  4553205748455245 205441424C455F54   ES WHERE TABLE_T  ............<.^.
 0090  59504520494E2028 275441424C45272C   YPE IN ('TABLE',  .&...+......<...
 00A0  275649455727 2C27 53594E4F4E594D27  'VIEW','SYNONYM'  ..........+!+.(.
 00B0  2C27414C49415327 292020414E442054   ,'ALIAS')  AND T  ...<........+...
 00C0  41424C455F4E414D 45204953204E4F54   ABLE_NAME IS NOT  ..<.^+.(.....+!.
 00D0  204E554C4C20204F 5244455220425920    NULL  ORDER BY   .+.<<..!........
 00E0  5441424C455F5459 50452C5441424C45   TABLE_TYPE,TABLE  ...<.^..&.....<.
 00F0  5F534348454D2C54 41424C455F4E414D   _SCHEM,TABLE_NAM  ^....(....<.^+.(
 0100  4520464F52204645 544348204F4E4C59   E FOR FETCH ONLY  ...!........!+<.
 0110  0056D00100020050 200C00442113C4C2   .V.....P ..D!...  ..}....&......DB
 0120  F2C3404040404040 4040404040404040   ..@@@@@@@@@@@@@@  2C
 0130  D5E4D3D3C9C44040 4040404040404040   ......@@@@@@@@@@  NULLID
 0140  4040E2D8D3D3F1F8 D5F3404040404040   @@........@@@@@@    SQLL18N3
 0150  4040404053417278 4E5A494F01290008   @@@@SArxNZIO.)..       ....+].!....
 0160  211400007FFF                        !.....            ....".

 6      DB2 fnc_data       gateway_drda_ar      sqljcrecv (1.35.10.81)
For Help, press F1
```

Figure 200. DDCS Trace Verifying the Usage of the DB2 ODBC Catalog

This DDCS trace shows an ODBC application retrieving table information from one of the DB2 ODBC catalog tables (CLISCHEM.TABLES) instead of SYSIBM.SYSTABLES.

For the last example, we set CLISCHEMA to SW6003A, which is our own schema name:

```
[DB2C]
AUTOCOMMIT=1
LOBMAXCOLUMNSIZE=33554431
LONGDATACOMPAT=1
PWD=AZUMA
UID=SW6003A
DBALIAS=DB2C
CLISCHEMA=SW6003A
; CLISCHEMA=CLISCHEM
```

Here is the DDCS trace for this case:

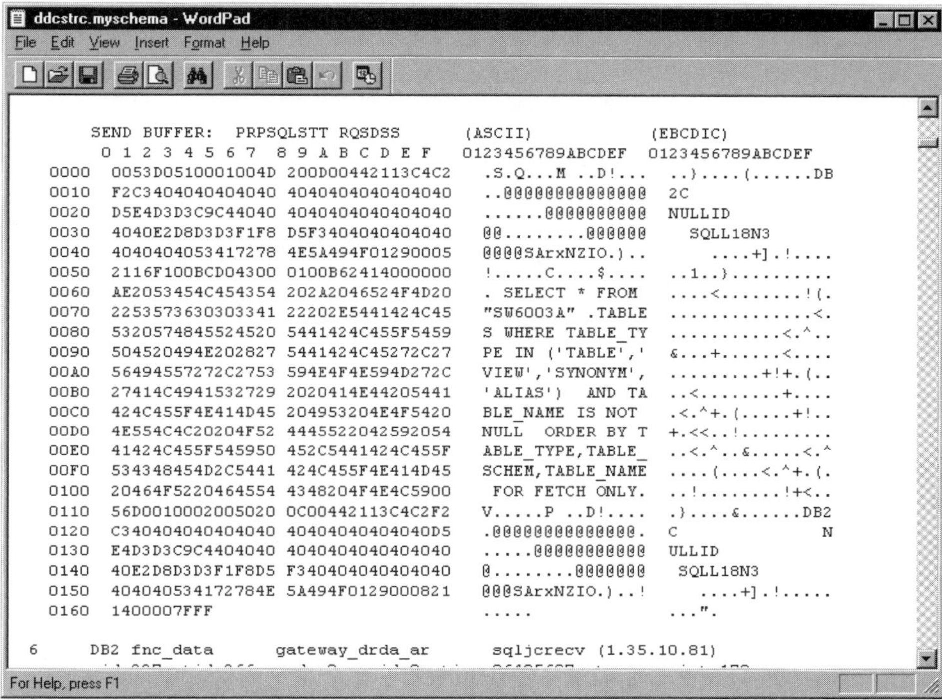

```
ddcstrc.myschema - WordPad
File  Edit  View  Insert  Format  Help

     SEND BUFFER:  PRPSQLSTT RQSDSS       (ASCII)           (EBCDIC)
      0 1 2 3 4 5 6 7  8 9 A B C D E F  0123456789ABCDEF  0123456789ABCDEF
 0000  0053D0510001004D 200D00442113C4C2   .S.Q...M ..D!...  ..}....(......DB
 0010  F2C3404040404040 4040404040404040   ..@@@@@@@@@@@@@@  2C
 0020  D5E4D3D3C9C44040 4040404040404040   ......@@@@@@@@@@  NULLID
 0030  4040E2D8D3D3F1F8 D5F3404040404040   @@........@@@@@@    SQLL18N3
 0040  4040404053417278 4E5A494F01290005   @@@@SArxNZIO.)..       ....+].!....
 0050  2116F100BCD04300 0100B62414000000   !.....C....$....  ..1..}..........
 0060  AE2053454C454354 202A2046524F4D20   . SELECT * FROM   ....<........!(.
 0070  2253573630303341 22202E5441424C45   "SW6003A" .TABLE  ..............<.
 0080  5320574845524520 5441424C455F5459   S WHERE TABLE_TY  ...........<.^..
 0090  504520494E202827 5441424C45272C27   PE IN ('TABLE','  &...+......<....
 00A0  56494557272C2753 594E4F4E594D272C   VIEW','SYNONYM',  .........+!+.(..
 00B0  27414C4941532729 2020414E44205441   'ALIAS')  AND TA  ..<........+....
 00C0  424C455F4E414D45 204953204E4F5420   BLE_NAME IS NOT   .<.^+.(.....+!..
 00D0  4E554C4C20204F52 4445522042592054   NULL  ORDER BY T  +.<<..!.........
 00E0  41424C455F545950 452C5441424C455F   ABLE_TYPE,TABLE_  ..<.^..&.....<.^
 00F0  534348454D2C5441 424C455F4E414D45   SCHEM,TABLE_NAME  ....(....<.^+.(.
 0100  20464F5220464554 4348204F4E4C5900    FOR FETCH ONLY.  ..!........!+<..
 0110  56D0010002005020 0C00442113C4C2F2   V.....P ..D!....  .}....&......DB2
 0120  C340404040404040 40404040404040D5   .@@@@@@@@@@@@@@.  C              N
 0130  E4D3D3C9C4404040 4040404040404040   .....@@@@@@@@@@@  ULLID
 0140  40E2D8D3D3F1F8D5 F340404040404040   @........@@@@@@@   SQLL18N3
 0150  404040534172784E 5A494F0129000821   @@@SArxNZIO.)..!      ....+].!.....
 0160  1400007FFF                          .....             ...".

 6      DB2 fnc_data       gateway_drda_ar      sqljcrecv (1.35.10.81)
For Help, press F1
```

Figure 201. DDCS Trace Verifying the Usage of the DB2 ODBC Catalog

This DDCS trace shows an ODBC application retrieving table information from our own view on the DB2 ODBC catalog tables.

8.5 DB2 UDB Enterprise-Extended Edition Considerations

DB2 UDB Enterprise-Extended Edition (EEE) provides the ability for a database to be partitioned across multiple independent computers using the same operating system. A single one of these partitions holds the System Catalog. It is referred to as the catalog partition or catalog node.

Both Capture and Apply programs have been packaged in EEE. However, there are some restrictions as to their usage.

8.5.1 Administration Considerations

If you use a EEE database in a replication configuration, the replication control tables will be created automatically when you define the first replication source or subscription (assuming you have not created them manually). If a EEE database is used as the target server, you must define these control tables on one node (partition). If a EEE database is used as the source server, then the control tables must be created on the catalog node (partition).

If you try to create the control tables over multiple nodes, you will receive the following negative SQLCODE:

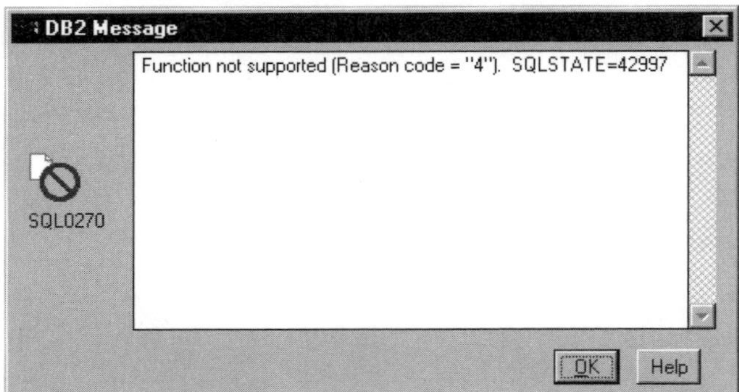

Figure 202. DB2 UDB EEE Control Table Error Message

The explanation of this message is as follows. Note that reason code 4 is the relevant reason in this case:

```
SQL0270N Function not supported (Reason code = "<reason-code>").

Cause:  The statement cannot be processed because it
violates a restriction as indicated by the following reason code:
1  The primary key, each unique constraint, and each unique
   index must contain all partitioning columns of the table
   (columns may appear in any order).
2  Update of the partitioning key column value is not supported.
3  A foreign key cannot include any nullable partitioning
   key columns when defined with ON DELETE SET NULL.  This
   is a special case of reason code 2 since defining such a
   constraint would result in attempting to update a
   partitioning key column.
4  A table defined using a multipartition nodegroup or a
   single-partition nodegroup on other than the catalog
   partition does not support DATA CAPTURE CHANGES.
```

You need to ensure that all the control tables are placed in a table space in a single partition nodegroup that uses the catalog partition.

For example:

```
DROP NODEGROUP MYGROUP;
CREATE NODEGROUP MYGROUP
       ON NODE (0)
;
drop tablespace dproprts;
CREATE TABLESPACE DPROPRTS in mygroup MANAGED BY SYSTEM USING
('/db/cont1')
;
```

The default settings for the replication control tables can be changed by editing the DPCNTL file for the required platform. There are four versions, all in the SQLLIB\SAMPLES\REPL directory. In this case, we edited the DPCNTL.UDB file. To store all the control tables in the DPROPRTS table space, we made changes such as this:

```
.......................................................
CREATE TABLE ASN.IBMSNAP_WARM_START (  SEQ CHAR(10) FOR BIT DATA,
AUTHTKN CHAR(12),AUTHID CHAR(18),CAPTURED CHAR(1),UOWTIME INT) in
dproprts;
.......................................................
```

8.5.2 Capture Considerations

The Capture program can't capture changes made to a source table defined over multiple nodes because the DB2 Log Read API that the Capture program uses does not support the Log merge capability (as DB2 for OS/390 does). The source table DDL requires the DATA CAPTURE CHANGES option. Therefore, your source table should also be placed in a table space on a single partition nodegroup that uses the catalog partition. The Capture program supports a source table that exist on the catalog node only.

8.5.3 Apply Considerations

The Apply program supports replication when using a EEE database as the target server. This is possible because the Capture program has an option to capture UPDATES to partition key columns as separate DELETE and INSERT operations.

To replicate to a EEE target server when the target table is located over multiple nodes, you must select the **Changed data for partition key columns captured as delete and insert** option while defining the replication source from the Control Center.

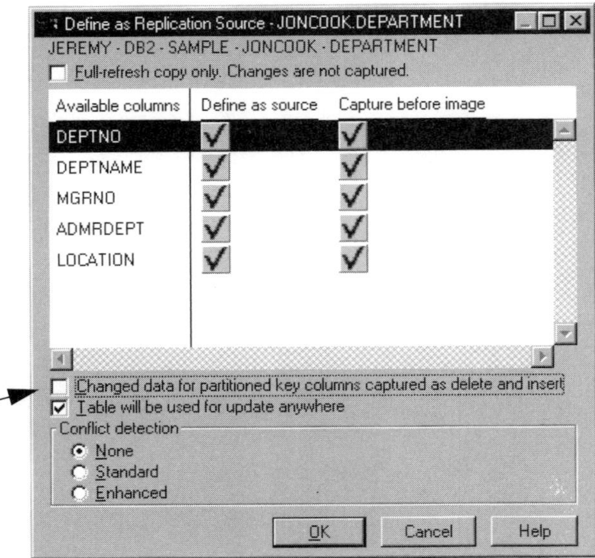

Figure 203. Define Replication Source - Custom

If you do not specify this option, and the target table data is spread over multiple nodes, the Apply program fails will the following negative SQLCODE.

```
SQL0270N  Function not supported (Reason code = "2").
SQLSTATE=42997
```

8.6 DB2 UDB Long Varchar Support

As a new feature introduced in DB2 UDB V5.2, LONG VARCHAR columns are supported by the Capture program. The Control Center recognizes this data type and generates a DATA CAPTURE CHANGES INCLUDE LONGVAR COLUMNS clause on the ALTER TABLE statement automatically during the source table registration phase. If you manually register your source table, this clause on the ALTER statement is also required.

For example, a source table is created as follows:

```
C:\azuma>db2 connect to copydb1

   Database Connection Information
Database server        = DB2/NT 5.2.0
SQL authorization ID   = AZUMA
Local database alias   = COPYDB1
```

```
C:\azuma>db2 create table longC1 (c1 smallint, c2 long varchar)
DB20000I  The SQL command completed successfully.
```

You must use the following registration definition to register this source table:

```
CONNECT TO COPYDB1;

ALTER TABLE AZUMA.LONGC1
DATA CAPTURE CHANGES
INCLUDE LONGVAR COLUMNS;

CREATE TABLE AZUMA.LONGC1_CD (
IBMSNAP_UOWID CHAR ( 10 ) FOR BIT DATA NOT NULL,
IBMSNAP_INTENTSEQ CHAR ( 10 ) FOR BIT DATA NOT NULL,
IBMSNAP_OPERATION CHAR ( 1 ) NOT NULL,
XC1 SMALLINT,
C1 SMALLINT,
XC2 LONG VARCHAR,
C2 LONG VARCHAR );

CREATE UNIQUE INDEX AZUMA.LONGC1_IX
ON AZUMA.LONGC1_CD
( IBMSNAP_UOWID ASC, IBMSNAP_INTENTSEQ ASC );

INSERT INTO ASN.IBMSNAP_REGISTER ( GLOBAL_RECORD, SOURCE_OWNER,
SOURCE_TABLE, SOURCE_VIEW_QUAL, SOURCE_STRUCTURE, SOURCE_CONDENSED,
SOURCE_COMPLETE, CD_OWNER, CD_TABLE, PHYS_CHANGE_OWNER,
PHYS_CHANGE_TABLE,
CD_OLD_SYNCHPOINT, CD_NEW_SYNCHPOINT, DISABLE_REFRESH, CCD_OWNER,
CCD_TABLE, CCD_OLD_SYNCHPOINT, SYNCHPOINT, SYNCHTIME, CCD_CONDENSED,
CCD_COMPLETE, ARCH_LEVEL, DESCRIPTION, BEFORE_IMG_PREFIX,
CONFLICT_LEVEL,
PARTITION_KEYS_CHG
) VALUES (
'N', 'AZUMA', 'LONGC1', 0, 1, 'Y', 'Y', 'AZUMA', 'LONGC1_CD', 'AZUMA',
'LONGC1_CD', NULL, NULL, 0, NULL, NULL, NULL, NULL, NULL, NULL, NULL,
'0201', NULL, 'X', '0', 'N');
```

The SYSCAT.TABLE will contain a value 'L' instead of 'Y' in the DATACAPTURE column after you run the above ALTER statement.

```
C:\azuma>db2 select tabname,datacapture from syscat.tables
where tabname='LONGC1
'

TABNAME            DATACAPTURE
------------------ -----------
LONGC1             L

  1 record(s) selected.
```

8.7 Summary

In this chapter, we covered some of the more advanced concepts and features of IBM DB2 Replication. This information should show you how diverse and powerful a product IBM DB2 Replication is, and how you can potentially use its many features in your own environments.

The information in this chapter will help you prepare for the certification exam for DB2 Replication; however it is not mandatory. It should help you understand the IBM DB2 Replication features and products in more depth.

Chapter 9. Troubleshooting

This chapter introduces some methods for troubleshooting problems in your replication environment. These methods should help you better understand how to identify the reason for a given replication problem.

At a high level, problems can occur during the three phases of replication:

- Replication Administration
- Running Capture
- Running Apply

The IBM Replication tools are essentially relational database applications. Typically, the replication control tables are created using DDL issued by the Control Center, and data is replicated by SELECT, INSERT, UPDATE, and DELETE statements issued by the Capture and Apply programs.

When an error occurs in a replication configuration, the error messages are very often relational database error messages, such as SQL messages and SQL states. You can refer to the *DB2 Message Reference* for your platform for more information about DB2 error messages and SQL states.

Note

Capture and Apply are cross platform tools. As such, command syntax may vary between platforms. Please see Chapter 3, "Capture and Apply" on page 59 for more details.

9.1 Replication Administration

Replication administration involves using the DB2 Control Center to define:

- Replication Sources
- Replication Subscriptions

The Control Center can encounter errors either when it is gathering information from source servers, target servers, or control servers to create the SQL statements for administration, or when it is actually running the SQL to set up the replication sources and subscriptions. The primary indicators are the SQL messages and SQL states that accompany the error. These SQL messages and states are issued in error message windows in the Control Center.

For example, what happens if you run the replication source definition SQL script twice? You will encounter a popup window, in the DB2 Control Center, similar to this:

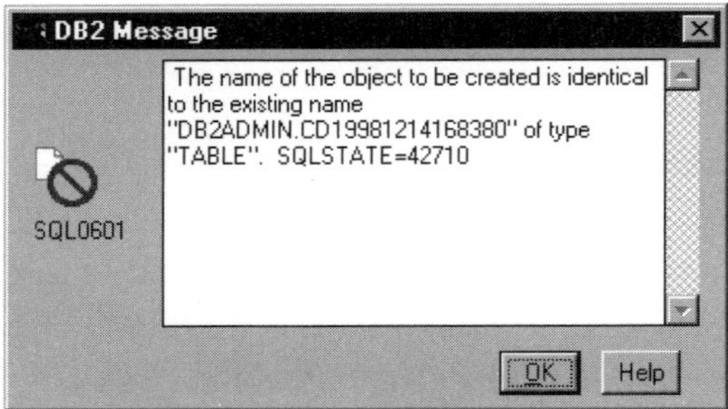
DB2 Message
The name of the object to be created is identical to the existing name "DB2ADMIN.CD19981214168380" of type "TABLE". SQLSTATE=42710
SQL0601
OK
Help

Figure 204. DB2 Control Center Replication Administration Error Message

Note the following:

- In the sidebar of the popup window, you can see the SQL error message number. This is SQL0601 in this case, which means that an object by the same name already exists.
- In the body of the popup window, the name of the object is given. In this case, this is a TABLE called DB2ADMIN.CD19981214168380.
- You also have an SQLSTATE (here, SQLSTATE 42710) relating to the SQL error message.

9.1.1 Replication Administration Messages

During replication administration, messages may be generated by the DB2 Control Center to alert you when a warning or error condition occurs. These messages are prefixed by DBA, and range from 6001 to 6110 (DBA6001 to DBA6110). As with SQL error messages, you should refer to the DB2 Messages Reference manual for further details on the error, including suggested causes and recommended actions.

Some examples are as follows:

1. **Message**: DBA6001I: The replication subscription set, "<subscription_set>", is in use. Please try again later.

   Cause: The Apply program is currently processing the replication subscription and this action cannot be deactivated. Wait until the Apply program has completed its processing and retry your command.

   Action: No action is required.

2. **Message**: DBA6002I: The replication source, "<source_name>", was defined successfully. To begin capturing changes to the replication source, start the Capture program from the command line.

   Cause: The Capture program requires a defined replication source in order to run.

   Action: Make sure the Capture program is running.

Refer to the *DB2 Replication Guide and Reference* and the *DB2 Messages Reference* for a complete list of the DBA error messages.

9.1.2 Replication Administration Problem Determination Checklist

1. Is the problem with a replication source or subscription?
2. What messages appear?
3. Can the user successfully connect to the source or target database from a command line or command prompt window?

9.2 Running Capture

The Capture program writes status and error messages to a trace table and a log file. In addition, a trace file can be generated if the trace parameter is used when starting the Capture program.

9.2.1 Capture Program Trace Control Table

The trace control table is located in the source server database where the Capture program maintains change data tables for replication sources. The trace control table, ASN.IBMSNAP_TRACE, contains basic information about the activities of the Capture program.

This table contains trace information for Capture for MVS, VM, VSE, and the supported DB2 UDB platforms. The information is added to it in a round-robin fashion until the row limit is reached. Capture pruning does remove entries from this table, and therefore a complete history of Capture may not be seen in this table. On a cold start, all of the entries in the trace table are deleted.

The message numbers ASN0100I, ASN0101W, and ASN0102W are issued for warnings and initialization information.

A description of the trace table columns is given in Table 32:

Table 32. Capture Trace Control Table Description

Column Name	Description
OPERATION: CHAR(8)	The type of Capture program operation, for example, initialization, capture, or error condition.
TRACE_TIME: TIMESTAMP	The time a row is inserted into the trace table.
DESCRIPTION: VARCHAR(254)	The message ID followed by the message text. The message can be informational or error. This column contains English-only text and is used by IBM service personnel.

You can query the ASN.IBMSNAP_TRACE table using SQL SELECT statements or query tools.

For example, to select all the entries from this trace table, you would use the following SQL:

```
SELECT * FROM ASN.IBMSNAP_TRACE
```

See "Capture Program Error Messages" on page 360 for an example of the contents of this table.

9.2.2 Capture Program Trace File

The Capture program can be started with the trace invocation parameter. This parameter specifies that problem determination records containing the Capture program internal logic flows should be sent to standard output. When starting the Capture program on workstation systems, to send the output to a file, precede the output file name with a 'greater than' symbol (>). It is important to understand that you cannot start trace for a particular instance of Capture once that Capture instance has been started. You must stop the Capture instance and restart it using the trace option.

To start the Capture program with trace on a workstation system, you issue the following command:

```
asnccp mysrcdb trace > cap.trc
```

Where:

- `mysrcdb` is the source server database for this Capture program instance.

- `trace` indicates that the Capture program traces all error and flow information.
- `cap.trc` is the file to which the output is directed.

If the optional parameters are not provided, defaults are assumed for the type of start (WARM, WARMNS, COLD) and pruning (PRUNE or NOPRUNE).

Refer to Chapter 3, “Capture and Apply” on page 59 for more details about the syntax of the `asnccp` command on the various supported platforms.

With the above invocation, the trace file is located in the directory from which the Capture program is started.

Here is an example of the output from the Capture trace:

```
sqlstr built in bld_prep_str is INSERT INTO
"DB2ADMIN"."CD19981214168380" VALUES(?,?,?,?,?,?,?,?,?,?,?,?,?)
length 19474908
 do_prep_isrt() - the PREPARE string for Insert 1 is INSERT INTO
"DB2ADMIN"."CD19981214168380" VALUES(?,?,?,?,?,?,?,?,?,?,?,?,?)

 before calling msgq_init retcode is 0
 the value of dwDdeInstance before DdeInitialize is 00000000
 the value of dwDdeInstance before DdeInitialize is
8.695304E+269
 trace_info called msg_type 16 retcode 0
REPORT_LOG
 using asnccp.dll
GET_NLS called w msg_type 16 retcode 0ASNLMSG msg_type in
msg_parm = 16

 isuue msg rtn_name  ptr 00446960
MSG_FILE msg_text ptr 00457010
 initialized msg_text to blanks  for 760
 MsgNumber  100 num_subs 0
 calling APPLWTO
 in APPLWTO

 before concat msg_text lmsg now 1998-12-17-09:33:22

 after concat msg_text lmsg now 1998-12-17-09:33:22 ASN0100I:
The Capture program initialization is successful.
```

9.2.3 Capture Program Log File

Upon invocation, the Capture program creates a log file whose name is based on a combination of the instance and source database plus the file extension of .CCP (on DB2 UDB platforms). For DB2 for MVS, this information is written to the console.

For example, if the Capture program is started using `asnccp mysrcdb`, the log file is named `mysrcdb.ccp` on OS/2 and `<db2instance name>mysrcdb.CCP` on all other DB2 UDB platforms. The Capture Program log file is located in the directory from which the Capture program is started.

The log file contains all error messages and other messages about processing status. This same information is also recorded in the trace control table; however, where the trace table is added to in a round-robin fashion until a row limit is reached, the log file can grow continuously and as such may contain the full history of Capture's execution.

For an example of the contents of this log file, see "Capture Program Error Messages" on page 360.

9.2.4 Capture Program Error Messages

Capture program error messages are prefixed by ASN0. Some examples are as follows:

If you invoke `asnccp` without a database name (from a DB2 command line processor in Windows NT):

```
c:\>asnccp
1998-12-14-11:15:20 ASN0002E: The Capture program could not connect to
DB2. The routine name is connect(); the SQLCODE is -1024.
```

If you invoke `asnccp` without first binding the relevant packages to the database (the bind files listed in the file capture.lst):

```
c:\>asnccp sample
```

The log file `sample.ccp` (on OS/2) shows:

```
1998-12-14-11:17:48 ASN0001E: The Capture program encountered an SQL
error. The routine name is create_trace(); the SQL request is SELECT
COUNT(*); the table name is ASN.IBMSNAP_TRACE; the SQLCODE is -805; the
SQLERRML is 15; the SQLERRMC is NULLID.ASNNN000.

1998-12-14-11:17:48 SQL0805N  Package "NULLID.ASNNN000" was not found.
SQLSTATE=51002
```

If you start Capture for the first time with the WARMNS option, the following message will be generated. Capture will always perform a cold start the first time it is invoked so that data can be fully initialized:

```
1998-11-20-10:41:29 ASN0122E: An error occurred while reading the warm
start information or DB2 log. The Capture program will terminate.
1998-11-20-10:41:29 ASN0123I: The highest log sequence number of a
successfully captured log record is 00000000000000000000.
```

A successful attempt at using the `asnccp` command generates the following `sample.ccp` contents on OS/2:

```
1998-12-14-11:43:15 ASN0102W: The Capture program will switch to cold
start because the warm start information is insufficient.

1998-12-14-11:43:15 ASN0100I: The Capture program initialization is
successful.

1998-12-14-11:43:15 ASN0103I: The Capture program started with
SERVER_NAME SAMPLE; the START_TYPE is COLD0000000000000051B382; the
TERM_TYPE is ; the PRUNE_TYPE is PRUNE.
```

To verify this, you can query the Capture program trace table by using the following SQL statement:

```
SELECT * FROM ASN.IBMSNAP_TRACE
```

The results are as follows:

```
INIT      1998-12-14-11.43.15.578001 ASN0102W: The Capture program will
switch to cold start because the warm start information is insufficient.

INIT      1998-12-14-11.43.15.718000 ASN0100I: The Capture program
initialization is successful.

PARM      1998-12-14-11.43.15.781000 ASN0103I: The Capture program
started with SERVER_NAME SAMPLE; the START_TYPE is
COLD0000000000000051B382; the TERM_TYPE is ; the PRUNE_TYPE is PRUNE.

  3 record(s) selected.
```

9.2.5 Capture Program Determination Checklist

1. Is the Capture program running?
2. If the Capture program is not running, what happens when a warm start of the Capture program is tried?

3. Is there error information in the ASN.IBMSNAP_TRACE table?
4. Is there error information in the Capture program log file?
5. What information do you see if you run Capture with the TRACE option?
6. What is the DB2 configuration?
7. Are data changes being successfully inserted into the CD (change data) tables?
8. Does the user ID running the Capture program have sufficient privileges to run the Capture program and to access the directory where Capture is being run from?

9.3 Running Apply

Apply program error messages can be found in the ASN.IBMSNAP_APPLYTRAIL table and the Apply program trace file. There is one trace file at the server associated with each invocation of the Apply program. The Apply program log file tracks the activities of the Apply program and can be a useful diagnosis tool. It is recommended that you start problem determination for Apply by examining the IBMSNAP_APPLYTRAIL control table.

9.3.1 The Apply Trail Control Table

There is an Apply trail control table (ASN.IBMSNAP_APPLYTRAIL) located at each control server where the subscription control tables are located. The Apply program inserts a new row in the Apply trail control table every time it attempts to replicate based on a subscription. There is a row for all successful and unsuccessful subscription cycles of each replication subscription.

The Apply trail table records a history of updates performed against subscriptions. The subscription statistics can be used to audit update activity. This table is a repository of diagnostics and performance statistics. Because this table is not automatically pruned, it is up to you to do so.

A brief description of the Apply trail table columns is given in Table 33:

Table 33. Apply Trail Control Table Description

Column name	Description
APPLY_QUAL	Identifies the Apply program for the platform instance that will run this subscription. The value must be unique among all Apply program processes maintaining dependent replicas of a user table or parent replica, and unique among all Apply program processes sharing a common set of control tables. This value is case sensitive. You must specify this value when you define a subscription.
SET_NAME	Names a subscription set. This value is unique within an Apply qualifier.
WHOS_ON_FIRST	Allows both the up and down replication subscriptions to be contained in the same set without the potential for multiple SOURCE_SERVER values for each APPLY_QUAL, SET_NAME pairing. When the value of this column is: - F (first): The target table is the user table or parent replica and the source table is the dependent replica-propagation is UP the hierarchy. 'F' is not used for read-only subscriptions. - S (second): The source table is the user table, parent replica or other source and the target table is the dependent replica or other copy that is lower in the hierarchy-propagation is DOWN the hierarchy. 'S' is also used for read-only subscriptions.
ASNLOAD	One of the following values: - Y or N: Indicates whether ASNLOAD was called during the subscription set process. - NULL: Indicates that an error occurred before the decision to call ASNLOAD was made.
MASS_DELETE	One of the following values: - Y or N Indicates whether MASS_DELETE was triggered during the full refresh of a subscription set. - NULL Indicates that an error occurred before the decision to issue a mass delete was made.
EFFECTIVE_ MEMBERS	The number of members associated with calls to ASNLOAD, or the number of members for which rows are fetched and inserted, updated, or deleted.
SET_INSERTED	The total number of rows individually inserted into any set members during the subscription cycle.
SET_DELETED	The total number of rows individually deleted from any set members during the subscription cycle.
SET_UPDATED	The total number of rows individually updated in any set members during the subscription cycle.
SET_REWORKED	The total number of inserts reworked as updates and updates reworked as inserts for any set members during the subscription cycle.

Column name	Description
SET_REJECTED_TRXS	The total number of rejected replica transactions due to a direct or cascading update conflict. Always zero if either source or target is a replica.
STATUS	A value that represents in-progress and completed work status for the Apply program: - '-1': A known failed execution. You can modify the definition. - '0': A stable definition row that can be modified. This value is the default. - '1': A pending or in-progress execution. Do not modify this definition or any rows related to this subscription in other control tables. - '2': A continuing execution of a single logical subscription that was divided according to the MAX_SYNCH_MINUTES control column and is being serviced by multiple subscription cycles. Do not modify this row or any row related to this subscription in other control tables.
LASTRUN	The estimated time that the last subscription definition began. This value is calculated by adding the LASTRUN value with the INTERVAL_MINUTES value.
LASTSUCCESS	The control server wall clock time of the beginning of a successful subscription cycle, recorded at the end of the cycle if STATUS=0 or STATUS=2. If not, existing value is unchanged.
SYNCHPOINT	The SYNCHPOINT value equals the SYNCHPOINT field value in the register table. This value is used to coordinate the pruning of change data tables. The Apply program sets this initial value to 0, indicating refresh. If the Apply program sets a nonzero value, the change data table can be eligible for pruning.
SYNCHTIME	A source server timestamp that can be added to any captured log records for any source table. This timestamp indicates that a change did not occur before this time. If the log records are individually timestamped, use those timestamps; otherwise, these values are approximate and are set by the Apply program at the start of a subscription cycle and after each subsequent cycle. These values are eventually appended into each change data table row.
SOURCE_SERVER	The RDB name of DB2 for MVS, DB2 for VSE, and DB2 for VM where the source tables and views are defined.
SOURCE_ALIAS	The name of the source server used by the Apply program on the DB2 Universal Database client interface. This alias identifies the location of the subscription definition and is later used to perform administrative actions on a subscription. This alias does not necessarily match the alias of the source server used by the Apply program for the DB2 Universal Database and can be null if the database has no DB2 Universal Database name.
SOURCE_OWNER	The middle qualifier of the source table, that names the owner of the source table whose updates are being captured.
SOURCE_TABLE	The third qualifier of the source table, that names the source table whose updates are being captured.

Column name	Description
SOURCE_VIEW_ QUAL	Supports join subscriptions by matching the similar column in the register table.
TARGET_SERVER	The RDB name of the MVS, VSE, or VM server where the target table and views are defined.
TARGET_ALIAS	The name of the target server used by the Apply program on the DB2 Universal Database client interface. This alias identifies the location of the subscription definition and is later used to perform administrative actions on a subscription. This alias does not necessarily match the alias of the target server used by the Apply program for the DB2 Universal Database.
TARGET_OWNER	The middle qualifier of the target name. Use the value in the SOURCE_OWNER column as the default.
TARGET_TABLE	The third qualifier of the target table name. Use the value in the SOURCE_TABLE column as the default.
SQLSTATE	If an error, the SQL error code. Otherwise, NULL.
SQLCODE	If an error, the database-specific SQL error code. Otherwise, NULL.
SQLERRP	If an error, the database product identifier. Otherwise, NULL.
SQLERRM	If an error, the string containing the SQL error. Otherwise, NULL.
APPERRM	The Apply error message text from SQLCA if there was an error, otherwise NULL. This value is constant for each copy derived, directly or indirectly, from the original source table.

The Apply Trail table is usually created automatically using the following CREATE TABLE statement:

```
CREATE TABLE ASN.IBMSNAP_APPLYTRAIL (
   APPLY_QUAL CHAR(18) NOT NULL,
   SET_NAME CHAR (18) NOT NULL,
   WHOS_ON_FIRST CHAR(1) NOT NULL,
   ASNLOAD CHAR(1),
   MASS_DELETE CHAR(1),
   EFFECTIVE_MEMBERS INT,
   SET_INSERTED INT NOT NULL,
   SET_DELETED INT NOT NULL,
   SET_UPDATED INT NOT NULL,
   SET_REWORKED INT NOT NULL,
   SET_REJECTED_TRXS INT NOT NULL,
   STATUS SMALLINT NOT NULL,
   LASTRUN TIMESTAMP NOT NULL,
   LASTSUCCESS TIMESTAMP,
   SYNCHPOINT CHAR(10) FOR BIT DATA,
   SYNCHTIME TIMESTAMP,
   SOURCE_SERVER CHAR(18) NOT NULL,
   SOURCE_ALIAS CHAR(8),
   SOURCE_OWNER CHAR (18),
   SOURCE_TABLE CHAR(18),
   SOURCE_VIEW_QUAL SMALLINT,
   TARGET_SERVER CHAR(18) NOT NULL,
   TARGET_ALIAS CHAR(8),
   TARGET_OWNER CHAR (18) NOT NULL,
   TARGET_TABLE CHAR(18) NOT NULL,
   SQLSTATE CHAR(5),
   SQLCODE INT,
   SQLERRP CHAR(8),
   SQLERRM VARCHAR(70),
   APPERRM VARCHAR(760) );
```

The Apply trail control table records one SQL code and one SQL state for a replication subscription that does not get replicated successfully. Additional SQL codes and states associated with the problem can be found in the Apply program trace file.

You can query the Apply trail control table for information about successful and unsuccessful replications. Some key fields in the table that have problem indicators are:

- STATUS: Contains -1 to indicate a failed execution.
- SQLSTATE: Contains the error SQLSTATE for a failed execution.
- SQLCODE: Contains the error SQLCODE for a failed execution.
- SQLERRM: Contains the text of the SQL error message.
- APPERRM: Contains the text of the Apply program error message.

Within the error message text, you also need to determine which database the Apply program was connected to when the error occurred; for example, did the error occur while the Apply program was connected to the source server or the target server.

The Apply trail control table has fields that identify the source and target databases and tables so that you can locate the Apply trail control rows that are causing replication errors. To reduce the number of rows that you examine, you can:

- Before starting the Apply program, delete all rows from the ASN.IBMSNAP_APPLYTRAIL table to clean out rows from earlier replication processing.
- Temporarily disable replications that are successful in order to capture rows in ASN.IBMSNAP_APPLYTRAIL only for replications that have problems before starting the Apply program.

To select specific columns we would be interested in from the Apply trail table, issue the following SQL query at the Apply control server:

```
SELECT TARGET_TABLE, STATUS, SQLSTATE, SQLCODE, SQLERRM, APPERRM FROM
ASN.IBMSNAP_APPLYTRAIL
```

9.3.2 Apply Program Trace File

The Apply program creates a trace file when an Apply program trace invocation parameter is used.

If you specify a trace option, specify the name of a trace output file and, for workstation systems, precede the output file name with a 'greater than' symbol (>). As with Capture, you cannot start a trace for an instance of the Apply program once that instance of Apply has been started. You must stop that instance of Apply and restart it using one of the two trace options. For example, in a DB2 command line processor window in Windows NT:

```
c:\>asnapply MYAPPLY mydbnt2 trcflow > apply.trc
```

Where:

- `MYAPPLY` is the Apply qualifier.
- `mydbnt2` is the control server where the Apply program finds the control tables.
- `trcflow` indicates that the Apply program traces all error and flow information.

- `apply.trc` is the file to which the output is directed.

The trace file is located in the same directory from which the Apply program is started.

For more details about the syntax of the Apply program, see Chapter 3, "Capture and Apply" on page 59.

After the Apply program is stopped, you can view the trace file with any editor.

You have two trace options:

- TRCFLOW: Provides very detailed information and is oriented toward helping IBM Service diagnose errors. When using TRCFLOW, we suggest isolating the subscription error, such as by running it in a test environment or disabling other error-free replication subscriptions to reduce the volume of information.
- TRCERR: Provides less detail and is a better choice when you are new to the replication tools.

Within the trace, particularly with the TRCFLOW option, entries are made into the trace file for the Apply program's activities. The following are examples of the recorded information:

- Connecting to the control server to obtain information on replication subscriptions to be processed.
- Connecting to source servers to fetch rows to be replicated from the CD table to the target table.
- Connecting to the target servers to insert, update, and delete rows into and from the target tables.

The Apply program inserts error messages and indicators in the trace file at points when it encounters an error.

For example, to invoke the Apply program with a qualifier of DEPTQUAL, on database PHING, with TRCFLOW tracing enabled, use the following command (from a DB2 command line processor window on Windows NT):

```
c:\>asnapply DEPTQUAL phing trcflow > apply.trc
```

The output captured in the apply.trc file is as follows:

```
Apply program compiled at 10:19:48 on Sep 11 1998 (Level 0058)
Apply qualifier is DEPTQUAL.
Control srvr name is PHING.
Issue Sleep msg.
Will not invoke ASNLOAD.
Will not invoke ASNDONE.
  IMSG: Instance name is DB2     .
  IMSG: The log file name is DEPTQUALB2PHING.LOG.
   CEXPC: connect to PHING
   CEXPC: CONNECT without USERID/PASSWORD
   CEXPC: serverIsolationUR is 1.
  CIMPC: serverIsolationUR is 1.
  CIMPC: The local_srvr is PHING.
  CIMPC: Userid is PHING
    MSGF: MsgNumber is 45.
   The NLS msg is ASN1045I: The Apply program was started using database
PHING.

.
   The NLS msg is ASN1045I: The Apply program was started using database
PHING.
```

9.3.3 The Apply Program Log File

The Apply program also has a log file containing messages with a summary of the Apply program's activities. The log file is in the directory from which the Apply program is started and any trace files are located.

On DB2 for MVS, this information is written to the console. On DB2 UDB platforms, the name of the Apply program log file is based on the following, with the extension of .LOG:

- The Apply qualifier associated with the control server.
- Instance name (if not on OS/2).
- The Control server name (if not on OS/2).

For example, for an Apply program operating on Windows NT with an Apply qualifier of MYAPPLY, a control server of COPYTEST, and using the default DB2 instance, the log file name is MYAPPLYDB2COPYTEST.LOG.

Because the Apply program log file information is high level, it typically directs you to the ASN.IBMSNAP_APPLYTRAIL table for more detailed information.

9.3.4 Apply Program Error Messages

Apply program error messages are prefixed by ASN1. Some examples are as follows:

If you invoke `asnapply` without a password file, using the following command:

```
asnapply DEPTQUAL phing trcflow > apply.trc
```

The Apply program log file, DEPTQUALDB2PHING.log, would contain the following:

```
1998-12-20-13:25:59 ASN1056E: The Apply program password file could not
be opened. The error code is 215601.
1998-12-20-13:25:59 ASN1097I: The apply program stopped due to the above
error.
```

The corresponding `apply.trc` file would contain:

```
Apply program compiled at 10:19:48 on Sep 11 1998 (Level 0058)
Apply qualifier is DEPTQUAL.
Control srvr name is PHING.
Issue Sleep msg.
Will not invoke ASNLOAD.
Will not invoke ASNDONE.
  IMSG: Instance name is DB2       .
  IMSG: The log file name is DEPTQUALDB2PHING.LOG.
 INIT: fopen failed. errcode is 215601.
 INIT: file DEPTQUALDB2PHING.PWD is not opened
 DOWN: retcode is 15
    MSGF: MsgNumber is 56.
   The NLS msg is ASN1056E: The Apply program password file could not be
opened. The error code is 215601.
.
   The NLS msg is ASN1056E: The Apply program password file could not be
opened. The error code is 215601.
.
   MSGF: MsgNumber is 97.
  The NLS msg is ASN1097I: The Apply program stopped due to the above
error.
.
  The NLS msg is ASN1097I: The Apply program stopped due to the above
error.
.
 DOWN: Apply is shutting down due to an error
```

If you invoke `asnapply` without first binding the relevant packages to the database (the bind files listed in the file apply.lst), the log file would contain:

```
1998-12-20-13:35:00 ASN1001E: The Apply program encountered an SQL
error. ERRCODE is 080102, SQLSTATE is 51002, SQLCODE is -805. SQLERRM is
NULLID.ASNM014, SQLERRP is SQLRACFI, server name is PHING, table name is
.

1998-12-20-13:35:00 ASN1097I: The Apply program stopped due to the above
error.
```

When you start the Apply program, if you specify the apply qualifier in lower case, no eligible subscriptions will be found. This message is generated:

```
ApplyTrace:CEXPC: connect to COPYTEST
 GCST: Control server timestamp is 1998-11-09-14.40.08.156001
  R1NES: No eligible named event subscription at this moment
  R1RTS: No eligible relative timer driven subscription at this moment
```

Even if you type the apply qualifier name in lower case in the subscription definition panel of the Control Center, it is automatically converted to upper case when the subscription is created.

In cases when a primary key is required for replication to take place, the lack of a primary key will generate a message similar to this:

```
Apply program compiled at 14:48:48 on Aug 12 1998 (Level 0053)
Apply qualifier is TESTKEYQUAL.
Control srvr name is COPYTEST.
Issue Sleep msg.
Will not invoke ASNLOAD.
Will not invoke ASNDONE.
BSSKC: Error: There are no key columns. errcode is 6B1903.
BSSKC: Error: There are no key columns. errcode is 6B1903.
```

A server name in the Apply password file must be specified in upper case. If you specify it in lower case, you will see a message similar to this:

```
in CEXPC: connect to SAMPLE
  CEXPC: CONNECT without USERID/PASSWORD
  SQLCA is
       00000000 53514C43 41202020 88000000 85FAFFFF SQLCA   ........
       00000010 00000000 00000000 00000000 00000000 ................
       00000020 00000000 00000000 00000000 00000000 ................
       00000030 00000000 00000000 00000000 00000000 ................
       00000040 00000000 00000000 00000000 00000000 ................
       00000050 00000000 00000000 53514C45 58415553 ........SQLEXAUS
       00000060 00000000 00000000 00000000 00000000 ................
       00000070 00000000 00000000 20202020 20202020 ........
      00000080 20202030 38303034                              08004
  CEXPC: IMPLICIT CONNECT failed. errcode is 130301. sqlstate is 08004.
sqlcode is -1403
 PSET: ROLLBACK
```

Finally, a successful invocation of the Apply program leaves the log file with the contents as follows:

```
1998-12-20-13:39:00 ASN1045I: The Apply program was started using
database PHING.

1998-12-20-13:39:00 ASN1045I: The Apply program will become inactive for
5 minutes and 0 seconds.
```

9.3.5 Apply Program Determination Checklist

1. Is the Apply program running?
2. If not, what occurs when the Apply program starts?
3. What messages appear?
4. Is there error information in the ASN.IBMSNAP_APPLYTRAIL table?
5. Is there error information in the Apply program log file?
6. Are data changes being successfully replicated to the target table?
7. Do all tables in a replication subscription have the same problem?
8. What table types (for example, user copy, point-in-time, CCD) are involved in the failure?
9. Did you run the Apply program with trace?
10. Are CALL procedures being used?
11. Is a CCD (consistent change data table) being used?

9.4 ASNLOAD Messages

When the ASNLOAD exit program is being used to provide an alternate load method (instead of the default select and insert approach used by Apply), any errors encountered during the initial load or full refresh are written to specific files on DB2 UDB. There is no facility to do this on DB2 for MVS.

On OS/2, the generated files are as follows:

- <Apply qualifier>.EXP - this is the file containing the export messages.
- <Apply qualifier>.LOA - this is the file containing the LOAD process messages.

On the other DB2 UDB platforms, the files generated are:

- ASNEXPT<Apply qualifier><DB2 Instance name><Target server>.MSG - this file contains the export process messages.
- ASNALOAD<Apply qualifier><DB2 Instance><Control Server>.MSG - this file contains the LOAD process messages.

9.5 Mobile Replication

To be able to generate a trace for a mobile replication situation, you need to specify the '-T' option on the ASNCOPY command as follows:

```
ASNCOPY -T <any other parameters>
```

In addition, if using the ASNMOBIL GUI, you would specify tracing on the panel as indicated in Figure 159 on page 266.

In this situation, any trace for Capture associated with the mobile replication will be written to the trace control table for Capture.

The trace information for Apply will be written to a file, whose name is:

- <Apply qualifier>.TRC on OS/2.
- APPLY<YYYYMMDDHHMMSS>.TRC on Windows 95/98/NT.

The Apply trace file will be created in the directory from which the ASNCOPY or the ASNMOBIL commands were initiated.

9.6 Summary

This chapter has discussed the IBM Data Replication tracing and diagnostic facilities that are available in addition to those provided with the DB2 product for each platform. These facilities can be used to isolate and better understand the normal functioning of your replication environment and also to determine the cause, and eventual resolution, of any problems you may encounter.

Appendix A. Sample Certification Questions and Test Objectives

To help you prepare for the DB2 UDB Certification exam #508 on Data Propagation/Replication, we provide for you a number of sample test questions and answers, as well as the exam objectives. These questions and objectives should help you determine if you are prepared for the exam and if you understood the topics and concepts in this certification guide.

A.1 Data Replication Exam Objectives for Exam #508

The following is a list of the test objectives broken down by category:

IBM Data Replication Products/Components

- Discuss the features/function of the IBM Data replication products
- Given a situation: Determine the IBM Data replication product(s) which best satisfy the requirements
- Identify the Product/Component requirements based on the customer's requirements
- Identify the connectivity requirements for the Data replication products
- Identify the components of the DPropR product
- Identify the functions performed by the DPropR components
- Identify the differences between DPropR and DPropN

DPropR Administration

- Grant privileges to DPropR users in the database
- Define the target table types
- Identify the target table attributes
- Register the source table(s)
- Register a CCD table
- Cancel existing registrations
- Create subscriptions
- Cancel existing subscriptions
- Start the Capture component
- Restart the Capture component
- Suspend the Capture component

- Resume the Capture component
- Reinitialize the Capture component
- Prune Capture data
- Start the Apply component
- Stop the Apply component
- Given a failure situation: Determine the correct recovery method
- Translate Encoded data
- Fast Load Tables
- Account for referential integrity

DPropR Configuration

- Identify the Data Server (Source Server)
- Identify the Copy Server (Target Server)
- Identify the Control Server
- Identify the Capture control tables
- Identify the function of the Capture control tables
- Identify the Apply control tables
- Identify the function of the Apply control tables
- Bind Capture package to the Source database
- Bind Apply package to the Source database
- Bind Apply package to the Target database

A.2 Sample Questions

1. Administering replication can be accomplished from the Control Center. Which of the following products does NOT contain the Control Center?

   A) IBM DB2 Connect

   B) IBM DB2 for OS/390

   C) IBM DB2 Universal Database

   D) IBM DB2 Universal Database CAE

2. Which of the following protocols can be used to connect from DB2 Connect to DB2 for OS/390?

   A) IPX/SPX

B) Named Pipes

C) NetBIOS

D) TCP/IP

3. Which of the following products will provide the necessary communication support for Apply to pull changes from DB2 for OS/390 to DB2 Universal Database?

   A) DB2 Universal Database CAE

   B) DB2 Universal Database Personal Edition

   C) DB2 Universal Database Workgroup Edition

   D) DB2 Universal Database Enterprise Edition

4. For the given operating system, where does Apply NOT obtain the userid and password for its database connections?

   A) OS/2 - UPM

   B) OS/390 - CDB

   C) Windows NT - SAM DB

   D) AIX - Apply password file

5. Capture communicates to Apply via which of the following tables?

   A) Apply Trail Table

   B) Critical Section Table

   C) Pruning Control Table

   D) Unit of Work Table

6. Which of the following parameters indicates that ASNCOPY will NOT call Capture?

   A) -F

   B) -H

   C) -L

   D) -T

7. Which of the following actions are NOT performed by Capture?

   A) Deletion of rows from the Change Data table

   B) Insertion of rows into the Register table

   C) Insertion of rows into the Unit of Work table

   D) Updating of rows in the Prune Control table

8. A target computed column which references before image columns must be defined with which of the following data type attributes?

   A) NULL

   B) NOT NULL

   C) UNIQUE

   D) NOT UNIQUE

9. Which of the following is the minimum privilege required for Apply to make changes to a target table on DB2 Universal Database server?

   A) CONTROL on the table

   B) DBADM for the database

   C) SELECT on the table

   D) SYSADM for the instance

10. Which of the following source table types can be used to support a fan out differential replication scenario without Capture?

    A) Point In Time

    B) Consistent Change Data

    C) Replica

    D) User Copy

11. Which of the following target table types uses only the source table as its input?

    A) Base Aggregate

    B) Change Aggregate

    C) Replica

    D) Consistent Change Data

12. Which of the following attributes must be specified for the Consistent Change Data target table to contain a complete history?

    A) Condensed/complete

    B) Condensed/noncomplete

    C) Noncondensed/complete

    D) Noncondensed/noncomplete

13. During which of the following tasks is the level of conflict detection specified?

    A) Defining a replication source

B) Defining a subscription set

C) Starting Capture

D) Starting Apply

14. Given that the Apply program is locking all replicas in the subscription set against further transactions and that it begins detection only after all changes made prior to the locking have been captured, which of the following levels of Conflict Detection was used when registering the source table?

A) None

B) Standard

C) Enhanced

D) Super Enhanced

15. In order for Capture to recognize a newly defined replication source, which of the following actions must be performed?

A) No action is required.

B) Capture must be reinitialized.

C) Suspend and resume Capture.

D) Stop and start Apply.

16. Which of the following actions will occur when removing a replication source using the Control Center with the default tool settings?

A) The Change Data table tablespace will be dropped unconditionally.

B) The Change Data table tablespace will be dropped if it is empty.

C) The target table tablespace will be dropped unconditionally.

D) The target table tablespace will be dropped if it is empty.

17. Given: The source table is located on a DB2 Universal Database Server and a column must be computed that is the numeric difference between the before and after image values for the column named AMT. Which represents the before image prefix of X?

A) AMT - XAMT

B) Coalesce(AMT - XAMT, 0)

C) Case

When IBMSNAP_OPERATION in ('I', 'U')

Then Coalesce(AMT - XAMT, AMT)

When IBMSNAP_OPERATION ='D'

Then AMT

End

D) Case

When IBMSNAP_OPERATION in ('I', 'U')

Then Coalesce(AMT - XAMT, AMT)

When IBMSNAP_OPERATION ='D'

Then -AMT}

End

18. At which of the following locations is the WHERE clause for a subscription set member evaluated?

A) Control server

B) Gateway server

C) Source server

D) Target server

19. What is the maximum amount of time an event driven subscription set will wait to be executed after the event time has passed?

A) 30 seconds

B) 1 minute

C) 5 minutes

D) 30 minutes

20. When removing one member of a multiple member subscription set using the Control Center, which two of the following control tables will be affected?

A) Subscription Set Table

B) Subscription Targets Member Table

C) Subscription Columns Table

D) Subscription Events Table

E) Subscription Statements Table

21. Which of the following is the default Retention Limit for Capture?

A) 1 minute

B) 60 minutes

C) 1440 minutes

D) 10080 minutes

22. In which of the following locations must the Capture packages be bound prior to Capture being started?

    A) Source Server

    B) Target Server

    C) Control Server AND Source Server

    D) Control Server AND Target Server

23. When issuing the ASNCMD command for Capture/NT, which of the following server names must be used for the DB2DBDFT environment variable?

    A) Control Server

    B) Gateway Server

    C) Source Server

    D) Target Server

24. Which of the following commands will continue Capture/MVS processing after it has been suspended?

    A) F jobname, RESUME

    B) F RESUME

    C) F jobname, CONTINUE

    D) F CONTINUE

25. Which of the following are valid reasons for issuing the REINIT command?

    A) Tuning parameters have changed.

    B) Source Table statistics have changed.

    C) A replication source has been removed.

    D) A replication target has been removed.}

26. Which of the following commands will refresh the control information for Capture/AIX?

    A) ASNCMD jobname, REINIT

    B) ASNCMD REINIT

    C) ASNCMD jobname, REFRESH

    D) ASNCMD REFRESH

27. Which of the following groups of tables completely identifies the tables which are modified by the Capture pruning process?

A) Change Data Tables, Unit of Work Table

B) Change Data Tables, Unit of Work Table, Register Table

C) Change Data Tables, Unit of Work Table, Consistent Change Data Tables

D) Change Data Tables, Unit of Work Table, Consistent Change Data Tables, Register Table

28. To cause pruning to switch from pruning by command to pruning automatically on a DB2 Universal Database source server, which of the following commands must be issued?

A) asncmd stop then asnccp prune

B) asncmd prune

C) asnccp stop then asncmd prune

D) asnccp prune

29. Which of the following tables & columns does Apply use to communicate to Capture which data has already been applied?

A) Subscription Set Table: SYNCHPOINT Column

B) Subscription Set Table: SYNCHTIME Column

C) Pruning Control Table: SYNCHPOINT Column

D) Pruning Control Table: SYNCHTIME Column

30. In which of the following groups of servers must the Apply packages be bound prior to Apply being started?

A) Source Server, Target Server

B) Source Server, Gateway Server

C) Source Server, Target Server, Control Server

D) Source Server, Gateway Server, Control Server

31. The source servers for an Apply process are specified in which of the following tables?

A) Subscription Qualifier Table

B) Subscription Set Table

C) Subscription Statement Table

D) Subscription Target Member Table

32. When starting Apply/MVS the DB2 subsystem name must be specified in which of the following parameters?

A) 1st parameter

B) 2nd parameter

C) 3rd parameter

D) 4th parameter

33. Which of the following commands will stop Apply/AIX?

A) ASNASTOP Apply_qualifier

B) ASNSTOP Apply_qualifier

C) ASNASTOP control server name

D) ASNSTOP control server name

34. Which of the following actions is required to synchronize the data between the source and target tables while minimizing the affect on subscription sets on other source tables if the source table is recovered to a point in time prior to the end of logs?

A) Apply will automatically synchronize the data.

B) Perform a cold start of Capture.

C) Force full refresh for all subscription sets that include the source table.

D) Set the SYNCHPOINT, LASTSUCCESS & LASTRUN in the Subscription Member table to NULL.

35. Given: A time interval execution of Apply is in the process of retrieving changes for the commit sequence range of 1000 to 5000 into the spill file. While Apply is retrieving a record with a commit sequence of 2000, it encounters an error. What commit sequence range of changes will Apply retrieve during the next time interval execution for the subscription set if the current commit sequence of Capture is now 8000?

A) 1000 - 5000

B) 1000 - 8000

C) 2000 - 5000

D) 2000 - 8000

36. On which of the following servers must the Unit of Work Table reside?

A) Control Server

B) Gateway Server

C) Source Server

D) Target Server

37. Apply CANNOT run on which of the following target servers?

 A) Windows NT

 B) VSE/ESA

 C) OS/2

 D) Windows 95

38. On which of the following servers is the Apply Trail Table located?

 A) Control Server

 B) Gateway Server

 C) Source Server

 D) Target Server

39. Which of the following tables is joined with the Change Data table to ensure transaction consistency?

 A) Commit Table

 B) Unit of Work Table

 C) Transaction Control Table

 D) Warm Start Table

40. Which of the following tables contains the column CONFLICT_LEVEL?

 A) Register Table

 B) Subscription Set Table

 C) Subscription Target Member Table

 D) Transaction Control Table

41. Given: The source and target tables have been defined with the same column and primary key definitions. You issue SQL UPDATE statements to modify the primary key column values of the source table. In order to ensure data consistency between the source and target tables, which of the following column settings must be specified in the Register Table?

 A) PARTITION_KEYS_CHG = 'Y'

 B) PRIMARY_KEYS_CHG = 'Y'

 C) PARTITION_KEYS_UPD = 'Y'

 D) PRIMARY_KEYS_UPD = 'Y'

42. In which of the following tables can the character identifying the before image column names be specified in the Change Data table?

A) Change Data Table

B) Register Table

C) Subscription Set Table

D) Subscription Target Member Table

43. Which of the following functions is NOT supported by the ACTIVATE column in the Subscriptions Set table?

A) -1 The subscription set is executed once.

B) 0 The subscription set is deactivated.

C) 1 The request is active indefinitely.

D) 2 The set can be copied immediately.

44. Which of the following actions must be performed upon detecting an entry in the Subscription Set table where STATUS = 0?

A) No action is required.

B) Apply restart is required.

C) The error information fields in the Trace table must be checked.

D) The error information fields in the Apply Trail table must be checked.}

45. Given: A source table mysource.tab1 and a subscription against it defining a Consistent Change Data (CCD) table mytarget.tab1_ccd. If mytarget.tab1_ccd is defined as an external remote CCD table, how is its replication source definition stored during the subscription process?

A) In the CCD_Owner, CCD_Table, CCD_Condensed, and CCD_Complete columns of the Register Table row where source_owner='mysource' and source_table='tab1' at the Source server

B) In the CCD_Owner, CCD_Table, CCD_Condensed, and CCD_Complete columns of the Register Table row where source_owner='mytarget' and source_table='tab1_ccd' at the Source server

C) In the Source_Owner, Source_Table, CCD_Condensed, and CCD_Complete columns of the Register Table row where source_owner='mysource' and source_table='tab1' at the Target server

D) In the Source_Owner, Source_Table, CCD_Condensed, and CCD_Complete columns of the Register Table row where source_owner='mytarget' and source_table='tab1_ccd' at the Target server

46. Which of the following source table attributes will cause Apply to issue an error when it needs to perform a full refresh?

A) CCD Condensed = 'Y', CCD Complete = 'Y'

B) CCD Condensed = 'Y', CCD Complete = 'N'

C) Target Condensed = 'Y', Target Complete = 'Y'

D) Target Condensed = 'Y', Target Complete = 'N'

A.3 Answers to Sample Questions

1. B
2. D
3. D
4. C
5. C
6. A
7. B
8. A
9. A
10. B
11. A
12. C
13. A
14. C
15. B
16. B
17. D
18. C
19. C
20. B,C
21. D
22. A
23. C

24.A

25.A

26.B

27.B

28.A

29.C

30.C

31.B

32.B

33.A

34.C

35.B

36.C

37.B

38.A

39.B

40.A

41.A

42.B

43.A

44.A

45.D

46.B

Appendix B. Replication Tables

ASN.IBMSNAP_APPLYTRAIL

(no primary key)

APPLY_QUAL	CHAR (18) NOT NULL
SET_NAME	CHAR (18) NOT NULL
WHOS_ON_FIRST	CHAR (1) NOT NULL
ASNLOAD	CHAR (1)
MASS_DELETE	CHAR (1)
EFFECTIVE_MEMBERS	INT
SET_INSERTED	INT NOT NULL
SET_DELETED	INT NOT NULL
SET_UPDATED	INT NOT NULL
SET_REWORKED	INT NOT NULL
SET_REJECTED_TRXS	INT NOT NULL
STATUS	SMALLINT NOT NULL
LASTRUN	TIMESTAMP NOT NULL
LASTSUCCESS	TIMESTAMP
SYNCHPOINT	CHAR (10) FOR BIT DATA
SYNCHTIME	TIMESTAMP
SOURCE_SERVER	CHAR (18) NOT NULL
SOURCE_ALIAS	CHAR (8)
SOURCE_OWNER	CHAR (18)
SOURCE_TABLE	CHAR (18)
SOURCE_VIEW_QUAL	SMALLINT
TARGET_SERVER	CHAR (18) NOT NULL
TARGET_ALIAS	CHAR (8)
TARGET_OWNER	CHAR (18) NOT NULL
TARGET_TABLE	CHAR (18) NOT NULL
SQLSTATE	CHAR (5)
SQLCODE	INTEGER
SQLERRP	CHAR (8)
SQLERRM	VARCHAR (70)
APPERRM	VARCHAR (760)

ASN.IBMSNAP_SUBS_EVENT

EVENT_NAME, EVENT_TIME

EVENT_NAME	CHAR (18) NOT NULL
EVENT_TIME	TIMESTAMP NOT NULL
END_OF_PERIOD	TIMESTAMP

ASN.IBMSNAP_SUBS_STMTS

APPLY_QUAL, SET_NAME, WHOS_ON_FIRST, BEFORE_OR_AFTER, STMT_NUMBER

APPLY_QUAL	CHAR (18) NOT NULL
SET_NAME	CHAR (18) NOT NULL
WHOS_ON_FIRST	CHAR (1) NOT NULL
BEFORE_OR_AFTER	CHAR (1) NOT NULL
STMT_NUMBER	SMALLINT NOT NULL
EI_OR_CALL	CHAR (1) NOT NULL
SQL_STMT	VARCHAR (1024)
ACCEPT_SQLSTATES	VARCHAR (50)

ASN.IBMSNAP_SUBS_SET

APPLY_QUAL, SET_NAME, WHOS_ON_FIRST

APPLY_QUAL	CHAR (18) NOT NULL
SET_NAME	CHAR (18) NOT NULL
WHOS_ON_FIRST	CHAR (1) NOT NULL
ACTIVATE	SMALLINT NOT NULL
SOURCE_SERVER	CHAR (18) NOT NULL
SOURCE_ALIAS	CHAR (8)
TARGET_SERVER	CHAR (18) NOT NULL
TARGET_ALIAS	CHAR (8)
STATUS	SMALLINT NOT NULL
LASTRUN	TIMESTAMP NOT NULL
REFRESH_TIMING	CHAR (1) NOT NULL
SLEEP_MINUTES	INT
EVENT_NAME	CHAR (18)
LASTSUCCESS	TIMESTAMP
SYNCHPOINT	CHAR (10) FOR BIT DATA
SYNCHTIME	TIMESTAMP
MAX_SYNCH_MINUTES	INT
AUX_STMTS	SMALLINT NOT NULL
ARCH_LEVEL	CHAR (4) NOT NULL

ASN.IBMSNAP_SUBS_COLS

APPLY_QUAL, SET_NAME, WHOS_ON_FIRST, TARGET_OWNER, TARGET_TABLE, TARGET_NAME

APPLY_QUAL	CHAR (18) NOT NULL
SET_NAME	CHAR (18) NOT NULL
WHOS_ON_FIRST	CHAR (1) NOT NULL
TARGET_OWNER	CHAR (18) NOT NULL
TARGET_TABLE	CHAR (18) NOT NULL
COL_TYPE	CHAR (1) NOT NULL
TARGET_NAME	CHAR (18) NOT NULL
IS_KEY	CHAR (1) NOT NULL
COLNO	SMALLINT NOT NULL
EXPRESSION	VARCHAR (254) NOT NULL

ASN.IBMSNAP_SUBS_MEMBR

APPLY_QUAL, SET_NAME, WHOS_ON_FIRST, SOURCE_OWNER, SOURCE_TABLE, SOURCE_VIEW_QUAL, TARGET_OWNER, TARGET_TABLE

APPLY_QUAL	CHAR (18) NOT NULL
SET_NAME	CHAR (18) NOT NULL
WHOS_ON_FIRST	CHAR (1) NOT NULL
SOURCE_OWNER	CHAR (18) NOT NULL
SOURCE_TABLE	CHAR (18) NOT NULL
SOURCE_VIEW_QUAL	SMALLINT NOT NULL
TARGET_OWNER	CHAR (18) NOT NULL
TARGET_TABLE	CHAR (18) NOT NULL
TARGET_CONDENSED	CHAR (1) NOT NULL
TARGET_COMPLETE	CHAR (1) NOT NULL
TARGET_STRUCTURE	SMALLINT NOT NULL
PREDICATES	VARCHAR (512)

Used by APPLY

Figure 205. The Replication Tables at the Control Server Database

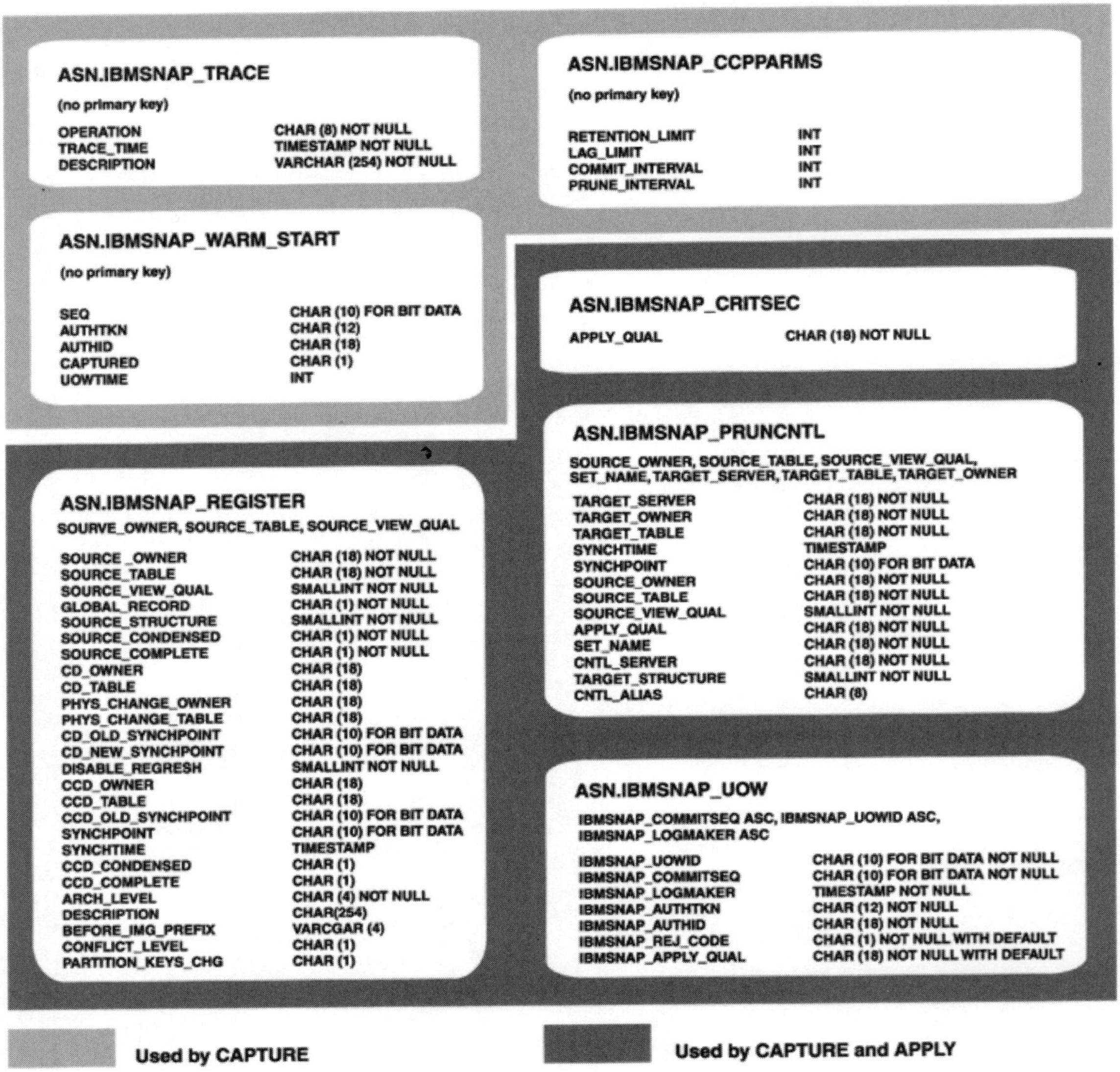

ASN.IBMSNAP_TRACE

(no primary key)

OPERATION	CHAR (8) NOT NULL
TRACE_TIME	TIMESTAMP NOT NULL
DESCRIPTION	VARCHAR (254) NOT NULL

ASN.IBMSNAP_CCPPARMS

(no primary key)

RETENTION_LIMIT	INT
LAG_LIMIT	INT
COMMIT_INTERVAL	INT
PRUNE_INTERVAL	INT

ASN.IBMSNAP_WARM_START

(no primary key)

SEQ	CHAR (10) FOR BIT DATA
AUTHTKN	CHAR (12)
AUTHID	CHAR (18)
CAPTURED	CHAR (1)
UOWTIME	INT

ASN.IBMSNAP_CRITSEC

APPLY_QUAL	CHAR (18) NOT NULL

ASN.IBMSNAP_PRUNCNTL

SOURCE_OWNER, SOURCE_TABLE, SOURCE_VIEW_QUAL, SET_NAME, TARGET_SERVER, TARGET_TABLE, TARGET_OWNER

TARGET_SERVER	CHAR (18) NOT NULL
TARGET_OWNER	CHAR (18) NOT NULL
TARGET_TABLE	CHAR (18) NOT NULL
SYNCHTIME	TIMESTAMP
SYNCHPOINT	CHAR (10) FOR BIT DATA
SOURCE_OWNER	CHAR (18) NOT NULL
SOURCE_TABLE	CHAR (18) NOT NULL
SOURCE_VIEW_QUAL	SMALLINT NOT NULL
APPLY_QUAL	CHAR (18) NOT NULL
SET_NAME	CHAR (18) NOT NULL
CNTL_SERVER	CHAR (18) NOT NULL
TARGET_STRUCTURE	SMALLINT NOT NULL
CNTL_ALIAS	CHAR (8)

ASN.IBMSNAP_REGISTER

SOURVE_OWNER, SOURCE_TABLE, SOURCE_VIEW_QUAL

SOURCE_OWNER	CHAR (18) NOT NULL
SOURCE_TABLE	CHAR (18) NOT NULL
SOURCE_VIEW_QUAL	SMALLINT NOT NULL
GLOBAL_RECORD	CHAR (1) NOT NULL
SOURCE_STRUCTURE	SMALLINT NOT NULL
SOURCE_CONDENSED	CHAR (1) NOT NULL
SOURCE_COMPLETE	CHAR (1) NOT NULL
CD_OWNER	CHAR (18)
CD_TABLE	CHAR (18)
PHYS_CHANGE_OWNER	CHAR (18)
PHYS_CHANGE_TABLE	CHAR (18)
CD_OLD_SYNCHPOINT	CHAR (10) FOR BIT DATA
CD_NEW_SYNCHPOINT	CHAR (10) FOR BIT DATA
DISABLE_REGRESH	SMALLINT NOT NULL
CCD_OWNER	CHAR (18)
CCD_TABLE	CHAR (18)
CCD_OLD_SYNCHPOINT	CHAR (10) FOR BIT DATA
SYNCHPOINT	CHAR (10) FOR BIT DATA
SYNCHTIME	TIMESTAMP
CCD_CONDENSED	CHAR (1)
CCD_COMPLETE	CHAR (1)
ARCH_LEVEL	CHAR (4) NOT NULL
DESCRIPTION	CHAR(254)
BEFORE_IMG_PREFIX	VARCGAR (4)
CONFLICT_LEVEL	CHAR (1)
PARTITION_KEYS_CHG	CHAR (1)

ASN.IBMSNAP_UOW

IBMSNAP_COMMITSEQ ASC, IBMSNAP_UOWID ASC, IBMSNAP_LOGMAKER ASC

IBMSNAP_UOWID	CHAR (10) FOR BIT DATA NOT NULL
IBMSNAP_COMMITSEQ	CHAR (10) FOR BIT DATA NOT NULL
IBMSNAP_LOGMAKER	TIMESTAMP NOT NULL
IBMSNAP_AUTHTKN	CHAR (12) NOT NULL
IBMSNAP_AUTHID	CHAR (18) NOT NULL
IBMSNAP_REJ_CODE	CHAR (1) NOT NULL WITH DEFAULT
IBMSNAP_APPLY_QUAL	CHAR (18) NOT NULL WITH DEFAULT

Used by CAPTURE **Used by CAPTURE and APPLY**

Figure 206. Replication Table at the Source Server Database

Appendix C. Replication Defaults File - DPREP.DFT

```
-- Sample replication default value file
--
-- PLEASE READ THIS FILE CAREFULLY IF YOU WISH TO CUSTOMIZE YOUR SQL SCRIPTS!!!
--
-- 1. Background
-- The purpose of this file is to be used as a template file for the customization of change table
-- names and the customization of indexes and tablespaces used during the define as replication
-- source and subscription actions.  You can specify this file inside the Replication page of the
-- "Tools settings" notebook, under the section entitled "Substitute user-defined values to define
-- replication objects".
--
--
-- 2. Usage
-- Please edit a copy of this file to follow your site-specific standards and place that file
-- For the Control Center (non-web): in the working directory for Control Center (\SQLLIB\BIN) to enable its
use.
-- For the Web Control Center: in the codebase path as specified in the db2webcc.htm page,
--                           (most likely \SQLLIB\JAVA) to enable its use.
--
-- When using the replication default value file, we recommend you choose the "Save SQL to file
-- and run later" option during Define replication source or subscription actions.  This will
-- allow you to verify the customization before running the SQL script file.
--
--
-- 3. Syntax
-- Comments are prefixed by '--'
-- Each default statement follow this syntax:  <keyword> = <value>
-- The keyword, such as SourceFQTable is not case-sensitive
-- The value, such as "OrgCopy" preserves case if delimited, otherwise is folded to uppercase by DBMS
-- Note that a semi-colon ';' cannot follow a default statement
--
-- Each record in the dprepl.dft file has the following syntax, as described below:
--
--
-- 3.1. SAMPLE DEFAULT RECORDS
-- 3.1.1. A default "Define as replication source" record can contain the following statements:
--   SourceServer         =<database alias *>                   -- such as SAMPLE
--   SourceFQTable        =<fully-qualified source table *>     -- such as USERID.ORG
--   SourceViewQualifier =<source view qualifier for "Define Join", this defaults to 0 if unspecified>
--   SourceDBMS           =<database platform>                  -- such as DB2/2
--   CDFQTable            =<fully-qualified change data table> -- such as USERID."OrgCD"
--   CDCreateTSStmt       =<create tablespace DDL for the change data table>
--   CDInClause           =<in clause for change data table>   -- such as IN USERSPACE1
--   CDCreateIndex1       =<create index DDL of first index for change data table **>
--   CDCreateIndex2       =<create index DDL of second index for change data table **>
--
-- 3.1.2. A default "Define as replication subscription" *** entry follows this syntax:
--   TargetServer        =<database alias *>               -- such as SAMPLE
--   TargetFQTable       =<fully-qualified target table *> -- such as USERID.ORGCOPY
--   SourceDBMS          =<source database platform>       -- such as DB2
--   TargetDBMS          =<target database platform>       -- such as DB2/2
--   TargetCreateTSStmt =<create tablespace DDL for the target table>
--   TargetInClause      =<in clause for the target table> -- such as IN USERSPACE1
--   TargetCreateIndex1 =<create index DDL of first index for target table **>
--   TargetCreateIndex2 =<create index DDL of second index for target table **>
--
-- Notes:  * marks mandatory default statements used for record lookup, all other statements are optional
--         ** see "CREATING ... INDEXES" sections below for recommended indexes
--         *** For replicas, you need an additional default "Define as replication source" record for
--             "auto-registration".
```

```
--
--
-- 3.2. CREATING A SUBSCRIPTION FOR A REPLICA TABLE:
--
-- In order to fully customize a replica member inside the subscription set, you should create a default
-- "Define as replication subscription" for the replica target table and also a "Define as replication
-- source" for the replica at the target server.  Remember to set TargetServer=<target server in GUI>,
-- TargetFQTable=<target table in GUI> for the default subscription entry and
-- SourceServer=<target server in GUI>, SourceFQTable=<target table in GUI> for the default source entry.
-- This is because the replica is automatically being defined as a replication source during the
-- "Define as replication subscription" action.
--
--
-- 3.3. CREATING TARGET TABLE INDEXES (TargetCreateIndex)
--
-- If you are using this file to create indexes on target tables, these are the recommended indexes:
--
-- Note:  for point-in-time, user copy, replica and "condensed" consistent change data tables on the
--        Universal Database (UDB) platform, unique indexes on the primary key are not required.
--
-- Note:  for DB2 MVS V4 and up, it is highly recommended that the indexes are created as TYPE 2 indexes.
--        In order to create type 2 indexes, add the clause "TYPE 2" after the CREATE keyword of the
--        CREATE INDEX statement.
--
-- For Point-in-time, User copy and Replica target tables (not required on UDB):
--    TargetCreateIndex1=CREATE UNIQUE INDEX USERID.ORGCOPYX ON USERID.ORGCOPY( <primary key columns> )
--
-- For Base Aggregate target tables:
--    TargetCreateIndex1=CREATE UNIQUE INDEX USERID.ORGCOPYX ON USERID.ORGCOPY( IBMSNAP_LLOGMARKER DESC )
--
-- For Change Aggregate target tables:
--    TargetCreateIndex1=CREATE INDEX USERID.ORGCOPYX ON USERID.ORGCOPY( IBMSNAP_LLOGMARKER DESC )
--
-- For "condensed" Staging (CCD) target tables (TargetCreateIndex1 not required on UDB):
--    TargetCreateIndex1=CREATE UNIQUE INDEX USERID.ORGCOPYX1 ON USERID.ORGCOPY( <primary key columns> )
--    TargetCreateIndex2=CREATE UNIQUE INDEX USERID.ORGCOPYX2 ON USERID.ORGCOPY( IBMSNAP_COMMITSEQ ASC )
-- For the OS/400 platform, the following three indexes (in addition to the previous two) are recommended:
--    TargetCreateIndex3=CREATE INDEX USERID.ORGCOPYX3 ON USERID.ORGCOPY( IBMSNAP_COMMITSEQ DESC )
--    TargetCreateIndex4=CREATE INDEX USERID.ORGCOPYX4 ON USERID.ORGCOPY( IBMSNAP_LOGMARKER ASC  )
--    TargetCreateIndex5=CREATE INDEX USERID.ORGCOPYX5 ON USERID.ORGCOPY( IBMSNAP_LOGMARKER DESC )
--
-- For "non-condensed" Staging (CCD) target tables:
--    TargetCreateIndex1=CREATE INDEX USERID.ORGCOPYX1 ON USERID.ORGCOPY( IBMSNAP_COMMITSEQ ASC  )
-- For the OS/400 platform, the following three indexes (in addition to the previous one) are recommended:
--    TargetCreateIndex2=CREATE INDEX USERID.ORGCOPYX2 ON USERID.ORGCOPY( IBMSNAP_COMMITSEQ DESC )
--    TargetCreateIndex3=CREATE INDEX USERID.ORGCOPYX3 ON USERID.ORGCOPY( IBMSNAP_LOGMARKER ASC  )
--    TargetCreateIndex4=CREATE INDEX USERID.ORGCOPYX4 ON USERID.ORGCOPY( IBMSNAP_LOGMARKER DESC )
--
--
-- 3.4. CREATING CHANGE DATA TABLE INDEXES (CDCreateIndex)
--
-- If you are using this file to create indexes on change data tables, these are the recommended indexes:
--
-- Note:  for DB2 MVS V4 and up, it is recommended that the indexes be TYPE 2 indexes.  In order to
--        create type 2 indexes, add the clause "TYPE 2" after the CREATE keyword of the CREATE INDEX
--        statement.
--
-- For DB2 for MVS, UDB, VM or VSE and OS/400:  you will need one index
--    CDCreateIndex1=CREATE UNIQUE INDEX USERID.ORGCDX ON USERID."OrgCD"( IBMSNAP_UOWID ASC,
IBMSNAP_INTENTSEQ ASC )
```

Appendix D. Script to Create Control Tables - DPCNTL.UDB

Note that other versions exist for other platforms (OS/390, VSE/VM and AS/400).

```
------------------------------------------------------------
--    Create Replication Control Tables
--    (UDB edition)
------------------------------------------------------------

-- BEGIN DPCNTL.UDB

-- UDB -- For the UDB platform, follow the directions given in the comments
-- UDB -- prefixed with "-- UDB --" (if any).


------------------------------------------------------------
--    Critical Section Table              (All IBM platforms  )
------------------------------------------------------------

CREATE TABLE ASN.IBMSNAP_CRITSEC (
    APPLY_QUAL           CHAR( 18) NOT NULL )
DATA CAPTURE CHANGES;

CREATE UNIQUE INDEX ASN.IBMSNAP_CRITSECX
ON ASN.IBMSNAP_CRITSEC ( APPLY_QUAL         ASC );


------------------------------------------------------------
--    Pruning Control Table               (All platforms      )
------------------------------------------------------------

CREATE TABLE ASN.IBMSNAP_PRUNCNTL (
   TARGET_SERVER      CHAR( 18) NOT NULL,
   TARGET_OWNER       CHAR( 18) NOT NULL,
   TARGET_TABLE       CHAR( 18) NOT NULL,
   SYNCHTIME          TIMESTAMP,
   SYNCHPOINT         CHAR( 10) FOR BIT DATA,
   SOURCE_OWNER       CHAR( 18) NOT NULL,
   SOURCE_TABLE       CHAR( 18) NOT NULL,
   SOURCE_VIEW_QUAL   SMALLINT  NOT NULL,
   APPLY_QUAL         CHAR( 18) NOT NULL,
   SET_NAME           CHAR( 18) NOT NULL,
   CNTL_SERVER        CHAR( 18) NOT NULL,
   TARGET_STRUCTURE   SMALLINT  NOT NULL,
   CNTL_ALIAS         CHAR(  8) )
DATA CAPTURE CHANGES;

CREATE UNIQUE INDEX ASN.IBMSNAP_PRUNCNTLX
ON ASN.IBMSNAP_PRUNCNTL (
   SOURCE_OWNER       ASC,
   SOURCE_TABLE       ASC,
   SOURCE_VIEW_QUAL   ASC,
   SET_NAME           ASC,
   TARGET_SERVER      ASC,
   TARGET_TABLE       ASC,
   TARGET_OWNER       ASC );


------------------------------------------------------------
--    Register Table                      (All platforms      )
------------------------------------------------------------
```

```
CREATE TABLE ASN.IBMSNAP_REGISTER (
    SOURCE_OWNER        CHAR( 18) NOT NULL,
    SOURCE_TABLE        CHAR( 18) NOT NULL,
    SOURCE_VIEW_QUAL    SMALLINT  NOT NULL,
    GLOBAL_RECORD       CHAR(  1) NOT NULL,
    SOURCE_STRUCTURE    SMALLINT  NOT NULL,
    SOURCE_CONDENSED    CHAR(  1) NOT NULL,
    SOURCE_COMPLETE     CHAR(  1) NOT NULL,
    CD_OWNER            CHAR( 18),
    CD_TABLE            CHAR( 18),
    PHYS_CHANGE_OWNER   CHAR( 18),
    PHYS_CHANGE_TABLE   CHAR( 18),
    CD_OLD_SYNCHPOINT   CHAR( 10) FOR BIT DATA,
    CD_NEW_SYNCHPOINT   CHAR( 10) FOR BIT DATA,
    DISABLE_REFRESH     SMALLINT NOT NULL,
    CCD_OWNER           CHAR( 18),
    CCD_TABLE           CHAR( 18),
    CCD_OLD_SYNCHPOINT  CHAR( 10) FOR BIT DATA,
    SYNCHPOINT          CHAR( 10) FOR BIT DATA,
    SYNCHTIME           TIMESTAMP,
    CCD_CONDENSED       CHAR(  1),
    CCD_COMPLETE        CHAR(  1),
    ARCH_LEVEL          CHAR(  4) NOT NULL,
    DESCRIPTION         CHAR(254),
    BEFORE_IMG_PREFIX   VARCHAR(4),
    CONFLICT_LEVEL      CHAR(  1),
    PARTITION_KEYS_CHG  CHAR(  1) )
;

CREATE UNIQUE INDEX ASN.IBMSNAP_REGISTERX
ON ASN.IBMSNAP_REGISTER (
    SOURCE_OWNER       ASC,
    SOURCE_TABLE       ASC,
    SOURCE_VIEW_QUAL   ASC );


------------------------------------------------------------
--    Trace Table                        (All IBM platforms  )
------------------------------------------------------------

CREATE TABLE ASN.IBMSNAP_TRACE (
    OPERATION          CHAR      (  8) NOT NULL,
    TRACE_TIME         TIMESTAMP       NOT NULL,
    DESCRIPTION        VARCHAR   (254) NOT NULL )
;


------------------------------------------------------------
--    Tuning Parameters Table            (All IBM platforms  )
------------------------------------------------------------

CREATE TABLE ASN.IBMSNAP_CCPPARMS (
    RETENTION_LIMIT    INT,
    LAG_LIMIT          INT,
    COMMIT_INTERVAL    INT,
    PRUNE_INTERVAL     INT )
;


------------------------------------------------------------
--    Unit-of-Work Table                 (All IBM platforms  )
------------------------------------------------------------
```

```
CREATE TABLE ASN.IBMSNAP_UOW (
   IBMSNAP_UOWID       CHAR( 10) FOR BIT DATA NOT NULL,
   IBMSNAP_COMMITSEQ   CHAR( 10) FOR BIT DATA NOT NULL,
   IBMSNAP_LOGMARKER   TIMESTAMP NOT NULL,
   IBMSNAP_AUTHTKN     CHAR( 12) NOT NULL,
   IBMSNAP_AUTHID      CHAR( 18) NOT NULL,
   IBMSNAP_REJ_CODE    CHAR(  1) NOT NULL WITH DEFAULT,
   IBMSNAP_APPLY_QUAL CHAR( 18) NOT NULL WITH DEFAULT )
;

CREATE UNIQUE INDEX ASN.IBMSNAP_UOW_IDX
ON ASN.IBMSNAP_UOW (
   IBMSNAP_COMMITSEQ  ASC,
   IBMSNAP_UOWID      ASC,
   IBMSNAP_LOGMARKER  ASC  );


------------------------------------------------------------------
--    Warm Start Table                         (All IBM platforms  )
------------------------------------------------------------------

CREATE TABLE ASN.IBMSNAP_WARM_START (
   SEQ                 CHAR( 10) FOR BIT DATA,
   AUTHTKN             CHAR( 12),
   AUTHID              CHAR( 18),
   CAPTURED            CHAR(  1),
   UOWTIME             INT )
;


------------------------------------------------------------------
--    Apply Trail Table                        (All IBM platforms  )
------------------------------------------------------------------

CREATE TABLE ASN.IBMSNAP_APPLYTRAIL (
   APPLY_QUAL          CHAR( 18) NOT NULL,
   SET_NAME            CHAR( 18) NOT NULL,
   WHOS_ON_FIRST       CHAR(  1) NOT NULL,
   ASNLOAD             CHAR(  1),
   MASS_DELETE         CHAR(  1),
   EFFECTIVE_MEMBERS   INT,
   SET_INSERTED        INT       NOT NULL,
   SET_DELETED         INT       NOT NULL,
   SET_UPDATED         INT       NOT NULL,
   SET_REWORKED        INT       NOT NULL,
   SET_REJECTED_TRXS   INT       NOT NULL,
   STATUS              SMALLINT  NOT NULL,
   LASTRUN             TIMESTAMP NOT NULL,
   LASTSUCCESS         TIMESTAMP,
   SYNCHPOINT          CHAR( 10) FOR BIT DATA,
   SYNCHTIME           TIMESTAMP,
   SOURCE_SERVER       CHAR( 18) NOT NULL,
   SOURCE_ALIAS        CHAR(  8),
   SOURCE_OWNER        CHAR( 18),
   SOURCE_TABLE        CHAR( 18),
   SOURCE_VIEW_QUAL    SMALLINT,
   TARGET_SERVER       CHAR( 18) NOT NULL,
   TARGET_ALIAS        CHAR(  8),
   TARGET_OWNER        CHAR( 18) NOT NULL,
   TARGET_TABLE        CHAR( 18) NOT NULL,
   SQLSTATE            CHAR(  5),
   SQLCODE             INT,
   SQLERRP             CHAR(  8),
```

```
    SQLERRM              VARCHAR(70),
    APPERRM              VARCHAR(760) )
;


--------------------------------------------------------------------
--    Subscription Columns Table              (All IBM platforms  )
--------------------------------------------------------------------

CREATE TABLE ASN.IBMSNAP_SUBS_COLS (
    APPLY_QUAL          CHAR( 18)     NOT NULL,
    SET_NAME            CHAR( 18)     NOT NULL,
    WHOS_ON_FIRST       CHAR(  1)     NOT NULL,
    TARGET_OWNER        CHAR( 18)     NOT NULL,
    TARGET_TABLE        CHAR( 18)     NOT NULL,
    COL_TYPE            CHAR(  1)     NOT NULL,
    TARGET_NAME         CHAR( 18)     NOT NULL,
    IS_KEY              CHAR(  1)     NOT NULL,
    COLNO               SMALLINT      NOT NULL,
    EXPRESSION          VARCHAR(254) NOT NULL )
;

CREATE UNIQUE INDEX ASN.IBMSNAP_SUBS_COLSX
ON ASN.IBMSNAP_SUBS_COLS (
    APPLY_QUAL          ASC,
    SET_NAME            ASC,
    WHOS_ON_FIRST       ASC,
    TARGET_OWNER        ASC,
    TARGET_TABLE        ASC,
    TARGET_NAME         ASC );


--------------------------------------------------------------------
--    Subscription Events Table               (All IBM platforms  )
--------------------------------------------------------------------

CREATE TABLE ASN.IBMSNAP_SUBS_EVENT (
    EVENT_NAME          CHAR( 18) NOT NULL,
    EVENT_TIME          TIMESTAMP NOT NULL,
    END_OF_PERIOD       TIMESTAMP )
;

CREATE UNIQUE INDEX ASN.IBMSNAP_SUBS_EVENX
ON ASN.IBMSNAP_SUBS_EVENT (
    EVENT_NAME          ASC,
    EVENT_TIME          ASC );


--------------------------------------------------------------------
--    Subscription Set Table                  (All IBM platforms  )
--------------------------------------------------------------------

CREATE TABLE ASN.IBMSNAP_SUBS_SET (
    APPLY_QUAL          CHAR( 18) NOT NULL,
    SET_NAME            CHAR( 18) NOT NULL,
    WHOS_ON_FIRST       CHAR(  1) NOT NULL,
    ACTIVATE            SMALLINT  NOT NULL,
    SOURCE_SERVER       CHAR( 18) NOT NULL,
    SOURCE_ALIAS        CHAR(  8),
    TARGET_SERVER       CHAR( 18) NOT NULL,
    TARGET_ALIAS        CHAR(  8),
    STATUS              SMALLINT  NOT NULL,
    LASTRUN             TIMESTAMP NOT NULL,
```

```
   REFRESH_TIMING      CHAR(  1) NOT NULL,
   SLEEP_MINUTES       INT,
   EVENT_NAME          CHAR( 18),
   LASTSUCCESS         TIMESTAMP,
   SYNCHPOINT          CHAR( 10) FOR BIT DATA,
   SYNCHTIME           TIMESTAMP,
   MAX_SYNCH_MINUTES   INT,
   AUX_STMTS           SMALLINT  NOT NULL,
   ARCH_LEVEL          CHAR(  4) NOT NULL )
;

CREATE UNIQUE INDEX ASN.IBMSNAP_SUBS_SETX
ON ASN.IBMSNAP_SUBS_SET (
   APPLY_QUAL          ASC,
   SET_NAME            ASC,
   WHOS_ON_FIRST       ASC );


-------------------------------------------------------------------
--    Subscription Statements Table          (All IBM platforms  )
-------------------------------------------------------------------

CREATE TABLE ASN.IBMSNAP_SUBS_STMTS (
   APPLY_QUAL          CHAR( 18) NOT NULL,
   SET_NAME            CHAR( 18) NOT NULL,
   WHOS_ON_FIRST       CHAR(  1) NOT NULL,
   BEFORE_OR_AFTER     CHAR(  1) NOT NULL,
   STMT_NUMBER         SMALLINT  NOT NULL,
   EI_OR_CALL          CHAR(  1) NOT NULL,
   SQL_STMT            VARCHAR(1024),
   ACCEPT_SQLSTATES    VARCHAR(50) )
;

CREATE UNIQUE INDEX ASN.IBMSNAP_SUBS_STMTX
ON ASN.IBMSNAP_SUBS_STMTS (
   APPLY_QUAL          ASC,
   SET_NAME            ASC,
   WHOS_ON_FIRST       ASC,
   BEFORE_OR_AFTER     ASC,
   STMT_NUMBER         ASC )
;


-------------------------------------------------------------------
--    Subscription Targets Member Table      (All IBM platforms  )
-------------------------------------------------------------------

CREATE TABLE ASN.IBMSNAP_SUBS_MEMBR (
   APPLY_QUAL          CHAR( 18) NOT NULL,
   SET_NAME            CHAR( 18) NOT NULL,
   WHOS_ON_FIRST       CHAR(  1) NOT NULL,
   SOURCE_OWNER        CHAR( 18) NOT NULL,
   SOURCE_TABLE        CHAR( 18) NOT NULL,
   SOURCE_VIEW_QUAL    SMALLINT  NOT NULL,
   TARGET_OWNER        CHAR( 18) NOT NULL,
   TARGET_TABLE        CHAR( 18) NOT NULL,
   TARGET_CONDENSED    CHAR(  1) NOT NULL,
   TARGET_COMPLETE     CHAR(  1) NOT NULL,
   TARGET_STRUCTURE    SMALLINT  NOT NULL,
   PREDICATES          VARCHAR(512) )
;

CREATE UNIQUE INDEX ASN.IBMSNAP_SUBS_MEMBX
```

```
ON ASN.IBMSNAP_SUBS_MEMBR (
   APPLY_QUAL         ASC,
   SET_NAME           ASC,
   WHOS_ON_FIRST      ASC,
   SOURCE_OWNER       ASC,
   SOURCE_TABLE       ASC,
   SOURCE_VIEW_QUAL   ASC,
   TARGET_OWNER       ASC,
   TARGET_TABLE       ASC );


------------------------------------------------------------------
-- Insert default values into Tuning Parameters Table
------------------------------------------------------------------

INSERT INTO ASN.IBMSNAP_CCPPARMS (
   RETENTION_LIMIT,
   LAG_LIMIT,
   COMMIT_INTERVAL,
   PRUNE_INTERVAL )
VALUES ( 10080, 10080, 30, 300 );


-- END DPCNTL.UDB
```

Appendix E. Related Publications

The publications listed in this section are considered particularly suitable for a more detailed discussion of the topics covered in this book.

- *DB2 Replication Guide and Reference*, S95H-0999-02
- *Data Where You Need It, The DPropR Way! DataPropagator Relational Solutions Guide*, GG24-4492-00
- *DPROPR Planning and Design Guide*, SG24-4771-00
- *DataJoiner for AIX Planning, Installation, and Configuration Guide*, SC26-9145
- *DataJoiner for Windows NT Systems Planning, Installation, and Configuration Guide*, SC26-9150
- *DB2 Universal Database Administration Guide*, S10J-8157-00
- *DB2 Universal Database for Windows NT, Quick Beginnings*, S10J-8149-00
- *DB2 Universal Database for UNIX, Quick Beginnings*, S10J-8148-00

Index

A

B

C

D

E

F

G

H

I

T

U

V

W